soggy
sneakers

fifth edition

A Paddler's Guide to Oregon's Rivers

Willamette Kayak and Canoe Club

MOUNTAINEERS
BOOKS

Mountaineers Books is the publishing division of The Mountaineers, an organization founded in 1906 and dedicated to the exploration, preservation, and enjoyment of outdoor and wilderness areas.

MOUNTAINEERS BOOKS

1001 SW Klickitat Way, Suite 201, Seattle, WA 98134
800.553.4453, www.mountaineersbooks.org

Printed in the United States of America
Third edition, 1994. Fourth edition, 2004. Fifth edition: first printing 2016, second printing 2022

Copy Editor: Sunny Parsons
Cover Design: Karen Schober
Interior Design: Peggy Egerdahl
Layout: Jennifer Shontz, www.redshoedesign.com
Cartographers: Moore Creative Designs and Red Shoe Design
Cover photograph: *Silache Rapid, Run 14, Siletz River, Oregon* (Photo by Gary Adams)

Library of Congress Cataloging-in-Publication Data

Names: Willamette Kayak and Canoe Club.
Title: Soggy sneakers : a paddler's guide to Oregon's rivers / Willamette
    Kayak and Canoe Club.
Description: Fifth Edition. | Seattle: The Mountaineers Books, [2016] |
    Revised edition of Soggy sneakers / Pete Giordano and the Willamette Kayak
    and Canoe Club. 4th ed. 2004.
Identifiers: LCCN 2016010990| ISBN 9781594858703 (paperback) | ISBN
    9781594858710 (ebook)
Subjects: LCSH: Canoes and canoeing—Oregon—Guidebooks. |
    Rivers—Recreational use—Oregon—Guidebooks. | Oregon—Guidebooks.
Classification: LCC GV776.O6 S63 2016 | DDC 917.95—dc23 LC record available at
http://lccn.loc.gov/2016010990

ISBN (paperback): 978-1-59485-870-3
ISBN (ebook): 978-1-59485-871-0

contents

REGION 1: NORTH COAST RIVERS

REGION 2: SOUTH COAST RIVERS

REGION 3: SOUTHERN OREGON RIVERS

REGION 4: UPPER WILLAMETTE AND MCKENZIE RIVERS

Upper Willamette River and Tributaries

REGION 5: MID-WILLAMETTE VALLEY RIVERS

REGION 6: LOWER WILLAMETTE VALLEY AND CLACKAMAS RIVERS

Silver Creek

Abiqua Creek

Butte Creek

Molalla River and Tributaries

Clackamas River and Tributaries

REGION 10: COASTAL SURF KAYAKING

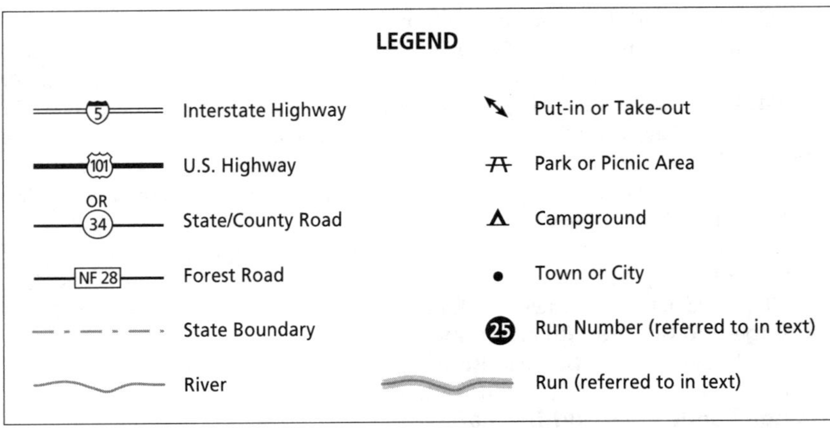

MAJOR RIVERS FEATURED IN *SOGGY SNEAKERS*

REGIONS

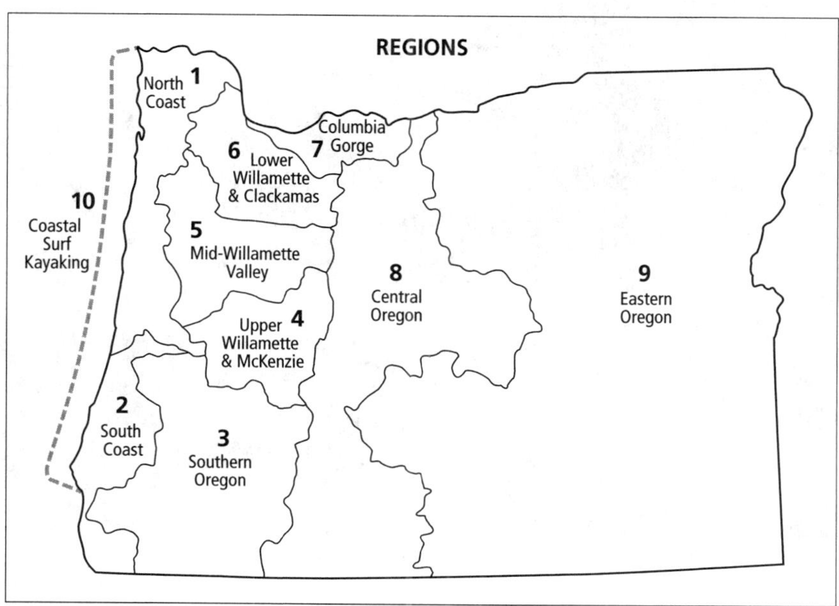

acknowledgments

A talented team of dedicated individuals contributed many hours of volunteer labor to make this new version of *Soggy Sneakers* possible. Major contributors to the fifth edition include: Tim Palmer, Marianne Musitelli, Teresa Gryder, Yann Crist-Evans, Rob Blickensderfer, Alex McNeily, Zach Urness, Al Grapel, Pete Schaefers, Gary Adams, and Mark Scantlebury. Mapping expert Jim Reed spent many hours checking the accuracy of existing maps, creating new maps where needed, and researching the gradients of each run. Thanks go to Laurie Pavey for coordinating the entire fifth-edition venture. Her countless hours of volunteer work gathering new descriptions, updating the existing runs, amassing map data, and collecting new photos have made this edition possible. And finally, a huge thank-you goes to all the boaters who have contributed their time and talents to keep *Soggy Sneakers* a vital paddling resource for the past thirty-five years.

Paddling a SUP above Foster Bar on the Rogue River (Thomas O'Keefe)

preface to the new edition

Since its humble beginnings in 1980, *Soggy Sneakers: A Paddler's Guide to Oregon's Rivers* has become the standard guidebook that boaters in Oregon use for information on where to go paddling. With more than 100 authors, it is undeniably a book written by and for the boating community.

I was a new paddler in 1979 when the idea for creating a book for paddlers came about during one of our Willamette Kayak and Canoe Club meetings. A year later, I was excited to own the first edition of the book, and also happy to know and paddle with some of the authors. Over the years, I was involved with the creation of the second and third editions of the book, and even became an author myself, writing descriptions of some of my favorite runs. I continue to paddle and explore new sections of rivers every year.

The size and breadth of the book has grown tremendously since the beginning. In this fifth edition, our publisher has chosen to keep the size of the book the same as in the fourth edition. In order to accomplish that goal, some of the runs that were in the fourth edition are no longer found in the main body of the book. Most of these absent sections are ones that are less stellar, at the extreme level of difficulty, or are runs that are no longer accessible due to locked gates or private property issues. New river runs have taken their place.

There are 26 new runs in this edition, many in the southern Oregon area. Some descriptions were written by new authors, others were written by paddlers who wrote descriptions for the first edition of *Soggy Sneakers*. The vast majority of the new runs are class 2 and 1+, but there are also a handful of class 3–3+ runs, and one class 4. These new runs address the needs of new boaters who have recently started paddling and have been asking for more information and guidance for running class 1+ to class 3+ rivers. We hope that the fifth edition will better help to fill that need.

Additional changes with this edition include a section titled "Popular and Favorite Runs," which is especially helpful for those visiting Oregon who have limited time to enjoy our lovely rivers. Also new is the "Water Trail Paddling Guides" section, Appendix B. Many more web links are included.

This new edition of *Soggy Sneakers* should inspire you to try some new river runs, paddle a new surf zone you haven't yet tried, or explore a whole new area of Oregon you've never seen. Hopefully, the pages that follow will help expand your paddling journeys on all of Oregon's many rivers.

Now, let's go boating! See you soon.

Laurie Pavey

introduction

We hope this book proves to be an effective guide for you in boating Oregon's whitewater rivers and streams and coastal surf. It is the voice of Oregon boaters past and present. They have invested in our future and in the future of Oregon's water resources. We owe them much for their unique boaters' view and for the skill and thoroughness they bring to the individual descriptions of runs in this guide.

One of the pleasures of compiling these many voices has been recording the new runs pioneered. Improvement in boater skills, a growing willingness to explore more distant rivers and streams, and better accessibility to streamflow data create these opportunities. Of course, boaters will continue to push into new watersheds to find additional runs.

Many of the known runs in Oregon are described, and all the popular runs are included. Most of the runs can be done in a day; some runs may be combined to provide multiday trips with river camping or car camping. A number of multiday runs in remote areas are described. The difficulty of the whitewater runs ranges from class 1 (least difficult) to class 5 (most difficult). A number of more difficult, remote, or logistically complicated runs are included in the section: "Other Rivers to Explore."

Region 10: Coastal Surf Kayaking is a unique feature of this guide. Surf kayaking represents the crossover in skills and equipment in the paddling community for those who surf the standing wave trains of rivers and those who surf the moving wave trains of the ocean. However, special problems and dangers that are not encountered on rivers are involved in paddling ocean surf. Regardless of skill, boaters engaged in surf kayaking must respect the power and unpredictability of ocean currents.

During the summers of 2020 and 2021 there were numerous wildfires in many river canyons. Some of the affected river basin drainages include the Clackamas, Santiam, McKenzie, Umpqua, Rogue, and Deschutes. Before paddling in these areas, perform some local research to determine whether access points are open. And always scout carefully on any Oregon river because fallen trees and landslides may cause river obstructions at any time. Prepare and stay safe.

Oregon whitewater will take you from the high desert to the ocean surf, from steep creeks to gentle streams and rivers, from runs within 1 hour of urban areas to remote rivers where hiking out is a serious event. Oregon whitewater is a year-round activity. We have fall and winter rains, spring snowmelt, and summer dam releases. Enjoy!

We will see you on the rivers.

The Authors

how to use this guide

Most of the known river runs in Oregon are described in this book. They are grouped into nine chapters organized around the seventeen drainage basins of the state. Multiple runs on one river are listed beginning upstream and heading downstream. All river runs reported in this book were run by the authors.

General river descriptions are given for major rivers and river systems. Each run begins with an information block that lists **class** designation, **flow** in cubic feet per second (cfs), **gradient** in feet per mile (fpm), **length** in miles, **character** of the surroundings (the most significant topographic, geographic, and/or scenic features), and **season** in which the river can be run. Because the class designation of a river varies depending upon the flow, multiple information-block entries, separated by semicolons, are given for some runs. Detailed information on some of these information-block categories and how they are used in this book is given later in this section.

Following the information block is a description of the run. The character of the river is described, as well as the rapids and landmarks that are found on the run. Unless otherwise indicated, "right" and "left" are used with respect to an observer looking downstream (river right and river left). Each run concludes with short sections on **hazards**, **access**, and **gauge** information (no gauge information is given for the surf sections in Region 10: Coastal Surf Kayaking).

The maps in this book show the principal rivers and roads, the sections for which runs are described, the locations of access points, and such major landmarks as campgrounds and towns. Although the main shuttle roads are shown, it is intended that a state road map be used with this book. (For more information on maps, see the end of this section.)

The appendices include important additional information. Appendix A lists the various online sources for river flow information. Appendix B lists water trail paddling guides that are available for some rivers. Appendix C lists some of the whitewater boating organizations in Oregon. These organizations provide an invaluable voice in the ongoing battles over how our rivers and streams are and will be used. Through clinics, workshops, and trips, they provide information and training on safety and paddling skills. Best of all, they put people in touch with a great bunch of paddlers and open the door to a rich agenda of river activities.

Following are the definitions of some of the categories used in this book.

Class. The class designations indicate the class of the majority of the run, according to the American Whitewater Affiliation International Scale of River Difficulty, as listed below. If the water temperature is below 50 degrees Fahrenheit, or if the run is remote, the American Whitewater Affiliation states that paddlers should allow an extra margin of safety between one's skills and the river's class rating. If only one or two spots are more difficult than the majority of the run, the class of these spots is given in parentheses; for example, Kilchis River as 2+(3) or Salmonberry River as 3(4). Rapids at the lower end or upper end of each class are designated "-" or "+," respectively. The letter T is given after the number designation for a run that is predominantly technical in nature, and the letter P indicates that at least one portage is mandatory.

Class 1. Moving water with a few riffles and small waves. Few or no obstructions. (Still water and class 1 are sometimes subdivided by water speed: Class A, standing or slow-flowing water, not more than 2.5 mph; Class B, current between 2.5 and 4.5 mph, but back-paddling can effectively neutralize the speed; Class C, current more than 4.5 mph, thus back-paddling cannot neutralize the speed of the current, and simple obstacles may occur that require a certain amount of boat control.)

Class 2. Straightforward rapids, with wide clear channels that are evident without scouting. Some maneuvering is usually required, but trained paddlers can easily avoid obstructions.

Class 3. Rapids with moderate, irregular waves that are often difficult to avoid and capable of swamping an open canoe. Narrow passages often requiring complex maneuvering. Strong eddies and powerful currents, especially on larger-volume rivers. Scouting from shore may be required.

Class 4. Intense, powerful rapids that often require precise maneuvering in turbulent waters. May include unavoidable waves, holes, or constricted passages. Scouting from shore is often necessary, and conditions make rescue difficult. Generally not possible for open canoes, except those navigated by experts. Boaters in covered canoes or kayaks should be able to Eskimo roll.

Class 5. Extremely long, obstructed, or very violent rapids. May include steep, congested chutes with complex and demanding routes, unavoidable holes and waves. Scouting from shore is recommended but difficult. Rescue conditions are difficult, and significant hazard to life may result in event of a mishap. Ability to Eskimo roll in kayaks and canoes is essential.

Class 6. Difficulties of class 5 carried to the extreme of navigability. Nearly impossible and very dangerous. For teams of experts only, after close study and with all precautions taken.

Flow. The rate of flow, which is normally measured at a nearby gauge location, is reported in cubic feet per second (cfs). The flow may differ significantly upstream or downstream of the gauge, depending upon flow in any tributaries. Where necessary, flows are estimated by the authors.

Gradient. The average gradient of the run is the elevation change over the length of the run, in units of feet per mile (fpm). The letters PD are used to indicate that a run is primarily pool-drop in nature; that is, relatively flat stretches are connected by relatively steep sections in which most of the elevation changes occur. The letter C is used to indicate that a run is primarily continuous in nature; that is, the elevation change is relatively uniform over its length.

Season. The time of year that a river can normally be run is related to the weather and the type of source for the river. Following are the classifications used in this book:

Year-round. There is adequate water all year for boating. The sources of these rivers are generally impounded or spring-fed.

Dam-controlled. The flow of these rivers is controlled by dams or irrigation diversions, but there is no requirement for minimum flow. Water may be shut off or reduced to less than runnable flows by the controlling agency.

Rainy. Runnable levels are reached after several days of rain. Many of the rivers of western Oregon are in this group, with a season from about mid-October to April.

Snowmelt. Most of the water comes from melting snow in the spring and early summer. Such rivers are at high elevations or in eastern Oregon.

Rainy/snowmelt. The water is received from both rain and snow. The rivers are runnable after a few days of good rain and into early summer because of melting snowpack.

Hazards. The most difficult rapids are described, and some suggestions are made about how they can be approached or portaged. Other hazards, such as sweepers, weirs, and dams, are also mentioned.

Access. Directions to the river, primary and optional put-ins and take-outs, and directions on running the shuttle are described.

Gauge. The name of the gauge closest to the actual run is listed first. If there is no gauge near the run, other helpful explanations on how to figure the flow are often given. When possible, the authors' opinions of *high runnable, low runnable,* and *optimum* flows are given. Appendix A lists the online sources where one can find the necessary information for obtaining current and predicted flows using the name of the gauge listed for each run.

Maps. This book's maps are intended to be used with a state road map. The Oregon Atlas and Gazetteer is probably the most useful single collection of maps for boaters in Oregon. It is extremely useful for locating all the runs and shuttle routes. California and Washington versions of this publication are similarly useful. Google Maps, an online source of mapping information, can also be used, but should not be relied upon as the sole source for navigation.

For smaller streams and forest roads, US Forest Service (USFS) and Bureau of Land Management (BLM) maps are useful. Most US Forest Service and Bureau of Land Management district offices sell paper copies of maps, and many have maps that are available online.

US Geological Survey (USGS) topographical maps are indispensable for exploratory boating. The 7.5-minute USGS maps with 40-foot contour intervals are the ones to obtain. Many sports stores and libraries carry some topographical maps. Online sources are also available.

Favorites. A ★ following the number of the run signals that it is included in the "Popular and Favorite Runs" list located in the back of the book.

river safety

The run descriptions in this book reflect the general character of a river, but the character can change dramatically in the course of a day, a season, or a year. Thus, while this book is a guide to the rivers and what to expect, it must in no way be regarded as the exact description of what you will find on a particular day. Each boater must accept personal responsibility for finding out what lies around the next corner; and for possessing sufficient skills to cope.

Persons running rivers are responsible for their own safety. This book is offered only as a guide. Neither the authors nor the publisher are responsible or liable for any loss of life or property that may befall others running the rivers.

People run rivers for different reasons; some seek a relaxing aesthetic experience, others seek adventure or challenge. Many seek a combination of the two. For whatever reasons you choose to boat, your river-running experience will be more fun and more rewarding if done safely. On any river, even apparently small ones, the price of ignorance or carelessness can be anything from lost or damaged equipment to personal injury or the loss of life.

A large part of safe boating lies in identifying potential dangers. Prevention is the key, not just reacting to a hazardous situation already in motion. Recognizing potential hazards requires experience. Boating clubs offer the novice a way other than trial and error to acquire that experience and learn boating safety. Clubs normally have people who teach boating and are willing to share their experiences and instill safe boating practices. Many clubs provide instruction in boat handling (for a listing of boating organizations, see Appendix C). Another way to learn boating skills and safety is in classes offered by city parks and recreation departments, community colleges, the Red Cross, the YMCA, and local paddling shops. Some of the books in the Bibliography at the back of this book discuss safety, rescue techniques, and safety equipment.

The Safety Code of the American Whitewater Affiliation, slightly condensed, is reprinted here with permission. Read it carefully.

T. R. Torgersen

I. PERSONAL PREPAREDNESS AND RESPONSIBILITY

1. Be a competent swimmer with ability to handle yourself underwater.
2. Wear a properly sized personal flotation device (PFD).
3. Wear a solid, correctly fitted helmet.
4. Keep your craft under control. Control must be sufficient to stop or reach shore before reaching danger. Do not enter a rapid unless you are reasonably sure that you can run it safely or swim it without injury.
5. Be aware of river hazards and avoid them. The following are the most frequent killers:
   A. High water. The river's power and danger, and the difficulty of rescue, increase tremendously as the flow rate increases. It is often misleading to judge river level at the put-in. Look at a narrow, critical passage. Be

aware that sun on a snowpack, hard rain, or a dam release may greatly increase the flow.

B. Cold. Cold quickly drains strength and robs one of the ability to make sound decisions. Dress to protect yourself from cold water and weather extremes. When the water temperature is less than 50 degrees Fahrenheit, a wet suit or dry suit is essential. Next best is wool or pile clothing under a waterproof shell. In the latter case, also carry matches and a complete change of clothes in a waterproof bag. If, after prolonged exposure, one experiences uncontrollable shaking or loss of coordination, or has difficulty speaking, one is hypothermic and needs assistance.

C. Strainers. These include brush, fallen trees, bridge pilings, and any other obstacle that allows river current to sweep through but pins boats and boaters against it. The water pressure on anything trapped this way can be overwhelming. Rescue is often extremely difficult. Pinning may occur in fast current with little or no whitewater to signal the danger.

D. Dams, weirs, ledges, reversals, and holes. When water drops over an obstacle, it curls back on itself, forming a strong upstream current that can hold boats or swimmers. Some holes make for sport; others are proven killers. Hydraulics around constructed dams and weirs are especially dangerous. Despite a benign appearance, such water can trap a swimmer. Once trapped, a swimmer's only hope is to dive below the surface, where downstream current is flowing beneath the reversal.

E. Broaching. When a boat is pushed sideways against a rock or log by strong current, it may collapse and wrap. Kayakers and decked canoe paddlers especially may become trapped and drowned. To avoid pinning, throw your weight downstream and lean downstream toward the obstacle. This allows the current to slide harmlessly underneath the hull of your craft.

6. Boating alone is not recommended. The preferred minimum is three craft.

7. Be honest with yourself about your boating ability. Do not attempt waters beyond that ability.

A. Develop paddling skills and teamwork to match the river you plan to boat. Attempts to advance too quickly compromise safety and enjoyment.

B. Be in good physical and mental condition. Make adjustments for loss of skills due to age, health, or fitness. Explain any health limitations to your fellow paddlers.

8. Be practiced in self-rescue, including escape from an overturned craft. The ability to Eskimo roll is strongly recommended.

9. Be trained in rescue skills, CPR, and first aid, with special emphasis on recognizing and treating hypothermia.

10. Be suitably equipped. Wear shoes that will protect your feet during a bad swim or a walk for help. Carry a throw rope, a knife, a whistle (required by Oregon law), and waterproof matches. If you wear eyeglasses, tie them

on and carry a spare pair. Do not wear ponchos, heavy boots, or anything that will reduce your ability to survive a swim.

11. Individual paddlers are ultimately responsible for their own safety and must assume sole responsibility for the following:
    A. The decision to participate on any trip.
    B. The selection of appropriate equipment.
    C. The decision to scout any rapids and to run or portage according to their best judgment.
    D. The continual evaluation of their own and their group's safety, voicing concerns when appropriate. The willingness to speak with anyone whose actions on the water are dangerous.

The Ten Essentials: A Systems Approach

Following is the revised version of the Ten Essentials that one should carry for safety and for emergencies, including in watercraft. The Ten Essentials have evolved from a list of individual items to a list of functional systems. The classic list has been expanded in the systems approach to include hydration and emergency shelter.
1. Navigation (map and compass)
2. Sun protection (sunglasses and sunscreen)
3. Insulation (extra clothing)
4. Illumination (headlamp or flashlight)
5. First-aid supplies
6. Fire (firestarter and matches/lighter)
7. Repair kit and tools (including knife)
8. Nutrition (extra food)
9. Hydration (extra water)
10. Emergency shelter

The Mountaineers

II. BOAT AND EQUIPMENT PREPAREDNESS

1. Test new and unfamiliar equipment before trusting it on a river.
2. Be sure craft is in good repair before starting a trip. Eliminate sharp projections that could cause injury during a swim.
3. Install flotation bags in non-inflatable craft, securely fixed and designed to displace as much water as possible. Inflatable craft should have multiple air chambers and should be test-inflated before launching.
4. Paddles or oars should be strong and of adequate size for controlling the craft. Carry sufficient spares for the length and type of trip.
5. Outfit your craft safely. Be certain there is absolutely nothing to cause entanglement when coming free from an upset craft, such as a spray skirt that will not release or will tangle around legs, life jacket buckles or clothing that might snag, canoe seats that lock on shoe heels, foot braces that fail or allow feet to jam under them, inadequately supported decks that collapse on the boater's legs when trapped by water pressure,

baggage that dangles in an upset, loose ropes in the craft, or badly secured bow and stern lines (painters).

6. Provide ropes to allow you to hold onto your craft in case of upset and so that it may be rescued. Following are the recommended methods:
   A. Kayaks and covered canoes should have grab loops attached to bow and stern. A stern painter, or line, 7 or 8 feet long may be used if properly secured to prevent entanglement.
   B. Open canoes should have bow and stern lines (painters) consisting of 8–10 feet of 1/4- or 3/8-inch rope. These lines must be secured in such a way that they are readily accessible but cannot come loose accidentally. Attached balls, floats, and knots are not recommended.
   C. Rafts and dories may have taut perimeter grab lines threaded through the loops that are usually provided. Flip lines should be carefully and reliably stowed.
7. Respect rules for craft capacity and know how these capacities should be reduced for whitewater use. When running rapids in open canoes, do not carry more than two paddlers.
8. Carry appropriate repair materials: cloth repair tape for short trips, complete repair kit and tools for wilderness trips.
9. Car-top racks should be strong and attach securely to the vehicle. Lash the boat to each crossbar, and then tie the ends of the boat directly to the bumpers.

III. GROUP PREPAREDNESS AND RESPONSIBILITY

1. Organization. A river trip, except an instructional or commercially guided trip, should be regarded by all participants as a common adventure. Participants share the responsibility for the conduct of the trip, and each is responsible for judging his or her own capabilities.
2. River conditions. Each member of the group should have a reasonable knowledge of the difficulty of the run. Be aware of possible rapid changes in river level and how these changes can affect the difficulty of the run. Secure flow information. If the trip involves important tidal currents, secure tide information.
3. Participants. Determine if the prospective boaters are qualified for the trip. All decisions should be based on group safety and comfort. Difficult decisions regarding the participation of marginal boaters must be based on total group strength.
4. Equipment. Plan so that all necessary group equipment is present on the trip: a minimum of one (preferably one per craft) 50- to 75-foot throw rope, carabiners, first-aid kit with fresh and adequate supplies, extra paddles, repair materials, and survival equipment, if appropriate. Check equipment as necessary at the put-in, especially life jackets, boat flotation, and any items that could prevent complete escape from the boat in case of an upset.
5. Organization. Keep the group compact, but maintain sufficient spacing to avoid collisions. If the group is large, divide into smaller groups, each with appropriate boating strength and a designated leader and sweep.

A. The lead paddler. Set the pace and do not get in over your head. Never run blind drops. When in doubt, stop and scout.

B. Keep track. Each boat keeps the one behind it in sight, stopping if necessary. Know how many people are in your group and take head counts regularly. Less-skilled paddlers should stay near the center of the group.

C. Courtesy. Do not cut in front of a boater running a drop. Always look upstream before leaving eddies to run or play. Never enter a crowded drop or eddy when there is no room.

6. Float plan. If the trip is into a wilderness area, or for an extended period, file plans before leaving with appropriate authorities or with someone who will contact authorities after a certain time. It may be wise to establish checkpoints along the way where people could be contacted if necessary. Knowing the location of possible help and preplanning could speed rescue.

7. Drugs. The use of alcohol or mind-altering drugs before or during river trips is not recommended since they dull reflexes and reduce decision-making ability.

IV. GUIDELINES FOR RIVER RESCUE

1. In case of an upset, recover if possible with an Eskimo roll. Evacuate your boat immediately if there is imminent danger of being trapped against logs, brush, or any other form of strainer.

2. If you swim, hold onto your craft. It has much flotation and is easy for rescuers to spot. Get to the upstream end so the craft cannot crush you against obstacles.

3. Release your craft if this improves your safety. If rescue is not imminent and water is numbingly cold, or if worse rapids follow, strike out for the nearest shore.

4. When swimming in shallow or rocky rapids, use a backstroke with your legs downstream and feet near the surface. If your foot wedges on the bottom, fast water will push you under and hold you there. Get to slow or very shallow water before trying to stand or walk. Look ahead. Avoid possible entrapment situations: rock wedges, fissures, strainers, brush, logs, and extreme hydraulics. Watch for eddies and slack water and be prepared to use them to your advantage. Use every opportunity to work toward shore. If rapids are deep and powerful, roll onto your stomach and swim aggressively toward shore, always looking ahead.

5. If others spill, help the boaters first. Rescue boats and equipment only if it can be done safely.

6. The use of rescue lines requires training. Never tie yourself into either end of a line without a reliable quick-release system.

V. UNIVERSAL RIVER SIGNALS

1. Stop: Arms extended horizontally or paddle held horizontally.
2. Help/emergency: Three blasts on whistle, or wave arm or paddle vertically above head.
3. All clear (come ahead): Paddle or arm held vertically.
4. I'm okay and not hurt: Hold elbow out toward the side, repeatedly pat top of head.

A Note About Safety

Please use common sense. This book is not intended as a substitute for careful planning, professional training, or your own good judgment. It is incumbent upon any user of this guide to assess his or her own skills, experience, fitness, and equipment. Readers will recognize the inherent dangers in kayaking, canoeing, and stand-up paddling, as well as in rivers and moving-water environments, and assume responsibility for their own actions and safety.

Changing or unfavorable conditions in weather, waterways, river flows, roads, trails, etc., cannot be anticipated by the author or publisher, but should be considered by any outdoor participants, as routes may become dangerous or water unstable due to such altered conditions. Likewise, be aware of any changes in public jurisdiction, and do not access private property without permission.

This book contains only the personal opinions of the authors. The publisher and authors are expressly not responsible for any adverse consequences resulting directly or indirectly from information contained in this book.

Mountaineers Books

river etiquette

Etiquette on the river means treating other people as you would like to be treated, and keeping the environment as clean and natural as you would like to find it on future trips. Landowners' rights, paddling and rowing etiquette, and camping conservation should be recognized and practiced. Run descriptions make note of private land when it affects the river runner; pay attention to these warnings and respect private property rights. Heed any "No Trespassing" signs.

Paddling and rowing etiquette involves all watercraft. Kayakers who stop at surfing waves should be aware of and yield to others paddling downstream. Rafters and drifters should be alert for smaller boats. Be courteous on the river.

Camping conservation is important. On long trips in fragile river environments, carry and use a fire pan if you have campfires. Pack out all coals and ashes. For less impact on the wilderness, the best practice is to use a gas (Coleman fuel or propane) stove.

Pack out your camping garbage, including bottle caps, cigarette butts, burnt aluminum foil, and orange peels. Buried human waste decomposes within a few weeks, but toilet paper may last a year or longer, so pack out all toilet paper or burn it in your firepan. Do not bury it. On many multiday river trips where a permit is required, carrying out solid human waste is usually mandatory. Be sure to read your permit regulations carefully and abide by the rules.

You river runners who are independent and enjoy wilderness, accept your responsibility.

Kim Hummer

river preservation

Oregon has a rich heritage of river conservation, and, historically, many river runners have risen to the challenge of protecting, preserving, and restoring our streams.

Early conservation activity was aimed at cleaning up egregious pollution from cities and industries. Efforts in the 1970s to reclaim the Willamette River by Governors Tom McCall and Bob Straub helped the waterway go from being a conduit of sewage to the attractive water trail we know today. Today it is one of the premier long river journeys in the West.

Stopping the construction of dams defined river conservation in the 1970s, and many boaters led the way by working to protect the lower half of the Snake River's Hells Canyon from dams. After stopping dams on the Illinois and South Santiam rivers and Elk Creek, Oregon's river enthusiasts launched a new age of river restoration with dam removals on the Rogue, Sandy, Hood, Sprague, Calapooia, and other streams. Efforts continue for the breaching of dams on the lower

Above Longbow Falls on section 1 of the South Santiam River (Zach Urness)

Snake River—four impediments that have helped to drive northeastern Oregon's salmon and steelhead toward extinction.

Another wave of conservation activity came in the 1990s with the Oregon Plan for Salmon and Watersheds, which created watershed councils and a source of funding for restoration of fish habitat statewide. Restoration efforts have included the planting of millions of trees to cool overwarmed river water, and the reinstatement of some logjams. Both techniques have improved fish habitat and aided the recovery of channel complexity, groundwater recharge, and spawning gravels in woodland streams.

Yet much remains to be done. Preservation of greenways along rivers, prevention of diversions that dry up the channels, and reduction of nutrient pollution from farms and cities will all become more important with the growing stress of a warming climate.

On the bright side, congressional protection from dams or other major developments through National Wild and Scenic River designation has safeguarded parts of 71 rivers and tributaries for nearly 2000 river miles in Oregon. The list of protected rivers grew greatly with the Oregon Rivers Omnibus Bill of 1988—a measure that members of the Willamette Kayak and Canoe Club worked hard to pass. More can be protected in this way and also through the similar state Scenic Waterways Program.

Paddlers have applied their own special abilities and insights to protect Oregon's rivers, creating a remarkable conservation legacy, and our role will be even more crucial with future challenges as the population grows and the climate warms. If you care about the rivers and streams in which you paddle or row, become involved with the conservation initiatives of your local paddling club or other river conservation groups. Substantial portions of the royalties from *Soggy Sneakers* are dedicated to river conservation organizations.

You can also help by taking others on river trips so that they, too, can feel the importance of these watery places we love. In Oregon, we're fortunate to have great rivers to run. But they won't stay that way without our involvement in their future and their fate.

Tim Palmer

Opposite: *Keeping it steady in the Wilson River Narrows* (Mark Scantlebury)

North Coast Rivers

Region 1

Nehalem River and Tributaries

1 Nehalem River
Spruce Run County Park to Nehalem Falls

Class: 3	Length: 14.6 miles
Flow: 2000–8000 cfs	Character: forested
Gradient: 16 fpm, C	Season: rainy

The Nehalem River flows westward from the northern Coast Range to the Pacific Ocean, and is among the largest rivers in the Coast Range. In earlier times many logs were floated down the Nehalem from the lush forests where they were cut. The terrain along the river is rugged, with very few inhabitants, and in places the hills rise 1200 feet above the river.

Spruce Run County Park, at the put-in, is a pleasant place with very few visitors in winter and spring. Below the put-in, the run is fairly straightforward for the first mile to Little Falls, a small river-wide ledge. For the next 6 miles below Little Falls, the river consists of long, flat stretches with occasional class 2 waves. At mile 7, the gradient increases and the river narrows in a long curve to the left through a scenic gorge with some class 2 waves.

The next river mark is at mile 8 where the Salmonberry River enters from the left. One may take out just above the bridge on river left for a shorter day or continue on downstream. Salmonberry Drop, the largest rapid on this section, is only 0.2 mile downstream. At low water, this drop contains a violent hole. Portage/scout on the right or from a small eddy on the left. Several other good class 3 rapids are separated by stretches of quiet water between here and the take-out. At moderate flows, many play spots are found in the river. At high water, the hydraulics become powerful, and many of the play spots are washed out. Nehalem Falls (class 3–4, depending on water level) can be run as a finale. The Falls, not a true waterfall, is formed by the river pinching between a concrete fish ladder and a basalt wall. The hydraulics in the rapids can be pushy, and the runout is turbulent.

The Tillamook County Water Trail guidebook for the Nehalem River provides useful information (see Appendix B).

Hazards

Salmonberry Drop should definitely be scouted. This drop cannot be seen from the road, but can be recognized from the river by a large rock at least 10 feet high on the right at the head of the rapids. The main chute can develop a violent hole at low water. Nehalem Falls, just below the normal take-out, can be scouted from the river on either side or by hiking through the park.

Access

To reach the put-in, take US Highway 26 west from Portland to the Nehalem River, 5 miles west of the highway summit. About 1 mile farther west, turn south on a secondary road or proceed another mile west on US 26 to Elsie and take the road south. In either case, Spruce Run County Park is about 6 miles beyond the

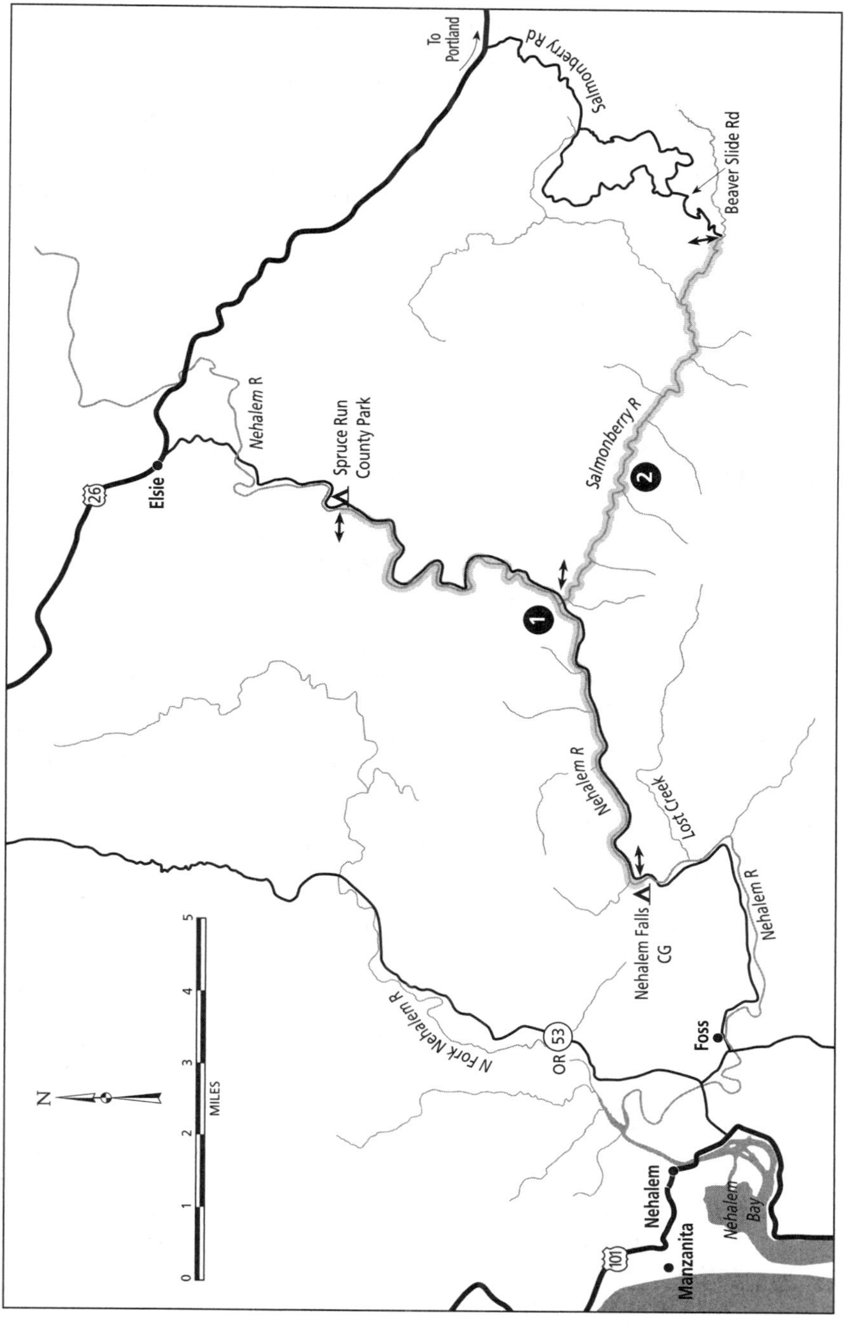

To Portland
Salmonberry Rd
Beaver Slide Rd
Nehalem R
Elsie
26
Spruce Run
County Park
Salmonberry R
2
1
N Fork Nehalem R
Nehalem R
Lost Creek
Nehalem R
Nehalem Falls
CG
OR 53
Foss
N
MILES
0 1 2 3 4 5
Nehalem
Manzanita
Nehalem Bay
101

turnoff. An alternative put-in is located approximately 7 miles farther downstream about 150 feet upstream of the Salmonberry River confluence. This divides the run into the upper 7-mile class 1 and 2 rapids and the lower 7-mile class 3 rapids.

The same road becomes rough and unpaved as it continues along the river to the take-out at Nehalem Falls Campground. An alternative take-out for those who run Nehalem Falls is near the bridge, less than 0.5 mile downstream. Boaters wishing to avoid the lower 7 miles of class 3 rapids can use the take-out above the confluence with the Salmonberry River.

Gauge

Nehalem River at Foss. Flow is unregulated.

Rob Blickensderfer and WKCC Editors

2 Salmonberry River
Beaver Slide Road to Nehalem River

Class: 3(4)	Length: 10.2 miles
Flow: 500–2000 cfs	Character: forested
Gradient: 72 fpm, C/PD	Season: rainy

First the good news: The Salmonberry River is a great intermediate run with a lot of great rapids and beautiful scenery. Now the bad news: The long shuttle and difficult road access to the put-in combine to make any run on the Salmonberry a long day, and they usually reduce the frequency of Salmonberry trips. Additionally, recent floods have washed out and devastated the railroad line that parallels most of the run.

The Salmonberry River is located in an isolated canyon just north of the more popular Wilson River. Access is limited to a few places, which makes hiking out of the canyon difficult in the event of an emergency. The railway right-of-way is the best option if considering hiking out of the canyon. Views of the canyon rim some 1000 feet above the river are plentiful from the river.

From the put-in at the bottom of Beaver Slide Road, the river consists of continuous class 3 rapids that are pleasantly technical at low water and a consistent flush at high water. At the confluence of the North Fork Salmonberry about 1.5 miles from the put-in, the river broadens, short pools develop between rapids, and the rapids begin to develop bigger hydraulics. Two significant rapids are found within a mile of the North Fork confluence. The first rapid, a class 3+, is a long boulder garden just upstream of a railroad tunnel. Scout on the left. The second rapid, Chew-Chew (class 4), is about 0.5 mile downstream just after Bathtub Creek, which enters on the left. Chew-Chew begins with a steep drop over some boulders and finishes with a few pushy waves and holes. Most people choose to punch several holes on the far left or to boof the large boulder in the center. Scout/portage on the right.

Below Chew-Chew, the river continues through several fun class 3–3+ rapids until it gradually flattens out. Some great views of the canyon are found in this section. The rapids pick up again as boaters approach the end of the run. Take out under the road bridge on river right. It's about 200 feet upstream of the confluence with the Nehalem River.

Hazards

Wood and other debris from the railroad could be dangerous anywhere along the run but especially in the first 1.5 miles. Scout Chew-Chew. Beaver Slide Road is very steep and can be very slick when wet. Four-wheel drive is recommended, although a high-clearance vehicle might be okay if the road is dry.

Access

Bring a good map to prevent getting lost on the shuttle. To reach the put-in, take Salmonberry Road south from US 26. Salmonberry Road is about 0.5 mile west of milepost 30. Stay straight at the four-way intersection about 1.2 miles from US 26. Turn left at the sharp turn about 4.4 miles from the highway. Turn left at the three-way intersection just over 8.5 miles from the highway, and after about a mile begin the long, 1.5 mile descent down Beaver Slide Road to the river.

As of this writing (2015), there is a plan to possibly gate the Beaver Slide Road closed during the summer months, but to keep it open for boaters during the winter paddling season. Before setting out, it would be wise to check with the Oregon Department of Forestry's Forest Grove office (phone: 503-357-2191) to find out about the road's condition and accessibility. One could also hike down the road to the put-in, if necessary.

To reach the take-out, return to US 26 and travel west. Turn south about 0.75 mile west of milepost 21 on US 26 and continue south along the Nehalem River to the bridge over the Salmonberry River.

Gauge

None. Generally, if the Wilson River is over 3000 cfs (Wilson River at Tillamook gauge), there will be enough water. The Salmonberry River drops more quickly than the Wilson River, so it is usually better when the Wilson gauge is rising.

Pete Giordano and WKCC Editors

Kilchis River

3 ★ Kilchis River
Confluence of North Fork and South Fork to Little South Fork

Class: 2+(3)	Length: 7.2 miles
Flow: 300–800 cfs	Character: forested
Gradient: 38 fpm, PD-C	Season: rainy

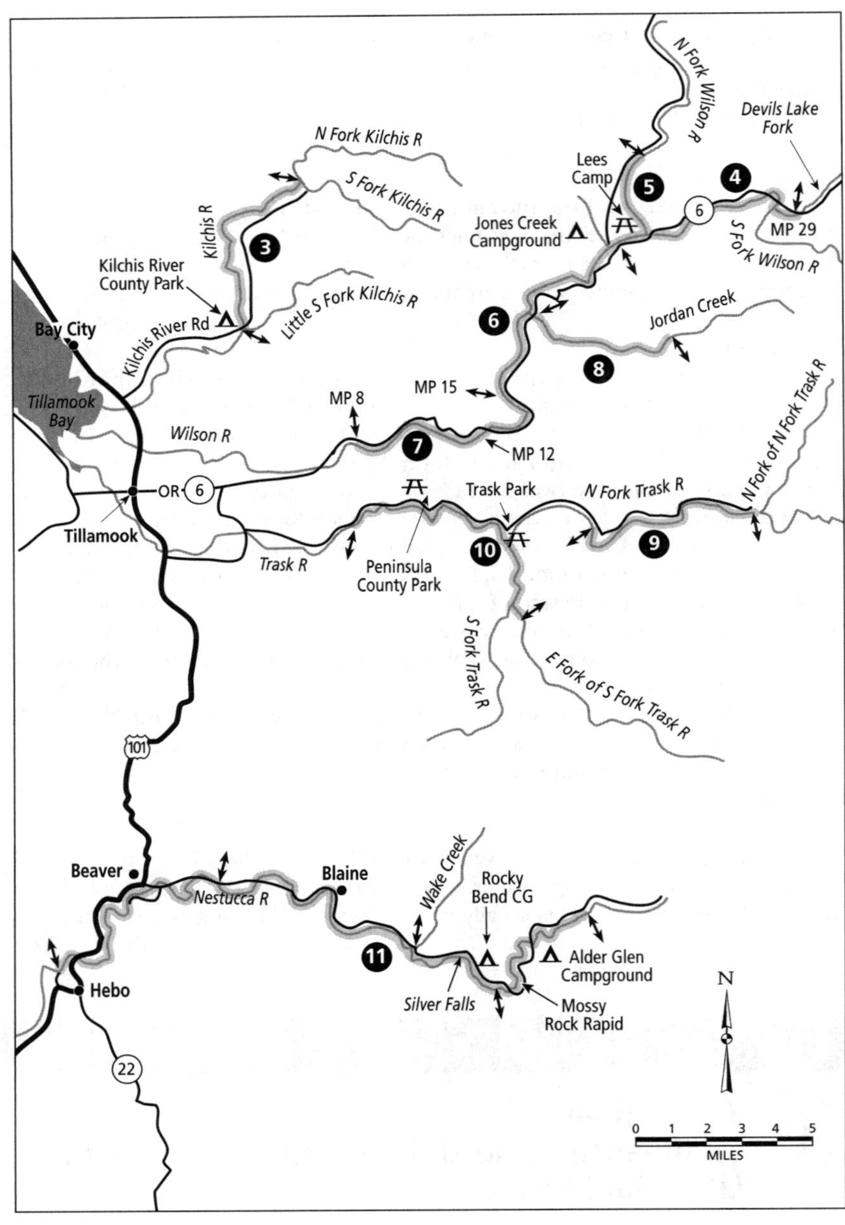

N Fork Wilson R
Devils Lake Fork
N Fork Kilchis R
S Fork Kilchis R
Lees Camp
5
4
Jones Creek Campground
6
MP 29
Kilchis R
S Fork Wilson R
3
Kilchis River County Park
Little S Fork Kilchis R
Jordan Creek
Kilchis River Rd
Bay City
6
8
Tillamook Bay
MP 15
MP 8
Wilson R
7
MP 12
N Fork of N Fork Trask R
OR 6
Trask Park
N Fork Trask R
Tillamook
Peninsula County Park
10
9
Trask R
S Fork Trask R
E Fork of S Fork Trask R
101
Wake Creek
Rocky Bend CG
Beaver
Blaine
Nestucca R
Alder Glen Campground
11
Hebo
Silver Falls
Mossy Rock Rapid
22
N
0 1 2 3 4 5
MILES

Beautiful clear green water, small waterfalls cascading in from steep banks, moss-laden trees, and few signs of civilization characterize this scenic coastal stream. The run from the confluence begins with several class 2 drops pushing around blind corners, with an abundance of eddies to catch. This section offers nice play spots and surfing waves. Toward the middle of the run are several 3-foot ledges. All the obvious chutes are runnable, but be sure to check for logs in the drops before committing yourself.

At about mile 3.5, the gradient increases and the river becomes more constricted. This section cannot be seen from the road but can be lined or portaged. Two good class 3 rapids in here can be run without scouting by eddy hopping. Soon the gradient eases and the river splits around several islands. At about mile 5 is a tricky drop. Here the river narrows and pours over a basalt ledge. The route seems clear but should be scouted. A large diagonal hole at the bottom loves to give the unwary open boater a twist (and often a swim). The remainder of the trip is a pleasant class 1+ to 2.

Hazards

The ledge at about mile 5 should be scouted. Be sure to keep an eye out for logs. At high water, this narrow run becomes a little pushier, but new surfing spots appear, and the major rapids are no more difficult.

Access

Take US Highway 101 north from Tillamook. Turn right on Alderbrook Road, following signs to Kilchis River. Drive upstream 2.3 miles from US 101 and turn right across the river. Continue up on Kilchis River Forest Road for another 2.7 miles until it crosses a sizable creek (Little South Fork Kilchis River). The take-out is on the left just above the confluence of the Little South Fork with the Kilchis River. It is advisable to walk to the river to ensure recognition of the take-out from the riverside view.

To reach the put-in, drive another 6.7 miles up the road to the bridge over the South Fork Kilchis. Put in just upstream of this confluence. Less steep put-in options may be found by driving upstream of this confluence along the North Fork Kilchis; however, lower flows and logjams may present a problem in this upper section. A class 3 rapid (Let's Make a Deal) is located about a mile up from the confluence put-in, and a bridge crossing the North Fork Kilchis is located 1.8 miles up from the confluence.

Gauge

None exists. Generally there will be enough water when the Wilson River gauge is over 1100 cfs and rising, but there is no consistent correlation. The Kilchis rises and falls more quickly than the Wilson. When the Wilson is too high to run, the Kilchis is usually a good alternative.

Alex McNeily and Paul Norman

Wilson River and Tributaries

4 Devils Lake Fork Wilson River/Wilson River Near Milepost 29 to Jones Creek Campground

Class 3+(4)	Length: 7 miles
Flow: 300–1000 cfs	Character: forested
Gradient: 55 fpm, C	Season: rainy

This is a great little run, just an hour from Portland. It shares the emerald water and lush coastal forest that make this and the rest of the Wilson River runs so beautiful. Significant ledge drops are mixed with steep, continuous whitewater. Oregon 6 follows the Devils Lake Fork and the Wilson and crosses the latter three times but does not intrude. Even if flows are too low on the Devils Lake Fork, the flow on the Wilson may be sufficient.

Put in at the normal put-in if there's enough water and you will be rewarded with a fast, continuous class 2–3 ride down to the confluence with the South Fork of the Wilson. If flows are too low, put in at the next bridge 0.5 mile downstream on the Wilson River, where the volume is approximately double. (The Devils Lake Fork joins the South Fork to form the Wilson River just above this highway bridge at milepost 28.)

Once on the Wilson, the action picks up. First one encounters a class 3 rapid followed by class 3+ Elk Creek Drop. Elk Creek Drop is a ledge drop with a boulder in the center and a rock wall at the bottom. Scout on the right and, normally, run on the right. Class 2+ water follows as one passes under the second highway bridge. The highway is on river right for the next 5 miles.

About 2 miles below the put-in, the river becomes braided into multiple channels. This area is clearly visible from the road. The middle channel is best. About 4 miles into the run is another multiple channel section. A short way downstream where a few homes are visible from the river is the start of the Lees Camp community. Keep off this private property. About 0.5 mile farther downstream, the North Fork Wilson River enters from the right. The remaining 1 mile of the run includes mostly class 2 water, but there is one class 3 drop just above the take-out at Jones Creek Campground. Take out under the campground bridge or 100 yards downstream on the right.

More adventurous boaters can put in 2 miles upstream from the usual put-in, adding several tougher rapids, which are class 4+ at lower levels and class 5 at higher flows. Check for logs, and keep in mind that road construction has resulted in sharp rocks in these rapids.

Hazards

Elk Creek Drop should be scouted before beginning the trip or from the river as logs could make this rapid very dangerous. Be especially alert for logs in the braided sections of the river.

Access

The Wilson River Highway, Oregon 6, follows the river. The normal put-in is between mileposts 28 and 29 on Oregon 6 at the bridge over the Devils Lake Fork. The turnout is on the south side and a trail leads to the river. Alternative put-ins are 0.5 mile downstream at milepost 28 at the bridge over the Wilson River, or 2 miles upstream at the Drift Creek Road bridge.

To reach the take-out, continue downstream to milepost 23, where the Jones Creek Campground road crosses the Wilson River. Parking is available on the north side of the river.

Gauge

Wilson River at Tillamook. Because this section is so far from the gauge, its flow is a fraction of the Tillamook value. The minimum gauge reading is about 3200 cfs. Optimal flows are 3400–4000 cfs on the gauge. Flows on the Wilson change quickly, so do not rely on 12-hour-old gauge readings.

Laurie Pavey, Alex McNeily, Paul Norman, and WKCC Editors

5 North Fork Wilson River Confluence with West Fork to Jones Creek Campground

Class: 3	Length: 2.6 miles
Flow: 500 cfs	Character: forested
Gradient: 93 fpm, C	Season: rainy

This short run with continuous rapids can be completed quickly on a cold, snowy day, but abundant play waves and holes invite a longer stay. Boaters can extend the run by putting in farther upstream on either the West Fork or the upper reach of the North Fork. The North Fork is more interesting and has more gradient (estimated at 140 fpm). Scout the river from the road to decide whether you want to do this, and pay particular attention to logs, which are a major hazard in this narrow upper section. An interesting plunge drop about 0.3 mile above the confluence with the West Fork deserves scouting.

About 1.5 miles below the West Fork confluence, a nice waterfall comes in from the left bank. Below the waterfall are several ledges that deserve caution because rocks and trees regularly slide into the river from the steep right bank. It is possible to scout and portage on the left. After the ledges, you pass the houses of Lees Camp. This is a private area with a private road and is not an alternative access. Watch out for a nasty midstream boulder on a right turn.

Below Lees Camp, the North Fork merges with the main Wilson River, which then splits into channels where the positions and status of logs and debris are subject to change. It is 1 mile to the take-out from here. Powerlines cross the river just above Jones Creek Rapid, a fun series of waves, which can be scouted from the bridge at the take-out. Below Jones Creek Rapid is a good take-out path a little below the bridge on river right.

Hazards

Watch for strainers at the ledges halfway through the run.

Access

The road to Jones Creek Campground, the take-out, is at milepost 23 on Oregon 6. The road to the camp crosses the Wilson River, and Jones Creek Rapid is visible from the bridge. Park at the day-use area across the bridge.

To reach the put-in, continue on Jones Creek Road 0.2 mile and take the first right turn. The North Fork road roughly follows the river, but you will not always see it. Take a left at the first fork (at 1.4 miles), bypassing the Diamond Mill OHV area, and then a right at the second (1.7 miles). It is 3 miles to the put-in from the take-out. Sometimes there are directional signs at forks and intersections to help you find your way, but do not count on them.

Gauge

None exists. If it looks like enough water at the confluence with the West Fork, it is probably runnable. If the Wilson River at Tillamook gauge is over 2000 cfs, enough water is probably present, but a gauge reading over 3000 cfs is usually better.

Linda Starr and WKCC Editors

6★ Wilson River
Jones Creek Campground to Milepost 15

Class: 2+ to 3; 4-	Length: 8 miles
Flow: 1200–2300 cfs; 7000 cfs	Character: forested
Gradient: 31 fpm, PD	Season: rainy

On this run, the Wilson River is relatively narrow as it winds between basalt rock walls. At medium flow, most rapids are pool-drop and eddies directly below major rapids are turbulent with eddies of their own. The river curves frequently, pushing curling rapids off rock walls. Many small tributaries and cascading streams join the river, and the volume increases as the run progresses.

The usual put-in is directly under the Jones Creek Campground bridge, or about 100 yards downstream. Some paddlers carry their boats upstream to run the class 3 drop just above the bridge. The first several miles have warm-up class 2 rapids. At about mile 2.5, an island divides the river. Most of the water flows through the right channel over a steep, rocky boulder garden. Scout from the island.

Below the island, the river narrows into a gorge. This section is extremely turbulent at high water and excitingly turbulent with good drops at medium levels. At medium levels, play spots are common throughout the gorge. Jordan Creek enters on the left about 1 mile below the gorge, and good play spots continue for the next 3 miles. The take-out is on a rock ledge on the left, before a right bend in the river. Look for parked shuttle cars.

The Wilson is a popular winter steelhead fishing stream; minimize your contact with the many anglers along this section. Do not play in their fishing holes.

Hazards

The river can rise from a mild run to a hair-raiser within 3–4 hours, so beware of fast runoff. The gorge section consists of several blind corners with no place to land or to scout from the river, so check the gorge from the road during the shuttle. Look for logs jamming the drops.

Access

Oregon 6 parallels the Wilson River throughout this run. The put-in at Jones Creek Campground is at milepost 23 on Oregon 6. Cross the bridge over the Wilson and park in the day-use area. The take-out is opposite milepost 15 on Oregon 6. Park on a small turnout overlooking a rocky ledge. The carry from the river is not too difficult. A common alternative for a 5-mile run is to take out just below the Jordan Creek confluence (milepost 18), which offers an easy carry up to the highway. Take care with traffic on this blind curve.

Gauge

Wilson River at Tillamook. Minimum flow is 1200 cfs. Optimal flows are 1500–2500 cfs.

Kim Hummer and WKCC Editors

7 ★ Wilson River
Milepost 15 to Milepost 8 Boat Ramp

Class: 2+(3); 3+(4)		Length: 7.7 miles	
Flow: 900–2300 cfs; 2400–7000 cfs		Character: forested	
Gradient: 25 fpm, PD		Season: rainy	

The Wilson River flows through some beautiful sunless canyons where spectacular hues of green and yellow lichens cover the trees and rocks. The clean white bark of the young alder trees contrasts with the large green Sitka spruces and red maples. Before the trees leaf out in the spring, young saplings and flowers can be seen growing from the thick moss of the tree limbs. This beauty can be enjoyed by boaters drifting in the glassy reflective pools and flatwater between the rapids. Oregon 6, never more than 0.5 mile from the river, and the homes overlooking the river do not detract from the scenery. One does not realize that the drifting speed is 4–7 miles per hour until one looks through the crystal-clear water to see the colored rocks flashing by. This run becomes more difficult as the flows increase above 1500 cfs. Timid or less experienced boaters can use the put-in at milepost 12 to avoid the harder rapids upstream.

The lead-in rapid just before The Narrows, Wilson River (Mark Scantlebury)

SECTION 1: MILEPOST 15 TO MILEPOST 12, 3.5 MILES, CLASS 3(3+)

The put-in has a set of nice waves that are perfect for warming up. After about 0.5 mile of short class 2+ rapids, the river begins to drop more steeply. This is a good time to stop and scout for logs in The Narrows—class 3+ at moderate flows—because a swim at the first drop might mean a swim through the narrow slot, which is only about 6 feet wide. Scout and/or portage on the right.

About 1 mile farther downstream, a small creek enters on the left near a wonderful ledge play wave that is about 20 feet wide. Just below is the second major rapid on this run, Yardsale. Here you will find a rock garden with room-size boulders scattered across the river. About halfway through this rapid, you can eddy out on river right to scout the steeper part of the drop. The usual run at moderate flows is in the middle-right channel to avoid the large hole at bottom right. Beyond, the river is filled with fun play spots interspersed with quiet water. Some paddlers like to put in 3 miles above, at Jordan Creek, to extend this section of class 3 whitewater.

SECTION 2: MILEPOST 12 TO MILEPOST 8, 4.2 MILES, CLASS 2

This section is a great run for novices, with beautiful scenery and fun, playful rapids at moderate flows. Although only 4.2 miles long, the run feels much longer and is good for cold, short winter days. Immediately below the put-in, the river enters an especially scenic part of the canyon. At 0.5 mile, a nice chute occurs between narrow rock walls spanned by a small bridge. For the next 2 miles, easy class 1+ to 2 rapids are interspersed with slower water, allowing one time to enjoy the scenic canyon.

Near the end of the run, after the river bends right, look for a boat skid with handrails and steps, the take-out. For a longer trip, one can enjoy an additional 2.3 miles of class 1 water ending at the Mills Bridge boat ramp.

Hazards

Section 1: The Narrows should be scouted every trip because logs in the slot would be a major problem. Yardsale Rapid should be scouted at least the first time down. *Section 2:* None in particular.

Access

The Wilson River Highway, Oregon 6, follows the river. The upper put-in is opposite milepost 15. Park on a small turnout overlooking a rocky ledge. The section 2 put-in is at milepost 12, just upstream of the highway bridge. Park in the pullout on the north side of the highway on river left and follow a trail down to the river.

The take-out is located just west of milepost 8 at a wide turnout: the Siskeyville drift-boat skid launch.

Gauge

Wilson River at Tillamook. Minimum flow is 1200 cfs. Optimal flows are 1500–2500 cfs.

Lloyd Likens, Laurie Pavey, and WKCC Editors

8 Jordan Creek
Hann Creek to Wilson River

Class: 3–3+	Length: 5.1 miles
Flow: 150–500 cfs	Character: forested
Gradient: 90 fpm, C	Season: rainy

This tight technical creek, which flows into the Wilson River, is a great introduction to creek boating and can be run after a good rain or when the Wilson is around 5000 cfs. Lots of maneuvering and tight turns are required. Many of the drops are blind and rather precipitous and possibly blocked by logs. At low water, you will find several ledges with narrow slots, and at high water big holes are common. Fun, technical ledge drops are interspersed with calmer sections of river. The last mile of the run cannot be seen from the road and contains several big rapids. The scenery is excellent throughout the run, despite the presence of the road. Take out at the confluence with the Wilson, or continue paddling down the Wilson a couple more miles for a few more good rapids.

Most boaters choose to put in at the end of the road at the Hann bridge for a 5.1-mile run. More adventurous paddlers can hike and bushwhack another 1.5–2 miles upstream of the Hann pedestrian bridge along the old roadbed. The uppermost put-in is just below a small, narrow waterfall in a rock gorge. From this put-in you are immediately confronted with a sharp 5-foot ledge. This ledge drop is very difficult to scout at river level, almost impossible to portage, and it develops a nasty hole at high water. If you do not want to run the difficult drop within the gorge, put in anywhere along the old road downstream of it.

Hazards

The biggest hazards are overhanging brush and logs. When the flow on the Wilson gauge is over 10,000 cfs, large holes develop and pools between rapids shrink. Several of the biggest rapids can be seen from the road and are good indicators of the difficulty of the run.

Access

From Oregon 6, which parallels the Wilson River, stop at a pullout by the bridge over Jordan Creek (near milepost 18); the take-out is here. Proceed upstream on Jordan Creek Road. Pass the Jordan Creek OHV Campground at mile 2. Continue upstream, staying on river right. There will be a side bridge near mile 2.5, and another at mile 4.5. It is worthwhile to stop and scout at each of the bridges. A final steel pedestrian bridge (Hann bridge) will be at the end of the drivable road, about 5 miles up from Oregon 6. This is the put-in.

Gauge

None exists. On a rising Wilson River gauge, Jordan Creek is usually runnable if the flow on the Wilson gauge is above 3000 cfs. On a falling Wilson River gauge, Jordan Creek is usually runnable if the Wilson gauge is above 6000 cfs; 5000 cfs on the Wilson is considered an optimal level.

Alex McNeily, Paul Norman, Stephen Duff, and WKCC Editors

Trask River and Tributaries

9★ North Fork Trask River
North Fork of the North Fork Trask River to Bridge

Class: 3	Length: 7.5 miles
Flow: 1600–3000 cfs	Character: forested valley
Gradient: 53 fpm, C	Season: rainy

The North Fork Trask River flows through second-growth coastal forest and drains an area of steep ridges punctuated by high rock walls, canyons, and frequent waterfalls. The upper half of this scenic run contains most of the significant rapids, including three drops approximately 3 miles from the put-in. The second of these drops is a river wide basalt ledge with the flow pouring over the right side. Shortly downstream is a rapid formed by a landslide. Scout/portage on the left. A significant boulder garden can be found downstream from the landslide rapid. Rock gardens and small play spots are plentiful. While rapids are less frequent on the lower half of the run, the road and river part company, providing a sense of isolation as well as a difficult hike out if problems arise.

The 4.3-mile section from the take-out to Trask River County Park has not been run by the authors, but has been run by others. The gradient is 37 fpm, continuous. About 0.4 mile upriver from Trask park is a difficult 8-foot drop through basalt that should be scouted on the shuttle if this section is to be run. The location of this drop is marked by a basalt outcropping above the road on river right and follows a sharp right bend in the river.

Hazards
All the significant rapids can be scouted from the river.

Access
About 1 mile south of Tillamook on US 101, go east on Long Prairie Road for 3.2 miles. Immediately after crossing the river, turn right on Trask River Road. (Boaters traveling west on Oregon 6 from Portland can turn south onto Trask River Road 2 miles before reaching Tillamook.) Proceed 10 miles upriver to the North Fork Road, 0.2 mile before Trask River County Park. Turn left and travel 3.5 miles on this dirt road to a prominent fork on a sharp right bend. The take-out is reached by traveling 0.7 mile down the right fork, crossing the bridge, and going upriver about 100 yards.

To get to the put-in, return to the fork and travel 7.8 miles upriver on the left fork. When a second fork is encountered, bear right and go several hundred yards to the put-in at the confluence of the North Fork of the North Fork Trask River with the Middle Fork of the North Fork Trask River.

Gauge
Trask River above Cedar Creek. The minimum recommended flow on this gauge is 1600 cfs, with optimal gauge flows at 2000–3000 cfs. (The flows listed above are gauge flows; actual flows will be less since the gauge is far downstream.)

Steve Cramer, Cliff Ryer, and Craig Colby

10 ★ Trask River
Fish Hatchery to Cedar Creek Boat Ramp

Class: 3(4)	Length: 9.6 miles
Flow: 1000–2500 cfs	Character: forested; residential
Gradient: 34 fpm, C	Season: rainy

Paddlers can combine sections 1 and 2 for a long day, or choose to do either section for a shorter run.

SECTION 1: FISH HATCHERY TO UPPER PENINSULA, 6.6 MILES, CLASS 3
The run begins just below the hatchery on the East Fork of the South Fork Trask River and passes through a lightly populated valley. The gradient is steepest in the first 2 miles, with several tight twisting drops. The last of these is recognized by

the remains of a log bridge hanging over the river 50 yards downstream. Scout the drops for debris.

After the confluence with the North Fork at mile 2.2, the gradient lessens but still provides interesting rapids and play spots. At mile 3.5 a busy class 2 rapid on a left bend leads immediately to a class 3 ledge drop with a reversal that must be punched. Paddlers in kayaks or decked single canoes should not be surprised when they disappear briefly in this hole. The remaining run is enjoyable class 2 water.

SECTION 2: UPPER PENINSULA TO CEDAR CREEK, 3 MILES, CLASS 3(4)

This run begins with easy class 1–2 water around the Trask "peninsula." At the tip of the peninsula, a class 2 wave train provides a fun ride, and several ledges provide surf opportunities at different flows leading to the Lower Peninsula boat ramp. After the Lower Peninsula, the river gets busier as it approaches the Upper Dam Drop (class 3) and the Lower Dam Hole (class 3–4 depending on flow). Both rapids can be portaged on the right, and both can be scouted from the road. The Upper Dam Drop gets more difficult at higher flows. The Dam Hole varies in difficulty as flow changes: at low flow (below 750 cfs), it's bony and prone to face-bashing; at medium flow (1500–2500 cfs), it becomes a fast chute; and at high flow, it transforms into a big class 4 hole. Fortunately, the Dam Hole drops into a large pool, enabling easier recoveries.

Below the Dam Hole, there is a great whirlpool at 1100 cfs—time to practice your mystery move! Class 2 water continues for another 0.75 mile until the start of Rocky Road. This continuous boulder garden runs for 1 mile with class 2+ (3+ at high flows) rapids. Eddy scouting is recommended due to pour-overs and potential wood problems, though at flows above 2000 cfs, this gets increasingly difficult as eddies wash out. Much of this section can be scouted from the road on the way up. After a brief let-up in the action, there is one final class 3 drop, and then class 2 rapids for 0.5 mile to the take-out at a drift boat launch on river right.

The best part of this section 2 run is that it can be run from the town of Tillamook in less than 2 hours, including the shuttle.

Hazards

Section 1: Scout the drops at roughly at 0.5 mile and 2 miles. The drop at 3.5 miles can be seen from the road. *Section 2:* Upper Dam Drop and Dam Hole.

Access

About 1 mile south of Tillamook on US 101, go east on Long Prairie Road for 3.2 miles. Immediately after crossing the river, turn right on Trask River Road. (Boaters traveling west on Oregon 6 from Portland can turn south onto Trask River Road 2 miles before reaching Tillamook.) Continue upstream 3.6 miles to the Cedar Creek boat slide, the take-out for section 2. Continue upstream another 2.4 miles to the Upper Peninsula boat ramp (the put-in for section 2). To reach the uppermost put-in, continue upriver from Upper Peninsula for 4.2 miles, go past Trask River County Park and across the North Fork Trask River. Continue another 1.9 miles up the South Fork Trask to a fork in the road. Turn left and go 0.3 mile to a turnout, the put-in, which is just before the fish hatchery. Note:

An alternative skid-rail launch is available to drift boats about 2.5 miles above the Upper Peninsula boat ramp. Watch for elk during the shuttle.

Gauge

Trask River above Cedar Creek.

Steve Cramer, Cliff Ryder, and Jake Mulder

Nestucca River

11 Nestucca River
Bridge BLM 3-7-28 to Boat Ramp near Hebo

Class 1–5	Length: 6–28 miles
Flow: 800–3000 cfs	Character: forested; farmland
Gradient: 10–65 fpm	Season: rainy

The Nestucca River, classified as a State Scenic Waterway, drops continuously through a lush scenic forest into a narrow valley populated by a few small farms. The upper reaches, in the Siuslaw National Forest, are uniformly steep, with numerous creeks entering over boulder shoals or waterfalls. After leaving the forest and entering private land, the river becomes pool-drop, and then eventually flattens out to a consistent low gradient. The lower reaches are heavily fished for winter steelhead from drift boats and from the bank. Please be courteous.

SECTION 1: BRIDGE BLM 3-7-28 TO ROCKY BEND CAMPGROUND

Class: 3	Length: 5.7 miles
Flow: 1250–3000 cfs, gauge	Character: forested
Gradient: 44 fpm, C	Season: rainy

The river in this section is almost continuous with drops that vary slightly in steepness. The flow nearly doubles in this section. Much of the river cannot be seen from the road high above it. About 2 miles down is Alder Glen Campground, with a fantastic waterfall. After passing the waterfall, continue under the main road bridge. A bit farther along are two relatively long islands. At the first island, the left channel has more water. At the second island, you will probably need to scout, because, in the past, the run-outs of both channels have been too full of boulders and logs to navigate. One of the small rapids below here is called Little Carnivore because of its resemblance to the hydraulics of Carnivore on the North Santiam River. Another mile downstream, Testament Creek, a large tributary, enters from the left. Immediately below is Mossy Rocks Rapid, class 3, identified by several large moss-covered rocks in the river. Much of the river flows onto a large boulder at the bottom of the rapids. During the last mile, after again passing under the main road bridge, enjoy a couple of steep, fast chutes that may remind you of a Disney ride. Take out on the right at Rocky Bend Campground.

Hazards
Beware of logs or trees in the river, especially in the upper reaches. Mossy Rocks Rapid can be scouted from the large turnout on the west side of the road near Bible Creek Road. Follow the small trail 200 feet east to the rapid.

SECTION 2. ROCKY BEND CAMPGROUND TO WAKE CREEK – NO TRESPASSING

Class 3 (4) (5)	Length: 3.7 miles	Gradient: 46 fpm

The first mile below Rocky Bend Campground is fast and includes a class 4 rapid. Below that are private land and a class 5 rapid, Silver Falls, and another class 4. Do not run this section, because the landowner has said she'll call the sheriff if she sees boaters trespassing. Near milepost 13, a private bridge crosses the Nestucca. The river is fenced and posted for another mile or so downstream. Do not trespass.

SECTION 3. WAKE CREEK TO WOLF CREEK ROAD

Class: 3	Length: 9.4 miles
Flow: 1000–2000 cfs	Character: rural, pastureland
Gradient: 28 fpm, C/PD	Season: rainy

Put in at the parking turnout along the river around Wake Creek, near milepost 10.5. This area is below the posted private property. The upper part of this section is fairly continuous, whereas the lower part is more pool-drop. This is a fine class 2+ to 3 run with surfing waves, pour-overs, and some nice wave trains. There are two class 3 rapids that can be scouted from the road. Three Rock Rapid, at milepost 9.5, is identifiable by three large rocks near the middle of the river. The best route is between the middle rock and the left rock. At milepost 7 is Z-Drop, an almost river-wide ledge with a serious reversal. It can be run at the far left. Less than a half mile downstream is the community of Blaine, with a drift boat slide near the community church. Below here, the river has long, slow pools between class 2 rapids. To shorten the run, take out at the boat skid on Bora Road. For the full run, continue on for 2 miles of class 1 riffles, pass under the highway bridge, and land at the boat ramp (also called "Fourth Bridge") on Wolf Creek Road.

Hazards
Three Rock Rapid and Z-Drop are easily scouted from the road.

SECTION 4. WOLF CREEK ROAD TO NEAR HEBO

Class: 1	Length: 9.3 miles
Flow: 800–3000 cfs	Character: rural, pastureland
Gradient: 11 fpm, C	Season: rainy

From the Wolf Creek boat ramp, the river continues through the rolling hills and dairy farms of Tillamook County. It becomes wider and flatter, yet still contains riffles. Drift boaters are commonly seen in this stretch. The length of the trip can be varied by the choice of access. The lower Nestucca River below Hebo is described by Philip N. Jones in *Canoe and Kayak Routes of Northwest Oregon*.

Access

From the northern Willamette Valley go to Carlton on Oregon 47. Go west on Meadow Creek Road, which becomes Nestucca River Road along the river.
From the southern Willamette Valley, go to Willamina. Follow Willamina Creek Road north, turn left onto Coast Creek Road, right onto Gilbert Creek Road, left onto Bible Creek Road to Upper Nestucca Road.

From the coast, take US 101 to the town of Beaver.

Section 1. For the put-in, go 19 road miles above Beaver using Blaine Road and Upper Nestucca Road, then turn right onto BLM 3-7-28 and go 0.1 mile. The take-out is at Rocky Bend Campground, 14.3 road miles above Beaver.

Section 2. Posted "No Trespassing." Access is denied due to private property from Rocky Bend Campground to approximately milepost 10.5.

Section 3. The put-in is at Wake Creek near milepost 10.5, measured from US 101 in Beaver. Parking is limited here. For the short run's take-out, turn north from the Upper Nestucca Road onto Borba Road 3.7 miles up from US 101 and proceed 1.1 mile to a boat skid. For the full run, turn north onto Wolf Creek Road at the bridge 2.6 miles upstream from US 101 and go 100 feet to the boat ramp.

Section 4. The put-in is the lowest take-out on section 3's run. Several take-out areas are available. The First Bridge take-out (off Blaine Road 0.4 mile above Beaver) enables a 3.2-mile run; Bixby Road, a 4-mile run; Farmer's Creek, a 6.8-mile run; and finally Three Rivers County Boat Launch (fee area, 0.5 mile west of Hebo), a 9.3-mile run.

Gauge

Nestucca River near Beaver. The gauge is 2 miles downstream of Beaver. The river has numerous side streams that raise the flow drastically between sections 1 and 4. The gauge is a good indicator of the flow in the lower miles (sections 3 and 4), but not a good indicator in sections 1 and 2. With a falling flow, a gauge of 1200 cfs is a minimum flow on section 1, a low-adequate flow for section 3, and plenty for section 4.

Note: Niagara Falls is well worth seeing. Near milepost 11, turn south onto Niagara Road. Go uphill about 4 miles, turn right at the sign, and go downhill another mile to the trail head. It's a 1-mile hike in.

For more information about paddling the Nestucca River, see the Tillamook County Water Trail information (Appendix B).

Rob Blickensderfer, Kathy Sercu, and Gary Hahn

Siletz River and Tributaries

12 North Fork Siletz River
Boulder Creek to South Fork Siletz River

Class: 3–4+(5), P	Length: 4.4 miles
Flow: 700 cfs	Character: forested; clear-cut
Gradient: 61 fpm, PD	Season: rainy

This is a short but fun section of the Siletz, containing significant whitewater. All major drops can be easily portaged and can be seen from the road.

A mile from the put-in is a smooth ledge that can develop a river-wide dangerous hydraulic. It is normally run on the right. Ten minutes later is Bombshell, a class 4 mini gorge on a hard right bend next to the road. Scout during the shuttle. Several miles farther is a narrow chute that drops into an even narrower chute between two badly undercut walls. A portage is recommended. However, this spot makes a good take-out as the remaining mile to the confluence with the South Fork is class 1 and 2.

Hazards

The first ledge, the gorge rapids, and the undercut chute mentioned above offer difficulty. These are serious class 5 drops at levels above 7.5 feet on the gauge.

Access

From the Central Willamette Valley, travel west on Oregon 20 and turn north on Kings Valley Highway (Oregon 223). Drive 6.4 miles north on Oregon 223 and turn left onto Hoskins Road. From here, follow the Luckiamute River, staying on the main road. Stay right at the bridge at mile 14.9 (from Oregon 223) and left at the bridge at 15.4 miles (staying south of the Valsetz Lake Bed). Cross the South Fork Siletz at mile 26.6 and continue 0.5 mile to the take-out at the North Fork–South Fork confluence.

To reach the put-in, drive up the South Fork Siletz and take the first left. Take the next left in an ugly clear-cut and follow the North Fork to the put-in. The best put-in for lower water runs is about 100 yards up Boulder Creek (5.4 miles from the South Fork turnoff) on river right.

Gauge

Just 5.5 feet on the Siletz River at Siletz gauge is not too bony. If you drive this far and the river is too high for your tastes, try the South Fork Siletz, the Luckiamute, or the Valley of the Giants section of the North Fork Siletz (yes, it has been run).

Eric Brown, Arthur Koepsell, and Chopper

13 Siletz River
Elk Creek to Buck Creek

Class: 3; 4-	Length: 4.3 miles
Flow: 1000 cfs; 3500 cfs	Character: forested; roadless
Gradient: 33 fpm, PD	Season: rainy

The river canyon here was extremely beautiful and remote once upon a time. Today, clear-cutting by the owner of these private lands is extensive, often reaching right to the river's edge. Once on the river, a boater has no contact with the road. The diversity of the rapids on this run gives intermediate boaters the chance to experience some interesting paddling.

Above the put-in for this run is Valsetz Falls. At the falls, the river squeezes through a basalt plug and plunges 70 feet within a few hundred yards. This awe-inspiring section of the river is absolutely unrunnable—but fun to view.

The put-in is at Elk Creek, 1 mile below Valsetz Falls. The two trickiest rapids (class 3) begin about a quarter mile from the put-in. The first is a right-to-left move to avoid a large wall at the bottom right. Following a brief pool, the second drop can be run on the right through a shallow boulder garden or on the left for a deep plunge off a ledge. The remainder of the river has fast, constricted chutes and broad V slicks leading to standing waves below. Take out at the Buck Creek bridge.

For a longer day's paddle, many boaters combine this run with parts of the next run (see the Siletz River: Buck Creek to Moonshine Park run). The bridge above Silache (Sil-at-chee) Rapid offers a possible take-out for those not yet ready for the class 4 Silache Rapid.

Hazards

The remoteness of the river dictates caution, since a broken paddle or boat would lead to a tough hike out.

Access

Note: The road upstream of Moonshine Park is a private logging road open for public use only on weekends.

From US 101 in Newport, take US 20 7 miles east to Toledo. Turn north on Oregon 229 to Siletz. Proceed 8 miles east on East Logsden Road to Logsden. From the Willamette Valley, Logsden is reached by taking US 20 west from Philomath to Blodgett; at Blodgett, turn north on Summit Highway and continue through Summit to Nashville. In Nashville, turn right on Rock Creek Road and proceed to Logsden. From Logsden, head north on Moonshine Park Road. About 5 miles upstream of the park, the road crosses the river at the head of Silache Rapid. Two miles farther upstream, the road forks. The right fork leads to the take-out at Buck Creek.

To reach the put-in, return to the fork and turn right, taking the left fork. Continue upstream for about 6 miles to the first and only place where the road meets

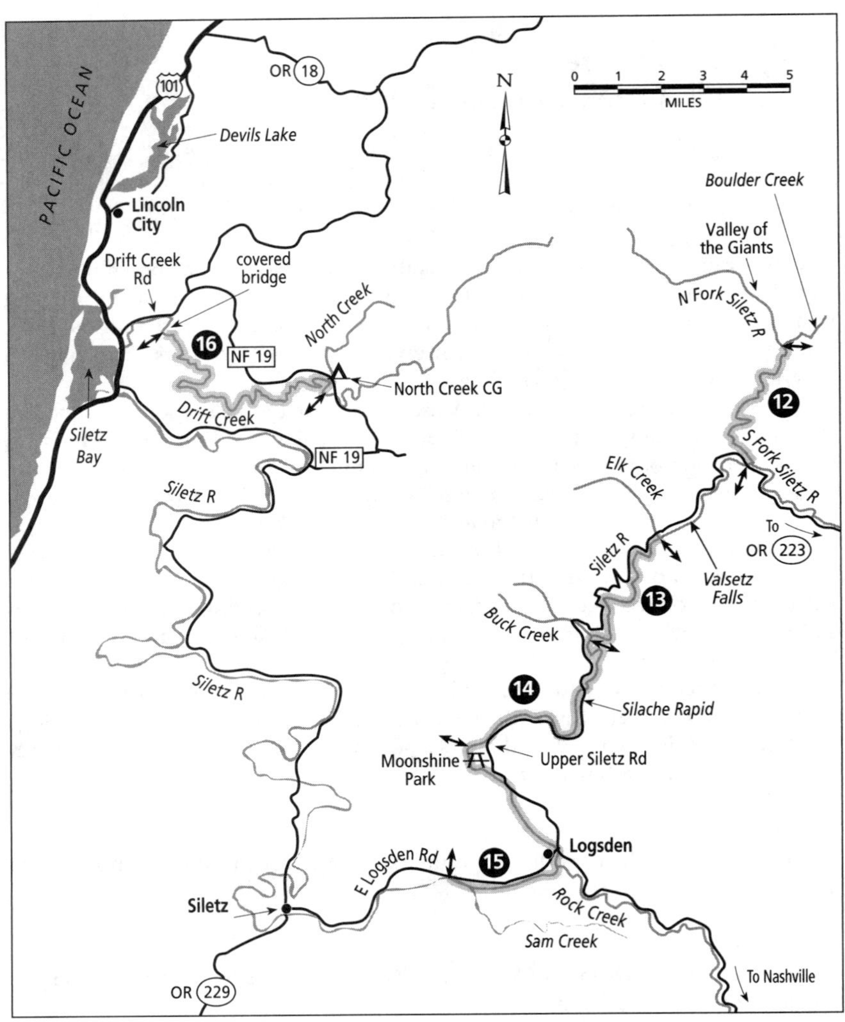

the river, at Elk Creek bridge, which is about milepost 11.5 on the forest road mileage system. This is the best put-in and avoids Valsetz Falls upstream.

To have a look at the falls, continue up the road for 1 mile. A small road to the right leads to the falls. At the head of the falls, some cable crosses the river, but there is no last eddy for unsuspecting boaters floating downstream to the falls.

Gauge

Siletz River at Siletz. A level of 900 cfs provides adequate water. At 3500 cfs, the rapids are faster and more plentiful and the run becomes pushier.

Lance Stein, Laurie Pavey, and WKCC Editors

14 ★ Siletz River
Buck Creek to Moonshine Park

Class: 3(4); 4(5)	Length: 6.1 miles
Flow: 860–4400 cfs; 4500+ cfs	Character: second growth; canyon
Gradient: 38 fpm, PD	Season: rainy

Of the 50 or more miles of boatable water on the Siletz River, this stretch has the most whitewater. Several possible put-ins vary the run's distance from 3 to 12 miles. At flows above 4500 cfs, the river is swift, and a 10.4-mile run from Elk Creek to Moonshine Park is an easy day. Buck Creek is the normal put-in and provides about 2 miles of warm-up class 2 rapids before Silache (Sil-at-chee) Rapid, the most difficult stretch on this run.

The steel bridge about 2 miles from the put-in marks the beginning of Silache Rapid. The hardest parts of Silache can be seen from the road on the way to the put-in, near Doris Falls. At low water, Silache is a class 3–4 rock garden with very distinct pools between drops. At moderate levels of 2500–4500 cfs, the pools become shorter and Silache turns into a long class 4 rapid that requires a boater to dodge rocks and holes. Above 4500 cfs on the gauge, Silache becomes a mile-long rapid with big waves and complex currents. The route through Silache straightens out, but the holes are large and the hydraulics powerful. As the flow increases, fewer and fewer eddies are available. At flows above 7500 cfs, expect the river to carry you through huge breaking waves and into big holes. Staying upright at high flows becomes very important, as there is little time to adjust your line.

Below Silache the gradient lessens and good surfing spots are plentiful. Two locations are of note. About 2 miles above the take-out is a gravel quarry on the side of the road opposite the river. At this spot, the river narrows into a rock-sided gorge called Quarry Drop. At the beginning of Quarry Drop are several holes on the right. These holes can be challenged or avoided by keeping left. The last hole, the biggest, is not noticeable from upstream. The second location of note is about 1 mile below the second bridge where the river is divided by a gravel island. The left channel has the most water and, although rocky, is the normal route. The right channel falls over about a 4-foot ledge.

At the end of the run, one can enjoy a boat shower at the base of the falls, just across the river from the take-out at the park. At low flows, many steelhead anglers will be on the river and on the shore. Please be courteous to them.

Hazards

During the drive to the put-in, scout Quarry Drop near the gravel pit about 2 miles upstream from Moonshine Park, as well as Silache Rapid and a few of the ledge drops.

Access

The shuttle road follows the river along most of this run. Follow directions to Logsden given in the Siletz River: Elk Creek to Buck Creek run. From Logsden,

Making the moves in Silache Rapid on the Siletz (Gary Adams)

follow Moonshine Park Road upriver about 3.5 miles to the park entrance. Turn left and go 0.5 mile to the take-out at the park (day-use fee) or use the boat ramp just above the park.

To reach the several optional put-ins, follow the gravel logging road that parallels the Siletz River. Please be careful on this road. It is a private road open for public use only on weekends. Continued access for boaters and anglers is dependent upon responsible use. Some boaters put in at the bridge marking the start of Silache Rapid or below Silache. The usual put-in is under the bridge over the Siletz River near Buck Creek. To reach that bridge, drive about 7 miles upstream from Moonshine Park. Just after the road crosses Buck Creek, take the right fork and continue 400 yards to the bridge over the Siletz River.

Gauge

Siletz River at Siletz. Minimum flow is 860 cfs; optimal is about 1200–3500 cfs (especially for first descents); see the description for flows above 4500 cfs.

Kim Hummer, Rick Starr, and WKCC Editors

15 Siletz River
Moonshine Park to Sam Creek Bridge

Class: 1; 2		Length: 6.6 miles	
Flow: 400 cfs; 2000 cfs		Character: rural; roads	
Gradient: 13 fpm, C		Season: rainy	

This is a pleasant and scenic run for beginning kayakers and intermediate open canoers. It is usually runnable in late spring or early fall when most of the other coastal rivers are too low to navigate. Numerous small rapids, shallow riffles, eddies, and a few small surfing waves provide enjoyable and easy boating. An occasional tree in the river is usually included. The river passes under the highway bridge (an alternative take-out) about midway through the run. After 3 more miles of easy paddling with a few riffles, the second bridge (concrete) marks the take-out at the boat ramp on the left.

Hazards

At high water, the large standing waves that develop in some places could swamp an open canoe.

Access

The take-out is 5.5 miles upstream from the town of Siletz on East Logsden Road (for directions to Siletz, see the Siletz River: Elk Creek to Buck Creek run). At Sam Creek Road, cross the river and park on the left in the lot adjacent to the boat ramp (which is called Twin Bridges boat ramp).

For the put-in, see the directions to the take-out for the Siletz River: Buck Creek to Moonshine Park run. From the parking area inside the park, it is a short carry to a nice pool put-in. If choosing to put in at the boat ramp upstream of the park, there's a class 2 rapid to negotiate just above the park.

Gauge

Siletz River at Siletz. Optimal surfing waves occur around 1500–2000 cfs.

Rob Blickensderfer

16 Drift Creek (Siletz River Tributary) North Creek to Covered Bridge

Class: 3(4) T	Length: 8.8 miles
Flow: 400–1100 cfs	Character: forested; canyon
Gradient: 28 fpm, PD	Season: rainy

Drift Creek is a small Coast Range stream that flows through a scenic forest, including 5 miles of old timber, and into Siletz Bay. The river is very beautiful, with large trees draped in moss and lichens and with many huge boulders, some as large as a house. In places the channel is very narrow—just enough to get a boat through.

The run starts in a small valley with a fairly gentle gradient, but soon flows into a steep-sided, narrow canyon with a gradient of 95 fpm. This is followed by a lower-gradient section below the canyon, which is followed by another steep, narrow canyon. It is important to remain alert at all times because logs could block almost any drop. If the water is much higher than 400 cfs, some of the channels and drops might be easier, but scouting from a boat might be more difficult. No signs of civilization appear until the last mile or so, which reveals a few buildings and fields and a view of the road. The last mile is flatwater.

Hazards

Several twisting rapids could be blocked by logs. Portages may be difficult depending on the water level. This run is in an isolated, steep canyon where climbing out to the road would be difficult. Given its remoteness and the potential for wood, class 4 skills are strongly recommended.

Access

Just south of Lincoln City, near milepost 119 on US 101, turn east onto Drift Creek Road. Go 1.6 miles to a T intersection and take a right, go 0.5 mile (past a fork to the left) to a bridge across Drift Creek, the take-out. A good parking area is located across the bridge on river left.

To reach the put-in, head back across the bridge for 0.2 mile and turn right on South Drift Creek Camp Road. In 0.8 mile you reach the junction of NF 17 and NF 19. Turn left on NF 17 and go 3.8 miles to NF 1929. Go right and head downhill for 2.5 miles to NF 19 and turn left. (NF 19 is partially blocked due to a landslide.) Follow NF 19 for 2.9 miles to the bridge across the river that serves as put-in.

Gauge

None exists. For an estimate of the flow see Pat Welch's flow page: Drift Creek (Siletz). The flow is about one-quarter of the Siletz River at Siletz gauge. Optimal flows are 800–1050 cfs.

Al Grapel, Bob Metzger, and WKCC Editors

Alsea River and Tributaries

17 Alsea River
Mill Creek Park to Boundary Road
Above Tidewater

Class: 1(2)	Length: 29.7 miles
Flow: 500–5500 cfs	Character: rural
Gradient: 7 fpm, PD	Season: rainy

The main stem of the Alsea River provides a number of runs that are used by many drift boat anglers, as well as beginning canoers and kayakers. The river usually becomes too low in the summer to negotiate in anything but a swimsuit and inner tube. Many possible runs can be designed between the various river access points described below. The milepost markers are along Oregon 34; river distances are greater than the road miles.

The 9 miles from the put-in at Mill Creek Park to Missouri Bend Recreation Site include several surfing waves at high water and rocks at low water. The 12 miles from Missouri Bend to Five Rivers is the most isolated section. It is relatively flat except for a class 2- technical rapid about 1 mile below River Edge Recreation Site. At milepost 26.7, Fall Creek, a major tributary, enters from the right. At Five Rivers Junction (milepost 20.1), Five Rivers, the largest tributary of the Alsea, enters from the left.

The next 5 miles include a nice combination of class 1 drops, eddies, and pools. During low to medium flows, this is a good introductory section of river for beginning boaters. Opposite Blackberry Campground is a small rocky shelf. The deepest slots are along the right third of the river. At milepost 15.6, Rock Crusher Rapid has a fast class 1 lead-in on a right curve, followed by a clean chute with waves at the bottom. Part of the river flows left at the head of the lead-in. Stay in the right channel.

The biggest rapid on the Alsea, Hellion Rapid (milepost 14.9), class 1–2, has swamped unwary drift boaters. The rapid tends to push boats to the right onto exposed rocks. Below the next bridge, Boundary Road bridge (milepost 13.2), the river is fairly flat. The last public access before Tidewater is 0.4 mile below the bridge (milepost 12.8). In about 2 miles, tidewater begins and continues to Alsea Bay and Waldport.

Hazards

None in particular.

Access

From Philomath, take Oregon 34 to Alsea. The first put-in is 2 miles west of Alsea at the boat ramp in Mill Creek Park, in Benton County (milepost 38.3).

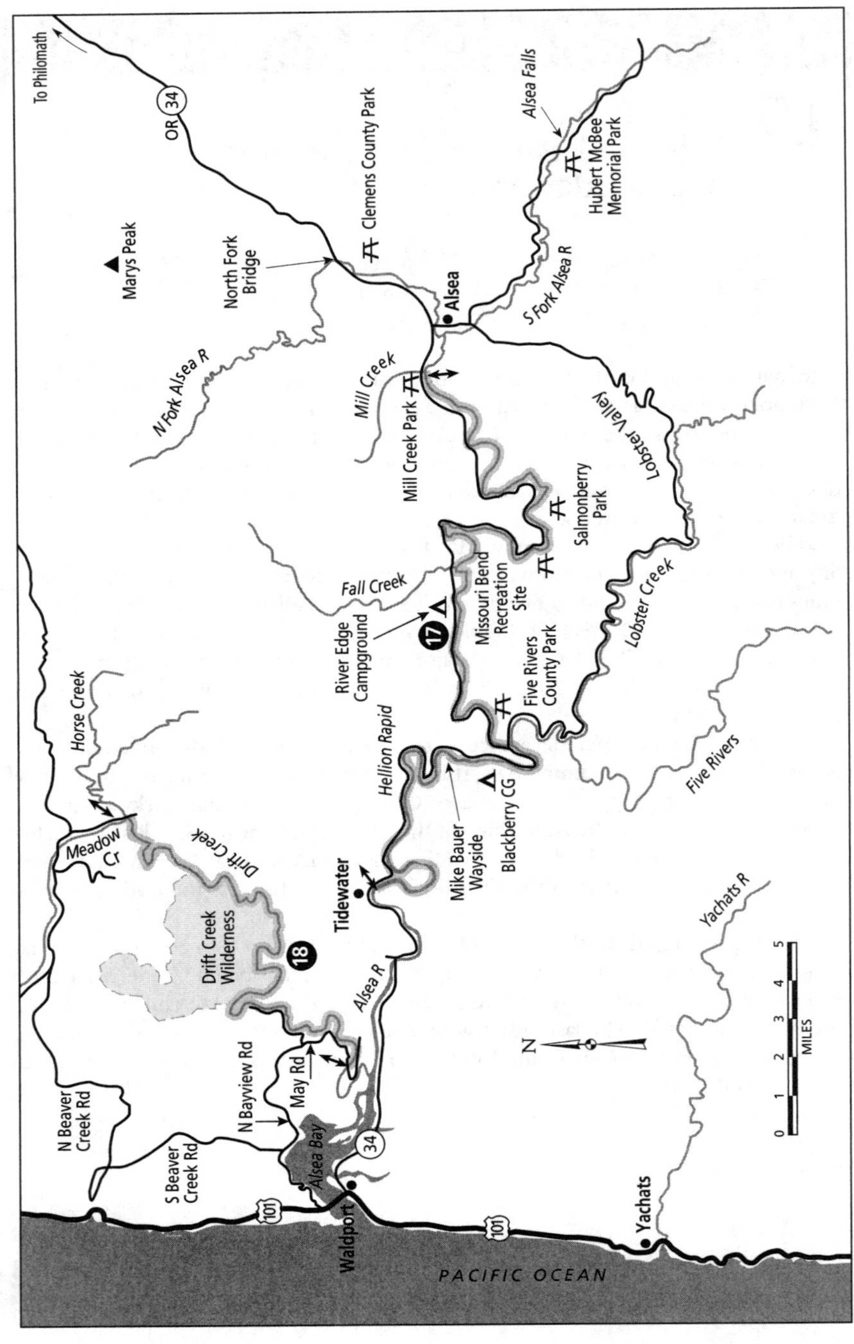
To Philomath
OR 34
Marys Peak
N Fork Bridge
Clemens County Park
Alsea Falls
Hubert McBee Memorial Park
S Fork Alsea R
N Fork Alsea R
Alsea
Mill Creek
Mill Creek Park
Lobster Valley
Salmonberry Park
Fall Creek
Missouri Bend Recreation Site
River Edge Campground
17
Five Rivers County Park
Lobster Creek
Horse Creek
Hellion Rapid
Five Rivers
Meadow Cr
Drift Creek
Mike Bauer Wayside
Blackberry CG
Tidewater
Drift Creek Wilderness
18
Yachats R
Alsea R
N Bayview Rd
May Rd
N
MILES
0 1 2 3 4 5
N Beaver Creek Rd
S Beaver Creek Rd
Alsea Bay
34
101
Waldport
101
Yachats
PACIFIC OCEAN

To reach the lowermost take-out, continue west on Oregon 34. The lowest take-out (which is not a boat ramp) is just below the Boundary Road bridge, a pullout near milepost 12.8.

Other accesses include Campbell Park (milepost 34.7); Salmonberry Park (milepost 33.1); Missouri Bend Recreation Site (milepost 31.2); River Edge Recreation Site (milepost 23.1); an unimproved boat ramp (milepost 20.5) a short distance above Five Rivers Junction that is a good place to launch paddle craft; a Siuslaw National Forest boat ramp (milepost 19.4); Blackberry Campground (milepost 17.7); and Mike Bauer Wayside (the Thissell Road bridge) is an access for paddle craft (milepost 16.5).

Gauge

Alsea River at Tidewater. A reading of 700 cfs is adequate to cover most rocks; 2000 cfs is plenty of water.

Rob Blickensderfer and WKCC Editors

18 Drift Creek (Alsea River Tributary) Meadow Creek to Lower Bridge

Class: 3	Length: 15.7 miles
Flow: 500–1000 cfs	Character: wilderness
Gradient: 24 fpm, C	Season: rainy

Drift Creek flows through the Drift Creek Wilderness Area in one of the most remote regions of the Siuslaw National Forest. It is a rare experience to paddle through a magnificent wilderness surrounded by the hush of an old-growth forest and to return home the same day. Farmland is found only along the last 5 miles.

From the put-in below Meadow Creek the gradient is fairly continuous with many class 2 rapids and an occasional more difficult rapid. Lower flows require much rock dodging. About one-third through the run, boaters enter the Wilderness Area, the largest in the Coast Range. Around mile 11, a fairly narrow and steep class 3 drop is the last significant rapid and signifies fewer and easier rapids ahead. The gradient decreases for the rest of the trip. In a couple of miles, the creek flows under a private bridge where take-outs are not allowed. About 3 miles farther is an impressive high waterfall on the left. It's a flat 2 miles farther to the take-out. An outgoing tide can be helpful.

Hazards

Expect one or more portages around fallen trees or logs in the creek. They seem to move from year to year.

Green paradise in the Drift Creek Wilderness (Tim Palmer)

Access

Bring good detailed maps (such as Siuslaw National Forest map and the Oregon Atlas and Gazetteer) for both the put-in and take-out vehicles. It is easy to get lost in this area.

Go to the take-out first. From US 101 on the coast go to North Bayview Road at the northeast end of the Waldport bridge. Drive 6.7 miles east and turn right onto May Road. Continue 2.7 miles to the bridge over Drift Creek, the take-out. Park on river left downstream of the bridge.

To reach the put-in, return to North Bayview Road, then continue 5 miles back toward US 101. Turn right (north) onto South Beaver Creek Road and go 5.2 miles to the intersection with North Beaver Creek Road. Turn right and continue for 10.4 miles to the intersection with 1000 Line Road. Turn right and continue 4.6 miles to the second turnoff to the right. Go through the gate. After the road crosses Drift Creek, you can put in anywhere along this road. There is a nice put-in just before the road ends, about 2 miles below the gate.

Gauge

None exists. For an estimate of the flow see Pat Welch's flow page: Drift Creek (Alsea). With the Alsea River at 2000 cfs and the Siletz River at 1800 cfs, Drift Creek has adequate flow.

Carl Landsness, Rich Brainerd, Rob Blickensderfer, and WKCC Editors

Siuslaw River and Tributaries

19 Siuslaw River
Clay Creek to Smith Creek

Class: 2	Length: 28.7 miles
Flow: 300–1000 cfs	Character: forested; logging
Gradient: 7 fpm	Season: rainy

The Siuslaw flows through thick forests and large clear-cut areas. The narrow, paved Siuslaw Road follows close to the river for much, but not all, of the run. However, paddlers will have only a few views of this road, even when it is close to the river.

From the put-in at the Bureau of Land Management's (BLM) Clay Creek recreation site down to the milepost 3 take-out, there are 30 miles of river with a beautiful medley of tight riffles, pools, and deeply wooded shores. Paddlers will probably find only one (or a few) logjams before the community of Austa, and probably none below there. Intermediate access points are available, including at Wolf Creek, Whittaker Creek, Austa, and Linslaw Park. This reach makes a fine overnight expedition; while campsites are not ideal, spots are available on National Forest land for a small group. **Note:** The 34 miles upstream of this reach, from

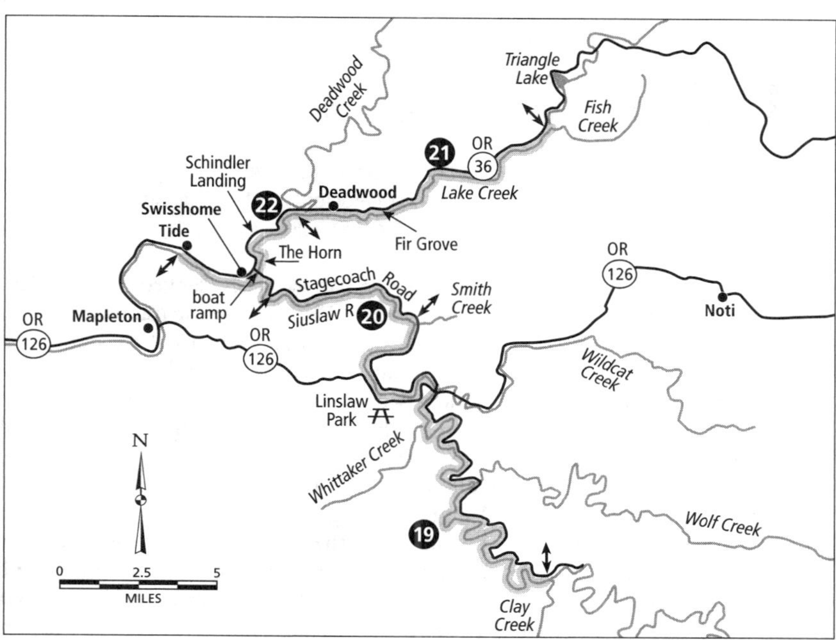

Siuslaw Falls to Clay Creek, are best described as "logjam boating" due to the numerous portages required on this upper reach.

Hazards

Watch for strainers and logjams. The BLM has placed rocks in the river to pond water intended to trap spawning gravels, effectively creating class 2 rapids in many locations down to Whittaker Creek. A few of these may require lining or portage at low flows, scouting, and special caution by inexperienced boaters. Avoid high flows, which would make logjams far more hazardous.

Access

To reach Clay Creek, go west on Oregon 126 from Noti for 15 miles. Turn left at the Siuslaw bridge and go south on Siuslaw River Road for 16 miles. Whittaker access is 1.6 miles south (upstream) of the Oregon 126 bridge. The Linslaw Park and boat ramp (fee area) is east of Mapleton 9.8 miles on Oregon 126. For the Smith Creek take-out directions, see the following run, Siuslaw: Smith Creek to Swisshome.

Gauge

None for the upper river. The Siuslaw River at Mapleton gauge can be used for estimating purposes. Good low flows have been found with 2800 cfs at Mapleton.

Tim Palmer

20 Siuslaw River
Smith Creek to Swisshome

Class: 1+(2+)	Length: 7.3 miles
Flow: 1100–2700 cfs, gauge	Character: forested; logging
Gradient: 13 fpm, C	Season: rainy

The Siuslaw River along this stretch flows in a narrow valley flanked by a one-lane gravel road, a working railroad, and a few houses. Few of these intrusions of humanity are noticeable from the river, and the run has a pleasant, rural character. The paddling is easy, the current is strong, and small creeks and waterfalls are frequent.

Be prepared for three class 2+ rapids. Each is conveniently marked by a railroad bridge. The first is a sloping drop under the first railroad bridge at 2.5 miles. A short quiet section is followed by a sweeping left bend and class 2+ rapids under the second railroad bridge at 2.8 miles. The third is at 6.5 miles, about 0.3 mile below the third railroad bridge. A cliff overhanging the road and a large rock on river right mark the rapids. The remainder of the run is relatively easy. Between the fourth bridge and the take-out is an island that cannot be seen from the road. The best route is usually left of the island. The take-out is at an access on river right, 1 mile below the fourth railroad bridge at a left bend in the river marked by cliffs and a high waterfall on the right. Alternatively, one can continue down past the confluence with Lake Creek for 2 miles to a take-out in Tide.

Hazards

Scout the three class 2+ rapids during the shuttle. The second has a broad clear channel on the left. The center bridge piling hides the main drop from view. The third has a hole at the bottom that becomes large at 2500 cfs and takes much of the flow; it can be portaged more easily on the left.

Access

Oregon 126 is near the put-in, and Oregon 36 is near the take-out. From Oregon 126, 19 miles west of Noti, drive to an intersection approximately 1 mile below Linslaw Park. Turn right, go 150 yards, and cross a concrete bridge. Turn left onto Stagecoach Road/Richardson Upriver Road, and travel downriver to the put-in, an access area at milepost 3.5. A pedestrian bridge crosses the river just below the put-in.

Continue driving downriver for about 7 miles to the take-out, which is 1 mile below the fourth railroad bridge and 0.8 mile above the intersection with Oregon 36 at Swisshome.

Gauge

Siuslaw River near Mapleton. Suggested flows listed above are gauge flows. Actual flows on the river will be substantially less (perhaps fifty percent less) since the Mapleton gauge includes the flow from Lake Creek, a major tributary of the Siuslaw.

Steve and Sandy Cramer, and WKCC Editors

21 Lake Creek
Fish Creek to Deadwood Creek

Class: 1+(2)	Length: 12.2 miles
Flow: 600–1200 cfs	Character: forested; pastureland
Gradient: 14 fpm, C	Season: rainy

This run is in a beautiful and somewhat secluded valley. One passes numerous houses along the way, and yet the creek often wanders away from the road giving the run a remote feeling. The scenery, which is mostly woodland and pastureland, includes some fine specimens of older alders and maples and lush understory growth. Small surf waves are abundant.

The first 3 miles are class 1+ with a few small boulders and ledges to navigate around. Routes are easy to discern, and the riverside brush doesn't present a problem. The next 3 miles are mostly class 1 with lesser gradient than the upper stretch.

The Nelson covered bridge is about halfway down the run. About 1.2 miles beyond it, one passes the alternative put-in, Fir Grove. A half-mile farther, the river makes a sharp left bend where the river spreads out over a boulder garden. This marks the start of a long class 2 rapid. The first half of the rapid is above a small bridge, and the second half is below it, as the river bends to the right. In a mile, the next small bridge has a sign on it with an arrow pointing to the right channel. This rapid features a short drop over a small rock weir. The right channel is the easiest route, although the left channel is also clear. The island just downstream is usually navigable on both sides, but keep an eye out for strainers.

Near the end of the run, one passes under a bridge that crosses the river diagonally. Stay alert because 0.33 mile farther down the current tends to run into the brush on the far right channel. Deadwood Landing take-out is another 0.5 mile downstream.

An alternative for a day offering more whitewater action would be to combine parts of this run with the following one (see Lake Creek: Deadwood Creek to Tide for details). An alternative put-in could be at the Fir Grove turnoff, where a short road drops down to the river near milepost 16. Combined with a take-out at Schindler Landing (milepost 10.5), this would allow one to paddle about 6 miles of class 1+ to 2+ water with many good surfing opportunities.

Hazards

Logs and strainers could be a problem at any time. Higher flows will likely increase the difficulty due to the scarcity of eddies. The class 2 rapid in the lower half of the run might involve a lengthy swim if one were to have trouble at the top.

Access

To reach the put-in, go 24 miles east of Mapleton on Oregon 36. At 0.2 mile east of milepost 24, turn right on Fish Creek Road (BLM 16-7-30). Park near the bridge over Lake Creek, then cross the bridge and put in on the upstream side. Parking is limited at this spot. Take-out is at the Deadwood Landing boat ramp (milepost 13.3), where a Lane County parking pass is required. (Alternatively, park at the Deadwood post office lot across the street from the boat ramp if it is a Sunday.)

Gauge

Siuslaw River at Mapleton. Lake Creek itself has no gauge. For estimating purposes, use the Siuslaw gauge. The flow of Lake Creek at Fish Creek is about one-fifth of the flow of the Siuslaw at Mapleton. At Deadwood, the flow is approximately one-third of the Mapleton flow. Optimal flows for this stretch would be about 4000–6000 cfs on the Mapleton gauge.

Laurie Pavey

22 ★ Lake Creek
Deadwood Creek to Tide

Class: 2+(3); 3(4)	Length: 7.6 miles
Flow: 1900–5000 cfs; 10,000–31,000 cfs	Character: rural
Gradient: 26 fpm, PD	Season: rainy

Lake Creek flows from Triangle Lake in the Oregon Coast Range. Immediately after or during a major storm, it is an excellent big-water run. At lower flows, it is a superb class 2+ to 3 river with good action and lots of surfing waves. Emerging from the lake, the creek meanders a few hundred feet, turns a swift corner, and drops over several falls into logjams and difficult rapids. A common put-in, 12 miles downstream of the lake near Deadwood Creek, provides paddlers with a good warm-up for the more difficult rapids below. Boaters who wish to vary the length of their run can choose access points several miles upstream or downstream of Deadwood. A popular play run put-in is at Schindler Landing 2.8 miles below Deadwood.

The first few miles of the run have several small holes and innumerable waves to play on. Below Schindler, after turning a corner, you will be engulfed in a series of drops and big waves at Ledges (class 2+ to 3), the lead-in rapid above The Horn. The Horn is a unique rapids, formed by a hard volcanic formation. It starts with small waves and keeps building up to bigger waves and holes. The last set of gigantic waves forms below a monster rock that bisects the river. A common run is to keep far left. Once in the rapids, stay upright. A large wave near the bottom crashes down on boats and can even stand decked double canoes (C-2s) on end. This rapid may also be run to the far right of the huge center rock. At low flows, The Horn is class 3.

The 4-mile run from The Horn to the take-out continues with big waves and holes. Just below The Horn, where the river bends right, a significant shelf produces a very wide and unfriendly hole at some levels. It is easy on the far right at all flows. Immediately below this, at the bottom of the left bend, is Bus-stop, another significant shelf hole. Safe passage is usually on the far left, or one can sneak cautiously between the right side of the hole and the rock wall on the right river bank. Grassy Lawn waves are next, followed by the Grassy Lawn hole on the left. The last few miles are on the Siuslaw River where the flow now doubles in size. Many surfing waves and holes, including Mill Wave and Red Hill, are found below the confluence. A few more good rapids lead to the take-out in Tide, which is marked by a cable crossing the river overhead.

Hazards

The Horn can be road-scouted (near milepost 9) but cannot be portaged along the river due to private property. The Bus-stop hole should be avoided. About 2 miles above the take-out, where a small tributary comes into the Siuslaw River, is an artificial structure on the left bank. It is often submerged at higher flows and should be avoided.

Access

Oregon 36, which connects the Eugene area to Florence on the coast, parallels this section of river. Deadwood Landing put-in is about 12 miles west of Triangle Lake at milepost 13.3. Alternative put-in areas are the informal launch at Green Creek turnout (milepost 12.2) and Schindler Landing (milepost 10.5).

Five miles downstream from Deadwood, Lake Creek flows into the Siuslaw River. Just above the confluence, there is access on river left, the Konnie Memorial Park access. To reach it, take Stagecoach Road across the Siuslaw River in Swisshome, immediately turn left and go upstream 0.5 mile.

The take-out is 3 miles downstream of the confluence at the small park Tide Landing. The access points Deadwood, Schindler, and Tide landings, all of which have concrete boat ramps, require a Lane County parking pass, which may be purchased in Mapleton or Eugene.

Gauge

Lake Creek itself has no gauge. The flow of Lake Creek at Deadwood is approximately one-third of the flow of the Siuslaw at Mapleton. For estimating purposes use the gauge: Siuslaw River at Mapleton. 1900 cfs on the gauge is a good minimum. 7000–10,0000 cfs is optimum for playing, and a level of 13,000 is beginning to be big water.

George Ice and WKCC Editors

Opposite: *A tight move in the South Fork Gorge, South Fork Smith River, CA* (Kathy Shelby)

South Coast Rivers

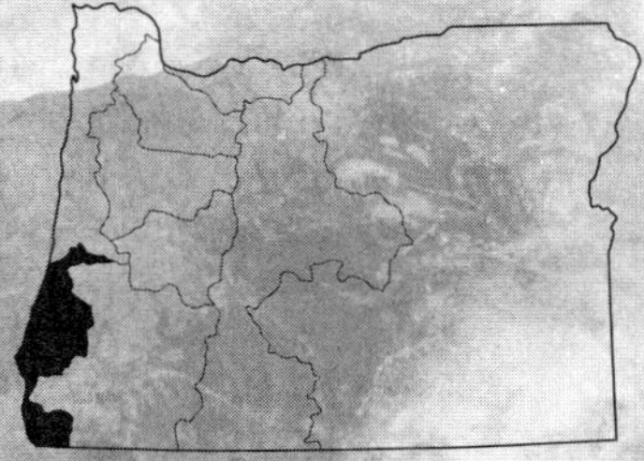

Region 2

Smith River and Tributaries (Umpqua River Basin)

23 North Fork Smith River (Umpqua Tributary) Cedar Creek to Harlan Creek

Class: 2(3)	Length: 9.3 miles
Flow: 450–600 cfs	Character: forested; residential
Gradient: 26 fpm, PD	Season: rainy

This run on the North Fork Smith, a tributary of the Smith in the Umpqua River drainage, is a great class 2–2+ run with a couple of short class 3 rapids. Although it is a bit of a drive from major population centers, the beauty of the forest you paddle through makes the drive worthwhile. The large maples, cedars, and firs tower overhead, and the river has a feeling of wilderness to it since the road often loops away from the river. You pass under eight bridges, yet only a few houses dot the banks, mostly in the last mile. Large areas of sandstone bedrock, sometimes filled with dozens of potholes, are common.

The run begins just upstream of Cedar Creek. In 0.2 miles you pass under Bridge 1. (It's a good idea to count bridges as you paddle.) A fun class 2 rapid is just above Bridge 3. Above Bridge 5 is a house on the left. Just past Bridge 5, the West Branch of the North Fork Smith enters on the right, increasing the flow. A mile farther, as the river bends left, stop on the right to scout Big Drop, class 3. It's an easy portage for this short 5-foot drop. About 0.7 mile below Big Drop is another steep drop that might be class 2+ to 3 at medium to high flows. It's worth a scout.

Below this second drop, in 0.3 mile, you pass under Bridge 6, which is followed by a large horseshoe bend in the river. At Bridge 7, you begin to see a few houses and the gradient lessens. Bridge 8, the final one, follows in about 0.5 mile. In about 0.7 mile, a water cable crossing overhead marks the take-out that is just above a class 2 rapid.

Hazards

Paddlers should be aware that there is potential danger posed by the leftovers of a faulty "fish-enhancement project." These dangers include logs in the river with loops of cable dangling out of them and rebar sticking up out of the river (mostly close to shore, thankfully). For this reason, only strong class 2–2+ boaters with good maneuvering skills should attempt this run. Also, there might be some logjams to sneak or portage. Big Drop and the smaller second drop should be scouted.

Access

From Reedsport, travel upstream on the Lower Smith River Road for 15 miles. Turn left onto North Fork Smith River Road and travel 6 miles to a small public lane on the right, the take-out.

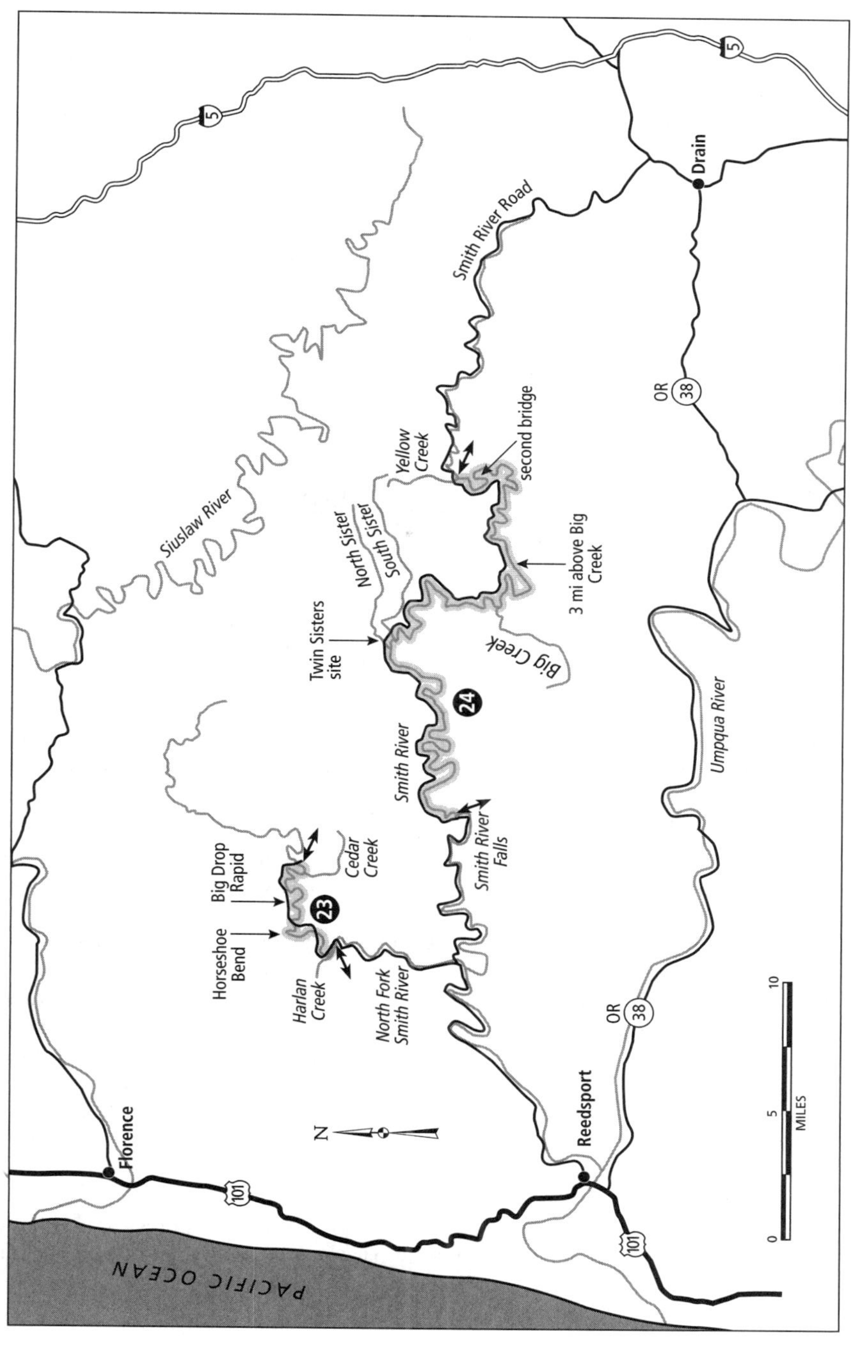
PACIFIC OCEAN
Florence
Siuslaw River
Smith River Road
Drain
OR 38
Yellow Creek
second bridge
North Sister
South Sister
Twin Sisters site
3 mi above Big Creek
Big Creek
Smith River
24
Big Drop Rapid
Cedar Creek
Horseshoe Bend
23
Harlan Creek
North Fork Smith River
Smith River Falls
Umpqua River
OR 38
Reedsport
N
0 5 10
MILES

To reach the put-in, travel upstream another 6.6 miles (on NF 48 and NF 23). After crossing a bridge near Cedar Creek, turn left down a small, brushy lane that leads to a primitive camping area near the river. Alternatively, you can approach the river from the Eugene area using directions to the Kentucky Falls hiking area, which is just a few miles upstream of the put-in.

Gauge

There is no gauge on this run. The flow is approximately one-third of the Smith or one-ninth of the Siuslaw. For estimation, check the Siuslaw River at Mapleton gauge and Pat Welch's estimated flow of the Smith River. About 4000 cfs on the Siuslaw gauge (or about 1350 cfs on the Smith) would be a good minimum. The author ran it when the Siuslaw was at 2900 cfs and dropping, but the river was very bony at that level. **Note:** Plastic kayaks don't slide very well on sandstone rock.

Laurie Pavey

24 Smith River (Umpqua Tributary) Yellow Creek to Smith River Falls

Class: 2(2+)	Length: 41.4 miles
Flow: 300–800 cfs	Character: forested; logging
Gradient: 12 fpm	Season: rainy

The Smith is a largely undiscovered gem, and even with its valley-length narrow road, it ranks as one of the wilder, long river passages through the Coast Range. The route is heavily logged, but old-growth tracts remain on some BLM and National Forest land. The river has no dams or development.

Rarely run, the Smith has 43 essentially wild miles of class 2 boating in a tightly winding path with one or more logjams likely. Camping is possible at very small sites along the river, on brushy banks, or at two BLM campgrounds at the lower end of this reach.

Below an informal put-in at Yellow Creek, a large logjam soon appears, avoidable by putting in at the second bridge below Yellow Creek. Then, 12 miles below Yellow Creek, a low-water bridge (3 miles above Big Creek) is easily portaged, with alternative access there. Another 15 miles wind to Twin Sisters Creek, with access on a steep path. A final 16 miles end with mandatory take-out just above BLM's Smith River Falls Campground. Below there, the falls is an impressive 8-foot drop with a concrete fish ladder on the right. Class 3+ ledges lie both above and below the falls. The Smith's long tidal reach begins a few miles downstream.

Hazards

One or more logjams are likely, and the low-water bridge requires care. Ledges above and below the falls are significantly harder than the rest of the river, and Smith River Falls is a major hazard below the take-out.

Access

To reach the upper river from Drain, take Oregon 38 east 2 miles and turn north on Smith River Road. After crossing the Umpqua–Smith divide, the road winds downriver for 53 miles to Smith River Falls and then along mostly tidal river to US 101. (Yellow Creek is 24 miles from the turnoff.) Or, drive up Smith River Road from US 101 just north of Reedsport.

Gauge

None. Pat Welch's flow page gives a calculated estimate of the Smith's flow near the mouth. Adequate low flows have occurred when the Siuslaw River at Mapleton ran 2100 cfs.

Tim Palmer

West Fork Millicoma River

25 West Fork Millicoma River Henrys Falls to Stonehouse Bridge

Class: 3(4)	Length: 8.5 miles
Flow: 400–2000 cfs	Character: canyon; forested
Gradient: 36 fpm	Season: rainy

The river's sandstone bedrock creates wide, shallow rapids and ledge drops. Numerous small play holes and waves enhance the upper end of the run. At moderate levels, only two significant rapids interrupt the run's class 3 character. Both can be scouted by car, although the road does not parallel most of the river. Flowing beneath a canopy of maple, cedar, fir, and aromatic myrtle, the river attracts many new sweepers annually.

Henrys Falls, a class 4 10-foot drop, occurs 1.6 miles into the run. It is scouted left, run in the chute, or easily portaged river right. This encounter is always stimulating. About 0.8 mile below is a low-water river crossing. At 4 miles into the run is Girl Scout Triple Drop, named for the old scout camp below. It is located 0.3 mile inside the Elliott State Forest boundary; look for sweepers here during the shuttle. Girl Scout Triple Drop begins with a turbulent chute into a small pool, directly above a 5-foot diagonal ledge drop. This is a tough portage on the left. An ender wave is encountered after the S turn below. Drift another 1.3 miles to The Green Gate, a 6-foot ledge, which is usually run right. The first take-out is on the right after another 0.2 mile. Medium to high flows may permit continuing downriver through another class 3 rapids, near some cabins, and on to Stonehouse Bridge. This adds another 3.2 miles of paddling.

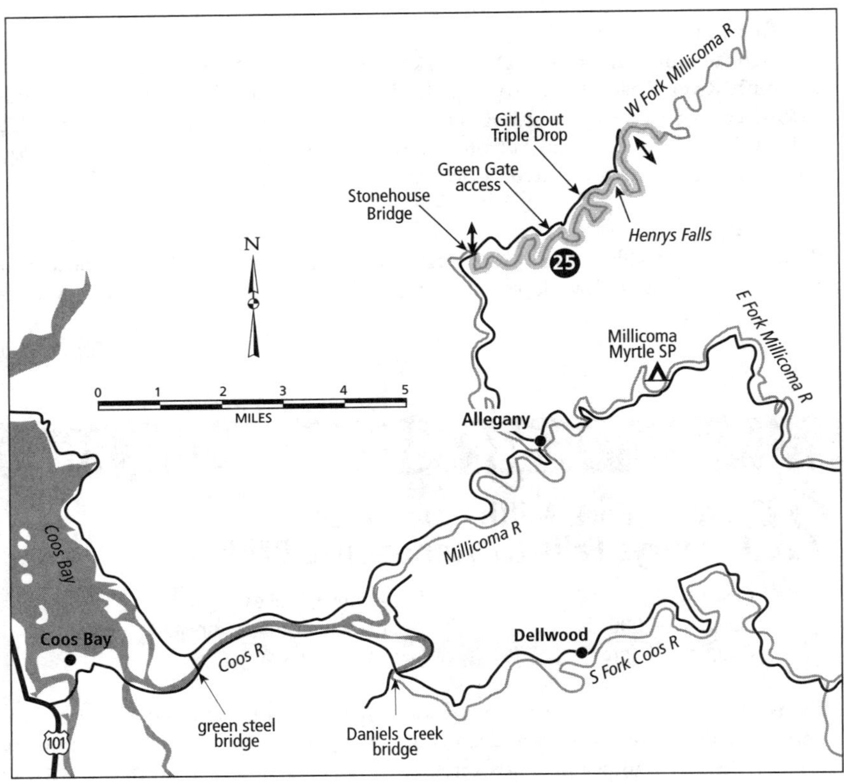

Hazards

The easy portage to the right of Henrys Falls can be difficult to reach after scouting on the left because of the lead-in class 3 rapids. The keeper hole in the center grows at higher flows. At flood, Henrys is a huge, river-wide hole, and the rest of the run is class 4- to 5-.

Access

From south Coos Bay, turn east off US 101 toward Allegany/Coos River; begin counting mileage. Cross the Isthmus Slough bridge and stay left. At the four-way stop, mile 1.1, turn right onto the Coos River Highway ("D" Street). Cross the Ross Slough bridge at 2.1 miles and continue to the green steel bridge, 3.5 miles from US 101. Cross over the bridge, stay right, and follow the road for 10.4 miles, to where it crosses the West Fork bridge into Allegany, 13.9 miles from US 101. Restart your mileage as you proceed left up the West Fork Millicoma Road. Go 4.8 miles to Stonehouse Bridge, and park the take-out vehicle there. Check the river flow (see Gauge). If it is necessary (or desirable) to drive to the lower-flow take-out, continue driving upstream a half-mile to the Deans Mountain junction, where the pavement ends. Stay right (do not take Deans Mountain

Road). At mile 7.9, park on the left in the pullout (just before the green steel gate on the right at mile 8). The river access trail is on the right.

The gravel road is normally passable with two-wheel drive all the way to the put-in, but occasionally after winter storms it may have severe washouts, especially upstream of the low-water crossing near mile 9.1, making four-wheel drive mandatory.

To reach the put-in, continue driving up the road to mile 8.7 where you can scout Triple Drop, then go past the low-water crossing at mile 9.1. An overlook at mile 10.1 is 260 feet directly above Henrys Falls. The road then leads downhill to the put-in, which is 10.8 miles from Allegany. Park on the right, next to three large red cedars. The old Vaughn Ranch gate, a little farther on, confirms your location. The turnaround is quite small.

Gauge

West Fork Millicoma River. The gauge is located on the right at the far end of the Stonehouse Bridge (see Access) as you approach it. Below 3.5 feet, expect an abrasive run. Water around 5–6 feet indicates great fun for the advanced boater. Above 6 feet, expect pushiness and sticky holes. This river requires an amazing amount of rain to come up, and it drops very quickly afterward. The Coos Watershed Association provides Internet readings of this gauge: www.cooswatershed.org/wfk.php.

Richard Dierks and Pete Schaefers

South Fork Coquille River

26 South Fork Coquille River
16-Mile Bridge to Milepost 3.2

Class: 4(5), T; 4+(5)	Length: 12.9 miles
Flow: 400 cfs; 3000 cfs	Character: forested; gorge; canyon
Gradient: 55 fpm, PD; C	Season: rainy

Deeply cut into sedimentary formations of the coastal mountains, the South Fork Coquille River offers some of the finest technical whitewater in Oregon. Historically, this is timber and mining country but, surprisingly, the excellent scenic quality of the corridor has been maintained. Campsites are available at China Flat, Daphne Grove, and Myrtle Grove. The run is divided into four sections in acknowledgment of the varied gradient and character of the river. At medium flows, the three upper sections are usually run together, but a more demanding combination is provided by sections 3 and 4. During low water, only section 3 is enjoyable. High runoff provides a fast, turbulent run from the top to Coal Creek.

SECTION 1: 16-MILE BRIDGE TO KELLY CREEK, 3.6 MILES, CLASS 4

Put in at the bridge or 100 yards upstream. Beware of rebar. The whitewater is technically demanding class 3+ to 4 with a gradient of 86 fpm involving boulder gardens that are difficult to scout or portage. Most of it is not visible from the road, and sweepers are abundant. About 2 miles below the put-in, 0.5 mile after passing under the concrete bridge at Daphne Grove Campground, an 8-foot vertical drop is followed by a boulder garden. The 8-foot drop can be scouted from the road 0.7 mile up from Kelly Creek at the gravel turnout. The take-out is 0.2 mile below Kelly Creek.

SECTION 2: KELLY CREEK TO MYRTLE GROVE CAMPGROUND, 4 MILES, CLASS 3

The action slows down as the gradient decreases to 33 fpm. An easier put-in is at China Flat Campground, 1.5 miles below, with a class 3+ section just below it. The section ends at Myrtle Grove Campground, alongside a class 3 rapid. (Check to see that the exit from this rapid is not boulder-choked.)

SECTION 3: MYRTLE GROVE CAMPGROUND TO COAL CREEK, 3.1 MILES, CLASS 4–5

Deep within vertical canyon walls, beautiful side-stream waterfalls exceed 100 feet, aromatic myrtle trees crowd the channel, and beaver sign is plentiful. The narrow class 4 pool-drops are more demanding than the gradient of 45 fpm implies. Immediately below the put-in is a series of blind drops followed by a short flat section. As the river sweeps back to the road, it begins an exciting descent into Roadside Narrows, which should be scouted from the road. Next up: Hole-in-the-Wall, which features a dangerous outlet among the boulders on the left of the pool. Note the ender hole below. Nearly continuous whitewater continues to Coal Creek, which enters through two large culverts on the right. Because of its narrowness, this upper section remains runnable at lower flows than the others.

SECTION 4: COAL CREEK TO MILEPOST 3.2, 2.2 MILES, CLASS 4(5)

Even more demanding rapids lie a short distance below Coal Creek as the gradient increases to 111 fpm for the first mile. It begins with a steep and narrow portion that narrows into a boulder field that has captured many logs. The canyon then tends left and constricts into a class 5 jumble, which is scouted and run or portaged right. Negotiating the approach through the reversal and around the large boulder can be tricky: No safe route can be found to the left. Rather, the safe route is located at a point even with milepost 5 on the road high above. More rapids and 1 mile of flatwater follow. The take-out is at the gully-washed site of an old footbridge, following a nice cliff exposure of shale.

Hazards

Sweepers are always a problem and must be aggressively scouted. Undercut rocks are found throughout the run. Section 1 is quite technical at intermediate flows. At high flows the rapids become easier, except for the 8-foot drop, which forms a class 5 keeper hole. In section 3, below Myrtle Grove Campground, Roadside Narrows and Hole-in-the-Wall become class 5 at high water. Hole-in-the-Wall is dangerous because of the person-size outlet among the boulders on the left of the

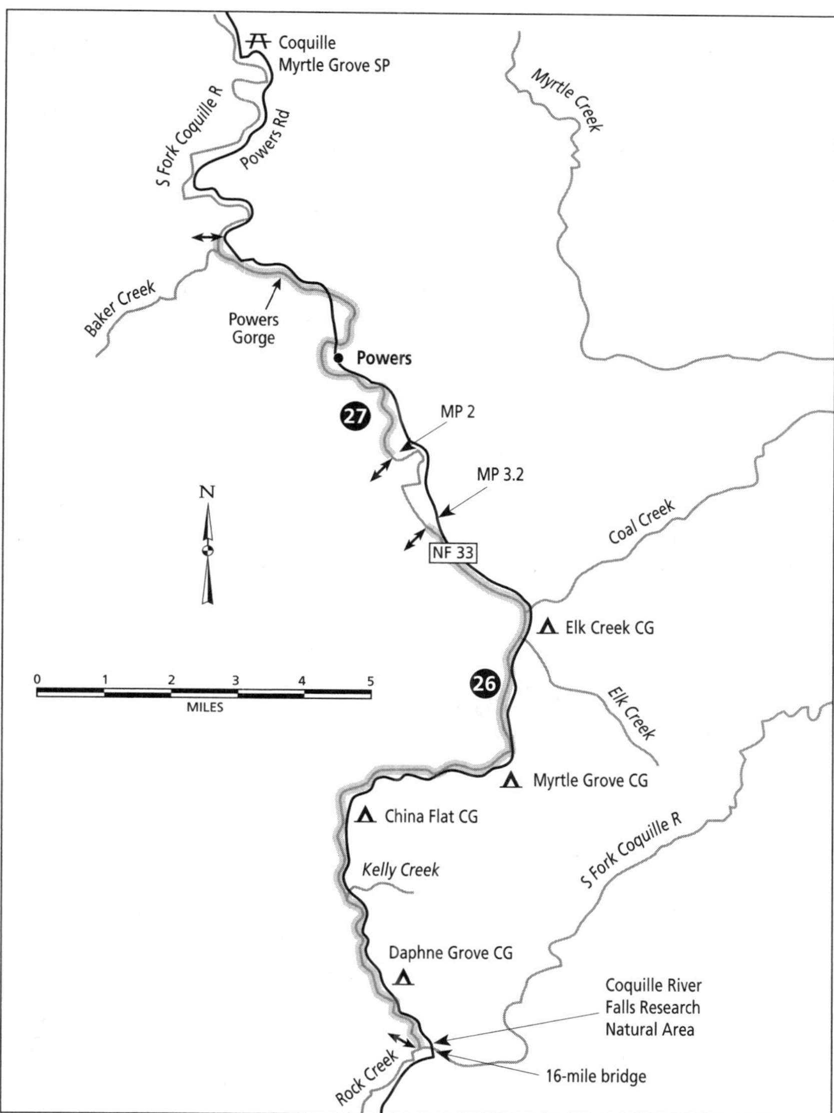

pool. Section 4 below Coal Creek requires increasingly advanced abilities as the water levels rise. At high water the canyon becomes 1 mile of wild froth with major log hazards. To avoid a reversal, the first walk may come after a short distance. A second portage will avoid the river-wide log barricade. About halfway through, the class 5 rapids must be scouted or portaged.

Access

To reach Powers, see the South Fork Coquille River: Powers to Baker Creek run. Several accesses are available along the road upstream from Powers. The lower take-out is at milepost 3.2 at the end of the field on the right. An overgrown trail leads to the river. Parking is available, clear of the gate, a couple of hundred yards before the trail.

Continuing upriver, the road becomes NF 33. Accesses are available at Coal Creek, 5.3 miles above Powers; Myrtle Grove Campground at 8.4 miles; China Flat Campground at 10.6 miles; Kelly Creek at 12.2 miles; and Daphne Grove Campground at 14.0 miles. The upper put-in is at the bridge 15.8 miles above Powers, with parking at the Coquille River Falls Research Natural Area.

Gauge

South Fork Coquille River at Powers. Also use the river-right pillar on 16-Mile Bridge. When the water just touches the pillar, the reading is 0 feet. Low is 1.5 feet, medium is 3 feet, and high is 5 feet. The maximum flow recorded at Powers is 48,000 cfs. When the water is up to the pillar (0 feet), section 3, Myrtle Grove Campground to Coal Creek, is the only runnable section. A gauge of 1.5 feet indicates that section 3 is runnable with only some class 4, but section 4 is tight and technical. The premium level for all sections is probably 3 feet.

Richard Dierks and WKCC Editors

27 South Fork Coquille River
Powers to Baker Creek

Class: 2+(4)	Length: 7 miles
Flow: 400–1500 cfs	Character: wooded; rural
Gradient: 21 fpm, C	Season: rainy

The upper 2 miles of this run are wide and shallow, and the scenery is open and pleasant. As the South Fork Coquille River meanders through Powers, high riverbanks hide the town, but the scenery is occasionally contrasted by washed-out bridges and Powers' dual solution to old automobile disposal and riparian erosion. Farther on, the river enters a scenic canyon and flows over a fisheries weir. About a half-mile below the bridge at the north end of town the gradient increases in the Powers Gorge, first with some class 3 activity and then a 10-foot class 4 drop. Run the drop on the right, off the pillow, or portage through the boulders on the right. After 1 mile of easier water, take out on the right just upstream of the next bridge.

Hazards

Beware of artificial hazards such as rebar. During the shuttle, the Powers Gorge can be seen from the road by driving 0.8 mile up Powers Road from the Baker Creek junction and looking down into the canyon. Although a pool sits above the drop, beginners should take note of the lead-in class 3 activity. The new weir can be seen from the Forest Service station, just before Powers.

Access

The Powers Highway joins Oregon 42 at the confluence of the Middle Fork and South Fork Coquille River, 4 miles southeast of Myrtle Point. The community of Powers is 17.5 miles upstream on Powers Road. To reach the take-out, drive 15.5 miles toward Powers, turn right at the Baker Creek turnoff, and proceed 0.3 mile to the boat ramp, river right, just upstream of the bridge across the river.

For the put-in, continue upstream through Powers (following the signs to China Flat, Illahe, and Agness) to the parking area at milepost 2, just past Orchard City Park.

Gauge

South Fork Coquille River at Powers.

Richard Dierks and WKCC Editors

Elk River

28 Elk River
Butler Creek to Fish Hatchery

Class: 4	Length: 11.4 miles
Flow: 400–3000 cfs	Character: canyon; forested
Gradient: 37 fpm, PD-C	Season: rainy

The Elk River is a beautiful pool-drop stream with continuous rapids at high flow. The green waters carve narrow passages beneath tall timber and large trees flanking the river. Some of the run can be scouted from the road. High flows last only as long as the storms producing them.

SECTION 1: BUTLER CREEK TO PURPLE MOUNTAIN CREEK, 5.5 MILES, CLASS 3(4)

The first 0.5 miles of this section are fairly continuous class 2 until a class 3+ to 4 slot with log complications, which can be portaged. After the slot rapid, the river continues with class 2 rapids until the gradient increases and the river drops through a long boulder garden (class 4) created by an immense landslide. Scout this drop from the right at the first sign of large boulders blocking the main channel and the large landslide on the right. Run center to right through several large holes at high water, which become several fun ledges at low water. Portage on the right. Several more fun class 3–3+ rapids separated by flatwater follow this boulder garden. Take out on the left at Purple Mountain Creek or continue down through the class 4 gorges of the next section.

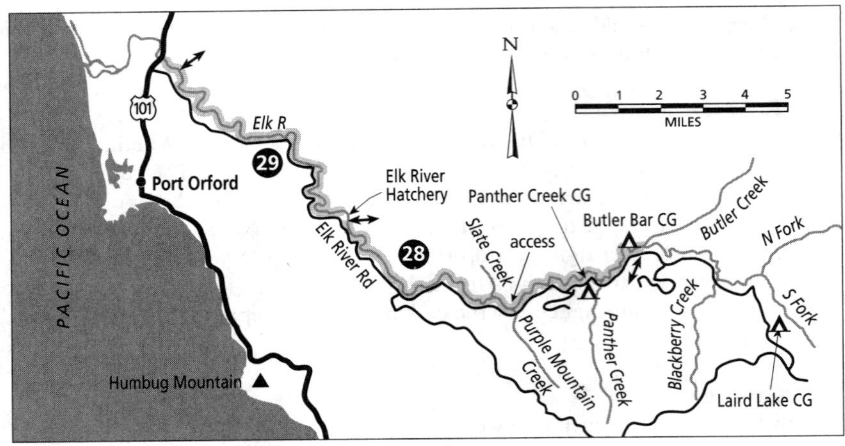

SECTION 2: PURPLE MOUNTAIN CREEK TO ELK RIVER HATCHERY, 7 MILES, CLASS 4

The first 1.5 miles are active class 3 and 4, dropping at 60 fpm. Successive rapids intensify and merge with higher water. Be careful of rocks in the bottom of several drops at low water. This fine upper series ends at mile 1.6 with a drop through a strong reversal into a turbulent pool exiting hard right. The next 3.6 miles are class 2 and 3. Just downstream of a tight S turn around a boulder is a pushy class 4. Near mile 5, begin the 0.3-mile class 4 lower gorge, dropping 150 fpm. Not easily scouted from the water, the final class 4 is a couple of hundred yards farther and is usually run right. Paddle another mile, and take out left on the gravel bar past the hatchery gates and trolley cable crossing.

Hazards

Most rapids cannot be seen from the road. At high water, the gorges in section 2 become more difficult and continuous. Be careful of sweepers at high water. Log hazards can occur at any time.

Access

Between Langlois and Port Orford, 47 miles south of Coos Bay, turn east onto Elk River Road (US 101, milepost 297.5). Drive upriver 7.5 miles to the Elk River Hatchery, the take-out and the gauge location.

The paved road upstream parallels the river for 7 miles to the section 2 put-in at the bridge over Purple Mountain Creek. For the section 1 put-in, continue upstream another 5.5 miles and turn left onto Butler Creek Road. Put in at the bridge over Butler Creek.

Gauge

Located at the end of the parallel concrete fish returnways at the most down-stream part of the Elk River Hatchery. Good low to moderate flows are 4–5 feet. Above 7 feet, the river begins to pump. Oregon Department of Fish and Wildlife (ODFW) announces gauge levels during the winter fishing season. Call 541-332-7025 for the level.

Richard Dierks and WKCC Editors

29 Elk River
Fish Hatchery to US Highway 101

Class: 2	Length: 9 miles
Flow: 300–1000 cfs	Character: forested; ranch; rural
Gradient: 15 fpm	Season: rainy

The Elk's spectacular gorge section of class 3–5 whitewater eases to class 2 at the ODFW hatchery. However, immediately after putting in there, the hatchery weir creates a steep straightforward drop. The rest of the run is a scenic mix of forest and ranchland with some houses. The river meanders sharply with brushy banks and swift flows. Take-out is about a mile upstream of US 101 at an ODFW access area on the left, but flag the riverfront—you won't see your car from the water. Or go on to US 101.

Hazards

The steep class 2 plunge at the hatchery weir can be carried on the left. Beginning boaters should be cautious with swift bends and brushy shorelines throughout this run, and avoid high flows.

Access

From Port Orford go north on US 101 for 3 miles and east on Elk River Road. In 0.8 miles, the ODFW access lies on your left; flag this take-out. Or, take out on the right at the US 101 bridge. There's a steep path to the highway and limited parking. To reach the put-in at the fish hatchery, see previous run: Elk River: Butler Creek to Fish Hatchery.

Gauge

ODFW announces gauge levels during the winter fishing season; 4–5 feet are good low to moderate flows. Call 541-332-7025.

Tim Palmer

30 Sixes River
Sixes River Campground to Cape Blanco

Class: 1+ (2+)	Length: 18 miles
Flow: 300–800	Character: forested; ranch; rural; tidal
Gradient: 9 fpm	Season: rainy

This accessible, mostly easy paddle offers a fine cross section of the southern Coast Range habitat. It starts with an enchanting rainforest gorge for 2 miles with lively class 2 rapids, and quickly eases to swift riffles. Access is good 8.5 miles below the put-in (Sixes River Campground) at BLM's Edson Creek Campground. Then it's another 9.5 miles of riffles to the Hughes House access in Cape Blanco State Park near the tide line, with a rare chance to paddle almost to the ocean: At high tide, paddle beyond the Hughes House another quarter mile to a beach (and back) with spectacular views of the Sixes mouth, rocky islands, and Cape Blanco.

Hazards

The class 2+ gorge can be seen from a high logging road bridge crossing 1 mile west of Sixes River Campground. Winds can be strong on the lower river. If probing to the Pacific, avoid the river's final bend, which swiftly sucks out to sea.

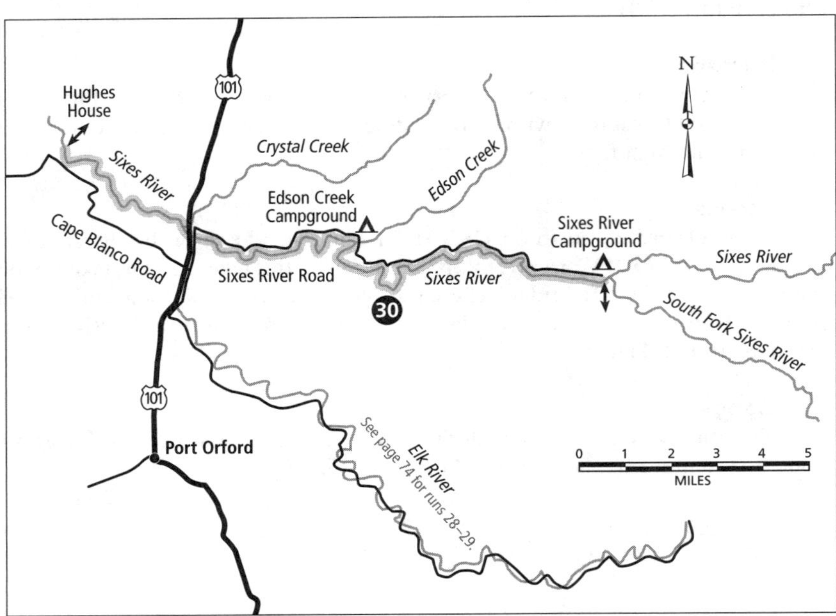

Access

From Port Orford, go north on US 101 for 6 miles and turn east on Sixes River Road. Go 4 miles to Edson Creek Campground or 11 to Sixes River Campground. To reach the take-out and mouth of the river, go 5 miles north from Port Orford on US 101 and turn west on Cape Blanco Road, turn right at the sign for Hughes House, and park by the tidal river.

Gauge

None. Good low flows occur when the Elk River runs at 4–5 feet; call ODFW at 541-332-7025 during the winter steelhead season.

Tim Palmer

Chetco River

31 Chetco River
Tolman Ford to South Fork (Lower Gorge)

Class: 3–4 (5)	Length: 10 miles
Flow: 200–3000 cfs	Character: rugged, inaccessible, forested canyon
Gradient: 25 fpm, PD	Season: rainy/snowmelt

The Chetco, a designated National Wild and Scenic River, is arguably the wildest river on the West Coast south of the Olympic Peninsula. The upper 30 miles through the Kalmiopsis Wilderness has no roads, dams, or development. The section described here has minimal four-wheel-drive access, ending at Low Water Crossing. Even the lower class 2 run, from South Fork to Loeb State Park, has very little development. The river is stunningly clear at low to moderate flows.

SECTION 1: TOLMAN FORD TO STEEL BRIDGE, 6 MILES, CLASS 3(4)

This section starts with about 2 miles of class 2 drops separated by deep pools. After the river turns to the south, the gradient increases with numerous boulder drops, mostly class 3 with a couple of class 4s. Most can be scouted by boat. These taper off just as the steel bridge comes into view.

SECTION 2: STEEL BRIDGE TO SOUTH FORK, 4 MILES, CLASS 4(5)

A short distance below the steel bridge lies the lower gorge, which includes two class 5 drops requiring arduous portages by most paddlers. The first of these, Radiolaria (or Candy Cane)—named for the undersea protozoa whose skeletons make up the unusual striped rock—is a massive pileup of car- and bus-size rocks. The second impressive blockage, just below Radiolaria, is Conehead—even more intimidating, with occasional logs interspersed among undercut boulders. Both drops can be portaged on the right. From there, it's a class 2 paddle to the Low Water Crossing access (the road is washed out, but one could hike out there), then another mile to the easier South Fork take-out.

Fun on the Chetco above the steel bridge (Tim Palmer)

While some expert paddlers run the Chetco gorges on boatable flows, others can experience the remarkably wild and rugged river with inflatable kayaks at flows as low as 50 cfs (200 on the Brookings gauge at the mouth of the river is comparable). The athletic portages and many boulder problems are still challenging.

Note: Above this run, the long (27 miles, 41 feet per mile), class 4 upper canyon of the Chetco is one of the ultimate rigorous wild river expeditions in the West, reached only by a 10-mile hike from Onion Camp on the east side of the Siskiyou Mountains or a 4-mile trail (usually unavailable because of a gated road) from Chetco Pass.

Hazards

At boatable flows of several hundred cfs, rocks here are chronically undercut, and Radiolaria and Conehead are formidable obstacles usually requiring rock-scrambling portages. At low flows, frequent wading and dragging is needed over large rocks—beware of foot entrapment.

Access

From US 101 in Brookings, take North Bank Chetco River Road north for 15.9 miles. Just before crossing the South Fork, take the short spur road to the left, the take-out. For Low Water Crossing, cross the South Fork, bear left, go less than a mile and left on NF 1407 (beware, the road end is washed out). For the steel bridge access point: Cross the South Fork, bear left, and continue 3 miles on NF 1376, cross the Chetco, and in 100 yards, turn left. Access is under the steel bridge. For the Tolman put-in, cross the South Fork, bear left, and go less than a mile, turn right on NF 1917, go 2.8 miles, then left on unsigned NF 060, go 4.4 miles, then left on unsigned dirt NF 067, and drop with four-wheel drive 1 mile to the river. Tolman Ranch (private) is directly across from the put-in.

Gauge

Chetco River near Brookings. Flows in the gorge will be much lower, perhaps up to one-quarter of the Brookings flow.

Tim Palmer

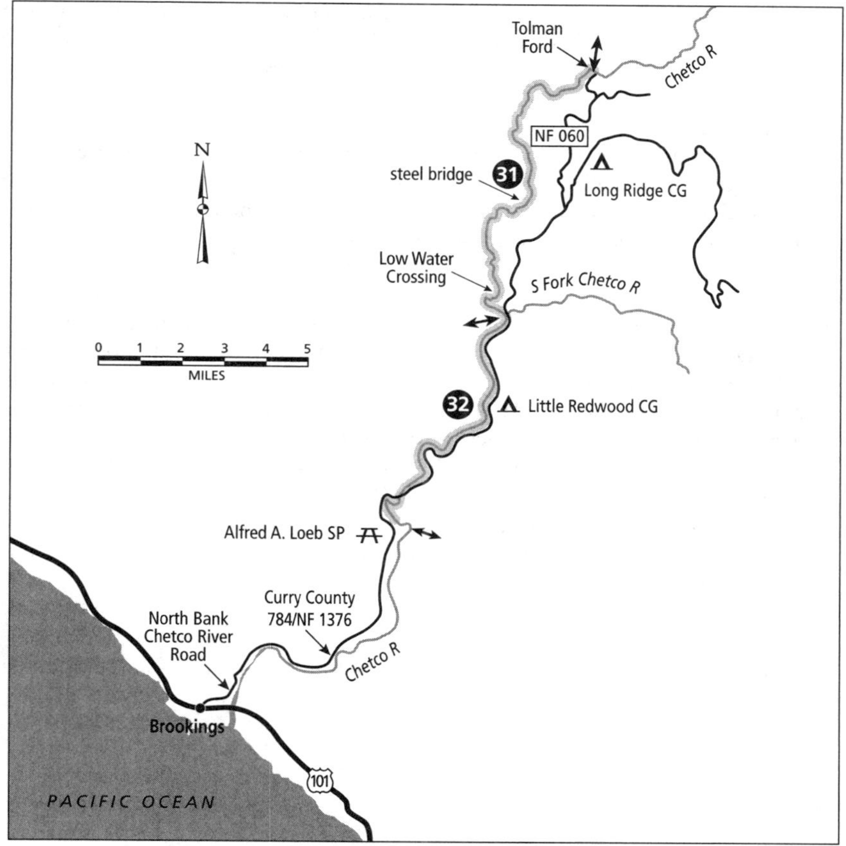

32 Chetco River
South Fork to Alfred A. Loeb State Park

Class: 1(2)	Length: 8.5 miles
Flow: 200–3000	Character: forested; rural
Gradient: 8 fpm	Season: year-round

The lower Chetco is like a miniature lower Rogue without the jet boats: crystal clear, turquoise blue water with riffles and pools the whole way to tide line without major rapids. Gravel bars in the upper half are excellent for camping. High flows in winter and spring have a big-river feel, with wide, swift flows of blue-gray water sweeping past Alaskan-scale cobble bars. Summer boating is possible on extremely low flows owing to low-water channelizing of the gravel, along with long flatwater pools, excellent for swimming and snorkeling. The best scenery and public land lie above Alfred A. Loeb State Park, although some may choose to paddle an additional 10 miles down to Brookings Harbor.

Hazards

The Chetco in winter can spike from 1000 to 60,000 cfs in a few days; even moderately high levels are relentlessly fast. In summer, trees block the entire channel in places, with hazards often not recognized by beginners who are drawn to this run. Wading around sweepers is sometimes required.

Access

From US 101, turn east on North Bank Chetco River Road. The take-out is at Alfred A. Loeb State Park, 7.6 miles from US 101. Other access points along the run are: Miller Bar in another 2.6 miles, Nook Bar in another 0.3 mile, and Redwood Bar in another 1.4 miles. At 15.9 miles from US 101, just before crossing the South Fork, turn left on a short access road to the easy put-in spot. Alternatively, one may drive across the South Fork bridge, bear left, continue less than a mile, then turn left on gravel NF 1407 to Low Water Crossing. (This road is washed out near its end, and a carry to the river is required.) Tempting as it is, the South Fork drive-in campsite is rowdy on summer weekends; leaving vehicles there overnight is not recommended.

Gauge

Chetco River near Brookings. Nice flows continue down to 200 cfs. Summer floating/wading is surprisingly possible at even lower levels.

Tim Palmer

Smith River and Tributaries (California)

If Oregon boaters decide to annex the best rivers outside Oregon, the Smith River in California should be first on the list. Beautiful, clear water, spectacular scenery, paddling and camping among 15-foot-diameter redwoods, and a bunch of runs of varying difficulty—the Smith has it all. The gorges can be run with less than 1000 cfs on the Jed Smith gauge, but water levels can go up and down like a yo-yo. Torrential winter rains can bring the water up to 40,000 cfs overnight, with big hydraulics even in some innocent-looking places, then the water drops to 20,000 cfs a day later. Plan a long weekend or even a week. The watershed is protected by Wild and Scenic River and National Recreation Area designations. The designations are largely the result of relentless work by the Smith River Alliance (www.smithriveralliance.org), a grassroots organization started and run by paddlers with roots in the Willamette Valley.

33 ★ North Fork Smith River Browns Flat to Gasquet

Class: 3+ to 4; 5	Length: 13 miles
Flow: 800–4500 cfs; 12,000 cfs	Character: wilderness; clear water
Gradient: 45 fpm, PD	Season: rainy/snowmelt

This is a run of rare isolation and beauty, unique in the Smith River drainage for its length and separation from roads. Even at high levels, the water is crystal clear, like a river of bubbling champagne. The North Fork is home to several spectacular waterfalls and the carnivorous insect-eating pitcher plant (*Darlingtonia californica*), and when the wild azaleas bloom, you float through clouds of their delicate perfume. Although the authors have run this stretch in as little as 1.5 hours at high water, it is best to start early and plan a long day. Hiking out after dark would spoil all the fun.

Many distinct drops, as well as a couple of small gorges, are found on this run, but the entire trip is less severe than the Middle and South Fork gorges and ranks between them and the stretches above them in terms of difficulty. Big (but generally friendly) hydraulics develop at high water.

Hazards

This is a long run with a long shuttle, so give yourself plenty of time. The isolation makes walking out or getting help difficult, so plan to be self-sufficient.

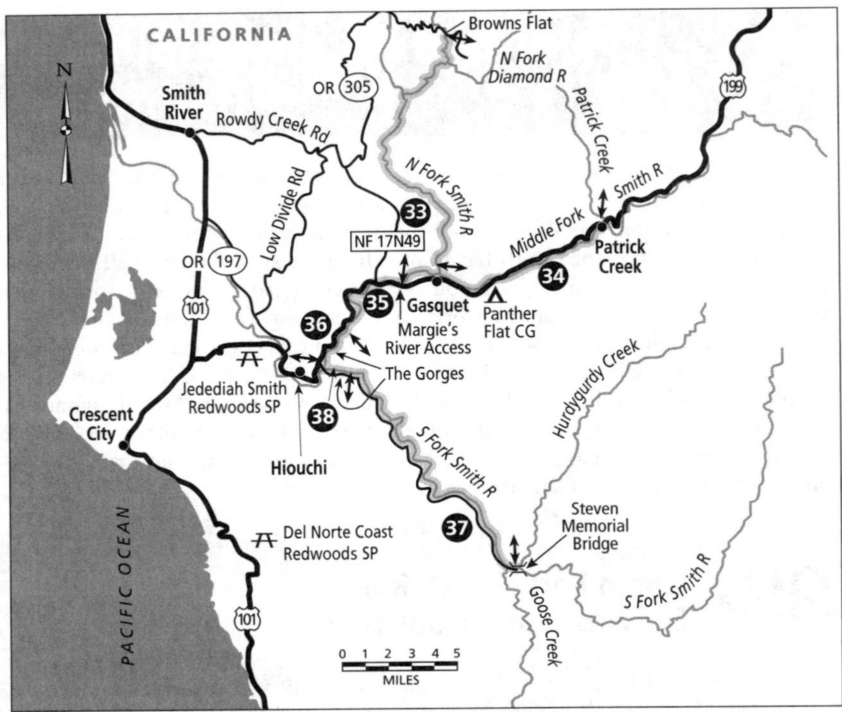

Access

The shuttle is about 1.5 hours one way, and the roads are mostly unpaved, although they are usually well maintained. Parts of these shuttle roads may be impassable because of snow at certain times of the year. Most boaters hire a shuttle driver in Gasquet: Bearfoot Brad, 707-457-3365, bradcamden@earthlink.net. He can also tell you the status for the shuttle roads, if you're doing your own shuttle.

The take-out is in Gasquet, California, at the confluence of the North Fork with the Middle Fork Smith River. Gasquet is on US 199 east of Crescent City, which is on US 101. To drive to the take-out, take Middle Fork Gasquet Road from the east end of Gasquet and turn right on Gasquet Flat Road. Go 0.2 mile and cross the bridge. Park and walk down a dirt road about 200 yards to the North Fork Smith River. From the river, the confluence and large rock outcropping on river left are obvious. An alternative take-out with better raft access is Margie's River Access, described as the put-in for the Middle Fork Smith River: Gasquet to Oregon Hole Gorge run.

To reach the put-in, take US 199 west from Gasquet for about 2 miles. Just after crossing the Middle Fork Smith River (the Mary Adams Peacock Memorial Bridge), look for the NF 17N49 road on the right. Travel up this road for 7.7 miles. Turn right onto Del Norte County Road 305 (Low Divide Road) and continue for 15 miles, climbing and then descending, until you reach the North Fork Smith River at an area called Browns Flat (also known as Major Moores). The launch site is on the left, just upstream of the bridge over the river. There is no camping at the launch, but just across the bridge and to the right, there's camping at the Forest Service's North Fork Campground.

Browns Flat can also be accessed off of California Route 197 (North Bank Road) via County Road 305 (Low Divide Road) or from US 101 near the town of Smith River, using County Road 308 (Rowdy Creek Road). Consult a map for details.

Gauge

Smith River at Jedediah Smith Redwoods State Park. The flow is approximately 33 percent of the flow at the gauge. Also, the steel pipe at the confluence of the North and Middle Fork Smith can be checked. A good level for first descents is 8.0–10.5 feet on the pipe gauge. The run is solid class 4 from 10.5 to 11.6 feet on the steel gauge, and really cranking above 12 feet.

Bo and Kathy Shelby

34 Middle Fork Smith River
Patrick Creek to Gasquet

Class: 3(4)	Length: 9.7 miles
Flow: 1000–5000 cfs	Character: forested; clear water
Gradient: 52 fpm, PD	Season: rainy/snowmelt

This beautiful run is often overlooked because of the allure of the gorges, the visibility of other stretches of the Smith along US 199, or the enticing remoteness of the nearby North Fork. However, with more than a dozen class 3 rapids in the first 5 miles, it has fairly continuous action. The road is often visible from the river, but isn't overly intrusive. The only class 4 rapid, named CalTrans, is about 2 miles downstream of the put-in, just below the first bridge. Scout or portage on river left. Most paddlers take out at Panther Flat, but the extra 2–3 miles to Gasquet offer a few more good rapids and wave trains.

Hazards

CalTrans, the class 4 rapid, should be checked for wood.

Access

The Smith River flows alongside US 199. The put-in is at Patrick Creek picnic area, 7.7 miles upstream of Gasquet. Panther Flat Campground is 2.9 miles upstream of Gasquet. The Gasquet access points include the North Fork Confluence (see the North Fork Smith River description for the directions) or Margie's River Access, which is located at the downstream end of Gasquet, near the sign welcoming you to Gasquet.

Staying busy at CalTrans Rapid, Middle Fork Smith River (Pat Fleming)

Gauge

Smith River at Jedediah Smith Redwoods State Park near Crescent City. The flow is approximately 17 percent of the flow at the gauge. Alternatively, obtain the calculated, estimated flows for this stretch of river using Pat Welch's flow page, Middle Fork Smith, California.

Bo and Kathy Shelby

35 Middle Fork Smith River
Gasquet to Above Oregon Hole Gorge

Class: 2+; 3	Length: 4.3 miles
Flow: 1000 cfs; 22,000 cfs	Character: clear water
Gradient: 28 fpm, PD	Season: rainy/snowmelt

This delightful run on the Middle Fork Smith River provides a good warm-up for the more demanding runs on the Smith. Several good rapids and play spots can be enjoyed.

Hazards

No particular difficulties are present.

Access

At the downstream end of the town of Gasquet on US 199, put in at Margie's River Access, the first place where the river is right next to the highway. An alternative put-in (with a steeper trail to the river) is downstream 1 mile at Mary Adams Peacock Memorial Bridge.

The take-out is approximately 4 miles downstream at Middle Fork Gorge river access (milepost 9.1), where a small dirt road angles down to the river (the river is not visible from the road here). Walk down and scout the take-out; it is not obvious from the river.

Gauge

Smith River at Jedediah Smith Redwoods State Park near Crescent City. The flow is approximately 55 percent of the flow at the gauge.

Bo and Kathy Shelby

36 ★ Middle Fork Smith River
Oregon Hole Gorge

Class: 4; 5	Length: 2 miles
Flow: 500 cfs; 22,000 cfs	Character: gorge; clear water
Gradient: 25 fpm, C	Season: rainy/snowmelt

The only thing wrong with this gorge is that it is over too soon. The character of the run changes dramatically with the water level. At low water, the drops are steep but distinct, requiring some tricky moves around big boulders. At high water, the gorge becomes an awesome, turbulent flush in which eddies are hard to find. Oregon Hole Gorge is also known as Middle Fork Gorge.

Hazards

Most of the gorge is visible from US 199, but the road is several hundred vertical feet above the river, luring the unsuspecting paddler into an inappropriate complacency. Be sure to take the time and effort to scramble down to river level and scout carefully; the water is bigger and faster than it appears from above. The last major rapid in the gorge is just barely visible downstream; it can be scouted from river left.

Access

Put in at either Margie's River Access on US 199, or just above the gorge at Middle Fork Gorge river access (both access points are described in the Middle Fork Smith River: Gasquet to Above Oregon Hole Gorge run).

Take out at the Myrtle Beach river access, at the bridge where the South Fork Road crosses the river (paddle under the bridge and land on river right at a small gravel beach). A steep trail leads up to a parking area where the South Fork Road takes off from US 199. An alternative with easier raft access is downstream on river left at the Smith River National Recreation Area river access, which is reached via South Fork Road.

Gauge

See the Middle Fork Smith River: Gasquet to Above Oregon Hole Gorge run.

Bo and Kathy Shelby

37 South Fork Smith River
Steven Memorial Bridge to South Fork Gorge

Class: 3(4)	Length: 10 miles
Flow: 1000–20,000 cfs	Character: forested; canyon
Gradient: 35 fpm, PD	Season: rainy/snowmelt

Most of the drops on this run are gradual and straightforward, with the exception of Pillow Rapid. This sharp drop is visible from the road several miles up from the gorge (past the point where the road climbs away from the river and then returns). The only class 4 rapid, Surprise Rapid, is located 0.25 mile above the take-out. It can be scouted (or portaged) on river right.

Hazards

Pillow Rapid develops a nasty hole at some water levels; it can usually be avoided by running river left. Surprise Rapid is worthy of a scout.

Access

From US 199, about 1 mile northeast of Hiouchi Hamlet, turn onto South Fork Road. Cross the Middle Fork and the South Fork, then turn left and go up the South Fork. The take-out is about 1 mile above the South Fork bridge (2 miles from US 199), where Craig's Beach river access has several trails to the river. At this point, the river is not visible from the road. Scout the take-out if you do not want to run the gorge; it is not obvious from the river.

To reach the put-in, proceed upstream, crossing the river twice on bridges high above the river. The put-in is at Steven Memorial Bridge about 10 miles upstream. The river is generally visible from the road. It is possible to shorten the run by putting in or taking out at Sand Camp river access near the middle of the run.

Gauge

Smith River at Jedediah Smith Redwoods State Park. The flow is approximately 45 percent of the flow at the gauge. A nice medium-level flow is about 4200 cfs on the Jedediah Smith gauge.

Bo and Kathy Shelby

38 South Fork Smith River
South Fork Gorge to Bridge

Class: 4; 5	Length: 1.5 miles
Flow: 500 cfs; 9000 cfs	Character: gorge; clear water
Gradient: 41 fpm, PD	Season: rainy/snowmelt

This gorge is a bit longer than the Oregon Hole Gorge, but it still is not nearly long enough. Although the South Fork Road follows the river, the water is generally out of sight. With persistence and scrambling, it is possible to scout most of this stretch from the road; do this before committing yourself to the run. This is one of the most beautiful gorges anywhere, complete with all the classic gorge characteristics: steep blind drops, tough landings for scouting, and powerful turbulent water. This run is particularly difficult and potentially dangerous at high water levels.

Hazards

The run has several distinct drops, which vary markedly with the water level. Be prepared to do your own scouting and make your own decisions.

Access

Put in at Craig's Beach access 1.6 miles above the South Fork bridge (2 miles from US 199). For a longer run, choose an upstream access point (see South Fork Smith: Steven Memorial Bridge to South Fork Gorge run).

Take out at the South Fork bridge by paddling under the bridge and landing at the small beach on river right. A trail goes sharply up the bank to the end of the bridge.

Gauge

Smith River at Jedediah Smith Redwoods State Park. The flow is approximately 45 percent of the flow at the gauge.

Bo and Kathy Shelby

Opposite: *Paddling the fish ladder near Rainie Falls, Rogue River* (Kathy Shelby)

Southern Oregon Rivers

Region 3

Umpqua River and Tributaries

39 Jackson Creek
Cover Campground to NF 31 Bridge

Class: 4	Length: 8 miles
Flow: 400–1000cfs	Character: forested
Gradient: 60 fpm	Season: rainy/snowmelt

This run on Jackson Creek contains numerous ledges and rapids, far too many to remember. Although most rapids are straightforward, three drops are definitely worth mentioning.

After putting in at Cover Campground (below a mandatory portage log), the first mile varies between mini-gorge and something a bit wider. After a mile, Squaw Creek enters on the left over a nice 4- to 5-foot falls, and the volume of the creek increases noticeably.

In another mile, you will pass the NF 2950 bridge. A mile farther, an anchored log spans 95 percent of the streambed. It could be boofed at higher flows, but might need to be portaged. After several straightforward class 2 and class 3 ledges and rapids, you will reach a definite horizon line with river mist coming up over it. Scout left. This drop is nicknamed Da Bootie Call (class 4–4+). The more than 8-foot-high, river-wide ledge is nastier than it looks. All the water pours over a width of about 10 feet. At higher flows, a boof on the left might be an option.

About 0.5 mile farther downriver is Second Thought. Scout left, but portage right. This is a class 3+ to 4- 8-foot slide that runs into the rocks on river left, then makes a hard right turn. Another 0.75 mile downstream is The Gate-Keeper (class 4). This is an easy rapid to run, but the consequences for a missed line are severe. As above, scout left, but portage right. The rapid is best described as a ledge shaped like a 30-foot-wide letter J followed by a constriction to about 6 feet at the bottom. At low water, the left 15 to 18 feet may be unrunnable but can be boofed at higher flows. The right side forms a terminal keeper. However, a 4- to 5-foot-wide path of clean water on far river right may permit access around the hole. A strongly recirculating eddy on the right allows enough breathing time before running the gate. This is a 4- to 5-foot-slide into a benign hole that can be very sticky at higher flows. It is imperative not to get sideways here as a boat could easily wedge.

After a relatively quiet mile, Beaver Creek enters on the left, increasing the flow substantially. The NF 31 bridge is just below the creek, with its take-out on the right. You can run some nice class 3 ledge drops by continuing downstream another 0.5 mile before taking out. Or continue on to the South Umpqua for an additional 3 miles of class 2+ paddling, and take-out below the confluence, 0.5 mile on river right.

Hazards

The three class 4 drops as well as the logs present challenges. Da Bootie Call and The Gate-Keeper can be seen from the road on the drive up, at approximately 6.2 and 4.8 miles, respectively, upstream from the Jackson Creek turnoff. All are easily river scouted. Watch for wood.

Access

From Canyonville, go east on County Road 1, following the South Umpqua River upstream. Turn left onto County Road 46 (South Umpqua Road) at the town of Tiller. Continue on County Road 46 for about 5.2 miles and turn right on NF 29. Go 3.7 miles to the NF 31 bridge over Jackson Creek.

To reach the put-in, continue another 8 miles upstream on NF 29 to Cover Campground.

Gauge

None exists. This section of Jackson Creek is estimated to have 30–35 percent of the flow of the South Umpqua River at Tiller.

Mike Haley and WKCC Editors

40 Cow Creek
Glendale to West Fork of Cow Creek

Class: 3 (4)	Length: 15 miles
Flow: 400–1000 cfs	Character: forested; narrow valley
Gradient: 27 fpm, C-PD	Season: rainy

Cow Creek, sometimes referred to as the Coast Fork of the South Umpqua, flows west from Glendale and then northeast to Riddle, where it flows into the South Umpqua River. The fine forests along this river consist mostly of madrone, cedar, and fir. However, during the catastrophic 2013 fire in this canyon, much of the forest was burned. Most of the trees closest to the river survived, so the riverside view as one paddles is not so bad.

The flow on this run rises and falls quickly, causing difficulty with catching it at precisely the right flow. Parts of the run can be scouted by road in the lower third of the run.

The first 4 miles of river below the Glendale put-in allow ample opportunity to get warmed up for the action below. After this gentle section of easy class 1 and 2 rapids, the canyon begins to narrow, and the road begins to climb high above the river on the right. Most of the next 6 miles of the run are not in view of the road. The pool-drop rapids are separated by class 1+ water. Some nice wave trains and a few fast chutes are encountered.

About 5 miles from the put-in is a steep class 3, which is straightforward at 1000 cfs, but somewhat technical at 500 cfs. The scout is on the right. An easier class 3 rapid follows in about a mile, where the first railroad tunnel is seen on the right. The next major rapid, Concrete Wall (class 3+ to 4), is identified by a high concrete wall along the right. The river runs straight for about 100 yards, at which point, boulders and pour-overs at the bottom demand maneuvering.

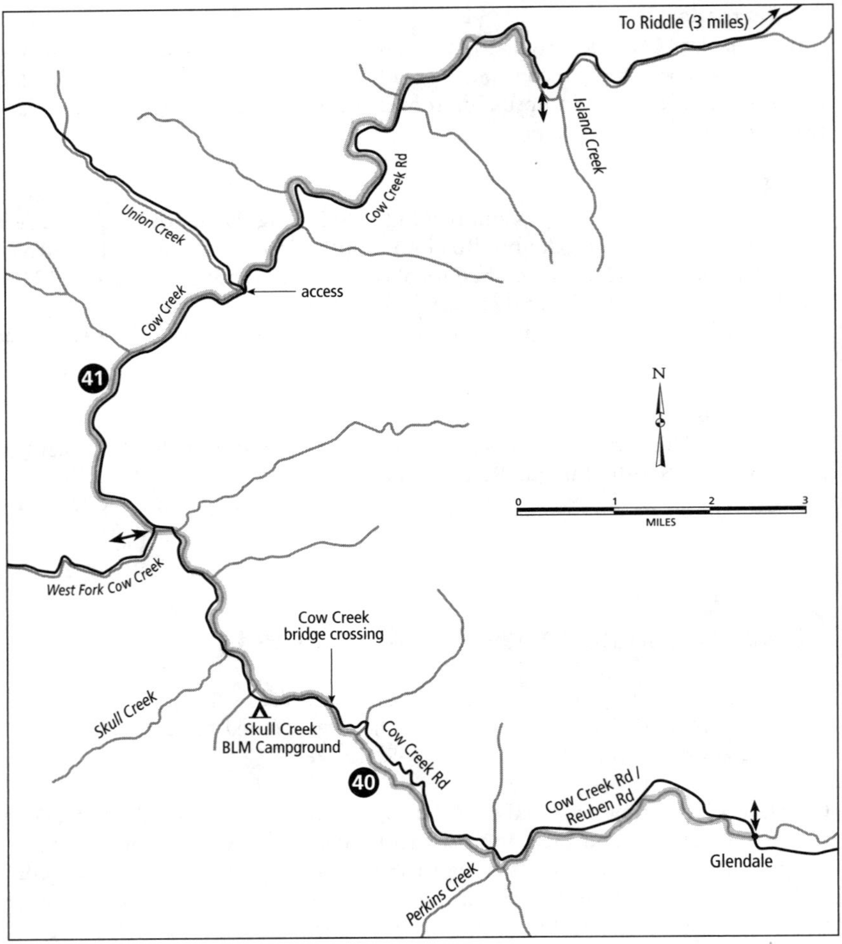

At mile 11, a bridge over Cow Creek appears with a nice alternative take-out on the right before the bridge. Around mile 12 is a long, ill-defined island ahead of Island Rapids, visible from the road. The left channel is easier, class 3, but requires navigation at the entrance. The right channel has a big pour-over, class 4-, at the bottom. The next rapid is Moo Cow (class 4), the biggest and steepest of the drops. Moo Cow curves right, and the bottom part of the drop is hidden from view. The final rapid, Chinese Wall (class 3), is just before a high rock wall on the right. The wall was built by Chinese laborers building the railroad in the 1880s. Near the end of the run, you pass under a railroad bridge and past a highway bridge on river right over Middle Creek, a tributary. From here, it's only 0.5 mile to the take-out on the left at the West Fork bridge.

Hazards

Several drops on this run are blind and should be scouted. Watch for wood.

Access

From the north take Interstate 5 exit 103, Riddle. Continue west on the Riddle bypass, which curves southward. At 5.9 miles from the interstate, note the bridge on the left over Cow Creek. Mileage markers start here at 0 and count upward. Continue upstream along the river. At milepost 19.2, turn right onto West Fork Road. Cross the bridge and park in the large gravel area on the left, the take-out.

To reach the put-in, return to the main road, turn right and follow Cow Creek Road upstream. In 4 miles, you pass Skull Creek Campground. An alternative put-in or take-out spot is located 5 miles upstream, where the road crosses the river (near milepost 24). The access is on river right upstream of the bridge. From the bridge, it's another 9.8 miles up to the put-in at Glendale. (Cow Creek Road changes its name to Reuben Road along the way.) Just past the lumber mill, turn right at the three-way intersection of Brown Road and Reuben Road. Take the dirt road down to the put-in spot, which is immediately downstream of the bridge over Cow Creek.

From the south, and alternatively from the north, take Interstate 5 exit 80 and follow Glendale Valley Road toward Glendale. Upon entering Glendale, pass a lumber mill on the left, go two blocks and turn right onto Brown Road. Cross the bridge over Cow Creek and turn hard left, taking the dirt road down to the put-in area. To reach the take-out, follow Reuben Road northwest and downstream for 15 miles.

Gauge

Cow Creek at Glendale. Cow Creek at Riddle. Flow in the middle and lower sections of this run is a little higher than the flow at Glendale, and at least half the flow at Riddle. Minimum flow on Glendale gauge is approximately 400 cfs.

Steve Cramer, Larry Hodges, Rob Blickensderfer, and WKCC Editors

41 Cow Creek
West Fork of Cow Creek to Island Creek

Class: 2(3)	Length: 15.9 miles
Flow: 700–1400 cfs	Character: forested
Gradient: 16 fpm, PD	Season: rainy

This is a pleasant run through steep terrain thickly wooded with manzanita, madrone, red cedar, and Douglas fir. While plenty of clear-cuts can be seen high on the slopes, lush riverside stands generally contain tall older trees. Cow Creek Road and a railroad run parallel to the creek, but are not obtrusive. The creek moves along quickly, even at low flows, and 10 miles of river can usually be paddled in 3 hours or less.

SECTION 1: WEST FORK COW CREEK TO UNION CREEK, 6.2 MILES, CLASS 2+(3)

The run is a mixture of continuous moving water and numerous class 2 and 2+ rapids. The only class 3 rapid is the boulder garden located 1.2 miles from put-in. It can be scouted from the road near milepost 18. Take out on the left just below the Union Creek bridge.

SECTION 2: UNION CREEK TO ISLAND CREEK ACCESS, 9.7 MILES, CLASS 2 (2+)

Just below the Union Creek bridge is a short class 2+ rapid. After a mile or two of very flat moving water is another class 2+ rapid. The river below is mostly class 1 with easy class 2 rapids interspersed with long stretches of moving water. About 2 miles above the take-out, a rapid under the road bridge may require some maneuvering. The take-out is on the left at Island Creek Day Use Area.

Note: Below Island Creek is a 10-mile run to the mouth of the river that is nearly all class 1. The one exception is the class 4 rapid that is located 2 miles down from Island Creek, near milepost 1.5. It can be portaged on river left. The take-outs for this lower run are at the Glenwood Loop Bridge (river left) or at Lawson Bar, on the South Umpqua (river right).

Hazards

None in particular, but always stay alert for possible sweepers. Occasional small trees are sometimes found growing in the river, and it may require some maneuvering to avoid them.

Access

See the Glendale to West Fork of Cow Creek run for general directions to the Cow Creek area.

Section 1: The put-in for this run is at the West Fork Cow Creek bridge, at milepost 19.2. The take-out is at the Union Creek bridge, river left, at milepost 13.5.

Section 2: For put-in, use the Union Creek access. The take-out is at Island Creek Day Use Area access at milepost 3.5.

Gauge

Cow Creek at Glendale (upstream of put-in). Cow Creek at Riddle (downstream of take-out). The flow is approximately 150 percent of that of the Glendale gauge and 75 percent of the flow of the Riddle gauge. Minimum flow on Glendale gauge is about 400 cfs.

Steve Cramer, Larry Hodges, Rob Blickensderfer, and WKCC Editors

42 ★ South Umpqua River
Campbell Falls to Three C Rock

Class: 3(4+); 4(5)	Length: 9.4 miles
Flow: 600 cfs; 4000 cfs	Character: forested
Gradient: 33 fpm, PD	Season: rainy/snowmelt

The run starts with a bang at Campbell Falls and its 14-foot vertical drop into a pool with a narrow exit. There is a chute along the far left wall, but the falls seems to be the saner route at most water levels. An alternative put-in is 75 yards downstream on river right.

The major rapids downstream change from narrow chutes through rock outcroppings to powerful river-wide ledge drops as the flow increases. The first major rapid, Diversification Drop, is located 1.9 miles down from the put-in. Two distinct chutes appear at low flows. River left is fairly straightforward; however, the right chute requires a quick left turn just as you drop over the 5-foot falls. Just 0.5 mile farther, Boulder Creek enters on the right, and 200 yards below is a drop similar to Diversification Drop. Both drops can be scouted from the road. Dumont Creek, with campground and rest rooms, is less than 1 mile downstream.

The third rapid worth mentioning, Triple Drop, is located about 6 miles farther down, just a couple of miles before the take-out. Three distinct drops in this 100-yard-long rapid give a great ride.

Hazards

Campbell Falls and the three other rapids mentioned above present difficulties. Scout or portage.

Access

The run is east of Interstate 5 between Roseburg and Medford. From the north, take Douglas County Road 1 east from the Canyonville city center; proceed 23 miles east to Tiller. From the south, take Oregon 62 from Medford to Oregon 227 to Tiller. In Tiller, take County Road 46 (South Umpqua Road) upstream for 4.5 miles to the take-out at the Three C Rock Campground.

The put-in is 9.2 miles farther upstream at Campbell Falls. Hike about 200 yards on a fairly good trail down to the river.

Gauge

South Umpqua River at Tiller.

Terry K. Wyatt and Jeff S. Wolfe

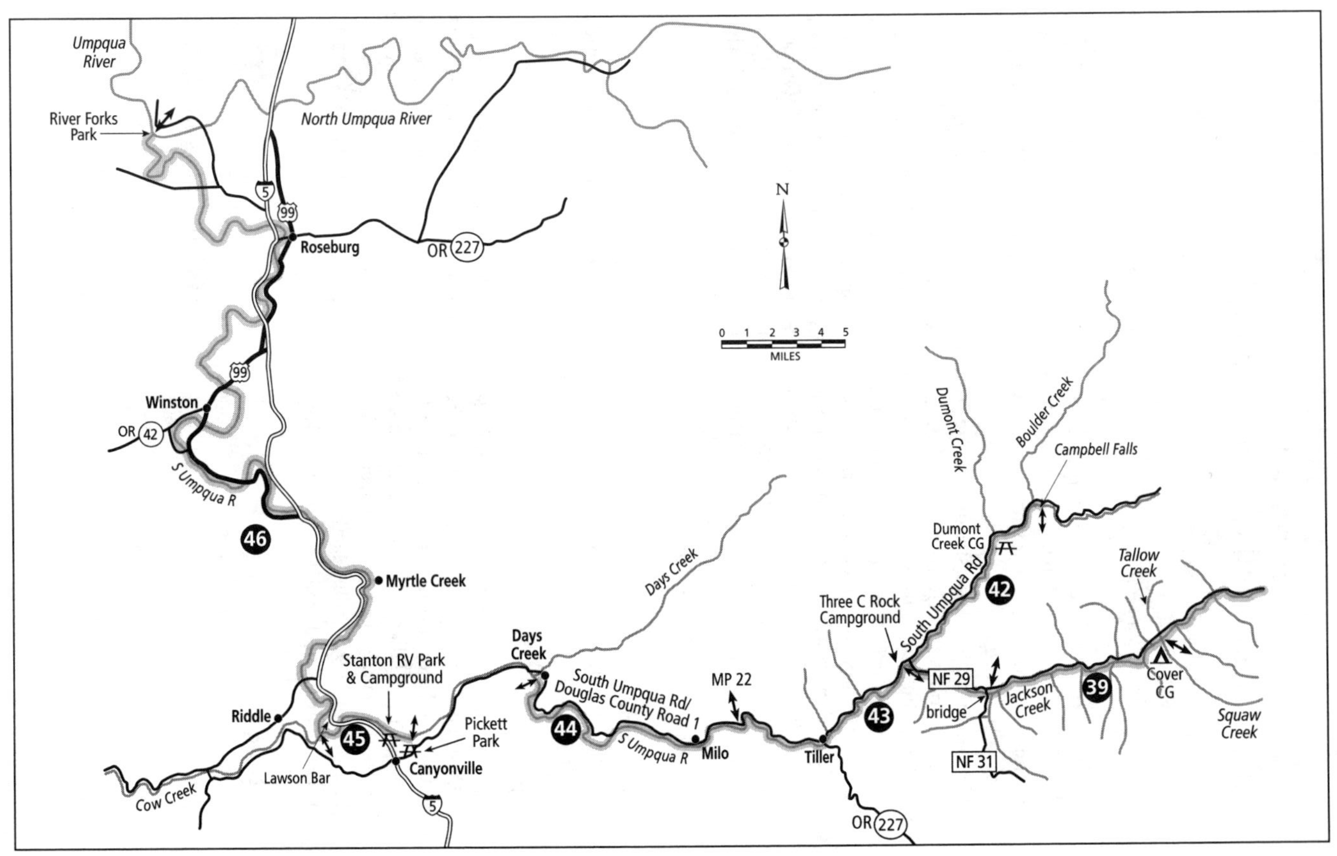

Umpqua River
River Forks Park
North Umpqua River
5
99
Roseburg
OR 227
N
0 1 2 3 4 5
MILES
99
Winston
OR 42
S Umpqua R
46
Myrtle Creek
Days Creek
Dumont Creek
Boulder Creek
Campbell Falls
Dumont Creek CG
South Umpqua Rd
42
Tallow Creek
Three C Rock Campground
Days Creek
Stanton RV Park & Campground
Days Creek
South Umpqua Rd/ Douglas County Road 1
MP 22
NF 29
Jackson Creek
39
Cover CG
Riddle
45
Pickett Park
44
S Umpqua R
Milo
43
bridge
NF 31
Squaw Creek
Lawson Bar
Canyonville
Cow Creek
5
Tiller
OR 227

43 South Umpqua River
Three C Rock to Milepost 22

Class: 3(4)	Length: 8.4 miles
Flow: 1000–4000 cfs	Character: wooded
Gradient: 22 fpm, C	Season: rainy/snowmelt

Although the nature of most of this run is class 1 and 2, several class 3 and class 4 rapids appear at high flows. From the put-in, the river flows at a nice tempo through a small canyon. After passing a concrete bridge at mile 1.6, it is another mile to a demanding class 3 rapid. This rapid should be run well left of center to avoid a large upstream pour-over hole on the right. The hole is followed by a massive rock in midstream with most of the water smashing directly into it.

At mile 3.6, a class 4 rapid can be scouted on the right. It is a river-wide ledge with a sticky reversal, followed by a hole of raft-flipping proportions.

The river passes under the Oregon 227 bridge in Tiller at mile 4.7. The last major rapid is at mile 7.2, near the downstream end of a recent major road cut. The river piles up against a huge boulder on the right bank as it makes a tight left bend. Sometimes, logs and debris get trapped here. Scout this rapid from the road during the shuttle or from the left shore.

Hazards

The rapids at mile 2.6 and mile 3.6 are both difficult. The class 3 drop at the road cut is potentially dangerous.

Access

The put-in for this run is the take-out for the South Umpqua River: Campbell Falls to Three C Rock run.

The take-out for this run is at about milepost 22.5 on South Umpqua Road/ Douglas County Road 1, where the river makes a sweeping left bend close to the road through a broad area of low rock outcroppings. Parking can be found on the riverside shoulder of the road.

Gauge

South Umpqua River at Tiller.

Steve Cramer, Rob Blickensderfer, and WKCC Editors

44 South Umpqua River
Milepost 22 to Days Creek

Class: 2+(4)	Length: 13.8 miles
Flow: 1000–4000 cfs	Character: rural
Gradient: 14 fpm, C	Season: rainy/snowmelt

The scenery varies at almost every turn; low rock cliffs, volcanic tuff, extensive gravel bars, and rolling hills. The river has many pleasant riffles over gravel bars that become very fast and turn into big waves at higher flows. It passes under a covered bridge at mile 2.1, and from there it is only about 0.5 mile to the concrete bridge in Milo. At mile 3.6 is a low ledge with a sticky reversal. After several miles of slow water, one hardly suspects the major class 4 rapid at mile 11.2, where the river slices through a low rock outcropping. Below this drop, the river bounces through delightful water with many play spots to the take-out.

Hazards

The class 4 rapid at mile 11.2 consists of a fast chute leading into a river-wide hole with a collapsing upstream wave that takes the full flow of the river. This rapid can be easily portaged on either side.

Access

The put-in for this run is the take-out at milepost 22.5 for the South Umpqua River: Three C Rock run to milepost 22.

The take-out is a boat ramp on river right located 50 yards upstream from the Douglas County Road 1 bridge in Days Creek.

Gauge

South Umpqua River at Tiller.

Steve Cramer and Rob Blickensderfer

45 South Umpqua River Pickett Park to Lawson Bar

Class: 2(3)	Length: 5.1 miles
Flow: 600–4000 cfs	Character: rural
Gradient: 12 fpm, PD	Season: rainy

A classic example of a pool-drop river can be experienced on this short run. After putting in at the pleasant Pickett Park, it is about 0.5 mile to the first drop, a straightforward class 2- rapid just as a bridge comes into view. A little farther along, a park is seen among large fir trees on the left. This is Stanton Park on the road just north of Canyonville, and it offers an alternative access to the river. About 0.25 mile below the park is the most difficult rapid on this section, consisting of class 3 channels over ledges. It can be scouted or portaged on the left. A mile farther is a class 2 rapid with several channels through willows. The next rumble heard is not a rapid but the traffic on the Interstate 5 bridge overhead. Below the bridge are enjoyable small rapids among scenic rock formations. An extensive gravel bar on the left indicates the approach to the mouth of Cow Creek, entering on the left, followed by Lawson Bar on the right. One may take out on the right either above or below the class 2 rapid at Lawson Bar.

Hazards

The class 3 rapid mentioned above can be quite technical at low flows. Above 3000 cfs, the class 2 rapid may be class 3.

Access

Take Interstate 5 exit 94 at Canyonville. Go east to Main Street, turn right, and in two blocks, turn left on Third Street following signs to Tiller. This road, Douglas County Road 1, travels up the South Umpqua River. In 1.1 mile, turn left on Pickett Lane. The put-in is at the end of the road at the boat ramp.

The take-out at Lawson Bar can be reached by returning to Interstate 5 and proceeding northward. Take exit 102, turn west, and then south following Lawson Bar Road to the river.

Gauge

South Umpqua River at Riddle.

Rob Blickensderfer and Steve Cramer

46 South Umpqua River
Lawson Bar to River Forks Park

Class: 1(2)	Length: 46.6 miles
Flow: 500–2000 cfs	Character: forested; ranch; rural; urban
Gradient: 6 fpm	Season: rainy/snowmelt

Even with the Interstate 5 corridor, small towns, one of the biggest sawmills in the West, and the city of Roseburg right nearby, this reach includes a lot of pleasant class 1 paddling with some easy class 2 rapids and long sections where you see little but riparian forest. With lower headwaters than the North Umpqua and less high-elevation volcanic rock (with its groundwater discharge), the South Umpqua's flows drop sooner and to far lower levels. But many accesses and easy water make this a great community river and a fine early-summer float. It's also Oregon's most productive smallmouth bass fishery and a popular steelhead stream for drift boaters in winter.

For an extended expedition, put in farther upstream at Tiller and paddle 76 miles to the mouth of the South Umpqua with one class 4 carry 2 miles above Days Creek and a few class 2+ drops. And, if you really like long trips, Tiller to the end of the main stem Umpqua at sea level is the third-longest river expedition that can be done in Oregon without dams or multiple major rapids—176 miles with long pools, hundreds of class 2 drops, three class 3 rapids on the main stem, and one carry for canoeists at Sawyers Rapid above Scottsburg.

Hazards

None in the Lawson to River Forks reach.

Access

To reach Lawson Bar put-in, take Interstate 5 exit 102, go west, and immediately left to the access.

For take-out just below the mouth of the South Umpqua, go to River Forks Park: Take Interstate 5 exit 125 at Roseburg, go northwest on Garden Valley Boulevard for 6 miles, turn left after the North Umpqua bridge, and go 2 miles. For intermediate access, Templin Beach Park in Roseburg is good; find US 99 south in downtown Roseburg, go west on Mosher Avenue, south on Fullerton, and right on Templin. Other intermediate accesses are available.

Gauge

South Umpqua River near Brockway (or South Umpqua River near Winston). 500 cfs is adequate.

Tim Palmer

47 Canton Creek
6.5 Miles Above Steamboat Creek to Steamboat Creek

Class: 3+(5); 4(5)	Length: 6.4 miles
Flow: 300 cfs; 2000 cfs	Character: forested
Gradient: 63 fpm	Season: rainy

This scenic tributary of Steamboat Creek is an excellent choice for intermediate paddlers. The road is always close by, but it never intrudes on the run. The ledgy nature of the creek provides many nice surfing holes and waves between rapids, all of which add up to one of the best all-around runs in the area.

Below the put-in bridge, the creek flows over many small drops and several long class 3 boulder gardens that have generous eddies for boat scouting. The creek is always quite wide, so generous flows are necessary for an enjoyable day.

Once you pass under the third bridge below the put-in, the water accelerates over several smaller ledgy drops and then enters a long, moving pool. The pool leads to the lip of a 15-foot waterfall (class 5) with no obvious route except at very high water. The portage around this drop is very easy on the left, and the entire drop is visible (and scoutable) on the shuttle.

Below the falls, two more significant rapids should be scouted. The first is a 5-foot ledge that is visible from the road just below a fun, twisty chute. The second drop is just downstream and contains a significant river-wide hole. More continuous rapids and surfing lead to the confluence with Steamboat Creek, where you can take out or continue down to the North Umpqua.

Hazards

The creek is always very wide, so logs are usually avoidable, but be watchful. The two lower ledges develop formidable holes at high water. A moderately challenging drop just above the class 5 waterfall may cause problems.

Access

From Oregon 138, turn up Steamboat Creek Road and drive 0.5 mile to the lower Canton Creek bridge. This is the take-out.

To reach the put-in, turn up the one-lane asphalt road that parallels Canton Creek. About 2.1 miles from the take-out is the class 5 waterfall, just before the second bridge over the creek. Continue upstream for a total of 6.4 miles to the fourth bridge, which is the put-in.

Gauge

Visible. Good medium flows occur after heavy rains when the North Umpqua River at Glide is between 6000 and 10,000 cfs, and Steamboat Creek is 3500–5000 cfs. Due to the wide nature of the creek, lower flows are not recommended.

Jason Rackley

48 Steamboat Creek
Steamboat Falls to Canton Creek Campground

Class: 4(5)	Length: 5.4 miles
Flow: 600–2500 cfs	Character: forested
Gradient: 43 fpm	Season: rainy/snowmelt

Steamboat Creek enters the North Umpqua River 1 mile west of Island Campground. Its feeling of isolation and good class 4 action make dipping a paddle into it worthwhile.

The put-in is just below Steamboat Falls where the road is near the river. Steamboat Falls can be run, but it is not recommended because of cement and steel rebar at its base. A line down the center-right has been relatively clean. A mile of easy play water allows a warm-up before a class 4 rapid. After 0.2 mile, a class 5 rapid can be scouted or portaged on the right. The remaining portion of the run is class 2 and 3 with an occasional easy class 4. Little Steamboat Falls lies at the end of the canyon and ranges in difficulty from class 4 at moderate flow to class 5 at high flows. It makes an excellent take-out.

Hazards

At levels above 5 feet (3000 cfs), the portage around the class 5 rapid becomes very difficult, as does the rapid. Check for logs.

Access

From Oregon 138 along the North Umpqua River, take Oregon 38 northward up Steamboat Creek. Canton Creek Campground, 0.5 mile upstream, is the take-out.

From the campground, drive 5.5 miles upstream. Put in where the road comes near the river. An alternative put-in is 100 yards up Steelhead Creek, which provides a short class 3 section.

Gauge

Steamboat Creek near Glide. A good low flow is 3.7 feet (1600 cfs).

Eric Brown

49 ★ North Umpqua River
Boulder Flat to Gravel Bin

Class: 2–3(4)	Length: 13.9 miles
Flow: 750–2000 cfs	Character: forested
Gradient: 35 fpm, PD	Season: year-round

The clear turquoise water, knock-out scenery, and exciting whitewater are just a few reasons why the North Umpqua River is loved and visited by thousands of people each year. With the river protected as a Wild and Scenic River, the area offers numerous campgrounds to accommodate boaters, hikers, mountain bikers, and anglers.

SECTION 1: BOULDER FLAT TO HORSESHOE BEND, 7 MILES, CLASS 2–3

Most of this run can be scouted from the road. The river is characterized by swiftly moving water and fairly continuous activity in moderate-size waves amid numerous rocks and other obstacles. In several spots, large holes and bigger waves are encountered. Snags are a hazard at times, and it is not unusual to encounter a tree spanning all or most of the stream. Good surf spots are at the first bridge and shortly below there.

Weird Weir Rapid is just beyond the second bridge. Here, a rocky ledge spans 80 percent of the river, creating a very narrow chute along the right bank. At lower water levels, this chute is virtually the only runnable spot. The force of the current may easily slam you into the wall on the right. It is a potential spot for lodged debris.

SECTION 2: HORSESHOE BEND TO GRAVEL BIN, 7 MILES, CLASS 3–4

This section is more pool-drop than the upper one. Between Horseshoe Bend and Apple Creek campgrounds, the river passes through a narrow gorge full of short, steep rapids that vary in difficulty. Some can be scouted from the road. Several of them require meticulous maneuvering between rocks and holes.

Pinball is a boulder-choked class 3+ to class 4 rapid located about 0.3 mile downstream of the bridge below Apple Creek Campground. Scouting is advised. The rapid, which cannot be seen from the road, occurs on a right bend of the river with a large gravel bar just above it on the left. At water levels that allow for the bar to exist, it is possible to pull into an eddy below the bar and scout from the left bank. Use caution at Alligator Rapid (class 3-), which is just above Pinball. Alligator is best run left to avoid the diagonal curler that forms at lower flows.

Below Pinball, the pool-drop pattern of the river continues all the way to the Gravel Bin take-out with many fine surf waves.

Hazards

All sections—watch out for sweepers and logs.

Section 1: Just above the take-out, Weird Weir should be checked for debris in the right chute. The ledge may need to be portaged.

Section 2: Pinball Rapid should be checked for wood.

An informational guide is provided by the U.S. Forest Service: "North Umpqua Wild and Scenic River Users Guide" (see Appendix B).

Access

Boaters are asked to avoid floating between 6:00 PM and 10:00 AM, July 31–October 31. This is to give anglers undisturbed time on the river during peak fishing hours.

The put-in at Boulder Flat Campground is approximately 50 miles east of Roseburg on Oregon 138.

The take-out for section 1 is at Horseshoe Bend Campground; turn right off Oregon 138 near milepost 46. Most boaters take out at the access located 500 feet downstream of the North Umpqua bridge on river right, just upstream of the campground.

For section 2, put in at any of the Horseshoe Bend Campground accesses. An alternative put-in is at the small turnout across from the Dry Creek Store, which is on Oregon 138 about 0.8 mile above the Horseshoe Bend turnoff.

The take-out is 0.2 mile below Island Campground at Gravel Bin access.

Gauge

North Umpqua River at Copeland Creek. North Umpqua River at Glide (below the run). The river is dam-controlled and runnable all year, although in late summer it can get very rocky and technical on the upper reaches. Flows above 2000 cfs on the Copeland gauge can be quite pushy and increase the difficulty.

Kent Wickham and WKCC Editors

50 North Umpqua River
Gravel Bin to Bogus Creek

Class: 2(3)	Length: 4.7 miles
Flow: 800–3000 cfs	Character: forested
Gradient: 24 fpm, PD	Season: year-round (with restrictions)

This 5-mile stretch of the river is a world-class fishing area. The mouth of Steamboat Creek is a holding area for migrating steelhead. This run is accessible only during the winter, early spring, and fall, and not during the summer. See the Access section below for details on the restrictions.

The Steamboat Inn marks the site of a rocky rapid in the left channel and a sometimes runnable falls in the right channel. Per the current owners, the inn welcomes visitors for lunch. This is the only class 3 rapid on this section. Several class 2 rapids follow with long pools between them. Take-out is at the Bogus Creek access.

Hazards

Watch for wood. Scout Steamboat Rapid.

Access

Restrictions: Boaters are asked to avoid floating between 6:00 PM and 10:00 AM, July 1–July 14. Additionally, boaters should avoid floating anytime between July 15 and October 31. This is to give anglers undisturbed time on the river during peak fishing hours and days, and also to protect the important steelhead spawning areas. The Steamboat Inn, accessed via the highway, is open seasonally for dining and lodging.

For directions to Gravel Bin, see North Umpqua: Horseshoe Bend to Gravel Bin.

For directions to Bogus Creek, see North Umpqua: Bogus Creek to Cable Crossing.

Gauge

North Umpqua River at Copeland. North Umpqua River at Glide (downstream of run).

Kent Wickham and WKCC Editors

51 ★ North Umpqua River
Bogus Creek to Cable Crossing

Class: 3(4)	Length: 12.3 miles
Flow: 1000–3000 cfs	Character: forested
Gradient: 20 fpm, PD	Season: year-round

This stretch, although highlighted by several of the North Umpqua's biggest rapids, is generally less technical than the upstream runs. Rapids are separated by long, flat stretches.

SECTION 1: BOGUS CREEK TO SUSAN CREEK, 6.3 MILES, CLASS 3

Four class 3 rapids are found on this run. Burial Rapid is found 0.7 mile below put-in. It is just above the Wright Creek Bridge. This is followed in another 0.2 mile by Bathtub Rapid; scout on river left. Bathtub has a very narrow channel on river left at low flows.

Small fun drops continue for several more miles. A very large cliff rising from the water's edge on the left is seen 200 yards above Island Rapid. At Island Rapid, the river divides into a broad, shallow left channel, which fizzles out to nothing, and a roaring right channel that approaches class 4 at higher flows. The usual run is right of the island but on the left side of the channel to avoid some large holes below. Island can be scouted from the road with difficulty.

One mile below Island Rapid is another class 3, Ledges Rapid. It is marked by the Bureau of Land Management boundary sign at the side of the road and can be scouted by road during the shuttle. Ledges is a long rapid that starts out easy but requires a very tricky cut at the end to avoid a very large hole (a large rock at low flows) on the right. Ledges becomes more difficult at higher flows. A class 2 rapid at Susan Creek State Park is 0.5 mile above the take-out on river right. Study the take-out area before launching; it's hard to spot from the river.

SECTION 2: SUSAN CREEK TO CABLE CROSSING, 6 MILES, CLASS 2(3)

The 4 miles of river below the Susan Creek put-in has many riffles, a couple of class 2 rapids, and some nice long pools. At Richard G. Baker County Park, a steep drop is followed by the 5-foot falls known as Baker Falls. Cable Crossing, a half-mile downstream, is the last convenient take-out above Deadline Falls. Study your take-out area well.

"The North Umpqua River Wild and Scenic River Users Guide" also offers helpful information (see Appendix B).

Hazards

Below the recommended take-out at Cable Crossing are two very demanding class 5 rapids, Deadline Falls and The Narrows. These rapids should be considered by experts only. Rafters might find it necessary to portage Bathtub at low flows due to the narrowness of the chutes. Island Rapid and Ledges both deserve a scout. Keep an eye out for wood.

Access

Boaters are asked to avoid floating between 6 PM and 10 AM, July 31–October 31. This is to give anglers undisturbed time on the river during peak fishing hours.

The section 1 put-in is at the river access at Bogus Creek Campground, approximately 35 miles east of Roseburg on Oregon 138. The Susan Creek picnic area/boat launch take-out (or put-in) site is on Oregon 138 at milepost 28.5.

The take-out for section 2 is at Cable Crossing, a poorly marked but very good dirt-road access 0.2 mile up from Deadline Falls. It is near milepost 23 on Oregon 138.

Gauge

North Umpqua River at Copeland. North Umpqua River at Glide (downstream of run). The river gets pushy and fast at flows over 3000 cfs.

Kent Wickham and WKCC Editors

52 North Umpqua River Lone Rock to Winchester

Class: 2+(3)	Length: 23.5 miles
Flow: 600–4000 cfs	Character: rolling hills
Gradient: 11 fpm, PD	Season: year-round

This lower section of the North Umpqua moves through terrain transitioning from forested mountain canyon to hilly pastureland. Near sunset, the hills of scattered oak become a masterpiece of shadow and gold. By June, the river is comfortably warm, yet mountain clear with plenty of flow, a rare treat for Oregon boaters. Additionally, this run contains a fairly continuous offering of class 2 whitewater, great for open canoeists and novice kayakers.

In the 3 miles from Lone Rock to Colliding Rivers, there are many class 1+ and 2 pool-drop rapids with fairly straight routes through 2- to 3-foot standing waves. At Colliding Rivers, the river is constricted by several large rock formations; it makes a sharp right turn after colliding head-on with Little River. An island divides the channel above the rapid. Left of the island, the standard route, is a class 3- to 3 drop with a rather tight right turn midway. Right of the island, a narrow class 3–3+ drop makes a shortcut turn to the right and pushes hard onto a rock with a big eddy below. Scout this drop from the island or by ferrying above the drop. Both sides change with the flow, and the left side may not be boatable at low summer flows.

The North Umpqua then starts its transition into open hills with a much wider streambed. The river takes on more of a gravel bar nature with longer rapids (mostly class 2), but also longer flatwater stretches that develop occasional afternoon headwinds. The waves get smaller, but the drops become more technical, especially at summer flows under 3000 cfs.

About 6 miles below Colliding Rivers, the river makes a bend to the north, announcing Whistlers Park Falls, a class 3- drop with several relatively turbulent

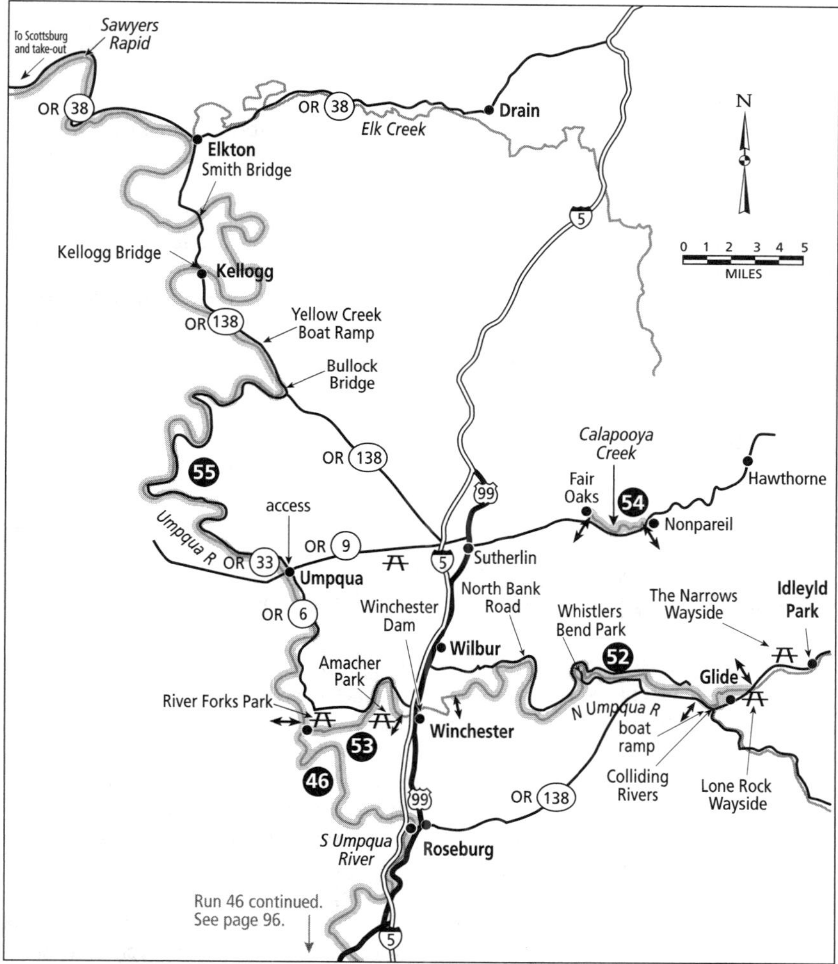

routes. From here, the river makes a horseshoe bend around Whistlers Bend Park, an alternative access, and begins the final 13 miles. About 4 miles down is Dixon Falls, a class 3 drop around the right side of an island. It starts with a slightly technical approach with poor visibility. The drop itself is a turbulent chute with side curlers and a pool finish. The left channel around the island is a possible alternative, but it is very rocky and technical.

Downriver about 0.5 mile from Dixon Falls are three more class 2 rapids. After another 2–3 miles, the river makes a big horseshoe bend to the south, with Umpqua Community College visible high on the right bank. When the water slows to a halt due to the Winchester Dam, start looking for a small boat ramp on river left, the take-out.

Hazards

Colliding Rivers, Whistlers Park Falls, and Dixon Falls are rated as class 3.

Access

The put-in is at the BLM Lone Rock access on river left, about 1 mile east of Glide off Oregon 138. Follow the signs to the launch. Most drift boaters put in at the Colliding Rivers boat ramp 0.3 mile below Colliding Rivers rapid, just west of the Oregon 138 bridge. Whistlers Bend Park is a convenient access point about 7 miles west of Glide on County Road 223. Access is also available across the river from the park at Jackson Wayside on North Bank Road.

The take-out is reached from Winchester, located on US 99 a few miles north of Roseburg. Take Page Road east out of Winchester along the south side of the river. A small boat ramp is upstream about 1 mile.

Gauge

North Umpqua River at Glide.

Carl Landsness and Marianne Musitelli

53 North Umpqua River
Winchester to River Forks Park

Class: 2	Length: 6.6 miles
Flow: 600–4000 cfs	Character: valley
Gradient: 9 fpm, PD	Season: year-round

Here the river makes another transition in character as it enters bottomland terrain and vegetation not unlike the Willamette River basin. Surprisingly few houses are visible, considering the proximity of roads. The frequency of rapids decreases, but those that exist have nice standing waves. A warm summer day can find many Roseburg-area residents leisurely rafting or tubing down to River Forks Park.

The first 4.5 miles to the Garden Valley Road bridge is intermittent class 1 and 2-. The mile following the bridge is a notoriously slow and flat stretch. The slow stretch ends abruptly at Burkhardt Rapid, a class 2+ ledge drop that can be a good ferry-practice spot at higher water levels. Another class 2+ drop with moderate waves quickly follows. A little more whitewater brings you to the confluence of the North Umpqua and the South Umpqua rivers, with a nice beach take-out on the right at River Forks Park.

Hazards

Burkhardt Rapid and several other class 2+ ledges present the only difficulties.

Access

Put in at Amacher RV Park and Campground on the south side of the US 99 bridge in Winchester, beneath the Interstate 5 high bridge.

To reach the take-out, cross the river on US 99, then follow Del Rio Road west 4 miles. At the three-way intersection turn right on Garden Valley Road. After 1.4 miles, turn left and go 0.6 mile south to a sign indicating River Forks Park on the right. Proceed to the take-out.

Gauge

North Umpqua River at Winchester.

Carl Landsness and WKCC Editors

54 Calapooya Creek
Nonpareil to Driver Valley Road

Class: 3+(4) T	Length: 3.1 miles
Flow: 300–800 cfs	Character: rural; narrow canyon
Gradient: 52 fpm, PD	Season: rainy

The first 1.5 miles are through open valley past the homes and outbuildings of the farming community of Nonpareil. The rapids are primarily broken ledges of increasing height. At about 1.0 mile is a 4-foot ledge that can be run up against the left wall at higher flows. At 1.5 miles, the creek enters a steep, narrow gorge. The first drop entering the gorge is through a narrow slot with the flow smashing into the right wall. At low water, the drop is not undercut, but there is risk of logs jamming here. The drop can be carried on the right along an abandoned road. Below the first drop, the action is nonstop for 1.9 miles. The drops are tight, technical, and abusive to boats at low water. At higher water, the drops are technical and the action is fast. With sufficient eddies for scouting, none of the drops are blind. If one has time to notice, the gorge walls are near vertical, rising 40 to 80 feet above the creek, and the gorge has a wonderful remote feel. Below the gorge is 0.25 mile of relaxing water on which to unwind.

Hazards

The first drop entering the gorge.

Access

From Interstate 5, take Nonpareil Road east through Sutherlin to Nonpareil (9 miles from Sutherlin). Put in on river left under the bridge just upstream of the store and downstream from the water treatment plant and dam.

Take out on river right at the first Driver Valley Road bridge out of Sutherlin (off Fair Oaks Drive). (A second Driver Valley Road bridge is 3.5 miles downstream.)

Gauge

None exists.

Steve Cramer and Larry Hodges

55 Umpqua River
River Forks Park to Scottsburg

Class: 1(2+ to 3)	Length: 84 miles
Flow: 1000–4000 cfs	Character: forested; agricultural; roaded
Gradient: 4 fpm, PD	Season: year-round

From the confluence of the North and South Umpqua Rivers west of Roseburg, the main Umpqua winds through the Coast Range to the Pacific Ocean near Reedsport. Numerous small farms and houses dot the river's banks, but many stretches show little development and the development one does see is fairly unobtrusive. Roads follow most of the river, but significant traffic is noticeable only on stretches below Elkton and along one short stretch near Kellogg. The predominant scenery is the forested hills of the Coast Range, enjoyable even with the considerable logging that has taken place.

The Umpqua's riverbed is quite wide, capable of holding typical winter storm flows in excess of 50,000 cfs and the occasional 100,000+ cfs flood. Yet summer flows are in the 1000–3000 cfs range. As one can guess from the low gradient, the Umpqua contains long stretches of slow or flatwater interspersed with riffles, many small rapids, and a few larger drops. As the river drops, it becomes restricted in places to narrow channels in the bedrock. Some of these develop into short class 2–3 rapids, depending on the river level.

The Umpqua is runnable year-round by experienced boaters able to deal with the hazards of high-volume rivers. The less adept should wait for summer, with its lower flows and warmer water.

The numerous boat ramps along this stretch allow boaters to choose any of numerous possible runs. Note the Bicycle Shuttler's Delight: A trip from Kellogg Bridge to Smith Bridge is about 14 river miles, mostly roadless, but the shuttle is just over 2 miles.

SAWYERS RAPID: 2.3 MILES, CLASS 2+ TO 3

Some whitewater boaters like to paddle a 2.3-mile stretch of river that includes class 3 Sawyers Rapid. After putting in just above the rapid on river right (pullout near milepost 27), paddle immediately over to river left to scout the drop. The narrow chute is turbulent at low water and is often portaged on the left by novice paddlers. A second class 3 rapid shortly follows and is run down the middle. Play spots are found below on far right and left. Take out at Scott Creek County Park, near milepost 24.5 on the highway.

Hazards

Rapids vary with water level, and some can be tricky. Be prepared to scout. Inexperienced boaters can get into trouble if they do not stay alert. Two class 2+ to 3 rapids lie between the two Oregon 138 bridges. Sawyers Rapid (class 3), 10 miles below Elkton, is a turbulent flume easily portaged on the left.

Access

The uppermost put-in (river mile 111) is the take-out for the North Umpqua River: Winchester to River Forks Park run.

There are many access points, a few are listed here. River miles (RM) differ from highway miles.

The Umpqua Landing launch is 1 mile west of the town of Umpqua (RM 103). To reach it, follow Garden Valley Road from River Forks Park; or from Interstate 5, take exit 136 (Sutherlin/Oregon 138), head west on County Road 9 to Umpqua. Bullock Bridge is on County Road 57 (RM 80). To reach it, follow County Road 33 (Tyee Road) north from the town of Umpqua, or follow Oregon 138 out of Sutherlin until it reaches the river (around milepost 13), or follow Oregon 138 south from Elkton. One can cross the bridge and go upriver a couple of miles to a boat ramp, or follow Oregon 138 north about 1 mile to the Yellow Creek boat ramp. Kellogg Bridge is on Oregon 138 (RM 71), near milepost 6. Smith Bridge is on Oregon 138 (RM 57), near milepost 4.

Bunch Bar access (RM 43) is on river right downstream of Elkton; go 6 miles west of town on Oregon 38. For Sawyers boat ramp (just above Sawyers Rapid, at RM 41) on river left, cross Mehl Creek Road bridge, turn right on Henderer Road, and travel downstream for 9 miles.

The Oregon 38 bridge is at Scottsburg (RM 27); the take-out is 0.6 mile below the bridge on river left at Scottsburg Park, near milepost 16 on Oregon 38.

Gauge

Umpqua River at Elkton. Typical summer flows are in the 1000–3000 cfs range.

Dan Valens, Richard Dierks, and WKCC Editors

Rogue River and Tributaries

56★ North Fork Rogue River
Natural Bridge to Woodruff Bridge

Class: 4(5); 4+(5) P	Length: 2.9 miles
Flow: 300–1000 cfs; 2000 cfs	Character: forested; fairly remote
Gradient: 62 fpm, PD	Season: year-round

Affectionately referred to as "Natty," Natural Bridge is one of many hidden gems in Southern Oregon. The river is always clear and cold, and consistently hovers around 300 cfs at its lowest summertime flows. The run contains many fun class 3 and 4 rapids set in a narrow canyon with beautiful forested banks and crystal clear water. If it's your first experience, be sure to take some time to stroll upstream on the paved walkways and gaze at the natural bridge, where the entire river plunges into a lava tube and emerges 100 feet downstream.

Immediately upstream of the recommended put-in is a tough class 5 rapid with

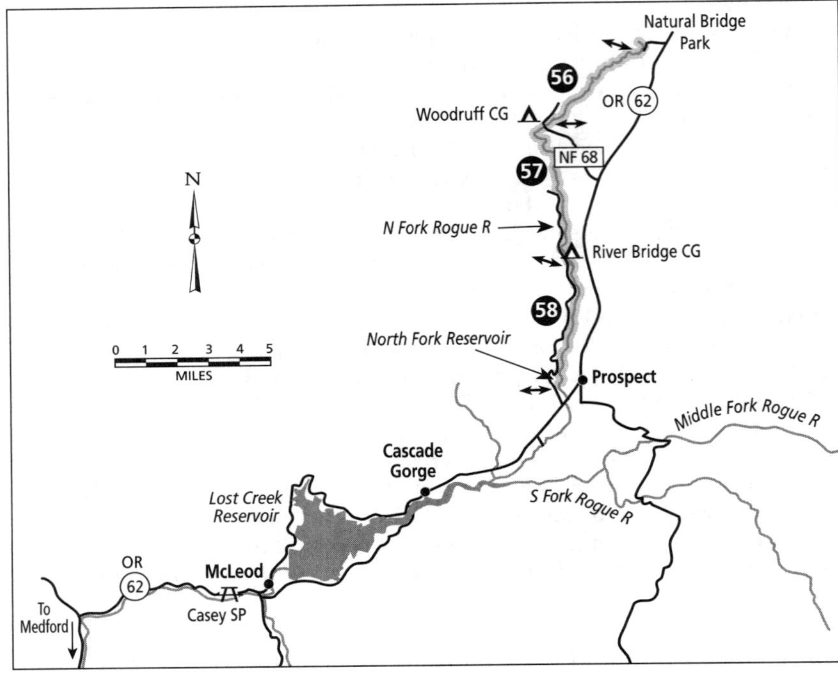

a cave on the left. Most boaters begin the run just below the footbridge on river left by seal-launching 10–15 feet into the pool below. Just downstream from the put-in, the action starts immediately with a long, steep class 4 drop featuring some big holes and interesting moves. The river then evolves into a pool-drop nature. After about a mile of some smaller class 3 rapids, paddlers arrive at Karma, identified by a tight horseshoe bend to the right. Although a fun entrance rapid called Pre-Karma just begs to be run, do not be fooled. Be sure to take out above it on river right to view Karma from above. This rapid is long, and the last part is not visible from the scout due to a left bend in the river. The classic middle boof line came back into play after the 2014 high water washed out a log in the drop. The end of the boulder garden leads to the center 8-foot boof down a sloping ledge, which drops into a pool with weird crosscurrents.

Below Karma, the river provides some easier drops, then slows its pace, taking a sharp turn to the right. Boaters need to be extra cautious as Knob Falls, a 20-foot, class 5 waterfall, lies 100 yards downstream. Exit on river left just before the bend to the right to portage the falls. The portage trail is clearly visible up the steep hill to the left. Although the portage is less threatening than the seal launch below the falls, the carry up and over the steep, loose-soiled hill is more work. Instead, many opt to carefully scramble across the right side ledge. Once a boater has traversed the ledge past the falls, he or she will be able to position the boat, and seal launch into the miniature gorge below.

Knob Falls has been run by a handful of boaters, but most people portage. Locals dubbed it "Therapy Falls," inferring that one might run it for therapy if ever diagnosed with a terminal illness.

Immediately below the falls are three successive rapids. The first is fairly small, and the second has a bizarre rock formation in the middle that can be avoided by starting left, then moving right just below the guard rocks. The third drop is just downstream and should be approached with caution as wood has been known to collect there. At least one member of the party should scout this rapid for wood and/or set safety. The river narrows and plunges into Blue Hole, a uniform hole that is easier than it looks, but is still best punched on the sides.

The river then mellows out for a time, with some long, scenic flatwater stretches punctuated by a couple of very narrow slots. The last significant rapid is through a tight slot created by a collapsed lava tube, where most of the flow is funneled through the boof squeeze appropriately dubbed Nozzle. To avoid getting pinched sideways in the 6-foot-wide passage, where boats have been known to wedge, start center-right with a final right-side boof stroke. The last and final drop is just above the take-out and visible from Woodruff Bridge. The river divides around a rocky island, where the left channel drops into a deadly undercut jammed with logs visible from the take-out bridge, while the right pours over a really nice 8-foot ledge ending the run.

Hazards

Use caution while portaging around Knob Falls. Watch for wood.

Access

To get to the take-out, take Oregon 62 east from Medford toward Lost Creek Reservoir and Prospect. Continue 6.25 miles past Prospect and turn left onto NF 68, following signs to Woodruff Bridge. The take-out is at the bridge over the North Fork Rogue 1.8 miles from Oregon 62.

To reach the put-in, return to Oregon 62 and turn left. Travel 3.5 miles and turn left at the sign for Natural Bridge Park. The parking lot is 0.5 mile ahead.

The usual put-in is a seal launch from a rock ledge just below the park's footbridge on the left. Access it by going upstream of the bridge and crossing under it. **Note:** There is no established access at this point, so be discreet and quick. Access could be closed altogether if conflicts arise with other park users or park staff.

Gauge

Rogue River above Prospect (USGS gauge), or Rogue River at Lost Creek Dam–Inflow. Flow at put-in is about half of the Prospect flow. In winter, flows are often much higher due to rainfall.

Jason Rackley, Pete Giordano, and Yann Crist-Evans

57 North Fork Rogue River
Woodruff Bridge to River Bridge Campground (Takelma Gorge)

Class: 4+	Length: 3.5 miles
Flow: 400–500 cfs	Character: forested
Gradient: 47 fpm, PD	Season: year-round

The Takelma Gorge section of the North Fork of the Rogue River is a short expert run, with year-round flows and great rapids. Do not be deceived by the mild gradient. The gorge in the middle of the run has a gradient of more than 100 fpm, with several difficult rapids and sheer walls on both sides. Climbing out of the gorge is next to impossible.

From the put-in, the run is scenic but flat for a mile before boaters enter the gorge. The first rapid, Entrance, is straightforward and marks the last realistic chance to exit the river before running the gorge.

The major rapids in the gorge are named Number One through Number Five. Number One is a steep drop over two river-wide ledges. The ledges produce big holes at high water, while at low water the second ledge has a severe sieve on the right and a narrow slot on the left. Several hundred yards downstream is Number Two: a relatively easy drop that pushes against the right wall a bit. Below Two the river slows a bit above Number Three, which is complicated by a river-wide log just above it. The log can be portaged pretty easily through the huge undercut in the wall on the right. Below the portage, you launch directly at the top of Number Three, which has a few big boulders blocking the main flow and then a river-wide L-shaped ledge. This ledge must be run either far left or right because in the middle is a large pothole/cave that has been explored by a few paddlers.

Another pool lies above Number Four, which is difficult to scout from the top of the gorge but can be scouted (but not portaged) from river level on the left. This three-part rapid develops a couple of powerful holes at high flows. A swim in Number Four would result in a long swim through the rest of the gorge (and rapid Number Five), as the walls are totally vertical here. Boaters finish the gorge by running through some big hydraulics and twisty moves in Number Five.

Hazards

Vertical walls make escape from the gorge virtually impossible except by running the rapids. For this reason, the entire gorge should be scouted before committing to the run. This is most easily done by hiking downriver from the put-in on a good trail. When you are peering down into the gorge from 30 feet up, it is difficult to estimate the size of the holes. Rapids that look inconsequential from above certainly do not feel that way when you are in them. Number One can be very dangerous at low water; scout carefully and set safety by having people on the banks to rescue someone if an accident occurs.

Access

The take-out is at River Bridge Campground. See the North Fork Rogue: River Bridge Campground to North Fork Reservoir run for directions.

To reach the put-in, return to Oregon 62 and turn left. Travel 2.2 miles and turn left on NF 68, following the signs to Woodruff Campground. The put-in is at the bridge over the North Fork Rogue 1.8 miles from Oregon 62. To scout via the trail, walk 0.3 mile east of the put-in bridge to the trailhead for the Upper Rogue River Trail No. 1034 and hike downstream.

Gauge

Rogue River above Prospect (USGS gauge), or Rogue River at Lost Creek Dam–Inflow.

Jason Rackley and Pete Giordano

58 ★ North Fork Rogue River River Bridge Campground to North Fork Reservoir

Class: 3+(4)		Length: 5 miles
Flow: 275–3000 cfs		Character: forested; side trail
Gradient: 40 fpm, PD		Season: year-round

The easiest of the three North Fork Rogue runs, River Bridge is an exceptional introduction to creeking for novice/intermediate kayakers and a great technical raft run at higher flows (which usually occur in the winter and spring). The river is surrounded by classic Oregon scenery where massive fir trees rise from the forest floors, and the clear, cold waters carve through the forest as the river feeds into the North Fork Reservoir. The North Fork Rogue is also one of the few rivers in Oregon where you can experience a combination of alpine boating and hot summer sun. Because the river is spring-fed, there is rarely ever a time when the flows actually get too low to kayak. In the winter during times of heavy rain, the river can swell to perfect flows for rafts.

The rapids in this run, though easier than the two runs upstream, have some of the same characteristics: lots of ledgy, mossed-over lava rocks and the constant potential for sweepers. Many of the rapids are fairly technical and require some frequent maneuvering around sleeper rocks and boulders. Occasionally, a passage under a log may offer the best option.

Just downstream of the put-in, the river cuts through a series of channels leading around a group of islands. Depending on the flow, boaters can go any number of ways, so just follow the deepest current. The first ledge drop, Boogie (class 3-) is a straightforward pool-drop, a good indication of the nature of what lies below. After a few easy class 2+ to 3- rapids, paddlers come to the first significant drop, Typewriter (class 3). Scout right. This ledge is about 3 feet tall at summer flows and, because of its shape, is not retentive, but rather flushy. More easy class 2+ to 3- rapids follow, then there's a calm pool with a large eddy on the right. Zoom Flume (class 3), a bending rapid to the right, presents a sloping and fairly steep ledge-like boulder garden with a flume in the middle of the bottom of the main channel.

A few more minor rapids lead to aptly named Double Drop (class 3+), recognized by a sweeping left turn in the river. Scout right. Double Drop starts out as a fun boulder garden with a boulder landmark that splits the flow between two channels. The channels can be run either way depending on skill level and flow. The right is the usual line at normal flows.

The next large rapid is a long, continuous class 3 boulder garden called Read-N-Run. A variety of lines exist here. A fun splashy boulder garden Up Next (class 3-) drops fast around an S-shaped turn, followed by Dogleg (class 3). This rapid winds around some boulders at the top then drops from left to right.

The final rapid, Rock Tumbler (class 3+ to 4-), can be tricky, so scout right at low water and left at higher flows. The four choices can be run at most flows with the easiest channel usually beginning on the far right. Proceed 0.5 mile along the reservoir to reach the take-out on the left either just before or just after the red buoys.

Hazards

Sweepers are a constant threat. Scout Typewriter, Double Drop, and Rock Tumbler. Some ledges can form sizable holes at gauge flows over 1000 cfs.

Access

To reach the take-out, drive an hour north from Medford on Oregon 62 past Lost Creek Reservoir until you see signs for the turnoff to Prospect. About 0.5 mile beyond the first turnoff for Prospect, Oregon 62 crosses an aqueduct. The dirt road immediately on the left past the aqueduct and paralleling it is the take-out road. Turn left and drive 0.3 mile to North Fork Reservoir, the take-out. (If you reach the Prospect Ranger Station on Oregon 62, you've gone too far.)

To reach the put-in, return to Oregon 62 and continue 3.8 miles past the Prospect Ranger Station to the sign "River Bridge Campground." Turn left and drive 1 mile to the river.

Gauge

Rogue River above Prospect (USGS gauge). When the gauge reads over 1000 cfs, the level is optimal, although lower flows are still fun.

Hayden Glatte and Yann Crist-Evans

59 Grave Creek
5 Miles to Confluence with Rogue River

Class: 3	Length: 5.9 miles
Flow: 500–1000 cfs	Character: forested
Gradient: 35 fpm, PD	Season: rainy

This is a small technical stream with short, twisting blind drops in the section not visible from the road and very few play spots, just nice scenery. The run continues down to the confluence with the Rogue River and can include Grave Creek Rapid.

Hazards

Possible hazards include low-swinging footbridges, brush along the bank, and wood in the river.

Access

The take-out is at the boat ramp beneath the Grave Creek Bridge across the Rogue River (see the Rogue River: Grave Creek to Foster Bar run).

To reach the put-in, take the road toward Wolf Creek from the northeast end of the bridge. Follow this for 4.8 miles to a point where it returns to Grave Creek after winding up the hill. Parking is limited. Do not trespass.

Gauge

None exists. Flow is flashy and depends on rainfall. The author made the run when the Rogue was running 4000 cfs at Marial; however, it is unlikely that a dependable correlation can be made between the Rogue and Grave Creek.

Karen Wilt

60 Rogue River
McGregor Boat Launch to Shady Cove

Class: 2	Length: 9.6 miles
Flow: 1200–3500 cfs	Character: rural
Gradient: 18 fpm, PD	Season: year-round

Located at Medford's back door in the town of Shady Cove, this is the best beginning canoe and kayak run in the Rogue Valley. Wide-open class 1 and 2 pool-drop rapids make a great training ground for novice paddlers to learn river dynamics, and practice eddy turns, peel-outs, and ferries. A handful of surf waves will interest intermediate-level paddlers as well. Thanks to dam-controlled releases, the river can be run most of the year. In the summer months of July and August, this favorite splash-and-giggle run will be crowded with rental rafts and inflatables

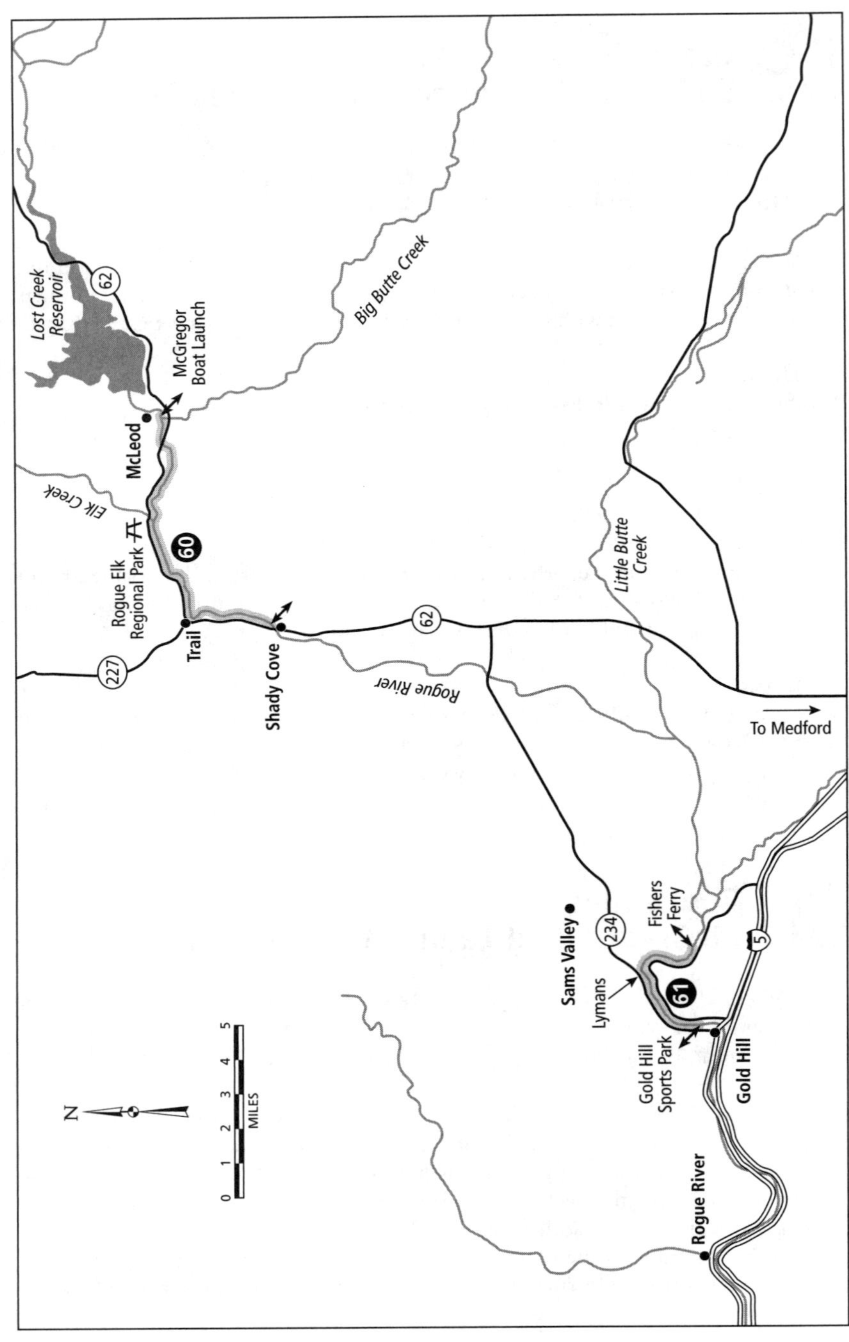
Lost Creek Reservoir
62
McGregor Boat Launch
Big Butte Creek
McLeod
Elk Creek
Rogue Elk Regional Park
60
227
Trail
Shady Cove
62
Rogue River
Little Butte Creek
To Medford
Fishers Ferry
Sams Valley
234
Lymans
61
Gold Hill Sports Park
Gold Hill
5
Rogue River
N
MILES
0 1 2 3 4 5

from the outfitters in Shady Cove. Before the Fourth of July or after Labor Day, paddlers can have the river to themselves, shared only with a handful of drift boat fishermen.

Notable class 2 rapids include Highway Hole (river mile 1.5) and Island Rapid (extending from river mile 1.8 to 2.2). Both are above Rogue Elk Regional Park, an alternative access point. Below the park are Big Gulp (river mile 7.0), where going right at the gravel bar is best, and Trail Creek Rapid (river mile 7.9), where going left is great for a big, bouncy ride down a wave train.

Hazards

Water for this section of river is controlled by releases from Lost Creek Reservoir and can remain cold, even in midsummer.

Access

From Medford, drive north on Oregon 62, the Crater Lake Highway, to the town of Shady Cove. Cross the bridge over the Rogue River and make the first left, following the signs to Upper Rogue Regional Park. This is the take-out. Leave a shuttle vehicle here. Return back to Oregon 62, turn left, and continue another 5 miles to Rogue Elk Regional Park (an alternative put-in) or another 8 miles to McGregor Visitor Center at the bottom of Lost Creek Reservoir. Turn left into the park. Continue past the turnoff to McGregor Visitor Center and turn right on Cole River Drive. Road signs here will direct you to the fish hatchery. At the first Y, veer right and continue into the parking lot for the McGregor boat launch. Jackson County Parks charges a day use/parking fee at Rogue Elk Regional Park and at Upper Rogue Regional Park.

Gauge

Rogue River near McLeod. Optimal flows are 1600–3500 cfs. Below 1500 cfs, the river is technical and bony.

Marianne Musitelli

61 ★ Rogue River
Fishers Ferry to Gold Hill Sports Park

Class: 4-	Length: 4.6 miles
Flow: 900–10,000 cfs	Character: residential; forested
Gradient: 16 fpm, PD	Season: year-round

This popular run on the Rogue provides enough good play spots and challenging rapids for an afternoon of boating. The run begins 0.8 mile below the old Gold Ray Dam site. (Gold Ray Dam was removed in 2010.) A few class 2 rapids present themselves before Bitterman, the first class 3 rapid of the run, which is about 1.5 miles from the put-in.

About a mile down river is Lymans (class 3), a fun, multifaceted drop that can be run from any point above. Lymans is commonly used as a park-and-play rapid with a fun surfing wave on the bottom right, providing paddlers with excellent eddy service, and an easy walk back to the top. Below this is a broken weir dubbed Enders Hole (class 3), that offers paddlers a fun ender spot for kayaks.

Just below the shallows ahead is Nugget Rapid (class 4). Nugget is a class 3+ or 4 drop that can be run down the middle of the left channel. It is tricky and should be scouted the first time down. Scout from the left, using a primitive trail that leads to the rock outcropping that defines the drop. A big surfing wave follows the drop.

About a mile of flatwater separates Nugget from Ti'lomikh Falls (formerly called Powerhouse), a class 4 rapid. Enter Ti'lomikh on the right side of the class 2, where the lava islands protrude out of the water. A marker indicating the drop below is the newer water treatment building on the right, where the current becomes swifter and the gradient drop is noticeable. Start right, then move back to the left through slack water, aiming for the middle braid of the river. Aim your boat to the left and adjust for the second hole above Ti'lomikh proper. Stay in the middle to line up for the bottom deep drop, which is known to stern-quirt boats. Once in the Green Room, take a moment to enjoy your surroundings. This is a sacred Native American salmon spawning location; an annual ceremony is held here. Ti'lomikh is a park-and-play site with access from above on river right, where a new gravel parking lot accommodates boaters and bike-path patrons alike. The remainder of the run is class 2 to the take-out boat ramp on the right.

Hazards

Nugget Falls and Ti'lomikh Falls present some difficulties. Ti'lomikh cannot be scouted from the river, so must be scouted from Upper River Road on the east side of the river. Go upriver about 1 mile from US 99 to a pullout on the left. The last drop can be seen from here, but the entrance is hidden by some trees. It may be a good idea to run Ti'lomikh with someone who has been through it before, since the entrance can be tricky.

Access

Gold Hill is near Interstate 5 between Medford and Grants Pass. Take Oregon 234 out of Gold Hill toward Sams Valley and Crater Lake. It is less than 1 mile to the take-out, the Gold Hill Sports Park boat ramp. For a short play run, continue upstream on Oregon 234 for another 2.7 miles to a gravel road that leads to a put-in just below Lymans.

To reach the uppermost put-in, backtrack to Gold Hill, cross the river again, and make a left onto Upper River Road. This road goes upstream on river left, the east side of the river. The put-in is 4.6 miles up this road at Fishers Ferry.

Gauge

Rogue River at Raygold. Flows can get very large in the winter.

Garvin Hamilton, Yann Crist-Evans, and WKCC Editors

62 Rogue River
Whitehorse Access to Hog Creek

Class: 1 C	Length: 11.4 miles
Flow: 1450–3000 cfs	Character: mixed woodland
Gradient: 9 fpm, C	Season: year-round; dam-controlled

The Rogue National Wild and Scenic Corridor begins at the confluence with the Applegate River just downstream of Grants Pass. The first river access point is at Whitehorse, approximately 0.5 mile below the confluence, and the next 26 miles between here and Grave Creek are classified as Recreational River. While whitewater paddlers usually prefer to launch at Hog Creek or below, this overlooked section of river between Whitehorse and Hog Creek provides moving-water paddlers with a taste of the beauty of the Wild Rogue. As boaters peacefully paddle through a park-like, woodland setting, wildlife sightings are common. Deer, ospreys, eagles, herons, songbirds, and a multitude of ducks and geese are commonplace. A few rural homes dot the riverbank, but most are fairly well hidden in the trees, and with the exception of the occasional passing jet boat, the overall experience is fairly pristine. There are several class 1 riffles along the way.

Josephine County Parks maintains a number of boat launches along this stretch of river, so the length of the trip can be adjusted as desired. Robertson Bridge, 8 miles downstream on river right, is a popular alternative take-out with an easy shuttle from Whitehorse. Hog Creek is 11.4 miles downstream from Whitehorse, and the shuttle requires drivers to return to the town of Merlin and then drive back out Galice Road, which can be a long, slow trip on country roads. A useful map of this area can be found in the "Rogue River Boater's Guide" (see Appendix B).

Hazards

Watch for jet boats. Hellgate Jetboat Excursions maintains a jet boat landing 2.75 miles downstream from Robertson Bridge. Courteous drivers will slow down for paddle craft, but the wake can still be significant.

Access

From Interstate 5, take exit 61, the Merlin exit. Drive 3.5 miles to Robertson Ridge Road. Turn left. Drive 3.1 miles to Lower River Road and turn left. Drive 4.6 miles on Lower River Road to Whitehorse Park. At the signed entrance, turn right into the park and drive 0.4 mile through the park to the boat ramp at the end of the road.

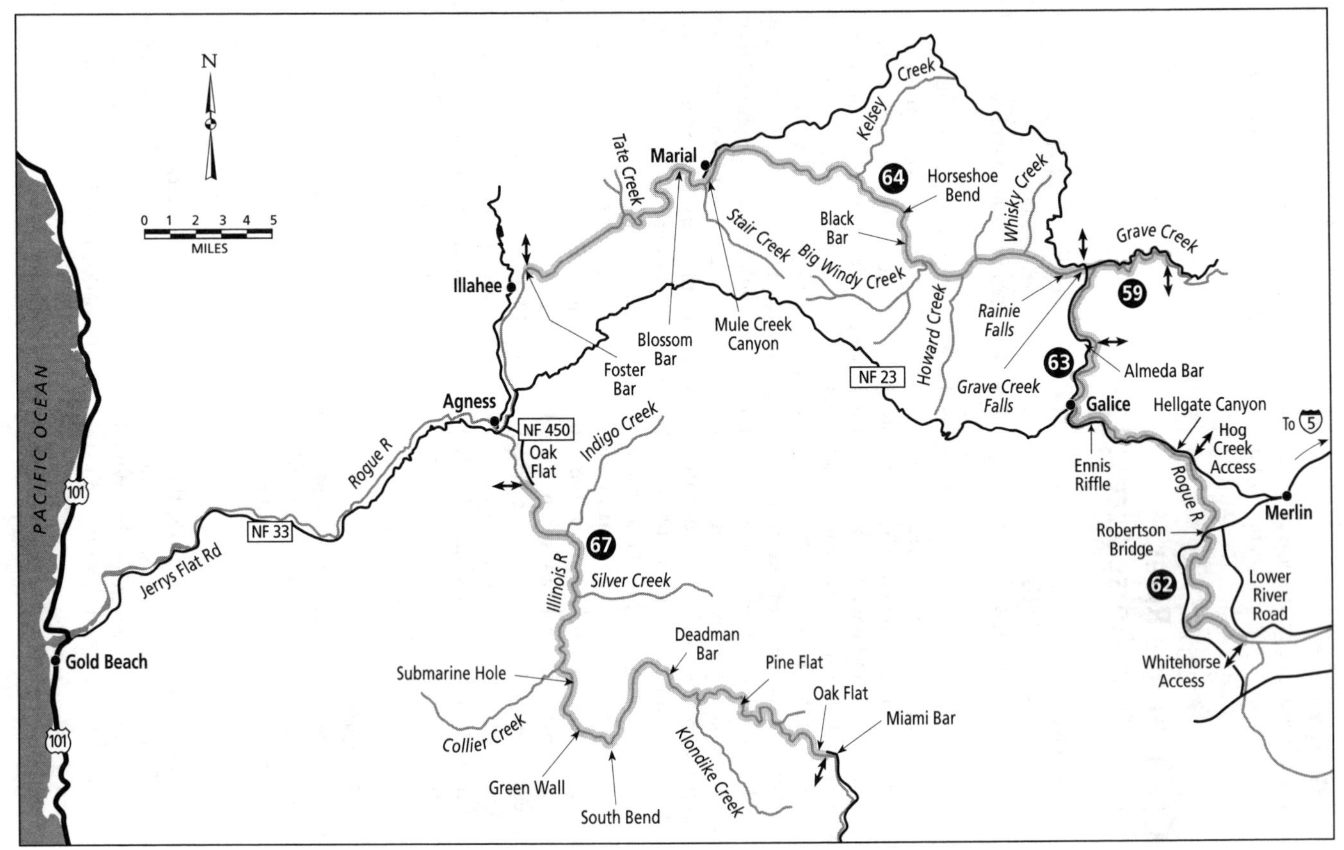
N
0 1 2 3 4 5
MILES
Kelsey Creek
Tate Creek
Marial
64
Horseshoe Bend
Black Bar
Whisky Creek
Grave Creek
Stair Creek
Big Windy Creek
59
Illahee
Howard Creek
Rainie Falls
Mule Creek Canyon
Blossom Bar
63
NF 23
Grave Creek Falls
Almeda Bar
Foster Bar
Agness
Galice
Hellgate Canyon
NF 450
Oak Flat
Indigo Creek
Ennis Riffle
Hog Creek Access
To 5
PACIFIC OCEAN
101
Rogue R
NF 33
Jerrys Flat Rd
67
Rogue R
Robertson Bridge
Merlin
Silver Creek
62
Lower River Road
Gold Beach
Illinois R
Deadman Bar
Pine Flat
Submarine Hole
Oak Flat
Miami Bar
Whitehorse Access
Collier Creek
Green Wall
South Bend
Klondike Creek
101

To reach the alternative take-out at Robertson Bridge, return to Lower River Road. Turn left and drive 4.9 miles to Robertson Bridge Access, which will be before you cross the bridge on the left side of the road.

To reach the Hog Creek take-out from Whitehorse, backtrack to the town of Merlin via Lower River Road and Robertson Bridge Road. Once back in town, at the intersection of Robertson Bridge Road and the Merlin/Galice Road, turn left. Drive 4.5 miles to the Hog Creek access. Free parking is in the paved lot near the road, above the river. At the lower lot (and also at many other access points along this run), there are day-use fees.

Gauge
Rogue River at Grants Pass.

Marianne Musitelli

63 ★ Rogue River
Hog Creek Access to Grave Creek

Class: 2(2+ to 3)	Length: 14.5 miles
Flow: 1450–3750 cfs	Character: oak woodland
Gradient: 9 fpm, PD	Season: year-round; dam-controlled

This very popular recreational section of the Rogue River is well loved by both private boaters and commercial trippers, who flock here on summer weekends to escape the heat of Grants Pass and Medford and enjoy the stunning beauty of the canyon. Immediately above the permitted Wild and Scenic section of the river, there is a good warm-up for the more challenging water below and a very small taste of what lies beyond Grave Creek. Long, slow pools give ample time to enjoy the scenery, and a handful of mostly class 2 rapids provide splash and excitement. This run can be done in its entirety in one day or broken up into sections of varying length and difficulty by virtue of a number of developed river access points along it. A useful map of this area can be found in the "Rogue River Boater's Guide" (see Appendix B).

SECTION 1: HOG CREEK TO ENNIS, 5 MILES, CLASS 1(2)
The trip begins with a float through majestic Hellgate Canyon. Dunn Riffle, a two-part class 2 starts about a mile below the put-in. At part one, far left is a clean line for open canoes and novice kayaks, although it involves some rock dodging at the top. Rafts and inflatable kayaks generally go straight down the center through some big ledge holes. Part two of Dunn is easiest on the left, or one can take the small, clean tongue between the two large pour-over boulders on river right. Riffles and long, slow pools continue to Ennis.

SECTION 2: ENNIS TO ALMEDA, 5.5 MILES, CLASS 2(2+)
Similar in character to the section above, section 2 includes many long, slow pools,

but has a few more class 2 rapids to break up its length. Upper Galice Rapid (class 2+) has the cleanest run on the far right, but watch out for the strong lateral wave at the bottom right and the pour-over boulder mid-channel. At Lower Galice Rapid (class 2+), a rock island splits the river channel, and at the bottom where the channels come together are two significant holes. Boils and turbulence are common, and many novice boaters survive the holes only to swim crossing a turbulent eddy line. Below Galice, a few more riffles and class 2 rapids lead to Almeda.

SECTION 3: ALMEDA TO GRAVE CREEK, 4 MILES, CLASS 2(2+ TO 3)

This section offers the most challenging whitewater on this run with some bigger class 2 rapids and one class 2+ to 3, Argo Rapid. The river begins to descend into a deep canyon at this point and leaves the road far above, giving a greater feeling of solitude. Perhaps for this reason and the higher level of difficulty, Almeda is often used as a launch point for those going through the permitted Wild and Scenic section below.

Argo is about 1.6 river miles below the Almeda access and 12.2 river miles from Hog Creek. It is difficult to scout from the river, and first-time boaters would be well advised to take a look at it from the road on the shuttle. At flows above 3500 cfs, the waves and holes in it can easily flip a raft, and at lower flows, the exposed rocks can cause rips in rafts and inflatable kayaks or possibly result in a wrapped boat. Far right can be a sneak route, but at low flows, this route becomes very rocky.

A number of small rapids provide some rock-dodging fun for the mile or so below Argo. The Grave Creek bridge signals the mandatory take-out at the boat ramp just below the bridge on river right for anyone without a permit for the Wild and Scenic section below.

Hazards

Watch for jet boats, particularly in narrow Hellgate Canyon. Argo Rapid can be scouted from the road.

Access

From Interstate 5 north of Grants Pass, take exit 61, the Merlin exit. Head west on Merlin Road through the town of Merlin. Once past Hugo Road on the outskirts of Merlin, the road's name changes and becomes Galice Road. Travel a total of 8 miles from Interstate 5 on the Merlin/Galice Road to the developed Hog Creek river access. Turn left and follow the road downhill to the launch area. Free parking is in the paved lot above, near the road.

To reach the take-out, return to Galice Road, turn left, and travel an additional 14 miles to Grave Creek river access. After you cross the second bridge over the Rogue, take the small road to the left. The road to the river access takes off steeply downhill from there.

Josephine County Parks charges parking fees at a number of the access points along the river, including Ennis, Galice, and Almeda. A parking fee is also charged for use of the lower lot near the launch area at Hog Creek. However, there is no launch fee.

Gauge

Rogue River at Grants Pass. Flows higher than 3500 cfs are not recommended for beginners.

Marianne Musitelli

64 ★ Rogue River
Grave Creek to Foster Bar

Class: 3+(4-)	Length: 35 miles
Flow: 800–10,000 cfs	Character: protected; popular
Gradient: 13 fpm, PD	Season: year-round

This run on the Rogue is one of the best-known whitewater runs in the United States. Flowing through the Siskiyou Mountains northwest of Grants Pass, it is classified Wild and Scenic, with the river preserved essentially in its natural condition. The banks vary from steep forested slopes to vertical rock walls. The river provides mostly class 3 rapids connected by slower stretches and deep pools.

Recreational use of the Wild and Scenic section has a long and diverse tradition. Private lodges and cabins are located in several places, and many of these are reached only by boat or trail. Jet boats from Gold Beach originally delivered the U.S. mail but later took passengers on popular excursions; these boats can be seen cruising at water-skiing speed along the lower 12 miles of the Wild and Scenic section. Drift boaters have long floated the river for the fine steelhead fishing, and Zane Grey's writings were inspired by the solitude and wild setting of his cabin at Winkle Bar.

The scenery, rapids, easy access, and possibility of two- to five-day float trips make this a very popular run. Permits, selected by lottery, are required from May 15 through October 15. Self-issue permits must be filled out the remainder of the year. During the lottery season, leftover or unclaimed launch dates sometimes become available. Permit information can be obtained from the Bureau of Land Management River Permits Office (541-479-3735, during summer months) or at www.blm.gov/or/resources/recreation/rogue/permit.php. The BLM gives out a one-page map with your permit, or sells a more detailed version.

The Wild and Scenic section is a forgiving and enjoyable stretch of water. Dam-controlled flows normally are above 2000 cfs, and the river is runnable throughout the year. Warm summer weather, warm water, rapids ending in pools, and sandy beaches for camping make this a great place for a laid-back trip. One should expect to see lots of other people during the summer season, although the author's first trip was a cold and snowy one in February, when he saw no one else.

Rainie Falls, 2 miles below the Grave Creek put-in, is the first of the two more difficult rapids on the Rogue (see "Hazards" below). In the next 20 miles, tributary streams, such as Russian, Howard, Big Windy, and Kelsey creeks provide pools for swimming, nice camps, and places to scramble up the streambeds.

Quiet moments on the Rogue River above Foster Bar (Kathy Shelby)

Numerous play spots can be found for kayaks, including an ender hole at Black Bar Rapid. Take care not to hurry.

At Marial, the river takes a sharp bend to the southwest and enters Mule Creek Canyon. The narrow canyon, with vertical walls, is one of the run's few continuous stretches of whitewater (about 0.5 mile). About 1 mile below Mule Creek Canyon, Blossom Bar (class 4-) is the Rogue's second major rapid; many rafts have been hung up or destroyed on the boulders there (see "Hazards" below). Tate Creek, about 7 miles below Blossom Bar, is a beautiful hike; about 0.2 mile up the creek is a pool with an exciting rock slide.

This section has lots of wildlife; it is common to see great blue herons, salmon, deer, otters, and bears. Protect food from bears. Please be friendly with the jet boats on the lower part of the river and pull to the side out of the main current so they may pass freely.

Hazards

At Rainie Falls, a short portage trail is located on the left bank and offers the best place to get a close-up view of the falls, always fun to look at. Although this "main falls" is run occasionally, most people run the small fish-ladder channel on the far right bank, while the more adventurous run the steeper "center chute" through the middle of the rock "island" between the fish ladder and the falls. The center chute can be scouted on river left from downstream of the main falls; the fish ladder can be scouted from river right.

In Mule Creek Canyon, the major problem is turbulence caused by constriction, rather than large waves or holes. Everything seems to wash out of here eventually, but several places have been known to hold boats, spin them around, or push them into the walls. Swimmers are difficult to pick up until they get out of the narrow part of the canyon, but even they should look around to appreciate this beautiful rock canyon. At Blossom Bar, stop on the right and clamber up the rocks to scout. The usual run starts on the left side in a channel that ends in a strainer of boulders called "the picket fence," so the next move is to the right into a center channel. At low water, this channel ends in boulders, so scout carefully and move fast. Dodge a few more rocks, and that's it. The picket fence occasionally claims a boat or a life, so be careful. A right side run opens up at higher flows.

Access

The put-in at Grave Creek is reached by taking the Merlin exit off Interstate 5, just north of Grants Pass, and proceeding west through Merlin and toward Galice. A popular put-in is 3 miles below Galice at Almeda Park. The Grave Creek put-in is another 4 miles downstream at the bridge.

The shuttle to the take-out goes back along this same road just past the town of Galice, then over the mountains and west toward Agness on Forest Service road 23 (also called Bear Camp Road). After joining Forest Service Road 33 at the Rogue River, follow it upstream about 1 mile, cross the river, and continue upstream to Foster Bar. Bear Camp Road climbs to 4600 feet and may be closed by snow early in the season, so check with the BLM for its status. If the road is impassable, drive to Grants Pass, take US 199 south to Crescent City, take US 101 north to Gold Beach, and proceed upstream toward Agness and Foster Bar. Shuttle services can usually be arranged at the Galice Resort.

Gauge

Rogue River near Agness (at the downstream end of this run).

Bo Shelby

65 Middle Fork Applegate River
Butte Fork Applegate River to
Applegate Reservoir

Class: 3+(5)	Length: 3.5 miles
Flow: 700–2000 cfs	Character: forested
Gradient: 103 fpm, C	Season: rainy/snowmelt

This stretch located above Applegate Reservoir, southwest of Medford, is one of the best runs in the Siskiyou Mountains. Clear water, forested canyons, and continuous class 2 and 3 whitewater make this run a local favorite. Since the run is short and a road runs alongside much of the river, doing laps is common. The whitewater is easiest at the low end of flows (700–1100 cfs) and gets pushier as the level rises past 1500 cfs.

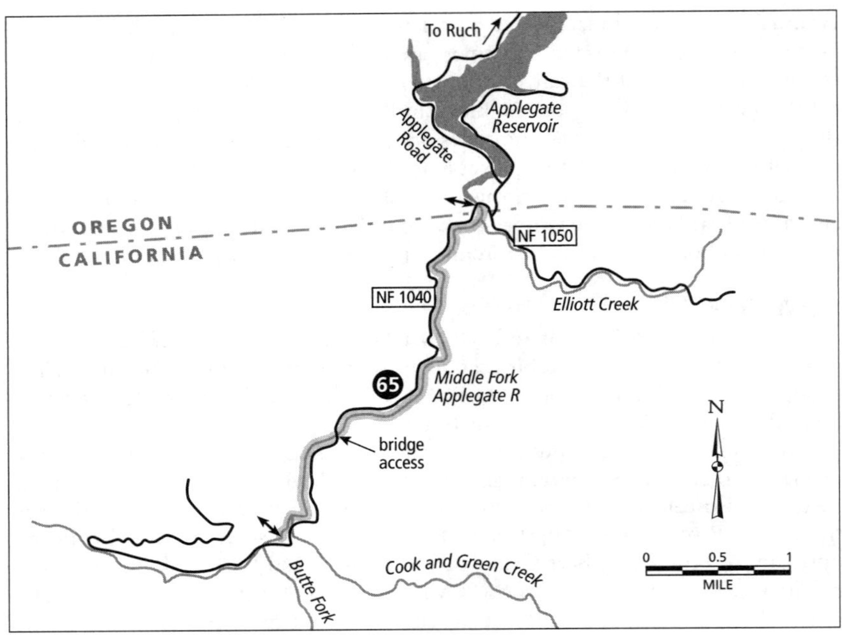

The run is typically seen as two parts, with the upper and lower sections separated by a nasty class 5 rapid that's normally portaged. The upper section of the run is a brushy and solid class 3+, while the lower half has better overall whitewater that is closer to class 3 in nature. Most boaters rate this run class 3+ due to the continuous nature of the rapids.

The put-in for the upper run is just below a narrow waterfall. You have to paddle out quickly to reach an eddy as the river bends left. The run is fast and continuous, with a couple of steep class 3+ rapids right away. The biggest can be scouted from the road.

After going a little less than a mile, keep your eyes open as the river narrows into the nasty class 5 undercut. Portage on the right.

Below is the beginning of the lower run, which is less steep but still busy. After you paddle under the bridge, the first rapid of note is a sweeping rapid called S-Turn (or Topless Weather Girl). Start on the right and sweep back to the left to avoid a retaining hole on river left. Downstream is Hydraulics on Crack, which at higher flows must be run far left to avoid a ledge hole. The run ends with a fun class 3 drop just below the take-out bridge.

Hazards

Wood can be an issue. The class 5 undercut rapid cannot be seen from the road and comes up quickly on the upper run.

Access

From Grants Pass, take Oregon 238 south for 25.5 miles to the small town of Ruch. Alternatively, travel 8 miles north from Jacksonville to Ruch. From Ruch, follow the Applegate River Road south for 15 miles, passing along Applegate Reservoir and driving to its upper end. At a paved T junction, turn left to stay on Applegate Road for 1.5 more miles to a gravel junction. Swing a sharp right onto gravel NF 1040 and drop down along the river. In 0.2 mile you'll see a bridge and parking area—that's the take-out.

From the take-out, continue up NF 1040 for 2.4 miles to the first bridge. Just over it, there's place to park on the side of the road and a put-in spot for the lower put-in.

For the upper put-in, continue upstream 1 mile. Drive just past a primitive campground and park on the side of the road. Hike down to the river through the campground to a put-in just below a 10-foot waterfall. If you reach a bridge over Butte Fork Applegate River, you have driven 0.15 mile too far.

Gauge

Applegate Reservoir—Inflow. Note that about two-thirds of the inflow comes from the Middle Fork Applegate River. When the gauge reads 700 cfs or more, the run is worthwhile. See also Dreamflows (Above Applegate Lake) in Appendix A.

Zach Urness

66 Deer Creek/Illinois River
US Highway 199 Bridge to Six-Mile Access

Class: 3 (3+ to 4)	Length: 8 miles
Flow: 1200–3000 cfs	Character: isolated canyon
Gradient: 25 fpm, PD	Season: rainy/snowmelt

The Illinois River is best known for its epic wilderness run downstream of this run, but the scenery is just as good, and the rapids a bit more manageable in this stretch. One the easiest ways to enjoy the Illinois canyon is by running a combination of Deer Creek and the Illinois, an easy day trip from Grants Pass or Selma. Paddlers can have easy access to the canyon and also avoid some of the hazards both upstream and downstream of this beautiful area. This run was a favorite of Cave Junction river advocate Barry Snitkin, who passed away in 2015, and who worked tirelessly to protect rivers in the Klamath-Siskiyou mountains.

The trip starts off on Deer Creek, a clear and pretty stream that is continuous class 2 and 2+. At lower-end flows (1200–1400 cfs on the Kerby gauge), it is quite rocky but still runnable. After about 4 miles, Deer Creek drops into the Illinois River, where the flow increases dramatically, and the landscape transforms into the big reddish-orange canyon that makes this area famous. The first part of the Illinois has few rapids and a fair amount of slow water.

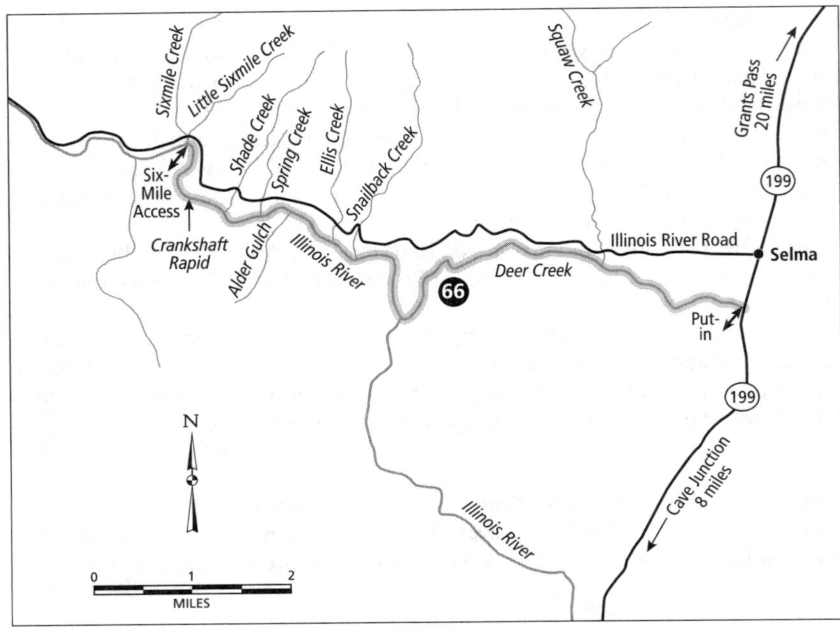

One hazard to watch out for is Snailback Rapid. It can be spotted by a big gravel bar on river right about a mile below the confluence of Deer Creek and the Illinois. There is a very large hole directly in the middle of this rapid, but can easily be avoided on the right or with a more challenging line on the far left. The next rapid of note is Ranch Rock, class 3, a large wave train that makes a left turn at the bottom. It can be identified by a large rock in the middle of the river. The standard line is just right of the rock and a gradual turn left.

The run's most challenging rapid is Crankshaft, class 3+ to 4. The rapid isn't too hard, but it requires hitting the correct line and should be scouted. Stop at a small pullout on river right where the canyon starts to close in on the river. The line is obvious once you view it, going over a small drop and threading the needle between a ledge pour-over on the left and a rock on the right before turning hard right at the bottom.

Below Crankshaft, the river is tight and fast, ending at upper and lower Six Mile rapids, class 3, right next to the take-out.

Hazards

Wood isn't typically an issue, but since most of the route cannot be scouted in advance, keep an eye out, especially on Deer Creek. Scout Crankshaft Rapid.

Access

From Grants Pass, drive on US 199 south for 20 miles to the small town of Selma. The put-in is at the US 199 bridge over Deer Creek. Park at the pullout on the northwest side of the bridge and carry down to the river. To reach the take-out, return to downtown Selma, go west on Illinois River Road for 8 miles. The Six-Mile Access parking area is on the left and next to a nice campground.

Gauge

There is no gauge on Deer Creek, so this run is measured with the gauge Illinois River at Kerby.

Zach Urness

67★ Illinois River
Miami Bar to Oak Flat

Class: 4+(5)	Length: 31 miles
Flow: 500–3500 cfs	Character: forested; remote
Gradient: 24 fpm, PD	Season: rainy

The Illinois, a crystal-clear tributary of the Rogue River, is one of the premier whitewater runs on the West Coast. In 1984 it received protection under the National Wild and Scenic Rivers Act. Flowing out of the Siskiyou Mountains south of Cave Junction, the Illinois runs in a northwesterly direction through the north end of the Kalmiopsis Wilderness. The canyons and mountains here are as steep and rugged as any in Oregon. The area is largely devoid of topsoil, but kalmiopsis, a plant in the heather family, grows here. Natural landslides and erosion are evident along the river. Look at the landscape and enjoy it, but treat it kindly. For a detailed description of the river, see *Handbook to the Illinois River Canyon*, by Quinn et al. (see Bibliography).

The Illinois is truly a wilderness river that tests both the skill and strength of boaters. Once a trip on this river is undertaken, boaters are on their own. The only trail is miles from the river and very difficult to reach except at Pine Flat. The whitewater is tough, even for the best boaters. Help is hard to get. Check the weather forecast, because a heavy rain can transform an 1800 cfs trip into an 8000 cfs nightmare overnight.

The river is technical at levels below 800 cfs. Flows of 1000–1500 cfs seem to be the easiest, when most of the technical drops are flushed over enough to make them easier to run. Flows over 3000 cfs turn the river into boiling holes and rapids.

The first 10–12 miles are characterized either by pools with very steep class 4 boulder-bar drops of up to 10 feet or by long rock gardens. Between miles 4 and 5 are three class 4 rapids, with the third one, York Creek Rapid, being the biggest. River mile 7 brings the boater to Pine Flat, where the canyon opens into large meadows on both sides of the river. About midway through Pine Flat, the river swings to the left, offering what appears to be two channels around a large rock in the middle of the river. On the left side is a class 2 route that can be run except at low water. On the right side is a chute with a raft-stopping hole at the

A sunny day at Green Wall on the Illinois (Gary Adams)

bottom. Scout this one carefully from the right. The hole is tougher than it looks. Rafts and kayaks have been flipped end over end in it. Pine Flat makes an excellent campsite for the first night of a three- to four-day trip. Backpackers are sometimes seen because this is one of the few places where they have access to the river.

From Pine Flat down to South Bend, the river continues in pool-drop fashion through beautiful deep green pools and many nice class 2+ to 3 drops. Klondike Creek, named for the mining done along its banks, enters from the left about 2 miles below the last meadow of Pine Flat. Deadman Bar is a long straight bench on the right about 2 miles farther downstream. It is difficult to spot from the river because it is up a 35-foot rock bank. Several groups can share the grassy area without intruding on each other. Beware of poison oak when scrambling up the rocks, especially in the spring when the plant is not in leaf.

South Bend, at mile 17, should be called "Last Chance" because it is the last chance to camp before Green Wall. South Bend Bar is located on the inside of a tight right turn in the river. A large creek cascades down the left bank; a large pink boulder on the right marks the spot. Sometimes this campsite gets washed away. The next 4 miles are the toughest of the trip. Immediately below South Bend is a good class 3+ drop, followed in 0.5 mile by Fawn Falls, the class 4 rapid before Green Wall. Fawn Falls does not look like much on the approach, but a sweeping rock garden leads to a solid 3+ drop that cannot be seen from above. An eddy on the left next to a boulder at the bottom of the rock garden provides a good spot to scout the remaining portion of Fawn Falls. Two alternatives are available: One is the falls on the left, the other is the tricky S turn on the right.

A short distance below Fawn Falls is Green Wall, class 5. An innocent-looking rock garden, Prelude, leads into the main drop. Land left, well above the class 3+ lead-in rapids, or, if confident, catch the eddy on the left at the end of it. A portage here is a tough 400 yards through a maze of truck-size boulders. Scout Prelude as carefully as the main rapids. Below the lead-in is a very short section of relatively calm water followed by a drop of 7–8 feet. Take the middle or left channel; the right side is a keeper for all but the largest of rafts. Below are more rapids with water rushing into the Green Wall itself on the right and a big hole in the middle. Stay off the right wall.

From Green Wall to Collier Creek are three class 4–4+ drops and six class 3–3+ drops that are quite technical and challenging. Do not hesitate to scout if in doubt. Submarine Hole, class 4+, 3 miles below Green Wall, can cause problems, especially for rafters. It is readily identified by the huge boulder in the middle at the bottom of the rapids. Avoid the right slots. The canyon is steep and rocky through this 3-mile section, and no campsites are available.

The end of the major rapids is signaled by Collier Creek on the left at mile 21.7. About 100–200 yards below Collier Creek, a campsite may be found up the left bank. Other campsites are located 2–3 miles downstream and less than an hour from the take-out. Most notable is a site high above the river on the right at Silver Creek. Land on the downstream side of the creek, climb 30 feet to the trail, and follow it upstream, across the bridge, and up to the top of the bluff.

From here to the take-out, the river flows placidly through country that is a feast for your eyes. Sit back and enjoy it. You are one of the lucky ones who have run the Illinois.

Hazards

Expect eight class 4–4+ rapids. Some of the named rapids are York Creek, Pine Flat, Fawn Falls, and Submarine Hole. Green Wall, class 5, is considerably more difficult and longer than the others. The 3-mile section below Green Wall has the greatest concentration of difficult rapids.

Access

To reach the put-in at Miami Bar, drive west on US 199 from Grants Pass to Selma. In the middle of town, turn west on Illinois River Road. This becomes NF 4103. It is 16.2 miles from Selma to Miami Bar, a boat launch area and outhouse.

To reach the take-out, return to US 199 and continue south to the Pacific Coast, then go north on US 101 to Gold Beach. Drive up Jerrys Flat Road (which becomes NF 33) along the south bank of the Rogue River for approximately 27 miles. After crossing the Illinois River, turn right onto Oak Flat Road, NF 450, and continue 3.4 miles to the broad grassy area of Oak Flat, the take-out.

Shuttle service can usually be hired at the Galice Resort in Galice.

River permits are required. Packing out human waste is required, as well as fire pans. The permits are free of charge at this time (2015) and can be obtained from the self-issue 24-hour kiosk at Ray's Food Place Market in Selma.

Gauge

Illinois River near Kerby. The recommended flows listed in this description are gauge flows. Since the run is far downstream of the gauge, the flow on the run may actually be double or even triple the flow that the gauge reads.

Ron Mattson

Opposite: *River fog on an autumn day, McKenzie River near Belknap* (Gary Hahn)

Upper Willamette and McKenzie Rivers

Region 4

Upper Willamette River and Tributaries

68 ★ Brice Creek
Champion Creek to Cedar Creek Campground

Class: 4(5) T	Length: 3.3 miles
Flow: 250–750 cfs	Character: forested
Gradient: 123 fpm, PD	Season: rainy/snowmelt

Brice Creek, a tributary of the Row River, drains a relatively uncut section of forest. Its clear water, beautiful scenery, and great rapids make it special. This narrow streambed has many class 3 and 4 pool-drop rapids, and is spiced up by several larger drops, all of which are easy to portage. Scout carefully.

The first mile is the most difficult. Several small ledges are followed by three big drops. The first is Trestle Rapid. Scout left. The best line is to boof off the left end of the L-shaped ledge. Just downstream is Arthur's Ledge; scout or portage left. At low water, the right route is advised, but at high flow, a nasty hydraulic develops. Downstream 50 yards is Pogo, a tricky drop that has been run by dropping through a slot just left of the bedrock island. Scout from this island. About 0.5 mile downstream is Cheese Grater; scout from the left. Runs down the center have been made, but take care.

From here, fun class 3 and 4 rapids break up occasional class 2 rapids. Around mile 1.8, logs have been a problem. At mile 2, a large class 3+ rapid named Fun (Gumdrop) splits around a house-size boulder; go left with enough speed to punch a sticky hole. The right can be clogged with debris. Just downstream, on a sharp left-hand bend, is Not Fun, which should be checked for logs. Above the take-out 0.2 mile, a class 3+ rapid leads to a small eddy above Laura's Thighs, a class 5 crack. Scout or portage on the right. A side creek enters here. Just downstream is Cedar Creek Campground, the take-out. One can extend this run 1.2 miles with class 2 and 3 rapids by continuing to the road bridge.

Hazards

Large drops occur over steep ledges with dangerous holes at the bottom or rocks that can likely pin a boat. Watch for wood.

Access

The take-out is reached by taking exit 174 from Interstate 5 near Cottage Grove and following Row River Road east to Disston. At Disston, take Brice Creek Road 4.5 miles to Cedar Creek Campground, the take-out.

For the put-in, follow Brice Creek Road another 3.6 miles to Champion Creek Road. Put in just west of the bridge.

Gauge

None exists. For a close estimate of the Brice Creek flow, see Pat Welch's flow page. The inflow to Dorena Lake should be 1200 cfs minimum; 2000 cfs is optimum on this gauge.

Eric Brown and WKCC Editors

69 Layng Creek
Rujada Campground to Above Wildwood Falls

Class: 3(4); 4(5)	Length: 4.2 miles
Flow: 750 cfs; 4000 cfs	Character: forested
Gradient: 44 fpm, PD	Season: rainy

This exciting run is on a tributary of the Row River. It is normally class 3–4, but becomes a challenging class 4–5 run at flood stage. The entire run can be scouted from the road while running the shuttle. When nearby Brice Creek is too high or too low, Layng Creek can be a fun alternative. At higher flows the river is unforgiving to the unprepared. Just below the put-in is Rujada Falls, a 4-foot drop. Run left. About 0.5 mile downstream is The Plunger. At high water, it can be quite dangerous and should be scouted from the road. Below the confluence with Brice Creek, now on the Row River, some of the most enjoyable whitewater of the trip is found. At high water, it is a fast, continuous flush, complete with large waves and big holes. Be sure to recognize the take-out just above Wildwood Falls. The falls have been run at high water.

Hazards

The Plunger and log strainers are hazards that should be checked from the road.

Access

Take exit 174 from Interstate 5 at Cottage Grove and drive about 16 miles east on Row River Road, past Dorena Reservoir. Turn left onto Lower Brice Creek Road at the signs to Wildwood Falls. Follow this road for 0.8 mile to the 16-foot falls. The take-out is above the falls in Wildwood Park on river right.

To get to the put-in, continue upstream to the intersection with NF 17. Turn left and go another 1.5 miles to Rujada Campground, the put-in.

Gauge

Row River above Pitcher Creek, near Dorena. Minimum flow is 1000 cfs; optimum is 2000–4000 cfs.

Jason Bates and WKCC Editors

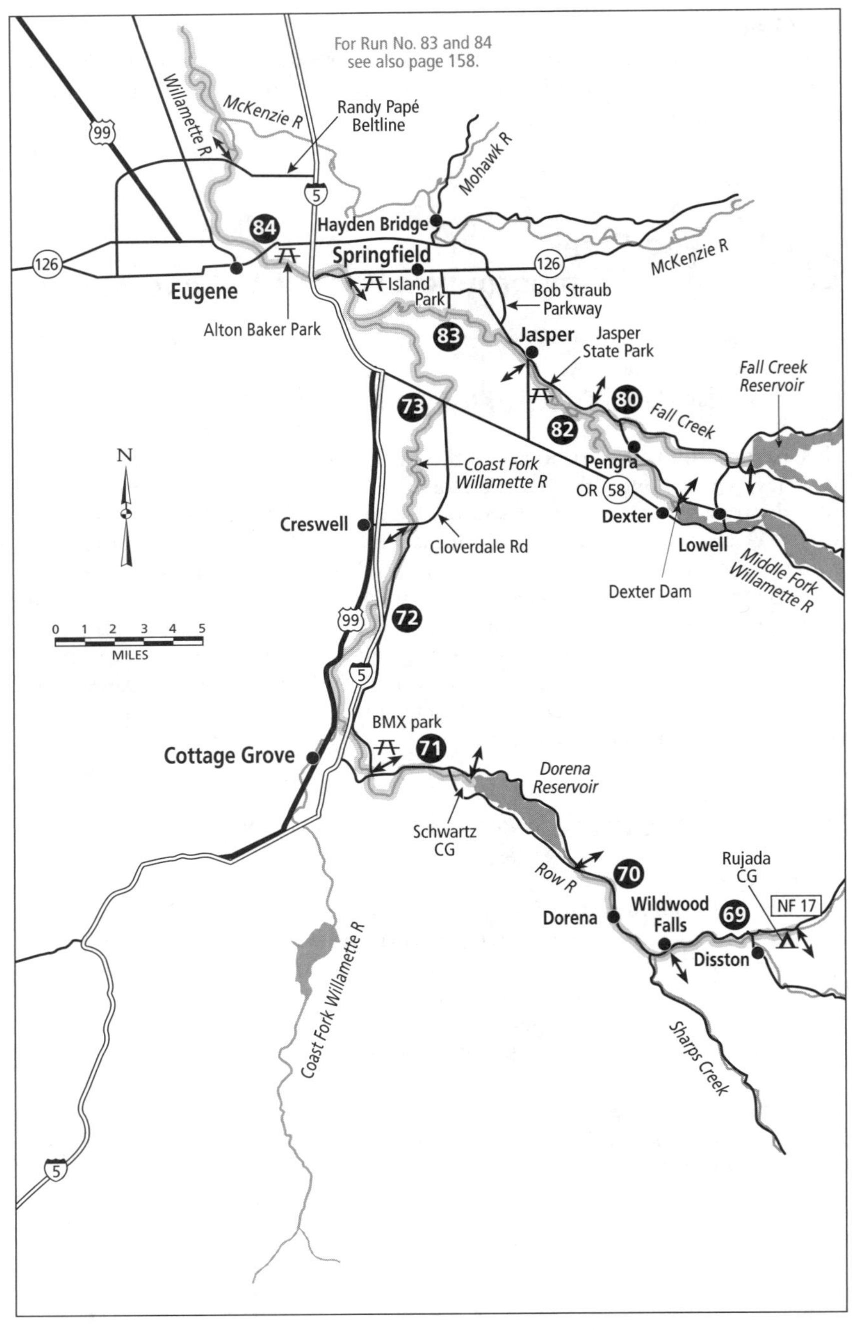
For Run No. 83 and 84
see also page 158.
Willamette R
McKenzie R
Mohawk R
99
Randy Papé
Beltline
5
Hayden Bridge
Springfield
126
McKenzie R
84
Eugene
126
Island
Park
Bob Straub
Parkway
Alton Baker Park
83
Jasper
Jasper
State Park
Fall Creek
Reservoir
73
80
Fall Creek
82
Coast Fork
Willamette R
Pengra
OR 58
N
Creswell
Dexter
Lowell
Cloverdale Rd
Middle Fork
Willamette R
Dexter Dam
0 1 2 3 4 5
MILES
99
72
5
BMX park
Cottage Grove
71
Dorena
Reservoir
Schwartz
CG
Rujada
CG
Row R
70
NF 17
Coast Fork Willamette R
Dorena
Wildwood
Falls
69
Disston
Sharps Creek
5

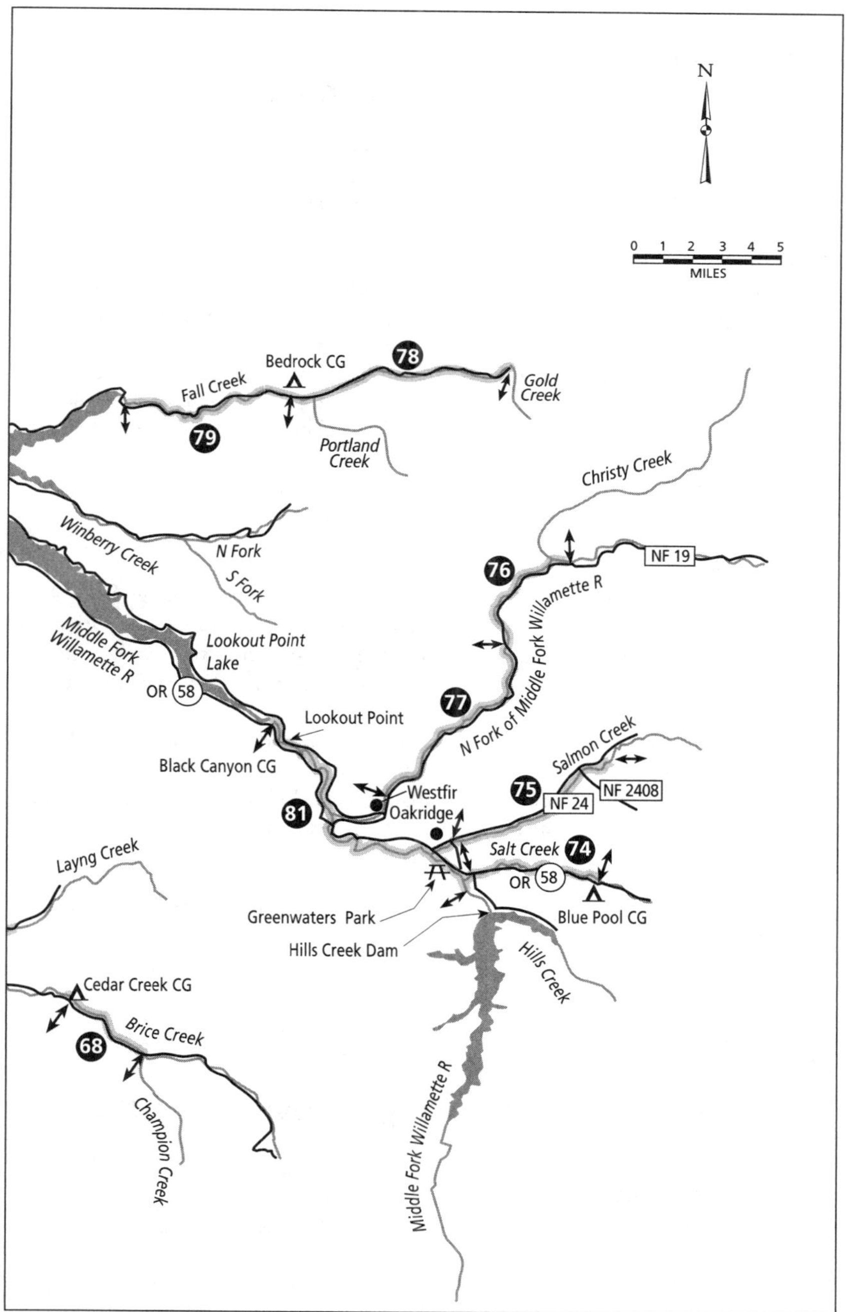
N
0 1 2 3 4 5
MILES
Bedrock CG
78
Fall Creek
Gold Creek
79
Portland Creek
Christy Creek
Winberry Creek
N Fork
S Fork
76
NF 19
Middle Fork Willamette R
Lookout Point Lake
OR 58
N Fork of Middle Fork Willamette R
77
Lookout Point
Salmon Creek
Black Canyon CG
75
NF 2408
NF 24
81
Westfir
Oakridge
Salt Creek
74
Layng Creek
OR 58
Greenwaters Park
Blue Pool CG
Hills Creek Dam
Cedar Creek CG
Hills Creek
Brice Creek
68
Champion Creek
Middle Fork Willamette R

70 ★ Row River
Wildwood Falls to Dorena Reservoir

Class: 2+(4); 3(4+)	Length: 6.2 miles
Flow: 500–2000 cfs; 3000 cfs	Character: rural
Gradient: 27 fpm, PD	Season: rainy

The name "Row" rhymes with cow. This nice short run of mostly class 2 water flows through little gorges, passing huge boulders and several houses. The class 4 rapid Pitchers Falls is a steep drop near the end of the run just above a covered bridge. Scout left initially. It is normally run on the far right, but watch out for the bow-crunching rock at the bottom of the final drop in the rapid there. An additional scout on the right is wise if running the right channel. This drop also has been run by experts in the left chute at low flows. The portage on the left is easy.

Hazards
The class 4 drop near the end should be scouted. Watch for wood.

Access
Take exit 174 from Interstate 5 at Cottage Grove and drive east on Row River Road. After about 4.5 miles, continue straight (right) onto Shoreview Drive and proceed to the head of Dorena Reservoir. After crossing the Row River, turn left onto Row River Road. Go 0.7 mile to a picnic area on the left that leads to the reservoir and the take-out.

To reach the put-in, return to Row River Road and head east toward Culp Creek and Disston. After 4.5 miles, at the junction with Lower Brice Creek Road, bear right and cross the bridge over the Row River. Go 0.5 mile and turn left into LaSells Stewart Park. The put-in is at the base of Wildwood Falls, river left.

Gauge
Row River above Pitcher Creek, near Dorena. Minimum flow is 500 cfs. Optimum is 600–2000 cfs.

Jason Bates and WKCC Editors

71 Row River
Dorena Dam to Cottage Grove BMX Park

Class: 3	Length: 4.1 miles
Flow: 300–1500 cfs	Character: rural
Gradient: 21 fpm, PD	Season: dam-controlled; rainy

This run includes four major drops (4–6 feet each) and several minor drops, all of which make this a quick, exciting run. The first quarter of the run winds through some narrow channels where riverside brush can be a hazard.

About 0.5 mile below the first bridge is a major drop that is 50–75 feet long. The rapid occurs on a hard right turn and scouting is advisable. At levels higher than 600 cfs, a narrow right channel can be used. About 100 yards below the first drop is a second major drop, which also should be scouted. It is usually run on the left, although at high water an exciting channel exists on the right. Within the next 0.5 mile is the third drop. Start on the right and navigate through the slot on the left, coming off the 3-foot drop at the bottom.

The last major drop is 0.8 mile downstream, right next to the road. Scout this rapid on the way up, and plan to hit the narrow slot. The remainder of the trip is less exciting, but it is still fun because of the many ledges that traverse the width of the river and the sneaky rocks that inhabit the streambed.

Hazards

Scout the first two class 3 rapids at the 0.5-mile mark. On the first trip down the river, scout the third major drop, 0.5 mile farther, and the fourth major drop, 0.8 mile after that.

Access

Take exit 174 from Interstate 5 at Cottage Grove and drive east on Row River Road. After about 1.5 mile, turn left into the Cottage Grove BMX bike park, which is the take-out.

To reach the put-in, continue east on Row River Road and then straight (right) onto Shoreline Drive for 0.4 mile. Turn left into Schwartz Campground and drive back to the river. The gate to the campground may be locked in the winter, necessitating a 0.2-mile carry.

Gauge

Row River near Cottage Grove. Minimum flow is 300 cfs. Optimum flow is 500–1000 cfs.

Larry Mooney and WKCC Editors

72 Row River/Coast Fork Willamette River
Cottage Grove BMX Park to Creswell

Class: 1+(2)	Length: 10.9 miles
Flow: 1000–2500 cfs	Character: rural
Gradient: 9 fpm, C	Season: rainy

The run starts on the Row River just east of Cottage Grove and ends on the Coast Fork Willamette River. The Row River section contains numerous enjoyable riffles and bends. The Row joins the Coast Fork Willamette 2.5 miles from the put-in. One mile farther downstream is a rapid identified by the Bohemia Lumber Mill on the left. Run the rapid on the far right, being careful of the overhanging branches.

After the bridge below the mill, there is a side channel on the left around a small island you can explore if the river is high enough, but the main channel stays on river right. In 1 mile, a second area of islands and braided channels is located alongside Lynx Hollow Park, where another interesting left side channel can be explored.

About 0.3 mile downstream of the park, there is a 3-foot rock dam that is partially broken through. This nearly invisible hazard is marked by powerlines overhead just upstream of the dam. Approach this dam on river right. If unsure of your maneuvering skills, land on the right to scout or portage. Safe passage is best accomplished by starting right, then moving left to avoid the rocks and the drop-off on the far right.

Near the end of the run, just after the interstate bridge, comes Cougar Mountain Rapid (class 2). It is fun to run the rapids on the left in the fast chute with some standing waves. If desired, scout this rapid on the right or during the shuttle. The take-out is a short distance downstream on river left at the bridge.

A water trail guide with maps for the Willamette River is currently available (see Appendix B).

Hazards

The 3-foot rock dam should be approached with caution. Cougar Mountain Rapid requires some maneuvering in waves.

Access

The take-out is reached by taking Interstate 5 to Creswell (exit 182), which is south of Eugene. Head east on Cloverdale Road for 1.2 miles. Just before crossing the bridge over the Coast Fork, pull off on the right and park. The put-in is just upstream of the bridge on river left.

To reach the put-in, cross over the bridge and turn right at the first road, Sears Road. Follow this road south for 9.8 miles until it intersects with Row River Road. Turn right and cross the bridge, and turn right again into the BMX park area. The put-in is at the boat landing just downstream of the bridge on river left.

Gauge

Row River near Cottage Grove. Coast Fork Willamette River near Goshen.

Herb Kielak, Mike Stevens, and Mark Murphy

73 Coast Fork Willamette River
Creswell to Springfield

Class: 1 C	Length: 13.5 miles
Flow: 1000–2500 cfs	Character: rural
Gradient: 8 fpm, C	Season: rainy

This run begins on the Coast Fork Willamette River, goes past the confluence with the Middle Fork Willamette, and then continues on (as the Willamette River) for 1.5 miles down to Island Park in Springfield. Large cottonwood trees along the banks are good places to look for wildlife.

The run begins with a class 1 rapid just below the put-in bridge. The left route is best, down the wave train. Several small riffles are encountered as one passes around a few tight bends in the next few miles. Near river mile 6, pass under the Oregon 58 highway bridge, where there's alternative access on the left (Dilley Landing).

The river makes a 90-degree left turn in the vicinity of Mount Pisgah and another big bend back to the right about a mile later. There are nice lunch spots and trails on river right in this area. A mile downstream of the next bridge (the entrance to Mount Pisgah) is one last island (most commonly run on the right of the island) and then a bridge. Past the bridge, the easiest route is to take the narrow left channel of the river. The Middle Fork of the Willamette River enters from the right at a grouping of islands. It is often turbulent here, as the flow often doubles or triples at this point. Novice paddlers usually have an easier time of entering the confluence on the far left side. The take-out is 1.5 miles downstream on river right. Just past the railroad bridge, move to river right for the take-out, which is located directly under the Oregon 126 twin bridges. Plan ahead since the river moves rather quickly with the increased flow.

A water trail guide with maps for the Willamette River is currently available (see Appendix B).

Hazards

Novice boaters should approach the confluence carefully, especially if the Middle Fork Willamette is at a high flow. Watch for strainers anywhere on the river.

Access

The put-in is reached by taking Interstate 5 to Creswell (exit 182), which is south of Eugene. Head east on Cloverdale Road for 1.2 miles. Just before crossing the bridge over the Coast Fork, pull off on the right and park. The put-in is just upstream of the bridge on river left.

To reach the take-out, continue east on Cloverdale Road for 5.3 miles. At the intersection at the end of the road, go left (west) on Oregon 58 for 2.2 miles. Take Interstate 5 north toward Eugene and Springfield. Exit almost immediately at exit 188-B. Go right at Franklin Boulevard and then right at the stop sign. Stay straight and follow signs toward Springfield. At the traffic signal, turn right onto Oregon 126 and cross the Willamette. At the first street, turn right onto Mill Street and follow it to the boat ramp, the take-out.

Gauge

Coast Fork Willamette River near Goshen.

Laurie Pavey and Mark Murphy

74 Salt Creek
McCredie Springs to Kitson Springs Road Bridge

Class: 3(4); 4(4+)	Length: 8.4 miles
Flow: 400 cfs; 1200 cfs	Character: forested
Gradient: 87 fpm	Season: rainy/snowmelt

Salt Creek is a small tributary that enters the Middle Fork Willamette River just east of Oakridge. It is fed mainly by snowmelt after warm spells in the spring, but large winter rainstorms occasionally bring the creek to a runnable flow. The continuous nature helps ease what many might call a steep gradient. Though play spots are few, the constant class 3 action creates an enjoyable cruising stream.

At mile 1.2, Luggage Inspector Rapid starts a series of class 3+ and 4 rapids. First-timers may want to scout on the right. At mile 1.3, Unclaimed Baggage Hole warrants a scout or portage on the right. At high flows, the river-wide hydraulic gets gruesome and a portage is recommended. For the next 1.3 miles, the river is an enjoyable 3+ roller coaster at high water and technical class 3 at lower flows. Remember to scout whenever the river drops out of sight. Beyond mile 1.6, the river maintains a steady class 2–3 personality, but watch out for blind turns and logs. A steeper class 3-plus drop is located about two-thirds of the way down the run.

Hazards

Logs are a constant problem, especially in the first and last miles.

Access

Take Oregon 58 to Oakridge. Continue past Oakridge for about 1 mile and turn right onto Kitson Springs Road toward Hills Creek Dam. After 0.2 mile, the road crosses Salt Creek at the take-out.

For the put-in, drive back to Oregon 58 and turn right. Proceed 8 miles and turn right into the parking area for McCredie Springs (near Blue Pool Campground).

Gauge

None exists. The flow can be approximated by subtracting the outflow of Hills Creek Reservoir from the inflow to Lookout Point Reservoir and dividing the difference by 5 (winter) or 4 (spring). Phone 541-937-3852 for the flows.

Eric Brown

75 Salmon Creek
1.5 Miles Above NF 2408 Bridge to Fish Hatchery Road Bridge

Class: 3+(4+); 4-(5)	Length: 7.5 miles
Flow: 300 cfs; 800 cfs	Character: forested
Gradient: 63 fpm, C	Season: rainy/snowmelt

Salmon Creek is great for intermediate to advanced paddlers wanting to boat smaller volume runs. For less excitement, the mile-long class 4–5 gorge can be avoided by putting in at the NF 2408 bridge. The 3–4 miles of Salmon Creek above the gorge are a combination of shallow braided channels and more continuous stretches of class 2–3 whitewater, both of which contain a substantial amount of wood (logjams, partial blockages, sweepers); thus, running this upper section is not recommended.

After about 150–200 yards of warm-up, the run drops into a deep mile-long gorge. The entrance into this section is denoted by a massive moss-covered cliff on river left. Immediately after going far right through the "guard" logjam, the first rapid is a class 3+ slalom that opens into a log-choked gravel bar. After carefully maneuvering, eddy out left and scout the first of two long, complex class 4+ boulder gardens. Runs down the center or far left are recommended. The next 0.5 mile contains numerous smaller class 3 and 4 rapids and ledges, interspersed with copious wood. Scout what you cannot see around. The second class 4+ rapid soon occurs and should be scouted right. Runs down the right side are best, but at higher flows this rapid can be sneaked on the left side. Class 2 rapids remain to the NF 2408 bridge.

Below the bridge, the creek gives paddlers another 1.2 miles of a splashy class 2 until arrival at Salmon Creek Falls Campground. Here the streambed makes a hard right turn and plunges through a class 3 rapid that contains several big boulders. Be certain to inspect the channels before committing because the narrow slots in this drop often collect wood. Below the boulders, boaters negotiate a fun series of waves and crosscurrents. A swim here would be bad, as a few hundred yards downstream is Salmon Creek Falls (class 4). At the falls, the creek divides around a bedrock island with the right channel a nearly vertical 12-foot drop and the left side a long slide into a hole. Both sides are run easiest on the far right.

About 0.5 mile downstream, the creek crosses under the NF 207 bridge and signals the beginning of a class 3 mini-gorge. This several-hundred-yards-long rapid is a series of small slides and ledges that develop into beefy holes at higher flows. The entire gorge can be easily scouted and/or portaged along a hiking trail on the right bank. The next 2 miles are class 2 water, but stay alert for logs and fallen alder. As you approach the railroad bridge, eddy out right and scout the fish hatchery diversion dam. This is an easy class 3 slide, but it has collected a large number of logs in recent years. The remainder of the run is class 2.

Hazards

The mile-long gorge contains quite a lot of wood debris and should be run with extreme caution. Salmon Creek Falls and the lower class 3 mini-gorge can be easily scouted on the drive up. Fallen trees are a problem, especially the last few miles. Be certain to scout the hatchery diversion dam before running it.

Access

From Eugene, take Oregon 58 to Oakridge. After crossing Salmon Creek just east of town, drive about 1 mile and turn left on Fish Hatchery Road. Continue up this road for 1.3 miles and again cross Salmon Creek. The north side of the bridge is the take-out.

To reach the put-in, turn right onto NF 24 and drive 5.2 miles to NF 2408. Less daring souls can put in at the bridge, while the more adventurous can drive 1.5 miles above the bridge and put in by scrambling down to the creek when it is again in sight of the road.

Gauge

None. The flow can be approximated by taking the difference of the inflow to Lookout Point Reservoir minus the outflow from Hills Creek Reservoir and dividing by 5 (winter) or 4 (spring). Call 541-937-3852 for the flows, or see Pat Welch's flow page for a calculated estimate: Salmon Creek.

Mike Haley

76 ★ North Fork of the Middle Fork Willamette River
Miracle Mile through The Gorge

Class: 4+(5) T; 5 T	Length: 5 miles
Flow: 300 cfs; 800 cfs	Character: old growth; canyon
Gradient: 107 fpm (first mile is 213 fpm), PD	Season: rainy/snowmelt

The North Fork offers exciting whitewater, superb scenery, and easy access. It flows into the Middle Fork Willamette River just below Westfir, near Oakridge. This section contains the Miracle Mile, a very steep, very tight, very technical section on which numerous professional and other hard-core kayakers have trained. Although many rapids along the Miracle Mile are named, it is best run for the first few times with someone who knows the complex, twisty routes, as well as the location of several dangerous logs. Eddies are small and difficult to catch. All except three drops can be scouted by boat. Whenever the run divides around an island, go left.

After 0.3 mile of easy class 2–3 water, the bottom drops out. In the mile between the two bridges, the gradient is 213 fpm. Zig and zag down the first few rapids (Initiation, Ricochet, Confusion). The left side of the first island is blocked by wood. Shark's Tooth soon follows. The latter requires careful maneuvering to run an extremely narrow slot. Whoop-de-do, class 5 is next. Scout or portage left. The left side of the island is also jammed by wood. The run is mainly class 4–4+ down to the confluence with Christy Creek, which marks the end of the Miracle Mile. Just around the bend below the second bridge is Dragon Slayer (class 5), which is perched against a cliff on river right. The scout requires wading through a jumble of rocks in the center of the river. The bottom hole can cartwheel boats, suck boaters out of boats, or pin boaters to the bottom. Within a mile, the river appears to turn right and plow into the canyon wall at Spinal Compression (a class 5 due to vertical pin possibilities). Runs down the center or far right are possible, but a portage left might be more advisable.

Below Spinal Compression, the river mellows to class 2–3 for 1.5 mile. Another road bridge and high cliff walls on river left signal the start of The Gorge, a 0.5-mile-long section of class 4 rapids ending in a class 5 boulder garden. At high water, the hydraulics in this section are very powerful. The Gorge has three main obstacles: a drop on the right, a very large curling wave/hole that crosses the entire river about halfway through the section, and a tight class 5 boulder garden at the end. The slots in the boulder garden are barely wide enough for boats. Scout carefully from river right. Take out another 0.2 mile farther, at the last bridge.

Hazards

The Miracle Mile and The Gorge. The latter can be scouted on the drive up. Logs are ever-present in the very steep sections. Pinning and broaching potential is very high. Several of the holes are also extremely treacherous. Also check for logs and cables in the class 5 rapid in The Gorge.

Access

To reach the take-out, see directions to the put-in for North Fork of the Middle Fork Willamette River: Bottom of the Gorge to Westfir run.

To reach the put-in, continue upriver another 4.8 miles to where the road is close to the river. Put in at one of the two muddy turnouts, 0.35 mile above the NF 1926 road bridge.

Gauge

For a close estimate of the flow of the river at Westfir, see Pat Welch's flow page for North Fork of the Middle Fork Willamette. The flow at the put-in is about half that at Westfir. There's a boater's gauge for the Miracle Mile on the bridge on NF 1925 3.4 miles up from the take-out. Flows around 1 foot are fine. At 2 feet, the run is solid white.

Jason Bates, Jim Reed, and Mike Haley

77 ★ North Fork of the Middle Fork Willamette River
Bottom of The Gorge to Westfir

Class: 3; 4	Length: 8 miles
Flow: 700–2400 cfs; 2500 cfs	Character: forested
Gradient: 34 fpm, PD	Season: rainy/snowmelt

This scenic river is protected under the Wild and Scenic Rivers Act. The run is mostly class 2+ to 3 in a forested canyon with clear water. Many good surf waves can be found at most flows. The run has four noteworthy rapids: Shotgun, Bullseye, Typewriter, and Ledges. Shotgun is a twisting left turn with a small 3-foot drop that can be seen from the road. It's about 0.2 mile above the NF 1912 bridge. Bullseye, located 0.5 mile above the NF 1910 bridge, can be recognized by a large rock that blocks the main channel on the left. Boaters may go either right or left of the rock, but some have been known to go straight over the top, giving it the name Bullseye. Alternatively, one can paddle the center chute for a short 3-foot drop. Typewriter, just below Bullseye, demands a right-to-left move to avoid a large hole on river right. Ledges, located near the end of the run, can be recognized by a wall of rocks on the left at the start of the drop. It is best scouted

Bullseye Rapid, North Fork of the Middle Fork Willamette River (Zach Urness)

from river left. A narrow channel on the far left becomes apparent only at the top of the drop. It is the most commonly run line, but other routes are also available in the middle and the right.

Hazards

Shotgun, Bullseye, Typewriter, and Ledges are class 3 rapids that present some difficulties. All can be scouted from the river or from the road. Keep an eye out for downed logs in the river and poison oak.

Access

Take Interstate 5, exit 188 and travel east on Oregon 58. Proceed 32 miles, turn left, and cross the Middle Fork Willamette River. Turn left again and proceed to Westfir. The take-out is at the former log weighing station located about 0.7 mile upstream from the covered bridged in Westfir. An alternative take-out, above Ledges, is at the NF 1910 bridge 3 miles upstream of the covered bridge in Westfir.

The put-in is 8.6 miles upstream from Westfir at the NF 19 bridge, below The Gorge where the road crosses to river right. For the best put-in spot, park at the large gravel turnout 500 feet downstream of the bridge. A good 500-foot-long trail leads to the river.

Gauge

For a close estimate of the flow see Pat Welch's flow page: North Fork of the Middle Fork Willamette. Optimum flows are 1000–2000 cfs.

Gene Ice and WKCC Editors

78 Fall Creek
Gold Creek to Bedrock Campground

Class: 3; 3+	Length: 7.8 miles
Flow: 500 cfs; 2000 cfs	Character: forested
Gradient: 56 fpm, PD	Season: rainy

This section of upper Fall Creek is paddled less often than the Bedrock run, even though it contains many of the same features as that section and is a bit easier. Class 3 paddlers who want to consider smaller creeks should find this to be a good training run. After 0.2 mile, the creek drops over a narrow 5-foot ledge. Scout and/or portage. Another mile down is another 4-foot ledge drop, sometimes with a log in it. At 5 miles into the run, just upstream of a bridge, is another steep and narrow drop. Check it for logs. In general, the run contains numerous play holes, surf waves, and a handful of smaller ledges.

Hazards

In addition to the first ledge, which must be scouted, this run usually contains a few logjams and several other near portages. Boaters should always remain alert for wood.

Access

The take-out for this run is the put-in for the Fall Creek: Bedrock Campground to Fall Creek Reservoir run.

To reach the put-in, continue on NF 18 another 7.5 miles to the bridge at Gold Creek, where there's a paved ramp with a locked gate. Fall Creek Falls is 1.1 mile upstream.

Gauge

Fall Creek above North Fork near Lowell. The flow is about 60 percent of that in the Fall Creek: Bedrock Campground to Fall Creek Reservoir run.

Mike Haley

79 Fall Creek
Bedrock Campground to Fall Creek Reservoir

Class: 3(4); 4(5)	Length: 7.1 miles
Flow: 800; 3000 cfs	Character: forested
Gradient: 28 fpm, PD	Season: rainy

The Bedrock section of upper Fall Creek is one of the more exciting and beautiful runs in the Eugene area. The drawback of this run is the unpredictable flow. With the exception of two difficult rapids, intermediate paddlers may consider the run.

Before launching, stop on the bridge that leads to the campground and look downstream. This is the site of past logjams; check to be sure it is clear. Also, the first class 3+ drop, which is downstream 0.3 mile, can be scouted by walking through the campground.

The put-in is on river right just above the bridge. It has a steep and often muddy trail. Sometimes boaters use an alternative put-in 1 mile upstream on Portland Creek, which has a put-in site that isn't as muddy.

The first rapid at 0.3 mile starts out with a river-wide ledge and then narrows considerably. The water in this slot is turbulent and can flip an unwary boater. This drop is usually run on the left. Below here is a series of ledges and pools. Several class 2 and 3 rapids are encountered in the miles below in this green Eden, somewhat scarred by some past forest fires.

Beyond the second bridge, begin preparing for Fish Ramp Rapid, which can be very difficult and potentially dangerous with a strong guard hole at the top. It is 0.2 mile below the bridge. Scout this rapid during the shuttle.

Between the third (final) bridge and the reservoir take-out lurks the second class 4 rapid. It is a 6- to 7-foot steep slide into a diagonal hole. Scout this drop before attempting to run it. It is possible to take out on river right or left at the bridge, or continue on into the reservoir for a take-out 200 yards down on the right shore. Sometimes the reservoir is high enough to cover this last class 4 drop.

Hazards

Scout Fish Ramp Rapid and the steep slide between the final bridge and the take-out. Intermediate boaters may wish to portage around Fish Ramp Rapid or take out above it. Be alert for fallen logs, such as the longtime log just below the Bedrock Campground bridge. At flows above 2500 cfs, this river is strictly for experts.

Access

Follow the Bob Straub Parkway south out of Springfield toward Jasper. The road becomes Jasper-Lowell Road and then becomes Pengra Road as you head south.

After passing the Jasper Market, drive 4.7 miles south, passing the Jasper-Lowell Road turnoff, and then turn left onto Place Road. Go 3.6 miles to the stop sign at the Unity covered bridge. Proceed straight (east). The road is now called Big Fall Creek Road. Follow this road along the north shore of the reservoir for 7.5 miles to the bridge crossing the river at the head of the reservoir. This is the take-out. Scout the class 4 drop from the bridge. Then proceed 1.8 mile above the take-out to scout Fish Ramp Rapid at the unmarked road leading down to a BLM ramp. (The gauge is also located near the ramp.) Continue another 5.7 miles upstream on NF 18 to the Bedrock Campground bridge, the put-in.

Gauge

Fall Creek above North Fork near Lowell. Minimum flow is 500 cfs.

Doug Tooley and WKCC Editors

80 Fall Creek
Fall Creek Dam to Middle Fork Willamette Confluence

Class: 2(3)	Length: 6.5 miles
Flow: 500–1200 cfs	Character: rural
Gradient: 18 fpm, PD	Season: dam-controlled

With the exception of the Willamette River and the McKenzie River at Hayden Bridge, this run on Fall Creek is the closest whitewater to the Eugene-Springfield area. It contains some excellent play spots that are good for beginners to try surfing. Because this portion of Fall Creek is not prone to flooding, fallen trees remain in the river, so watch for wood.

The first 0.5 mile of the run is the most interesting, with a nice series of short class 2 rapids. Throughout the run are many good play spots with eddies on both sides of the river. A class 3 rapid is located just downstream from the Pengra covered bridge. It can be easily scouted from the bridge. Open canoes risk swamping in the 3- to 4-foot standing waves. Boaters who do not wish to run the Pengra bridge rapid can take out on river left, at the base of the bridge, ending their run at the bridge. Paddlers wishing to continue on for another mile beyond the class 3 rapid can take out just above the confluence with the Middle Fork Willamette.

There's a pullout near milepost 3 with a short carry from the river. This run ends at the confluence. However, if a longer trip is desired, one can continue on past the confluence for another 4 miles on the Middle Fork Willamette to Jasper. See Middle Fork Willamette: Dexter Dam to Jasper for details on the Jasper take-out.

Hazards

Some boaters may opt to scout the class 3 rapid just below the Pengra covered bridge.

Access

Follow the Bob Straub Parkway south out of Springfield toward Jasper. The road becomes Jasper-Lowell Road as you head south. After passing the Jasper Market, drive 3 miles south. Park at the pullout on the right near milepost 3, this is the take-out and it is just above the confluence with the Middle Fork Willamette. Continue up the creek for 0.8 mile and turn left onto Jasper-Lowell Road. Go 2.2 miles (stop on the way to scout the rapid at the Pengra covered bridge, if desired) and turn right; stay on Jasper-Lowell Road. Continue 2.4 miles and cross Fall Creek on the Unity covered bridge. Turn left onto Big Fall Creek Road, go 0.6 mile, and take the short road on the right to the put-in just below the dam.

Gauge

Fall Creek below Winberry Creek. Optimal flow is around 1000 cfs.

Doug Tooley

81 ★ Middle Fork Willamette River Hills Creek Dam to Black Canyon Campground

Class: 2(3)	Length: 11.1 miles
Flow: 400–4000 cfs	Rural: forested hills
Gradient: 27 fpm, PD	Season: year-round

In this stretch of the Middle Fork Willamette, the banks are lined with trees and shrubs that largely hide the few houses along the river. The current is fast, creating frequent class 1 and 2 rapids. The run is available year-round because the minimum release from the dam is seldom below the 400 cfs minimum needed.

The run starts a short distance below the Hills Creek Dam. Salt Creek enters on the right a quarter mile from the put-in. At the half-mile mark is the first significant rapids, a class 2+. Here the river curves left and drops into a straight rapid followed by a curve to the right. The bank on the left is under continuous erosion, and occasionally sweepers are found here.

As you approach the town of Oakridge, note the boat ramp access at Greenwaters Park on the right, an alternative put-in. Just below the park, Salmon Creek enters on the right, identified by a large gravel bar.

The river calms down somewhat for the next 2 miles as it flows past Oakridge and then goes under the Oregon 58 bridge. A mile below this bridge, Hell's Gate Rapid (class 3) begins. An island splits the flow, and most boaters choose the left channel, but either channel is runnable.

A short distance below the rapid, a large gravel bar on the right marks the entrance of the North Fork of the Willamette River. During the rainy season, the flow below this confluence may be three or four times greater than the flow at put-in. The remainder of the run has lower gradient, but don't go to sleep because there are four class 2 rapids that require some technical maneuvering at low flows and paddling through strong hydraulics at larger flows.

Hazards

Watch out for wood at the class 2+ rapids just below put-in. Hell's Gate Rapid, just below the second bridge, is the most technically difficult of this section. It is easily scouted on the drive to put-in.

Access

Take Oregon 58 east from Interstate 5, just south of Eugene, and proceed upstream 27 miles to the take-out at Black Canyon Campground. The boat ramp is open all year.

To reach the put-in, continue east on Oregon 58 to Oakridge. (If a scout of Hell's Gate Rapid is desired, go 4 miles beyond Black Canyon Campground, and turn left at signs to Westfir. Proceed 0.4 mile to the bridge over the rapid for a look. Then cross the bridge and turn right to rejoin Oregon 58 in 1.3 miles.) Continue through the town of Oakridge. Near the east end of town, note Greenwaters Park, which is an alternative put-in. Continue 1 mile past Greenwaters Park and turn right on Kitson Springs Road at the sign to Hills Creek Reservoir. After 0.5 mile, turn right on NF 21. Go 0.2 mile and just before the bridge, turn left onto a narrow dirt road. Proceed several hundred feet to the put-in. Park on the west side of the bridge.

Gauge

Middle Fork Willamette River near Oakridge. The flow includes the dam discharge, plus Salmon Creek and Salt Creek. It ranges from 600 to 2000 cfs in summer and from 1500 to over 5000 cfs in winter. Below Hell's Gate Rapid, the North Fork Willamette enters. It adds little water in summer, but may add significant amounts during the rainy season. For the total flow below the confluence, see the gauge: Middle Fork Willamette River below North Fork Willamette.

Rob Blickensderfer, Rich Brainerd, and WKCC Editors

82 Middle Fork Willamette River Dexter Dam to Jasper

Class: 2	Length: 8 miles
Flow: 1200–5000 cfs	Character: rural
Gradient: 14 fpm, C	Season: year-round

In this section, the river makes its transition from the wild water of its upper reaches to the slower water found below Eugene. The trip begins at a brisk pace with a few small straightforward rapids. A short distance below the put-in the river splits and the right channel is preferred. Along the way several rock shelves require maneuvering at low water and develop large waves at high water. There are several chutes that may lead the unwary boater into overhanging brush. Numerous islands and channels occur. In particular, about 5 miles down, the river begins dividing into a number of channels of varying size with numerous trees in the river. The configuration of the channels and the location of logjams change from year to year. After these channels merge, the river broadens. A railroad bridge is passed around mile 6. At the next bridge, take out on the right where a little waterfall enters the river near the Jasper Store. If you are taking out at Jasper State Park, look for picnic tables about 1.2 miles downstream of the railroad bridge.

Hazards

Between miles 3 and 5 there are at least two low-water hazards where the river is squeezed by a gravel bar into a chute that flows directly into overhanging brush. Solid class 2 skills are needed in those areas. About 5 miles below the put-in, the river begins splitting into multiple channels in which logs and sweepers are always present. Approach with caution while looking for a possible landing, if needed. Usually the left channel is the largest and least likely to be blocked.

A water trail guide with maps for the Willamette River is currently available (see Appendix B).

Access

From Oregon 126 in eastern Springfield, travel south on Bob Straub Parkway, which merges with the Jasper-Lowell Road just after crossing the railroad tracks. Go 2.8 miles to Jasper. The take-out parking area for paddle craft is opposite the Jasper Store, just upstream of the steel bridge. Alternative take-outs are located under the steel bridge on river left or across the bridge and 0.2 mile upstream at Jasper State Park (open May 1–September 30; fee site).

To get to the put-in, follow the road upstream along the north side of the river toward Lowell. At 3.8 miles, stay straight. The road crosses over Fall Creek and becomes Pengra Road. An alternative put-in is the Pengra boat ramp a mile farther on the right. The main put-in is another 2.4 miles up. Turn right at a small river access sign. From the broad beach access at the put-in, Dexter Dam can be seen upstream.

Gauge

Middle Fork Willamette River near Dexter. Middle Fork Willamette River at Jasper.

Rob Blickensderfer

83 Middle Fork Willamette River
Jasper to Island Park

Class: 1(2-)	Length: 9.6 miles
Flow: 2000–6000 cfs	Character: wooded; residential; industrial
Gradient: 11 fpm, PD	Season: year-round

This lowest run on the Middle Fork Willamette is generally not too fast, but has some swift riffles and a few surfing waves in the first half of the run. Clearwater Boat Landing, an alternative access, is 4.2 miles downstream on the right. In about 4 more miles, look on the left for the mouth of the Coast Fork Willamette River. Below the confluence, you are now on the main stem of the Willamette. About 1.5 miles below the confluence, after passing under a railroad bridge, the Island Park access is on the right, just below the Oregon 126 twin bridges.

A water trail guide with maps for the Willamette River is currently available (see Appendix B).

Hazards

Watch for downed trees and root wads.

Access

For directions to the put-in, see the run Middle Fork Willamette River: Dexter Dam to Jasper. An alternative midway access is about 4 miles downstream at Clearwater Boat Landing, which is off Jasper Road in south Springfield.

The take-out is at the South Mill Street entrance to Island Park. From Interstate 5 N, take exit 194 to Oregon 126 East, and then take the first exit toward Springfield City Center. Turn right onto Pioneer Parkway West. Take a right onto Main Street and then the first left onto South Mill Street to the boat ramp. From Interstate 5 south, take exit 191 to Glenwood Boulevard and go north to Franklin Boulevard. Turn right and, just after crossing the Willamette, turn right again onto South Mill Street.

To reach the put-in from Island Park, take Main Street (Oregon 126–Business) east and then go south on South 42nd; follow signs to Jasper.

Gauge

Willamette River at Jasper. The flow is regulated, the minimum is runnable. Flows over 6000 cfs are not recommended for beginners.

Gene Ice, Al Grapel, and WKCC Editors

84 Willamette River
Island Park to Randy Papé Beltline

Class: 2-(2+)	Length: 7.4 miles
Flow: 2000–6000 cfs	Character: residential; commercial, city park lands
Gradient: 7 fpm, PD	Season: year-round

The river from Island Park to the Beltline is a popular summer run for Eugene and Springfield residents. Do not expect a wilderness run here; rather, enjoy plenty of happy folks, especially during the summer when hot weather drives rafts, canoes, inner tubes, pool toys, and other crafts of all pedigrees onto the water. Despite its popularity with novice paddlers, the river merits respect. During summer, the rapids are mild for experienced boaters, but not for novices; plus, rocks are plentiful, and a dangerous weir (low-head dam) and a rock-wall diversion are present. During winter and spring, the flows can often be very high and powerful.

About a half mile below the put-in, the right two-thirds of the river channel is usually exposed bedrock. The left side is a class 2- rapid known as Pizza Rapid. A half-mile-long flat section extends below Pizza Rapid with the D Street boat ramp located about halfway down on the right side. The flat section ends just above what is potentially the most dangerous part of the Willamette River between Dexter Dam and Willamette Falls. This is due to a combination of a low rock wall and a concrete weir with several slots that extend across the whole river except for a short, narrow S turn on the far right of the river. These features are located about 200 yards below the D Street boat launch and 100 yards upstream of the Interstate 5 bridge. Most boaters should use the S turn on the far right of the river. This won't be seen until you are just above it. It is worth scouting the S turn and taking a look at the reasonably long class 2+ rapid (I-5 Rapid) below the I-5 bridge. The slots in the weir are especially hazardous, because debris and the hydraulic reversal action can trap boats, inflatable floats, rafts, and even people just below the weir.

Below the I-5 Rapid, there are several other spots that are worth noting, the first being about 0.4 mile ahead, where a shallow ledge extends all the way across the river and requires careful rock dodging as it drops down to the left. About 0.2 mile below the ledge, the river passes under a footbridge. The main channel on the left drops steeply under the bridge and continues in a long series of narrow standing waves for a couple of hundred yards. In another few hundred yards, the Alton Baker Park boat ramp is located on the right. Rose Garden Rapid is a little more than a mile downstream from the Alton Baker Park boat ramp, and this also requires a lot of careful rock dodging. The last intermediate take-out is located another 0.5 mile down the river and is behind Valley River Center. It is almost hidden on the right side, so pay attention. Marist Rapid, class 2-, is located a little more than a mile farther downstream. It is fairly straightforward with large waves in the center. Scout on the left, if desired. Another 1.5 miles brings you to the take-out on the left under the Beltline bridge.

A water trail guide with maps for the Willamette River is currently available (see Appendix B).

Hazards

The rock wall and weir just above the Interstate 5 bridge are dangerous at all water levels. Do not attempt to run any slot except the far right S turn. The I-5 Rapid may swamp open boats at high water. Watch out for strainers.

Access

For directions to the put-in, see the previous run, Willamette River: Jasper to Island Park.

The intermediate access points include: the D Street boat ramp, which is reached via Aspen Street that takes off from Centennial Boulevard east of the Interstate 5 underpass; the Alton Baker Park boat ramp, which is near the Cuthbert Amphitheater in Alton Baker Park; and the Valley River Center mall access, which is behind the mall near the movie theaters.

The take-out is under the Randy Papé Beltline bridge, just off River Avenue, which takes off from River Road just south of the Beltline.

Gauge

Willamette River at Eugene. The flow is regulated, the minimum is runnable. Flows over 6000 cfs are not recommended for beginners.

Gene Ice and Al Grapel

McKenzie River and Tributaries

85★ South Fork McKenzie River Above French Pete Campground to Cougar Reservoir

Class: 3(4-); 4(5)	Length: 8.4 miles
Flow: 900–2000 cfs; 3000–4000 cfs	Character: forested
Gradient: 49 fpm, C	Season: rainy

For most McKenzie River boaters, the South Fork is just another tributary that enters the main river unnoticed somewhere between Rainbow and Blue River. Above Cougar Reservoir, however, lies the free-flowing South Fork McKenzie River, one of the more interesting rivers of the Upper Willamette system. At flows above 2500 cfs, the South Fork is a superb experts-only run. At flows below 2000 cfs, the long rapids are no longer continuous and the South Fork is suitable for paddlers with a dependable roll.

Although the South Fork McKenzie drainage is adjacent to the North Fork of the Middle Fork Willamette River, it has greater fluctuations in flow. It is usually runnable only during or shortly after a hard rain. Winter snowstorms often reduce road access. The spring snowmelt is undependable. Furthermore, some of the best rapids are exposed only during the fall and early winter when Cougar Reservoir is lowered. The first 5 miles of the run consists of shallow and rocky class 2+ to class

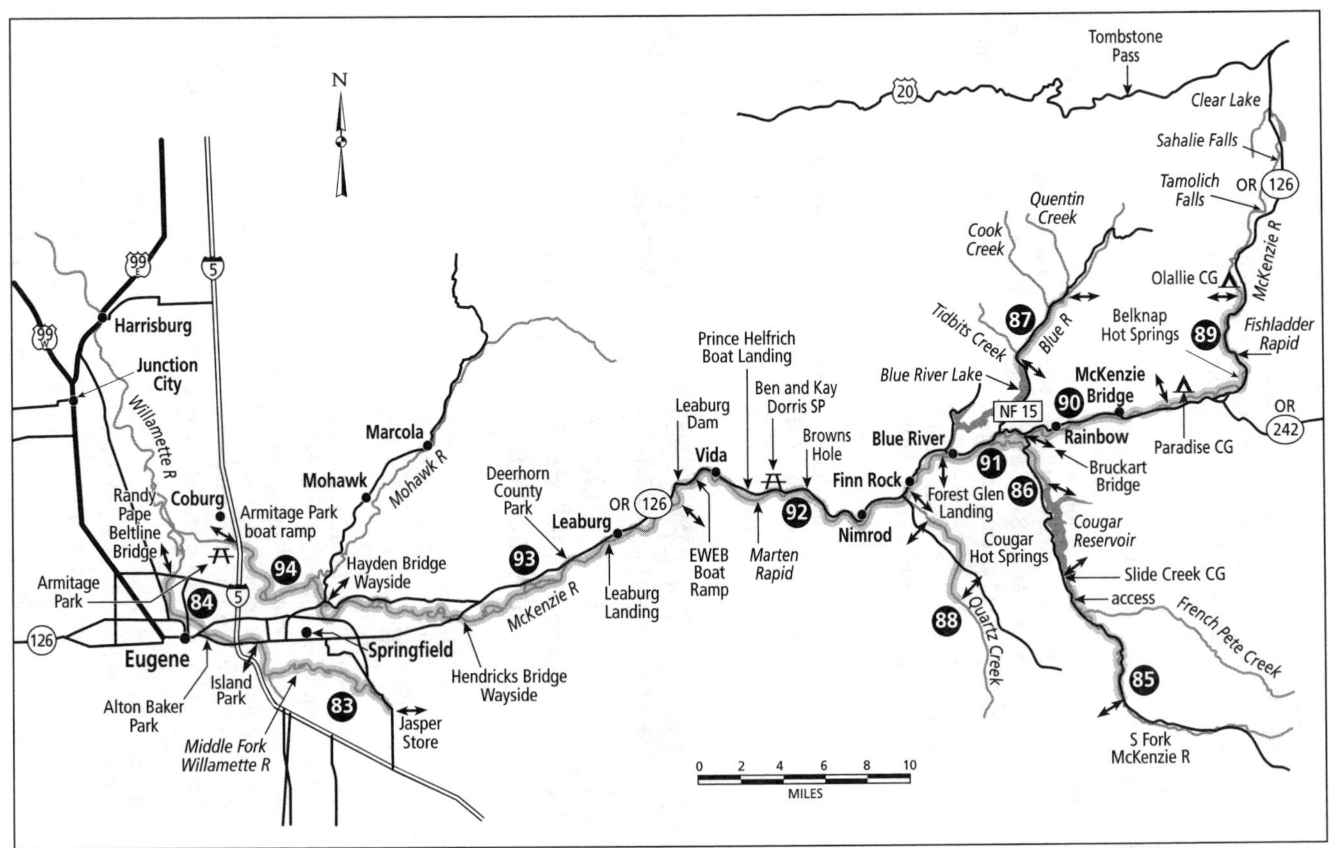
Tombstone Pass
20
Clear Lake
Sahalie Falls
Tamolich Falls
OR 126
McKenzie R
Quentin Creek
Cook Creek
Olallie CG
Belknap Hot Springs
89
Fishladder Rapid
87
Blue R
Tidbits Creek
Blue River Lake
McKenzie Bridge
NF 15
90
Rainbow
Paradise CG
OR 242
Prince Helfrich Boat Landing
Ben and Kay Dorris SP
Browns Hole
Blue River
Finn Rock
91
Bruckart Bridge
86
Leaburg Dam
Vida
Cougar Reservoir
N
99E
5
Harrisburg
99W
Junction City
Willamette R
Marcola
Mohawk R
Mohawk
Deerhorn County Park
Leaburg
OR 126
92
Nimrod
Forest Glen Landing
Cougar Hot Springs
Slide Creek CG
access
French Pete Creek
Randy Pape Beltline Bridge
Coburg
Armitage Park boat ramp
94
Hayden Bridge Wayside
93
McKenzie R
Marten Rapid
EWEB Boat Ramp
Leaburg Landing
88
Quartz Creek
Armitage Park
84
5
126
Eugene
Island Park
Springfield
Hendricks Bridge Wayside
85
S Fork McKenzie R
Alton Baker Park
83
Jasper Store
Middle Fork Willamette R
0   2   4   6   8   10
MILES

3 rapids. Soon, however, side creeks begin to add volume, and the gradient begins to pick up. Watch for logs.

The first bridge on the run is located immediately below the put-in. About a mile farther is a class 3 drop with a large boulder in the center to split the flow. This drop can be seen from the road during the shuttle. More class 2+ and 3-drops follow until you reach the second bridge, located at about river mile 5.5 near the confluence with French Pete Creek. The gradient now increases. About 0.2 mile below the bridge a long major rapid, Gauge Rapid (class 3+ to 4-), begins. Large waves and holes culminate in a tight right turn to avoid a large hole. A narrow left channel is sometimes available for sneaking left of the hole. The gauge itself is just below the final drop on river right. Parts of this rapid can be seen from the road during the shuttle.

After Gauge Rapid, the river quiets down for the half-mile paddle to the third bridge, the alternative take-out, on river right. Those wishing to tackle the difficult class 4 rapids below will continue on. Below this bridge, the river cuts deep into the mud walls of the lowered lake and the second major rapid follows. This rapid has two 90-degree right turns that can be run to the inside. Few eddies can be caught along this 0.8-mile stretch. The rapid finally comes to an end in the lowered reservoir.

The walk to the take-out is a bit muddy, but well worth the trouble. A welcome treat is a soak at the Terwilliger (Cougar) Hot Springs on the way home (be sure to hide and lock up your valuables here).

Hazards

The run is very fast. The final rapid below the alternative take-out should be scouted.

Access

To reach the put-in, take Oregon 126 east from Springfield past Blue River and take the Cougar Reservoir/Aufderheide Drive exit on the right. Stay on Aufderheide Drive and proceed to the top of Cougar Dam. From the dam, drive along the west bank of the reservoir until the road crosses the river at the top of the reservoir. Park here on the east side of the bridge for the alternative take-out. For the reservoir take-out, go left and continue downstream on a gravel road on the east side of the reservoir for about 1.5 miles to the boat ramp at Slide Creek Campground.

To reach the put-in, reset your odometer at the bridge and travel upstream (on the east side of the river) for 6.6 miles to a small, primitive campsite on the right, the put-in. Note: Just above the put-in, there are many wood problems in the streambed, including a massive log jam that has been in place for years.

Gauge

South Fork McKenzie River above Cougar.

Gene Ice and WKCC Editors

86 South Fork McKenzie River/McKenzie River Cougar Dam to Forest Glen Boat Ramp

Class: 2(3-); 2+(3)	Length: 7 miles (4.4 miles on the South Fork)
Flow: 500 cfs; 2000 cfs	Character: forested
Gradient: 28 fpm (overall); 40 fpm (on the SF), C	Season: rainy

This beautiful little run is intermediate in difficulty between the run on the South Fork above Cougar Reservoir and the main McKenzie where the confluence takes place. It is narrow, almost totally forested until it empties into the McKenzie, and feels like a run through a wilderness. The gradient might initially cause some newer boaters concern, but the elevation is lost uniformly with only one short, steep rapid, named Teardrop.

The run starts just below the Cougar Reservoir dam. Although the rapids are not large, much rock dodging is required. There is one very large boulder that appears to be blocking the entire channel almost a half-mile below the put-in. Narrow, runnable slots are on each side of the boulder. A tenth-mile farther, pull out on river right just below where a small stream enters to scout Teardrop Rapid. Walk downstream a couple of hundred yards to the large boulder that's adjacent to the drop. At low water, the easiest route through the rapid is on the far left, and at higher water, the far right is also okay. If running Teardrop is not appealing, there is a narrow sneak route down a side channel on the left side that takes off a couple of hundred yards above the rapid. Float down this channel a couple of hundred yards and take out where there seems to be a trail. Drag or carry across to the main river.

In about 0.7 mile, a sharp 90-degree left turn is required since going straight ends in a dead end. Another 0.7 mile brings you under the Aufderheide Drive bridge, an alternative put-in or take-out. In another mile there may be another 90-degree left turn needed to avoid a very shallow crossing into a side channel straight ahead. This crossing may need to be taken if the main channel to the left is blocked by wood. One more mile brings you to the confluence with the main McKenzie for a total of 4.4 miles on this delightful section of the South Fork. The remaining 2.6 miles to Blue River is class 1+ and easy 2. Forest Glen boat ramp is on river right of the large island just upstream of the confluence with Blue River.

Hazards

Watch out for strainers and other wood. Teardrop Rapid deserves respect.

Access

To reach the put-in, take Oregon 126 east from Springfield past Blue River and take the Cougar Reservoir (Aufderheide Drive) road on the right. Drive straight south (without turning when Aufderheide Drive does) to the end of the road at the base of the dam and the gate to the Cougar powerhouse and fish facility, about 2.4 miles. There is a rudimentary trail near the southern end of the gravel pullout.

The put-in is down a steep rip-rap slope; a rope is helpful.

Alternative take-outs are at Redsides (see McKenzie: Bruckart Bridge to Finn Rock run), which makes a shorter run of about 4.6 miles; or at Finn Rock, which makes a longer run of about 9.5 miles.

Gauge

South Fork McKenzie River below Cougar Dam (or South Fork McKenzie River near Rainbow).

Al Grapel

87 Blue River
Quentin Creek to Blue River Lake

Class: 4(5) T	Length: 5.1 miles
Flow: 250–900 cfs	Character: forested; logging
Gradient: 100 fpm, C,PD	Season: rainy/snowmelt

Blue River is a technically demanding, high-gradient tributary of the McKenzie River located east of Eugene. It is more like a creek than a river. Technical drops of 3–10 feet are numerous, as are extensive boulder gardens that require precise boat handling.

Approximately 0.5 mile below the Quentin Creek put-in is a class 5 triple drop called Food for Thought. This drop has been run successfully, but may require a difficult portage on the right. An alternative put-in is 1 mile below put-in at Cook Creek.

The remainder of the river is class 3–4, and extensive scouting both from the road and the river is strongly recommended. The largest drop in the lower 4 miles of the run, called Pincushion (or S-Turn), is easily visible from the road. Downstream of Tidbits Creek, during the final mile of the run, the river broadens and flattens, and then it drops steeply for one last, long boulder garden just before the take-out.

Hazards

Due to logging activity in the area, boaters should be wary of log debris and sweepers. In recent years, dangerous logs have been obstructing the exit of Food for Thought and also several of the boulder gardens immediately downstream. Avoiding the first mile is often the best option.

Access

Take Oregon 126 east from Springfield toward Blue River. About 2.8 miles east of the town of Blue River, turn north from Oregon 126 onto NF 15. The take-out is located at a boat ramp at the upper end of Blue River Lake, 3.5 miles from the Oregon 126 turnoff.

To reach the put-in, cross the bridge over Lookout Creek and continue up NF

15. The Cook Creek bridge put-in avoids the often log-choked, difficult first mile. It is 4 miles up from take-out. Quentin Creek bridge is 1 mile farther up.

Gauge

Blue River below Tidbits Creek. Optimal at 500–800 cfs.

Ron Mattson and WKCC Editors

88 Quartz Creek
Milepost 7.5 Bridge to Milepost 2 Bridge

Class: 3+(4) T	Length: 5.1 miles
Flow: 250–750 cfs	Character: forested; logged
Gradient: 120 fpm, C	Season: rainy

If you are an intermediate creek boater looking to hone your skills on harder runs, Quartz Creek is one of the best in the upper Willamette Valley. This continuous little alder-lined creek is technical rock dodging at low water and a nonstop class 3 to 4 slalom at higher flows.

The put-in is a log-choked bedrock ledge a hundred yards downstream of the mile 7.5 bridge. This class 4- ledge is runnable on the far left but some overhanging branches complicate the line. Warm up in the swirling eddy below the ledge because the continuous nature of the creek keeps paddlers occupied almost immediately. About 0.5 mile downstream, the creek splits around an island where the main right channel has an obvious horizon line. Scout this drop because wood often complicates maneuvers in this rapid. The portage is on the island. The next 2.5 miles are mainly class 2+ intermingled with several class 3 drops. After the first bridge, some large boulders signal the beginning of larger, pushier class 3+ rapids that continue for 0.75 mile. After this section, the creek mellows out a bit and the drops get less concentrated. The last mile contains numerous waves and holes to play in, though some can be a bit shallow. The take-out is the fourth bridge over the creek. Below the take-out, the creek flattens out dramatically and becomes braided and log-choked before finally flowing into the McKenzie below Finn Rock.

Hazards

The area surrounding the creek has been heavily logged, so wood is an ever-present danger. Remain alert for fallen alders and other sweepers, as well as for wood protruding from shore. The general fast pace of the creek could cause problems for swimmers.

Access

From Eugene, drive east on Oregon 126 along the McKenzie. Turn right onto Quartz Creek Road (NF 2618) just before the Finn Rock Store. Cross the McKenzie and continue up Quartz Creek Road for 2 miles to where a small road takes off to the right and crosses Quartz Creek, the take-out. To reach the put-in, continue up Quartz Creek Road 5.5 additional miles until you reach a bridge over the creek. The road closely parallels the creek all the way up, allowing paddlers to see much of the creek. Put in on the log-choked bedrock ledge a hundred yards downstream of the bridge.

Gauge

None. The gauge South Fork McKenzie River above Cougar provides guidance. Minimum flows on this creek correlate to gauge flows of around 1500 cfs (winter) and 1200 cfs (spring). A couple of days of heavy rain are usually needed.

Mike Haley, Jason Rackley, and Pete Giordano

89 ★ McKenzie River Olallie Campground to Paradise Campground

Class: 3	Length: 8.3 miles
Flow: 700–2000 cfs	Character: forested
Gradient: 49 fpm, C	Season: year-round

Within its tree-lined banks, the beautiful McKenzie rushes with almost nonstop rapids between Olallie and Paradise campgrounds. This continuous run has few play spots, but the lush forest scenery along the run is superb.

The first few miles are a fun, bouncy ride; however, stay alert for log blockages. At the first bridge, a good surf wave can be found at some water levels.

About 4 miles down from the put-in lies Fishladder Rapid, class 3, the most difficult rapid on this run. This rapid can be scouted from the left during the shuttle (see Access). The rapid starts at a left turn just as you see powerlines ahead across the river. To scout, land on the right. Several routes through the rapid are possible.

Below Fishladder, the river continues to offer miles of interesting rapids. About 0.2 mile past the second bridge, a shallow rock garden ends with a ledge hole on the right that has flipped many kayakers. It is directly against the right bank and can be challenged, or avoided by going left. Just below the hole is a sandy beach and eddy on the left, a perfect lunch stop.

The river then bends right, and just across from the Belknap Hot Springs resort, look for an eddy and plumes of steam arising on the right. The hot springs add some welcome hot water to warm your cold hands during winter runs. The fun read-and-run rapids continue for several more miles to Paradise Campground, a fitting name for the end of the trip. Take out on the left at the boat ramp.

Hazards

Fishladder Rapid should be scouted by those unfamiliar with it. Logs sometimes block the channels. At the put-in, look for signs warning of major log hazards, or call the McKenzie River Ranger District for updates on blockages.

Action at Fishladder on the McKenzie River (Mark Scantlebury)

Access

Drive east from Springfield on Oregon 126 to the take-out at Paradise Campground, located about 4 miles east of McKenzie Bridge. Paradise Campground is partially closed during the winter; however, the boat ramp usually remains open. Take a close look at the take-out to be able to recognize it from the river. To scout Fishladder during the shuttle, pull off onto a dirt road at milepost 16, about 5 miles above Paradise Campground, and walk 100 yards to the river.

The put-in is at Olallie Campground boat ramp, about 9 miles upstream on Oregon 126 near milepost 13. Snow may block access during the winter. An alternative put-in is at Frissell boat launch near milepost 17.

Gauge

McKenzie River below Trail Bridge (upstream of put-in). See Pat Welch's flow page for a calculated estimation of the flow near take-out: McKenzie River near McKenzie Bridge. The minimum flow is runnable.

Gene Ice and WKCC Editors

90 ★ McKenzie River
Paradise Campground to Bruckart Bridge

Class: 2+	Length: 9.2 miles
Flow: 700–4000 cfs	Character: wooded; cabins
Gradient: 39 fpm, C	Season: year-round

Below Paradise Campground, the McKenzie maintains its continuous nature, although the gradient becomes less, and there are occasional pools. The stretch that begins at the town of McKenzie Bridge and ends at the covered Rainbow Bridge is quite continuous and contains two of the most significant rapids on this run. One, called Dessert, is just below McKenzie River Campground and is easiest on the left. The other, starting about one-half mile below Rainbow Bridge, where the river makes a turn toward the main highway, is a long S curve that ends in a rocky stretch, with a strong diagonal wave on the right, called The Vortex. The Bruckart Bridge take-out is less than a mile below here on the right.

Hazards

The class 2+ stretches at Paradise, below McKenzie Bridge, and above the Rainbow Bridge are the most difficult. Serious log hazards come and go in this run every year. Look for hazard information posted at the put-in or call the McKenzie River Ranger District office (phone: 541-882-3381). And keep alert for wood on this run at all times.

Access

For the take-out, drive east on Oregon 126 from Springfield to the turnoff for Cougar Reservoir/Aufderheide Drive. After 150 feet, turn right (do not cross over the McKenzie River) and then immediately turn left to enter the Bruckart Boat Launch site. McKenzie Bridge Campground is an alternative take-out if a shorter trip is desired.

The put-in is at Paradise Campground about 4 miles upstream from McKenzie Bridge on Oregon 126 (see the McKenzie River: Olallie Campground to Paradise Campground run). Alternative put-ins are at the McKenzie trailhead about 1.5 river miles below Paradise Campground or McKenzie Bridge Campground, less than a mile below McKenzie Bridge.

Gauge

McKenzie River above South Fork. The gauge is located just upstream of Bruckart Bridge. The minimum flow is runnable.

Gene Ice, Al Grapel, and WKCC Editors

91 McKenzie River
Bruckart Bridge to Finn Rock

Class: 2(2+)	Length: 7.8 miles
Flow: 700–4000 cfs	Character: wooded; cabins; road
Gradient: 22 fpm, PD	Season: year-round

Below Bruckart Bridge, the river eases into a nice class 2 paddle for experienced kayakers, and open canoeists with a good back ferry. The only rapid of note that is more difficult is a class 2+ rapid that starts about 1.25 miles below the put-in. Here the river makes a right turn, steepens, and heads toward the highway. As the river makes a sharp left turn, keep left to stay out of very fast water with numerous rocks and holes along the bank. A sneak route is available at higher water on the far left before the river makes its sharp left turn. Play spots are few, but are highlighted by an excellent park-and-play area on the right called Redsides, about halfway down. Below Redsides, the river becomes flatter.

Hazards

The class 2+ rapid demands attention and aggressive paddling to keep from being pushed into the rocks and holes. As with the run above, log hazards come and go in this run every year. Look for hazard information posted at the put-in or call the McKenzie River Ranger District office (phone: 541-882-3381). Keep alert for wood and stay left at Redsides to avoid the hole if you don't wish to play there.

Access

Take Oregon 126 east from Springfield to the large pulloff between Quartz Creek Road and the Finn Rock Grill. Kayakers can take out here, but rafters will find the gentle bank across the river easier. To reach this, cross the river on Quartz Creek Road, take a left on the first gravel road, and then a left into the boat launch.

The put-in is at Bruckart Bridge Boat Launch (see Paradise Campground to Bruckart Bridge run). Alternative put-ins are at Redsides, about 5 miles upstream from Quartz Creek Road (near an old log-scaling pullout), Hamlin gravel boat ramp, about 0.5 mile above Redsides, or along the South Fork McKenzie below Cougar Dam where Aufderheide Drive crosses the South Fork (a run of about 7.5 miles). All the alternative put-ins miss the 2+ rapid.

Gauge

McKenzie River above South Fork. The minimum flow is runnable.

Gene Ice, Al Grapel, and WKCC Editors

92 ★ McKenzie River
Finn Rock to Leaburg Lake

Class: 2(3)	Length: 10 to 13.7 miles
Flow: 900–5000 cfs	Character: wooded; cabins
Gradient: 17 fpm, PD	Season: year-round

When people speak of "The McKenzie," they usually mean the 10-mile stretch from Finn Rock to Prince Helfrich Boat Landing. This run is one of the most popular day trips in Oregon. The scenic run consists of long, quiet stretches interspersed with exciting rapids and outstanding play spots. However, cold water is a danger to the unprepared.

Two miles below the put-in is one of the best play spots, Clover Point, just above and within sight of the bridge at Nimrod. It is identified by a large, flat rock outcrop on the right bank. About 0.8 mile downstream is Eagle Rock Rapid, class 2, identified by the rock cliff on the left. The best ride is down the chute near the left side. A short distance below Eagle Rock is a long series of surfing waves along the left side of the river. Pleasant class 1 and 2 water continues for several miles. Silver Creek Public Boat Landing is on the right at mile 4, followed in 2 miles by Rennie Public Boat Landing.

The most famous hole on the river, Browns Hole, is next. It can flip a small raft or swamp a drift boat, but it can be easily avoided by staying to the right. Barely visible from upstream, the hole is located near the end of a straight section. A rock wall on the left about 30 yards upstream of a right jog marks Browns Hole, about 15 feet from the left wall. For a thrill, kayakers can try to punch through the hole. If this isn't thrilling enough, they can return to the hole and enter it from either side.

About 3 miles farther downstream, the river passes Ben and Kay Dorris State Park, with a boat ramp. Ahead is Marten Rapid, class 3. Marten Rapid can be a fun ride, but many people end up swimming through it. To run Marten Rapid, look for the largest boulder in the center of the river in the middle of the rapid; a good channel is about 10 feet to the right of the boulder at most river levels. Beware of the large hole on the right toward the bottom of the rapid. Most people take out 0.5 mile downstream at Prince Helfrich Boat Landing, marked by a suspension footbridge across the river.

Boaters may continue on for 3.5 miles to the EWEB (Eugene Water & Electric Board) boat ramp at the head of Leaburg Lake for a dozen or so class 1 and 2 rapids. A significant rock garden occurs on a left turn just above an island. Going left of the island drops you into an area with a high, sheer bluff covered in ferns—one of the most beautiful spots along the McKenzie River. Just below this is class 2+ Gate Creek Rapid, which is easiest on the right side.

Hazards

Browns Hole can flip a raft and be very sticky for kayaks at some water levels. It can be totally avoided by going to the right. Marten Rapid can be more difficult than Browns Hole and demands precise maneuvering around large rocks and holes. The water temperature, even in the heat of the summer, is always cold. A long swim through Marten Rapid with little on but a swimsuit can be quite dangerous.

Access

Put in at Finn Rock on Oregon 126 east of Eugene, about 12.5 miles upstream from the covered Goodpasture Bridge. Cross the Quartz Creek Road bridge and turn left into the unimproved Finn Rock boat ramp, provided by Rosboro Lumber Company. Some boaters with limited time choose to put in at boat ramps about 4 and 6 miles below, at Silver Creek and Rennie boat landings, respectively. However, paddling down to the EWEB boat ramp at the head of Leaburg Lake provides a run from Silver Creek boat ramp of about 8.5 miles, or a run from Rennie boat ramp of about 6.5 miles.

The most common take-outs are at Ben and Kay Dorris State Park, located along the highway, or at Prince Helfrich Boat Landing (a fee site), located at the end of Thomson Lane, on the south side of the highway 1 mile below Ben and

Kay Dorris State Park. The final take-out is at the EWEB Goodpasture boat ramp at the head of Leaburg Lake at milepost 25.4 on Oregon 126.

Gauge

McKenzie River near Vida. The minimum flow is runnable.

Gene Ice and Al Grapel

93 McKenzie River
Leaburg Dam to Hayden Bridge

Class: 2	Length: 24 miles
Flow: 900–2000 cfs	Character: agricultural
Gradient: 12 fpm, PD	Season: year-round

This section of river is fairly quiet compared to the upper runs, but very enjoyable. The scenery is more typical of Oregon's agricultural countryside than the dense forests found upstream, although the banks are generally covered with trees. The river meanders around large islands and shifting gravel bars, and flows swiftly through sharp turns with tricky currents. Most of the channels around islands appear to be open, but the fast turns, routes through gravel bars, and the wood and root wads that litter the river require careful attention, especially at low water. Overall, the flow is characterized by moderately moving water with short, relatively easy drops and no major rapids.

This section of river breaks nicely into three runs: an upper, middle, and lower (see Access for details).

Hazards

On the middle run, about 1.5 miles below the Deerhorn County Park put-in, be sure to take the left channel. There are two narrow entrances to this channel that can be missed if boaters aren't paying attention. (The flow in the river's larger right channel goes into the Walterville hydroelectric canal and is not recommended.)

Also on the middle run, one rapid is noteworthy. It is about 0.5 mile above the Hendricks Bridge Wayside take-out, identified by the high ridge on the left that slopes down to river level. The river drops to the right, forms some high waves, and then runs swiftly out around some large rocks.

On the lower run, Hayden Bridge Rapid (class 2) is a difficult rapid. It occurs on or just after a sharp left turn a few hundred yards above Hayden Bridge. Get out and scout (or scout from the bridge), since wood often blocks this rapid and the situation can change almost yearly.

Access

UPPER RUN: LEABURG DAM TO DEERHORN COUNTY PARK, 7 MILES

The take-out is on the south side of the river. From the junction of Oregon 126 and East Main Street (Business 126) in Springfield, drive 11.4 miles east on

Oregon 126 to Holden Creek Lane. Take a right, go 0.2 mile, then turn right onto Bridge Street. Cross the bridge and Deerhorn Park is immediately on the left. The ramp is under the bridge.

To reach the put-in just below Leaburg Dam, return to Oregon 126, turn right, and go to the Leaburg Dam. Cross the dam, take the first right turn and use the drift-boat slide or the trail down to the river just below the dam.

An alternative ramp is at Greenwood. Go up Oregon 126 for 3.7 miles from Holden Creek Lane, turn right on Greenwood Lane, and go 1 mile to the ramp.

Another alterative ramp is Leaburg Landing. Go 2.1 miles up from Holden Creek Lane. Turn right off Oregon 126, and drive 0.1 mile on a gravel road to a sand/gravel ramp.

MIDDLE RUN: DEERHORN COUNTY PARK TO HENDRICKS BRIDGE WAYSIDE, 7 MILES

The take-out for this run is on the north side of the river. From the junction of Oregon 126 and East Main Street (Business 126) in Springfield, drive 5.3 miles east on Oregon 126 to the entrance to Hendricks Bridge Wayside, just across the river. Take a right off Oregon 126, then another right into the park.

To reach the put-in at Deerhorn County Park, follow the directions to the take-out for the Upper Run just above.

An alternative way to reach the put-in is to turn right onto Deerhorn Road on the south side of the river just before crossing Hendricks Bridge, drive about 7 miles, and turn left on Bridge Street.

An alternative ramp is at Taylor Landing, on the south side of the river, reached by going up Deerhorn Road 5.3 miles from Oregon 126.

LOWER RUN: HENDRICKS BRIDGE WAYSIDE TO HAYDEN BRIDGE, 10 MILES

The take-out for this run is just downstream from Hayden Bridge on the south side of the river. From Interstate 5 take exit 194A to merge onto Oregon 126 east. After 4 miles, take the 42nd Street/Marcola exit and turn left onto North 42nd Street. Go 0.5 mile, turn right onto Marcola Road. After 0.4 mile, just before reaching Hayden Bridge, turn left onto Hayden Bridge Road, go up the hill 500 feet and turn right into the boat ramp parking lot.

To reach the put-in at Hendricks Bridge Wayside, follow the directions to the take-out for the middle run just above.

One intermediate boat ramp exists for this run at Bellinger Landing. From Hayden Bridge, head northeast on Marcola Road for 0.1 mile. Turn right onto Camp Creek Road and drive 3.1 miles to a right turn on Oak Point Road, where the boat ramp and parking will be just ahead on the right.

Gauge

McKenzie River below Leaburg Dam. McKenzie near Walterville. McKenzie River above Hayden Bridge at Springfield. Gauges are listed in upstream to downstream order.

Gene Ice and Al Grapel

94 McKenzie River
Hayden Bridge to Armitage Park

Class: 1(1+)	Length: 7.5 miles
Flow: 900–2000 cfs	Character: agricultural; residential
Gradient: 9 fpm, C	Season: year-round

This run makes an excellent canoe and beginner kayaker paddle close to Eugene and Springfield. Although it offers very few rapids, it is pleasant. The most difficult rapids are just above Armitage Park, but can be avoided, if desired, by staying to the left. Take out on the left at the boat ramp, which is immediately downstream of the I-5 and Coburg Road bridges. One of the most enjoyable parts of this float is gliding by the Coburg Hills. After finishing the run, Armitage Park makes a fine spot for a picnic.

The remaining 3 miles to the confluence with the Willamette are class 1+ rapids. For more details about paddling below Armitage Park and on the Willamette downstream of the confluence, see the "Willamette River Water Trail Guide" (see Appendix B).

Hazards
None in particular.

Access
See the McKenzie River: Leaburg Dam to Hayden Bridge run for directions to Hayden Bridge, the put-in for this run.

The take-out at Armitage Park (day-use fee) is located on Coburg Road.

From the north: Take the Coburg exit 199 from Interstate 5, and turn south on Coburg Road. From the south: Take Interstate 5 to Belt Line Road. Follow Belt Line west to the first exit, Coburg Road, and go north. Follow signs to the park.

The shuttle may be run via Interstate 5 south and Oregon 126 east. An intermediate access on river left is located at Harvest Lane boat launch, at the north end of 14th Street in Springfield.

Gauge
McKenzie River at Springfield. The minimum flow is runnable.

Gene Ice and WKCC Editors

Opposite: *Mount Jefferson from Mountain View Eddy, North Santiam River* (Zach Urness)

Mid-Willamette Valley Rivers

Region 5

Marys River

95 Marys River
Wren to Philomath

Class: 1+(2)	Length: 8 miles
Flow: 500–900 cfs	Character: wooded; rural
Gradient: 20 fpm, C	Season: rainy

The Marys River flows east from the Coast Range to its confluence with the Willamette in Corvallis. This mild-mannered and isolated stretch of the river is ideal for canoers and kayakers who are interested in scenery and mild whitewater. The river loops away from the road for much of the run as one passes under one road bridge and five railroad trestles. About 5 miles into the run is a class 2 drop, The Ledge, where a 3-foot drop over the middle right of the ledge is usually the best option. Some very scenic oak-woodland hillsides and cliffs are passed in this section of the river. Take out on the right at the US 20 bridge, up a short but steep trail.

Note: The section of the Marys River below Philomath to its mouth is a poor choice for paddling because of the dense blackberry growth on the stream-banks and the muddy scarps, both of which combine to make it very difficult for portages of the log jams that are sometimes numerous along that stretch.

Hazards

The brushy banks and occasional downed trees can sometimes present problems for novice boaters on this narrow stream. Some maneuvering skills are required.

Access

For take-out, drive to Philomath on US 20 and go 1 mile west of town, where the US 20 highway bridge crosses the Marys. Take an immediate right onto the dirt road there and park. The access is under the bridge on river right.

For put-in, drive upstream 4 miles on the highway to where US 20 crosses the Marys again. Park just past the bridge on the right, well off the highway. Put in below the bridge on river left.

Gauge

Marys River near Philomath. Optimal is 650 cfs for medium-low flows.

Bill Ostrand, Richard Hand, and Laurie Pavey

Luckiamute River

96 Luckiamute River
Rock Pit Creek to 7.9 Miles Above Oregon 223
(Luckiamute Gorge)

Class: 4 T	Length: 4.8 miles
Flow: 200–1500 cfs	Character: forested
Gradient: 56 fpm	Season: rainy

The Luckiamute Gorge is a nearly unknown gem located about halfway between
Wren and Falls City on the eastern side of the Coast Range mountains. This

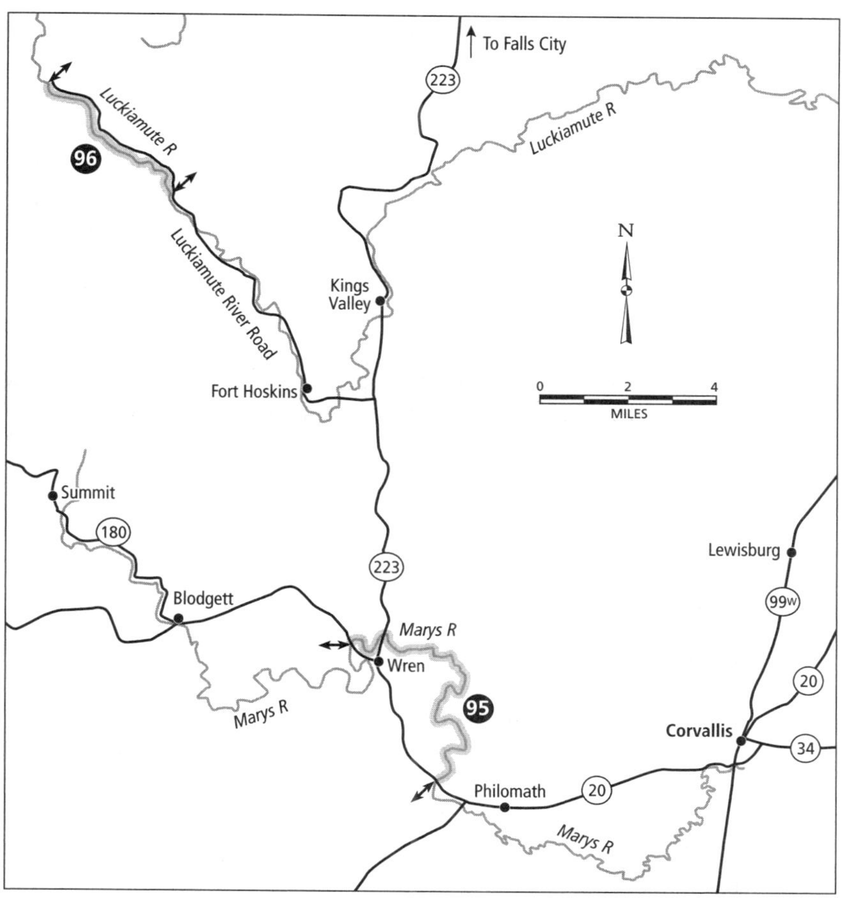

stretch starts out with a bang in the class 4 Gorge, which can be scouted from the road near the put-in. After the Gorge, it mellows to a tight, fast class 3 run until the last big class 3–4 drop, about 0.3 mile above the take-out. This drop features a wave/hole with a nice ledge drop on the left side and can be scouted by walking to the river on the old railroad bed, about 0.2 mile upstream of the take-out.

Hazards

Wood in the Gorge. The section below the take-out is class 4, but be aware that massive logjams at the old railroad bridge pilings are very common.

Access

Take US 20 west out of Philomath. At Oregon 223 near Wren, turn right. Go north 6.4 miles. Turn left onto Hoskins Road, pass Fort Hoskins, and continue up the Luckiamute River Road. At 7.9 miles up from Oregon 223, park at the take-out. There's a pullout on the left.

The take-out is about 0.5 mile upstream from the intersection of Wildwood and Gage roads near the old railroad bed.

The put-in is 4.2 miles farther upstream. There is no obvious put-in; it is a bushwhack down to the river from just above the Gorge.

Gauge

Luckiamute near Suver. The gauge is far downstream and not a reliable indicator. If the Suver gauge is over 2000 cfs and the Siletz is over 1000 cfs, the Luckiamute Gorge section is probably runnable.

Pat Welch

Calapooia River

97 ★ Calapooia River
Gate 9 Miles Above Holley to McClun Wayside

Class: 2+ (3)	Length: 6.8 miles
Flow: 700–3000 cfs	Character: forested; logging; rural
Gradient: 32 fpm, PD	Season: rainy

This class 2 river is a great winter run for class 2 boaters who want to fine-tune their paddling skills. It offers many opportunities to practice eddy turns, maneuver in rapids, and read the currents. The only class 3 rapid, Dollar Drop, is easily portaged.

The run begins just below the occasionally locked gate across the road that accesses the Weyerhaeuser-owned timberland above this run. The put-in is at a pullout a few hundred yards below the gate. Do not leave cars here.

After a half-mile warm-up, the river bends right, and the channel narrows. A class 2 ledge rapid with a tricky curl is followed by the short rapid named The Narrows. More class 1 and 2 water follows for about 1.5 miles.

After passing beneath a bridge, as the river bends left, pull out on the right to scout Dollar Drop. This 4-foot drop over a ledge is commonly run, but can also be easily portaged on the right. Another mile of easy class 1 and 2 water leads to an alternative access on the right, 0.2 mile below the next bridge. (This access is nicknamed "Old Couch" for the old couch that resided here for a long while.)

Below this access, in about 0.5 mile, the river sweeps around several bends in a long class 2+ rapid. The gradient then lessens after the third bridge (concrete), where the road crosses to river left. The last 1.5 miles are mostly class 1. After the fourth bridge, land on the left for the short carry up to McClun Wayside take-out.

Hazards

Scout Dollar Drop. A hazardous reversal forms along the left half of the base. The runout is reasonably good, with a good eddy on the right.

Access

From Interstate 5, take exit 216 for Brownsville and head east on Oregon 228. At the village of Holley, 4 miles upstream from McKercher Park, turn right on Upper Calapooia River Road. Drive 2.1 miles from Holley to McClun Wayside on the left, the take-out. Several short, brushy paths lead to the river.

For the "Old Couch" put-in, drive 5 miles up from Holley to a wide pullout on the right. The uppermost put-in is 8.7 miles upstream of Holley at a wide pullout about 0.1 mile downstream of the gate, where the river is close to the road. As of 2019, Weyerhaeuser owns all the land at and upstream of "Old Couch." Only the road itself is public access. Parking next to the road or walking on their property will result in fines.

Gauge

None exists. The flow is unregulated. For a close estimate of the river's flow, see Pat Welch's flow page: Calapooia River at Holley. An estimated flow of 700 cfs at Holley is low but good. At flows over 3000 cfs, the difficulty increases, eddies are few, and the river flows through brush and trees at the shoreline. Flow fluctuates widely and rapidly in response to rainfall. The flow does not correspond to the Albany gauge.

T. R. Torgersen and WKCC Editors

98 ★ Calapooia River
McClun Wayside to McKercher Park

Class: 2	Length: 7.8 miles
Flow: 400–2500 cfs	Character: rural
Gradient: 21 fpm, PD	Season: rainy

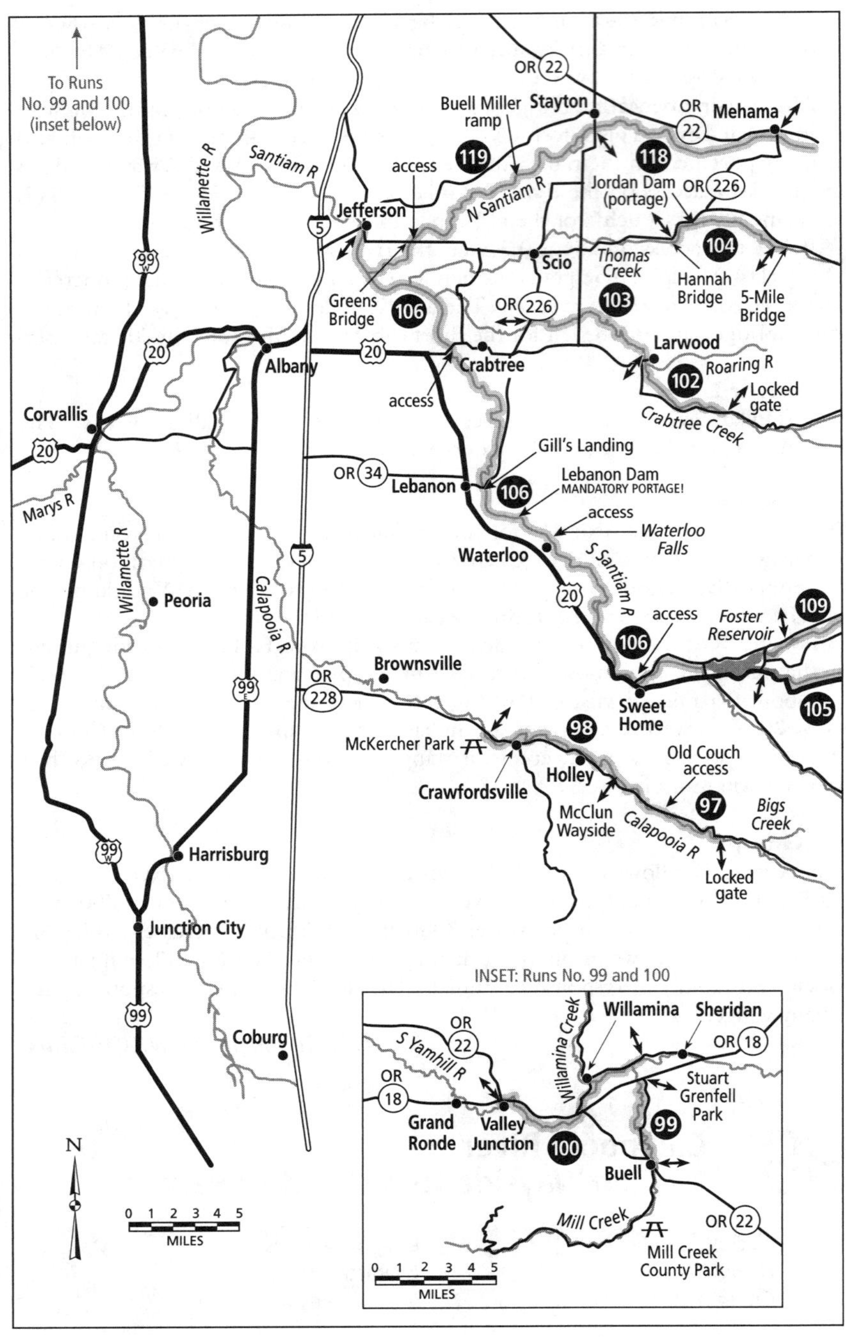
To Runs No. 99 and 100 (inset below)
Willamette R
Santiam R
OR 22
Buell Miller ramp
Stayton
OR 22
Mehama
access
119
118
Jordan Dam (portage)
OR 226
N Santiam R
Jefferson
5
104
Scio
Thomas Creek
Hannah Bridge
5-Mile Bridge
Greens Bridge
106
OR 226
103
99 W
Larwood
Roaring R
Locked gate
20
20
Crabtree
102
Corvallis
access
Crabtree Creek
20
Gill's Landing
Marys R
OR 34
Lebanon
106
Lebanon Dam MANDATORY PORTAGE!
access
Waterloo Falls
Waterloo
S Santiam R
20
Willamette R
access
Foster Reservoir
109
Peoria
Calapooia R
5
106
Brownsville
OR 228
Sweet Home
105
99
McKercher Park
98
Old Couch access
Crawfordsville
Holley
97
Bigs Creek
McClun Wayside
Calapooia R
99 W
Harrisburg
Locked gate
Junction City
INSET: Runs No. 99 and 100
99
Coburg
S Yamhill R
OR 22
Willamina Creek
Willamina
Sheridan
OR 18
OR 18
Stuart Grenfell Park
Grand Ronde
Valley Junction
100
99
Buell
N
Mill Creek
OR 22
0 1 2 3 4 5
MILES
Mill Creek County Park
0 1 2 3 4 5
MILES

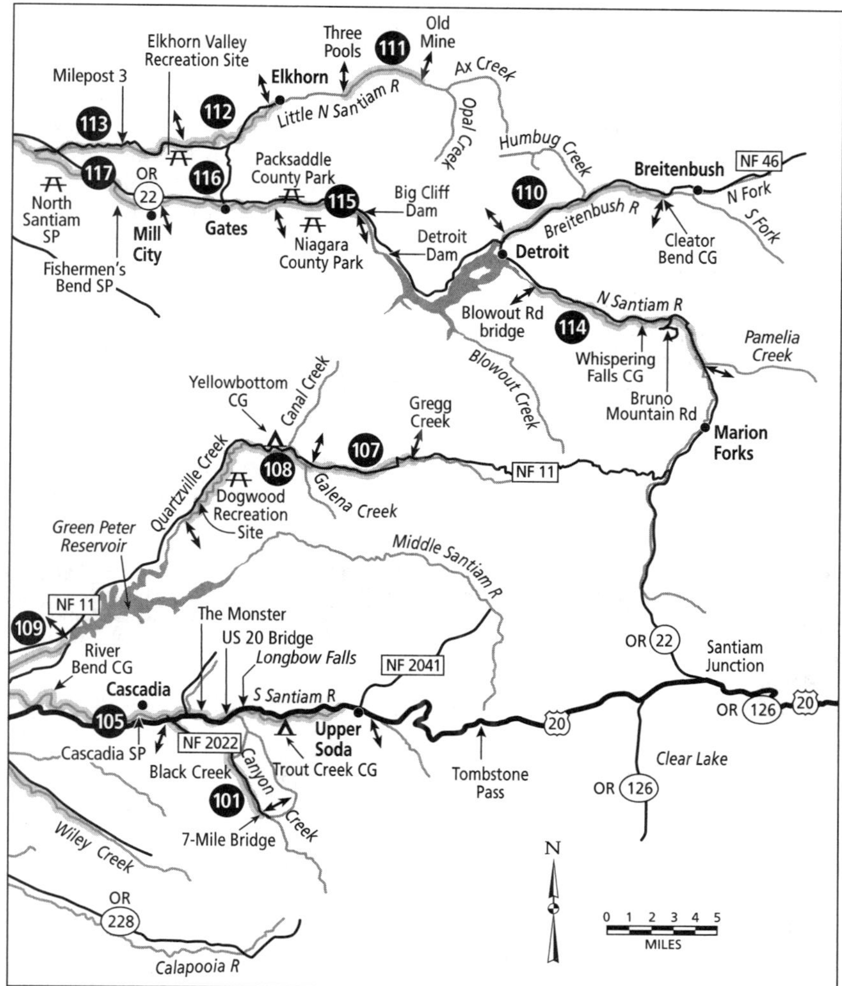

This pleasant run through farmland and alongside small towns exhibits lower gradient than the upper runs, but the river still maintains reasonable speed. There are a few class 2 rapids scattered throughout the run. The most difficult rapid is over a rocky shelf 0.2 mile below the double bridges at Crawfordsville.

Hazards

Widely fluctuating, storm-influenced flows make sweepers and debris jams potential hazards. The class 2 rapid just below Crawfordsville may warrant scouting; land on the left.

Access

From Interstate 5, take exit 216 for Brownsville and head east on Oregon 228. Leave a shuttle car 5.8 miles east of Brownsville at McKercher Park. Scout the take-out area at McKercher Park before launching. Most boaters opt to take out at the upper end of the park to avoid running McKercher Falls, class 4. If one chooses to run the falls, there is a take-out eddy on the right below the falls with a short carry back to the parking area. To get to the put-in, continue east on Oregon 228 for 4.6 miles to the town of Holley. Turn right at the Holly Market and reset your odometer. Follow Upper Calapooia Road upstream to the put-in at McClun Wayside Park. It is 2.1 miles up from Holley on the left. There are several brushy paths to the river.

If a longer trip is desired, boaters can add on the lower 3 miles of the run above this one by putting in above McClun at the access called "The Old Couch." See the run Calapooia River: Gate 9 Miles Above Holley to McClun Wayside for more details.

Gauge

See the run Calapooia River: Gate 9 Miles Above Holley to McClun Wayside.

T. R. Torgersen and WKCC Editors

Mill Creek

99 Mill Creek
Buell Park to Stuart Grenfell Park

Class: 2- T	Length: 5.6 miles
Flow: 500–1500 cfs	Character: forested; agricultural
Gradient: 23 fpm, C	Season: rainy

This run on Mill Creek is quite enjoyable at medium to high water when numerous class 2 surfing waves develop. When many other local rivers are too high to run, this one is usually a good choice. Large maples, oaks, alders, and cottonwoods line the banks of the creek. The scenery is better than one might expect so near agricultural fields. The take-out at Stuart Grenfell Park is on the right, just upstream of the highway bridge.

Hazards

Trees can block the entire river, but the alert boater will find it possible to land in time.

Access

Oregon 22 crosses Mill Creek about 22 miles west of Salem. Just west of the bridge, go north on Mill Creek Road. Drive downstream 0.2 mile to Buell Park on the right, the put-in.

To reach the take-out, continue north on Mill Creek Road for 0.4 mile and then turn right on Harmony Road. Continue north on Harmony Road for 4.2

miles. Before reaching Oregon 18, turn left into Stuart Grenfell Park and proceed west to the river, the take-out.

Gauge

None exists. The flow is unregulated. This run is runnable after long or hard rains; the flow fluctuates rapidly. If the South Fork Yamhill River at Willamina gauge is at 2000 cfs, the flow is probably good.

Rob Blickensderfer and WKCC Editors

South Fork Yamhill River

100 South Fork Yamhill River
Valley Junction to Willamina

Class: 2(3) T	Length: 8.5 miles
Flow: 700–3000 cfs	Character: wooded; flat
Gradient: 10 fpm, PD	Season: rainy

This run keeps open canoers busy and entertains beginning kayakers with many good surfing waves. The river has several 2- to 3-foot ledge drops and passes under three bridges. The optional take-out, at Hampton Park in Willamina, allows a boater to take out before the class 3 Willamina Ledge and shortens the run to 6.1 miles. The lower take-out is about 1 mile below the Willamina Ledge. Look for it on the left, just below the Mill Creek confluence.

Hazards

The Willamina Ledge, at mile 7.2, is difficult to scout because the riverbanks are so steep that it is hard to get out of one's boat. A fast riffle leading to the ledge makes it difficult to get close enough in a boat to pick a safe route. Parts of the ledge have potentially dangerous reversals. To scout, land on the left bank above the sawmill. The far left chute and the chute about one-third of the way from the right bank are feasible. Other ledges can be run by experienced boaters without scouting.

Access

From the Mid-Willamette Valley, take Oregon 18 west from McMinnville or Oregon 22 west from the Salem area toward Willamina. At the junction of Oregon 18 and 22, take Oregon 18 Business northward to Willamina. The first take-out is in downtown Willamina. Turn right on Northeast E Street, go two blocks, turn left on Yamhill Avenue and into Hampton Park. Drive to the end of the road and walk 100 feet farther to a good path that leads down to the river. For the longer run, start at the intersection of Oregon 18 and Willamina Creek Road in Willamina. Drive 2.4 miles northeastward, on Oregon 18, through Willamina, to a wide gravel parking area along the right side of the highway. Locate the electric power pole on the right and go 70 feet downstream to the small trail through the trees and brush.

For the put-in, drive back to the intersection of Oregon 18 and 22. From there, continue 4.2 miles toward Valley Junction. Stay on Oregon 22 where it turns right, then immediately turn right into the large parking area, which provides excellent access to the river.

Gauge

South Yamhill River at McMinnville. The flow is unregulated.

Rob Blickensderfer

South Santiam River and Tributaries

101 Canyon Creek
7-Mile Bridge to South Santiam River

Class: 5 T	Length: 7.4 miles
Flow: 200–1000 cfs	Character: forested; canyon
Gradient: 102 fpm, C/PD	Season: rainy

Canyon Creek is one of the few true class 5 creeks in Oregon. Steep, continuous drops with undercuts and log hazards make Canyon Creek an excellent run for expert boaters. Unstable geology also makes Canyon Creek one of the more dynamic creeks in Oregon, with rapids changing every few years after big flood events. Only a couple of the big rapids can be scouted beforehand, so consider carefully before committing to the run. A landslide has cut this run into a lower 5-mile class 4 run and a technically demanding 2.5-mile class 5 upper run.

On this upper section, the first 0.5 mile of the run is flat, with several logs, and it gives no indication of the intense rapids found farther downstream. The first major rapid, Chocolate Chips, consists of a tricky ledge drop at the top and a narrow slot into a hole at the bottom. Scout/portage on the right. Another 100 yards downstream is the beginning of Chicken Little, a long, complex boulder garden that often contains wood. Several sharp ledges and steep boulder gardens follow Chicken Little all the way to Terminator. Boaters must run the narrow slot on the right to avoid being pushed into a dangerous sieve on the left. Scout/portage on the right. Immediately below Terminator is a very steep boulder garden, Day of Judgment. This rapid changed dramatically in 2007 when a gigantic boulder fell into the rapid, turning it into a class 5++ rapid. Portage on the right. The lower run starts below Day of Judgment where Black Creek enters. Steep rapids continue for a mile before the gradient decreases and the rapids become smaller and less frequent.

Be on the lookout for a steep drop near the middle of this flatter section. Osprey Rapid can be scouted or portaged on the right. The mile above the take-out contains many fun class 3–4 rapids set in a beautiful canyon and is a great way to end the day after the challenging rapids upstream.

Hazards

Unstable geology can change rapids and deposit dangerous wood in many of the rapids. Large hydraulics develop at high water and make several of the harder rapids very dangerous.

Access

US 20, east of Albany and Sweet Home, follows the South Santiam River. East of Cascadia State Park 1.8 miles, US 20 crosses Canyon Creek. Turn north (left) on a short spur road that leads to the confluence of Canyon Creek with the South Santiam River, the take-out.

For the lower put-in, follow Canyon Creek Road (NF 2022) along Canyon Creek for 5 miles to a landslide that blocks the road. Follow the trail down to the creek. The 300-foot-long trail begins next to the bridge over Black Creek. In order to reach the upper put-in at 7-Mile Bridge, you must drive a long way around on forest roads that are often snowed in when the river is running.

To reach the upper put-in, drive east from the take-out on US 20 for 2.7 miles and turn right on NF 2032. Twist your way up for about 7 miles to NF 145, turn right. Go about 7 miles to the junction with Canyon Creek Road, turn right. Go 0.75 mile to the junction of NF 2026, turn left. Go 0.1 mile to the put-in bridge over Canyon Creek.

Gauge

None exists. For a close estimation of the flow, see Pat Welch's flow page: Canyon Creek. A good level is between 350 and 500 cfs.

Pete Giordano and WKCC Editors

102 ★ Crabtree Creek
Concrete Bridge (Locked Gate) to
Larwood Covered Bridge

Class: 3- T	Length: 5.5 miles
Flow: 650–1500 cfs	Character: forested; rural
Gradient: 57 fpm, C	Season: rainy

Crabtree Creek is located between the South Santiam River and Thomas Creek. From the put-in below the concrete bridge at the locked gate, the action begins immediately. Several large bedrock ledges throughout the run create class 2+ to 3- rapids. Many surfing waves spice up the action. In a number of places, the creek flows steeply into a curve, with the possibility of a tree or log partially blocking the route. Quick and careful maneuvering is required. Midway through the run, at a curve to the left, is Squeaker Rapid. Here the creek drops over a ledge producing a large hole on the right that surprises many paddlers. A safe route is to the left of the hole, squeaking by in the narrow left channel. In the lower half, the gradient lessens, but a couple of islands split the creek's flow and present opportunities for wood blockages. Be sure to scout on blind curves. Take out on the right just below the covered bridge.

Hazards

At high flows, the brushy banks and the speed of the water eliminate most eddies. Sweepers could be a problem in this narrow streambed. Portages through the brush can sometimes be difficult. Heavy logging in the basin and high water have combined to increase the presence of wood throughout the run. Most logs are on the bank, but can shift from year to year.

Access

To reach Crabtree Creek, take US 20 east from Albany 5.4 miles, then Oregon 226 eastward 4.7 miles, and turn right onto Fish Hatchery Road. After 6.5 miles, at the three-way intersection, turn left toward the Larwood covered bridge; cross the bridge and turn left into the parking area, the take-out.

For the put-in, go back across Larwood Bridge, turn left on Meridian Road, go 0.6 mile, and turn left on East Lacomb Road. Go 1.8 miles and turn left onto Island Inn Drive. Head upstream following the river for 1.7 miles, go right, and immediately left again. Continue upstream for 1.2 miles to the concrete bridge with a locked gate. The put-in is just below the bridge on river left.

Gauge

None exists. For a close estimate of the flow, see Pat Welch's flow page: Crabtree Creek. Flows over 2000 cfs are not recommended, due to the scarcity of eddies in which to stop.

Lance Stein, Rob Blickensderfer, and Laurie Pavey

103 Crabtree Creek
Larwood Covered Bridge to Oregon 226 Bridge

Class: 2-	Length: 8.3 miles
Flow: 600–1500 cfs	Character: rural; wooded
Gradient: 16 fpm, C	Season: rainy

The lower river contrasts dramatically with the upper as Crabtree Creek empties into lightly wooded farmland. The first 6 miles provide steady class 1+ and 2- water with a few play spots. The last few miles to Oregon 226 are still swift but with only occasional class 1+ riffles. The take-out is at the Oregon 226 bridge.

Note: It is possible to run below here for 16 miles of mostly class 1 water with a class 2 ledge drop about 4 miles down. The creek first enters the South Santiam and then the main Santiam, with a take-out at the bridge in Jefferson.

Hazards

None in particular, but always watch for strainers and downed trees blocking the channels.

Access

To reach the put-in, see the directions for the Larwood covered bridge in the run Crabtree Creek: Concrete Bridge to Larwood Covered Bridge.

The take-out is located 1.5 mile north of Fish Hatchery Road on Oregon 226. There's a pullout about 100 yards north of the bridge.

Gauge

None exists. For a close estimate of the flow, see Pat Welch's flow page: Crabtree Creek.

Carl Landsness and WKCC Editors

104 ★ Thomas Creek
5-Mile Bridge to Hannah Bridge

Class: 2+(3) P T	Length: 6 miles
Flow: 900–2500 cfs	Character: forested; logging; rural
Gradient: 49 fpm, PD	Season: rainy

From the bridge at the put-in, the river moves right along. Some rather steep rocky drops occur; most can be scouted by boat. The rapids seen from Oregon 226 between Hannah Bridge and Jordan Bridge are typical of the difficulty of this run.

A few river bends after put-in, look for the good surf wave next to a waterfall on the left. The rapids between mile 2 and 3 on the run are steeper and more continuous than other parts of the run. Around mile 4 look for the Jordan Dam portage area. The river bends sharply left just above the dam. Take out well above the dam on river right in the large eddy. Walk up to the road, then put in again underneath, or slightly downstream of, the road bridge.

The class 3 rapid below the bridge is in three parts, separated by short pools. This section of the run should be checked for log blockages during the shuttle. A superb surf play wave/hole is found at the bottom of this section on the right. The rapid below here has current that runs into an occasionally brushy bank on the left, with turbulence on the right; use caution.

The take-out is on river right at Hannah Bridge. Stay close to the pilings to avoid private property while ascending from the river.

Hazards

The old Jordan Dam and the chute below should be portaged on the right. The main current sweeps under brush in several places, especially at low flow. Watch for wood blockages.

Portaging Jordan Dam on Thomas Creek (Zach Urness)

Access
Take US 20 east from Albany for 5.4 miles; turn left and follow Oregon 226 north to Scio. Turn right, staying on Oregon 226, and go 6.5 more miles. Turn right onto Camp Morrison Drive, cross the Hannah Bridge, and park. This is the take-out.

To reach the put-in, return to Oregon 226, turn right, and go 2.5 miles. Take a right onto Thomas Creek Drive and go 4.6 miles to the locked gate. The land upstream of the gate is privately owned by Weyerhaeuser, and access is denied. The put-in is downstream of the bridge on river right.

Gauge
Thomas Creek at Scio. Optimal flow is 1200–1600 cfs. This run becomes class 3 at flows over 2000.

Mark Hower and Laurie Pavey

105 ★ South Santiam River Above Soda Fork to Foster Reservoir

Class: 3–4(5+) P	Length: 5 to 19 miles
Flow: 700–3000 cfs	Character: forested; canyon
Gradient: 40 fpm, PD	Season: rainy/snowmelt

The upper South Santiam is magnificent. This run can be made only after substantial rainfall or snowmelt. The rapids are pool-drop, and all the more difficult rapids can be portaged. The upper South Santiam can be divided into three sections.

SECTION 1: 0.8 MILE ABOVE SODA FORK TO US 20 BRIDGE, 7.9 MILES, CLASS 3

Many surf waves and short ledge drops in this section keep paddlers busy and entertained. Although mostly class 2+ in nature, the run has four short rapids that are rated class 3. It's a good idea to scout these rapids for wood blockages.

The run starts with some maneuvering through a shallow boulder garden, followed by a mini canyon, rated class 3-. Soda Fork soon enters on the right and increases the flow. Fernview Fun (class 3) is just above the bridge to Fernview Campground. It's an easy road scout from the bridge leading to the campground. Airplane Turn (class 3) is just below the first large observation platform on river right. Scout on river right or from the road (just downstream of milepost 49). Longbow Falls, a 4-foot drop, is the biggest single drop on this section. It can be scouted from the road at milepost 47.5. On the river, look for it about 0.2 mile below the second large observation platform, just after an area where the river takes a sharp turn to the left and the road is nearby. Most paddlers choose the far right chute at the falls. Cha-Cha-Cha is about 0.3 mile below Longbow Falls. Usually this short class 3 drop is read and run, but watch out for the hole in the bottom center. Scout the take-out eddy at the highway bridge, as it may be small depending on the flow; right and left eddies have both been used. Below this bridge, the rapids are much more difficult, so be sure to make your eddy if you're not up for the next section's rapids.

Note: The river above this section is very steep and choked with logs.

SECTION 2: US 20 BRIDGE TO CASCADIA STATE PARK, 5 MILES, CLASS 4 (5+, P)

This is the most challenging stretch of whitewater on the river. Most of these rapids are peppered with large rocks and require quick judgment, skillful maneuvering, and a good roll. As in most high Cascade rivers, logs can be a problem. The Monster, 2 miles after the US 20 bridge, is class 5+ and can be portaged either up the left bank to the road or over the rocks on the right. Crawdad Rapid, a small twisty drop only 20 yards below The Monster, looks easy but munches a lot of boaters.

A mile below The Monster is Tomco Falls, adjacent to the old Tomco Mill. This true waterfall has a 5- to 10-foot double drop. The height of the falls is usually about 8 feet; however, the estimate will vary as you scout it, go over it, and look back up at it. As the flow increases, the height of the drop decreases. The runout is turbulent but free of rocks and other rapids. The easiest portage is on the left, but at low water you may be able to portage over the rocks on the right. Some boaters seal launch the second part of the drop at low water.

Shortly after Tomco Falls, a series of large haystacks is followed by a small drop with a tricky hole that throws boats against the left wall. Eddies exist on both sides above the hole. Catch the right eddy and sneak the hole on the right. Shortly after this hole, the river narrows to less than 10 feet. The gap can be blocked by a log, hence the name The Plug. Below The Plug is a long gorge. On this very scenic stretch, the river runs for 1 mile between 30- and 50-foot-high rock walls. Notwithstanding the proximity of the road, you will likely feel incredibly isolated. The rapids in the gorge are less violent than those upstream. The gorge section ends at Cascadia Park. A gravel bar on the right, 200 yards upstream from the bridge, is the take-out. Stairs and a railed path lead to the parking lot. This lovely park is complete with rest rooms, picnic areas, and a soda spring.

SECTION 3: CASCADIA STATE PARK TO FOSTER RESERVOIR, 6.5 MILES, CLASS 3(4)

The first several miles include a few class 3 rapids that are interspersed with class 1 and 2 rapids. Tree Farm Rapid is a class 4+ maze of rocks, slots, and turbulence; scout or portage on the right. After Tree Farm Rapid, the river contains long, flat stretches between rapids with good surfing waves. Below the recommended take-out, the river flows through a deep canyon with a few easier rapids before reaching Foster Reservoir.

Hazards

Wood can be a problem. Do not run blind drops without checking for wood. Several rapids should be scouted before running: Longbow Falls, The Monster, Crawdad, Tomco, The Plug, and Tree Farm. The first three can be seen from the road. The Monster (class 5+) is seen near a left turn in the road (driving downriver) about 1.5 miles downstream of the US 20 bridge. The Monster can be portaged on either side and requires some effort. Tomco Falls, The Plug, and Tree Farm can all be scouted (and portaged) from the riverbanks.

Access

Section 1: US 20 east of Albany follows the South Santiam River. Upper Soda (formerly called Mountain House Restaurant, but now a private residence) is about 24 miles east of Sweet Home. The uppermost put-in is 0.8 mile above Upper Soda, at milepost 53.5. A pullout on the right is above a small trail to the river.

The take-out is at the US 20 bridge at milepost 46. Scout your take-out eddy; it may be small.

Section 2: Put in at the US 20 bridge. If you want to warm up, put in farther upstream along US 20.

The take-out is located at Cascadia State Park (milepost 41.3), about 11 miles upstream of Sweet Home.

Section 3: Put in at Cascadia State Park.

If you are camping at River Bend Campground near milepost 36.5, you can take out there. Otherwise, take out at the steep trail located at a small parking area at milepost 35.8 on US 20. The lowest take-out, requiring a 2.5-mile flatwater paddle, is at Quartzville Road (just off US 20) just east of Foster, or at the boat ramp below the road on the left.

Gauge

South Santiam River at Cascadia.

Chet Koblinsky, Rob Blickensderfer, and WKCC Editors

106 South Santiam River Foster Dam to Jefferson

Class: 1 P; 2(4) P	Length: 3 to 40 miles
Flow: 900 cfs; 1500–3000 cfs	Character: rural
Gradient: 8 fpm for the 40 miles	Season: year-round

The South Santiam below the dam has characteristics typical of most rivers within the Willamette Valley: tree-lined dirt banks, gravel bars, riffles, and sweepers. The river flows rather slowly in most places, but the scenery is better than one might expect so near population centers. The run is divided into five sections that can each be run separately, each with its own put-in and take-out. The sections can also be combined as desired.

SECTION 1: FOSTER DAM TO SWEET HOME, 3 MILES

This short section has the most action on this run, with small, evenly spaced class 1+ rapids at low flows. At high flows, canoers find an exciting class 2 run. At flood levels, kayakers find many excellent surfing waves. The put-in for this section is at Andrew Wiley Park at the base of Foster Dam on river left. The most difficult rapid is the S turn about 2 miles below Foster Dam. Just past the water intake for Sweet Home, a fine surfing wave is located where the river drops into the large pool near the end of the run. The take-out is at the Pleasant Valley Road boat ramp in Sweet Home on the south side of the river upstream of the bridge.

SECTION 2: SWEET HOME TO WATERLOO, 11 MILES

Warning: There is a falls at Waterloo. The put-in is the Sweet Home boat ramp (described above). The only major rapid, US 20 Rapid, occurs 2 miles below Sweet Home as the river bounds off the highway embankment on the left. Large standing waves and strong eddies here provide an excellent spot for practicing surfing and ferrying. Beyond are only a few more small shelves before the river flattens out for the rest of the way to Waterloo Falls. Expert whitewater kayakers sometimes run Waterloo Falls, class 4–4+. Unless you are prepared to run Waterloo Falls, take out on the left above the falls, in Waterloo Park.

SECTION 3: WATERLOO TO LEBANON, 5 MILES

The put-in is below the falls in Waterloo Park. The river flows nicely for the first 2 miles and then slows as gravel-pit workings are seen and a dam is approached. The fairly difficult but mandatory portage of the 10-foot dam is on the right. Never attempt to run the dam in any type of craft, because the backwash can hold bodies or rafts for hours or days. The take-out is on the left, just upstream of the bridge at Gill's Landing in River Park.

SECTION 4: LEBANON TO CRABTREE, 11 MILES

Put in on the left at River Park in Lebanon. The river is class 1 at flows up to 3000 cfs. It is characterized by flatwater, gravel bars, and sweepers. A poor take-out with no boat ramp is at the bridge on Oregon 226 about 1 mile west of Crabtree. A good take-out on river left about 0.1 mile downstream of the bridge is available upon prior purchase of a permit from the Linn County Road Department.

SECTION 5: CRABTREE TO JEFFERSON, 10 MILES

Put in at either of the take-outs mentioned above for the previous section. This section is similar in character to the previous section. After 8 miles, the North Santiam River enters from the right, and the volume increases for the last 2 miles on the Santiam River. The take-out in Jefferson is at a boat ramp on the right 100 yards downstream of the US 99E bridge.

Hazards

Rapids to watch for are those located 2 miles below Foster Dam and the US 20 Rapid. Waterloo Falls is usually portaged. The 10-foot dam below Waterloo must be portaged. Never attempt to run the dam in any type of craft. Watch for sweepers and downed trees in the river.

Access

Put-ins and take-outs are given above for each section. The put-in for the entire run is Andrew Wiley Park at the base of Foster Dam on river left. From Interstate 5 at Albany, take US 20 east to about 1 mile east of Sweet Home and follow the signs to the park, which is about 0.5 mile north of US 20.

The take-out for the entire run is in Jefferson, about 6 miles north of Albany. To reach the take-out, take exit 238 off Interstate 5 and follow the Jefferson Highway east for 2.5 miles to Jefferson. The take-out is about 100 yards downstream of the Jefferson bridge, on river right.

Gauge

South Santiam River near Foster. The flow is controlled at Foster Dam. A minimum flow of 900 cfs is maintained during the summer. Flows over 3000 cfs are not recommended for beginners.

Rob Blickensderfer and WKCC Editors

Middle Santiam River and Tributaries

107 ★ Quartzville Creek
Above Gregg Creek to Galena Creek

Class: 4+(5+); 5(5+)	Length: 5.2 miles
Flow: 700 cfs; 2000 cfs	Character: forested; mining
Gradient: 110 fpm, PD	Season: rainy/snowmelt

Clear water, old growth trees, and short, thrilling drops make a first trip down this section an unforgettable experience. That said, in a few places a missed line could have serious consequences, so be careful.

The run begins with a 0.5-mile warm-up section and then paddlers arrive at Technical Difficulties (TD), the longest single rapid on the run. TD starts out with a steep boulder garden and ends with an 8-foot ledge that is usually run middle or left. The boulder garden has a pin spot that has caused some problems in the past about halfway down. Look for a 2-foot pour-over and boof left here. The rock in the pour-over can be spotted from the road far overhead if you look carefully and the flows are right. Even grazing this rock can stall you enough that you slide back into the hole, so be careful here, too. Immediately below TD on a left turn with a small island in the middle of the river is Grocker, a fun ledgy drop that can be run on either side, although most boaters opt for the exciting 6-foot boof on the left side.

More fun drops continue as you work your way down the river. Immediately downstream of the first road bridge is Wrapped Bridge Rapid, a small rapid that contains the remains of the old road bridge on the right. Below Wrapped Bridge is Pick-Up Sticks, a rapid complicated by an enormous logjam blocking most of the flow. Some years it has been possible to run this rapid on the right, but it may be blocked with wood. Approach this drop carefully as most of the current plows into and under the logs in the middle—if you blunder into this one, you won't be found until summer.

The last major drop on this section is Double Dip, a very dangerous series of ledges that terminates in an evil, narrow pour-over backed up by the wall on the left. Double Dip is the kind of drop where you could do everything right and still get the beating of a lifetime (or drown, for that matter). Double Dip should only be run after taking every possible safety precaution.

Hazards

Double Dip is extremely dangerous and should be portaged on the left. Be on the lookout for wood in several of the steep, narrow drops.

Access

From Interstate 5 at Albany, take US 20 east to Sweet Home. Take Quartzville Road (NF 11), which follows the river on its north side past Foster Lake to Green

Peter Reservoir for approximately 25.8 miles to the bridge below Galena Creek. There is a take-out just above Double Dip at 27 miles, or an alternative take-out is at the bridge 27.8 miles from US 20.

The put-in is located about 31 miles from US 20 on the right before the bridge.

Gauge

Quartzville Creek near Cascadia. The gauge is very far downstream. Keep this in mind for estimating actual flows. Also keep in mind that snowfall and snowmelt are major factors in the runoff.

Jason Rackley and Pete Giordano

108 ★ Quartzville Creek
Galena Creek to Green Peter Reservoir

Class: 4; 5	Length: 9.4 miles
Flow: 800–3000 cfs; 7500 cfs	Character: forested
Gradient: 58 fpm, PD	Season: rainy/snowmelt

Lower Quartzville does not have quite the gradient and is not as intense as the upper run, but its pool-drop character still presents a challenge. At 800 cfs, stretches of relatively calm water culminate in 6- to 8-foot vertical or very technical drops; the whole run is quite rocky. At 1500 cfs, the run is at its easiest, and play spots abound. Above 2500 cfs, large waves and holes punctuate almost every rapid, but routes are fairly easy to find. At flows of 6000–7500 cfs, it is a hardy class 4+. Over 7500 cfs, the run is class 5.

The most serious drops/rapids occur within the first and last 2 miles of the run. The three big ledges upstream of Yellowbottom Campground are definitely worth scouting. The first occurs after a hard left bend and can be scouted on the right. Just downstream, a house-size boulder marks the spot of the second drop. At low flows, keep right and punch the hole between the boulder and the side of the cliff. At higher flows, a sneak chute on the far left is recommended. The third ledge is a bit farther downstream and is usually run on river left with momentum. The middle 6 miles are mainly class 2+ to 3. Do not get too complacent as the few class 3–3+ ledges in this section have sticky holes that have surprised good boaters. Bankshot and Tractor Beam, both class 3+ to 4 rapids, can be seen from the shuttle road. Bankshot, 0.2 mile below the second bridge, is a blind turn to the right against the left wall. Tractor Beam is an S-turn rapid a quarter-mile below Bankshot. Large waves, play spots, holes, and a few flatter stretches of river continue until passing Dogwood Recreation Site, an alternative take-out site on the right. In about 0.3 mile, just past a waterfall on the left, the action begins again. Several long class 4 boulder gardens spice up this last section as the river drops relentlessly toward the reservoir.

Hazards

Most of the ledges on this run have sticky holes that only get worse at higher flows. On the drive up, scout the first three ledges and the class 4 boulder gardens at the end of the run. Most other hazards are seen on the drive up or can be scouted easily once on the river.

Access

From Interstate 5 at Albany, take US 20 east to Sweet Home. At the east end of Sweet Home, turn left on Quartzville Road (NF 11) and reset your odometer. Follow this road as it passes Foster and Green Peter reservoirs. At approximately 16.5 miles past US 20, turn right at a camping area along the upper part of the reservoir. This is the take-out. Dogwood Recreation Site, 18 miles from US 20, is a convenient take-out for paddlers wanting to skip the class 4 gorge rapids in the last 2 miles of the run.

Next up the road is Yellowbottom Campground, at mile 23.6, which is a convenient put-in spot for boaters who wish to skip the upper 2 miles of class 4 rapids. And finally, reach the upper put-in at the bridge below Galena Creek, which is 25.8 miles upstream from US 20.

Gauge

Quartzville Creek near Cascadia.

Ron Mattson, Lance Stein, and WKCC Editors

109 Middle Santiam River
Green Peter Dam to Foster Reservoir

Class: 4	Length: 2.5 miles
Flow: 2000–4000 cfs	Character: canyon
Gradient: 21 fpm, PD	Season: dam controlled

Although short, this run offers some of the best whitewater available in the mid-Willamette area during the summer. Green Peter Dam has two generating turbines, each of which requires about 2000 cfs. The flow from the dam is determined by electricity demand. When one turbine is in operation (also called one "unit"), the flow is up to 2000 cfs. If both generators are operating, the flow can be up to 4000 cfs. The water released comes from the bottom of the lake and is very cold, even on a very hot day. Abrupt releases change the nature of the run very quickly.

The last three rapids—Swiss Cheese, Scrawley's Wall, and Concussion—are the major rapids on the run. Swiss Cheese consists of several ledge drops that produce nice play waves at a flow of one unit. At two units, the ledges produce many large holes. The right is the usual route. Parties can regroup at the short pool before the second drop, Scrawley's Wall, where the river forms standing waves and can push the boater very close to the left wall. Another short pool provides a second regrouping spot before Concussion, the grand finale. Concussion is formidable and has lived up to its name at both water levels. At all flows, the right chute is recommended. Boaters generally catch the eddy on the right at the top of the rapid and then ferry across the current to the middle of the river to avoid a large hole. Several large holes and waves confront boaters before the rapid ends abruptly in the slack water of Foster Reservoir. The center chute has been run, but it contains a very dangerous rock sieve. Several good boaters have had close calls, and rescue in the event of problems is very difficult. Once boaters reach the reservoir, it is a short paddle to the take-out.

Hazards

Swiss Cheese, Scrawley's Wall, and Concussion present difficulties. A dangerous sieve lies in the middle chute of Concussion. Concussion can be scouted by parking at a spot 3.3 miles from US 20 and hiking down the steep bank to the river. Beware of abrupt releases from Green Peter Dam. Even in the middle of summer, the water is extremely cold.

Access

From Interstate 5 at Albany, take US 20 east to Sweet Home. At Sweet Home, take a left onto NF 11, the road to Quartzville at the upper end of Foster Reservoir. The take-out is 2.6 miles from US 20 on NF 11. A wide turnout on the right offers several trails to the top end of the reservoir just past where the current ends.

To reach the put-in, continue up the road along the river toward Green Peter Dam. At 4.4 miles from US 20, park near the first road to the right. Because the gate is locked, boats must be carried 0.5 mile down the road toward the dam. When nearing the dam, go through the gate on the right near a small building and put in on the rocks below.

Gauge

The schedule for water releases from Green Peter Dam can be obtained from Foster Dam one or two days in advance. Call 541-367-5132.

Ron Mattson and WKCC Editors

North Santiam River and Tributaries

110 ★ Breitenbush River
Cleator Bend Campground to Detroit Reservoir

Class: 4 T	Length: 7.8 miles
Flow: 400–2500 cfs	Character: forested; canyon
Gradient: 66 fpm, PD	Season: rainy/snowmelt

The Breitenbush River starts at the crest of the Cascades north of Mount Jefferson and is one of the major tributaries of the North Santiam River. This run is one of the best intermediate runs in the Cascades, with numerous rapids, crystal-clear water, and beautiful scenery.

This run is rated class 4 because the drops are so closely spaced and require technical precision to run, although the individual drops are mostly class 3. It might be said that the whole is greater than the sum of the parts. The pools are short, and the route is often not apparent until you are almost at the brink of a drop, and sometimes it is not visible even then.

SECTION 1: CLEATOR BEND CAMPGROUND TO ROAD BRIDGE, 5.8 MILES

This upper section has tight and technical rapids, with many class 3 drops. Short pools are found between the rapids and many eddies. Chutes are narrow, twisting, swift, and deep. Several blind corners should be scouted for logs by at least one member of the party. The run starts with one warm-up rapid before you encounter The Slot. This rapid has a deceptively sticky 4-foot ledge. It then races another 25 yards between sheer rock walls. About 0.5 mile below the slot is The Notch, a V-shaped ledge that is best run on the far right. Run the sticky hole just below a narrow gorge with caution, on the right. Several larger rapids in the middle of this stretch should be scouted.

SECTION 2: ROAD BRIDGE TO DETROIT RESERVOIR, 2 MILES

This stretch is markedly different from the upper 6 miles. Big, pushy rapids are separated by small boulder gardens. About 0.7 mile below the bridge, boaters encounter an island on a sharp left turn. This is the lead-in to Barbell Rapid. Barbell Rapid should be scouted (though with some difficulty) on the drive upriver, 2.8 miles above Detroit, since it is even more difficult to scout from the river. The right channel contains a sticky ledge that should be run on the right with momentum. The left side is a steep boulder garden. Much of the current pushes into the right wall at the end of the rapid. Be careful, as this wall is undercut. A half-mile below Barbell is Woo-Man-Chew, a 7-foot waterfall that drops into a deep pool. Scout on the left by landing at the low concrete structure. Woo-Man-Chew looks a lot worse than it really is. At low and medium flows, a run down the middle with momentum is pretty forgiving. At high water, this drop can recycle boats and swimmers—particularly boaters using small boats—for extended periods of time. The usual take-out is on the left at the gauging station, about 0.5 mile below Woo-Man-Chew. Class 2 rapids continue to the reservoir. When the reservoir is full, the flatwater extends to just above the Upper Arm Day Use Area, an alternative access. When the reservoir is low, the rapids continue past the town of Detroit, but the access is steep below the highway bridge.

Hazards

This river requires a class 4 level of concentration and quick reactions. A quick reliable roll is mandatory. Logs are always a threat, especially in the narrower upper section, so be sure to scout all blind drops.

Access

From Interstate 5 near Salem, take Oregon 22 east to the town of Detroit, at the east end of Detroit Reservoir. From Detroit, take NF 46 east toward Breitenbush Hot Springs. The usual take-out is at the USGS gauge station 1.7 miles up the road where there's a pullout on the left. This is 0.8 mile upstream of the Upper Arm Day Use Area (fee site, open seasonally), which is an alternative take-out.

To reach the put-in, continue up NF 46 to Cleator Bend Campground, which is about 9 miles above Detroit. Put in at the bridge just above the campground. To avoid The Slot or The Notch rapids, carry boats down the steep trail opposite the small quarry about 1 mile below the normal put-in. This access is just below The Notch.

Gauge

Breitenbush River above French Creek near Detroit. Optimal flow for a first-time run is 400–800 cfs.

Rich Brainerd, Pete Giordano, and WKCC Editors

111 ★ Little North Santiam River
Old Mine to Three Pools (Opal Creek)

Class: 4(5)	Length: 3.8 miles
Flow: 700–2500 cfs (at Mehama)	Character: forested; canyon
Gradient: 104 fpm, PD	Season: rainy/snowmelt

Known to the boating community simply as Opal Creek, this section of the Little North Santiam is revered by advanced and intermediate boaters alike. The area has largely been protected from logging by old mining claims and the tireless effort of The Friends of Opal Creek and other local groups. From the put-in, boaters travel through spectacular old-growth forests, beautiful gorges, and an uncountable number of intermediate rapids with crystal clear water. The rapids are classic pool-drop with small pools and numerous eddies throughout the run. This is simply one of the best advanced-intermediate runs anywhere.

Expect to do a fair amount of scouting your first time down, although all the drops can be boat scouted by experienced boaters. All the hardest drops have good recovery pools at most flows. Be on the lookout for a steep rapid that plows into two large boulders on the left before squeezing through a narrow slot on the right. The boulders create a dangerous sieve that can be avoided by staying right. About 50 yards downstream from another sharp right-hand corner lurks Big Ugly. Catch the small eddy on the right to scout/portage. Boaters tend to get slammed into the left wall at most flows, so be sure to boof right and stay upright. At low flows, a dangerous pin spot in the left chute suggests a portage. Below Big Ugly, another narrow slot should be scouted for wood.

Do not relax below Big Ugly, as shortly downstream is Big Fluffy. At the sight of a dramatic cliff wall on the left and of mist rising below an imposing horizon line that disappears to the right, eddy out on the right to scout this 15-foot waterfall. Although Big Fluffy has been run at a variety of water levels, the hydraulic at the base has a reputation for punishing even the best of boaters. Scout carefully and set safety before deciding to run this one. The best portage route is to seal launch off the 16-foot rock "platform" directly below the falls, or jump into the pool below the falls and collect your gear at the end of the pool.

Below Big Fluffy, the gradient tapers off and the canyon walls open slightly, although many more fun rapids are ahead. This section provides plenty of time to soak in the great scenery. Just as the scenery lulls you into a fuzzy state of mind, it is time to run Thor's Playroom. Thor's is a long rapid that can be broken into three sections. Several technical slots at the top lead boaters into a pushy middle section with swirly currents. The final drop that can be seen from the take-out has a powerful hole at the base that can easily separate people from their equipment. A big recovery pool lies just below this rapid.

Hazards

Several drops could pin boaters. Scout for wood beforehand. Approach Big Ugly and Big Fluffy with caution. Scout Thor's Playroom by hiking down to the take-out.

Access

The 2020 Beachie Creek Fire burned the entire run; contact Marion County for access point status and road conditions.

From Interstate 5 near Salem, take Oregon 22 east to Mehama. Turn left at the flashing light 0.7 mile east of Mehama (21.8 miles east of Interstate 5) onto North Fork Road. Turn right after 16.5 miles on this road at the sign for Three Pools Recreation Site. Stay right at the next fork, and follow this road to its end at the parking area. A USFS Recreation Pass is needed here and at put-in.

To reach the put-in, return to the main road and turn right. Go 4.5 miles to the road's end, the trailhead to the Opal Creek Wilderness Area. Hike along the road beyond the gate for about 0.5 mile to an old road on the right just after the bridge at Gold Creek. Follow it down to the river.

Gauge

Little North Santiam near Mehama. This gauge is far downstream of the take-out, so it only approximates the actual water level of the run. The correlation between the gauge and the actual water in the run fluctuates depending on whether water is coming from snowmelt or rain. Optimum is about 1000–1500 cfs on the gauge.

Pete Giordano and Jason Rackley

112   Little North Santiam River
Salmon Falls to Elkhorn Valley Recreation Site

Class: 2(3–4)	Length: 5.6 miles
Flow: 800–1000 cfs	Character: forested; valley
Gradient: 37 fpm, PD	Season: rainy/snowmelt

Take time at the put-in to enjoy the view as the river pours over 25-foot Salmon Falls. From the put-in below Salmon Falls, the river flows through much of the Elkhorn Valley as class 1 with occasional technical class 2 rapids through rock gardens.

However, at river mile 2.5, the run enters The Slot, a 15-foot-wide entrance to a narrow basalt canyon. About 200 feet ahead of The Slot, the river divides around a steep gravel bar. The two flows converge at The Slot and roll off the cliffs with pulsating flows. At a low flow of 800 cfs, The Slot is class 3. Check for logs before running the drop. At higher flows, this rapid could be extremely difficult, probably class 4 or higher. So unless you are a class 4 boater, it would be wise to avoid paddling this stretch of river if flows are over 1000 cfs.

The current slows as the river passes under the bridge at mile 3 in the community of Elkhorn and enters the broad Elkhorn Valley. The valley narrows again at mile 4.5 as Elkhorn Valley Recreation Site appears on the left. For the next 1 mile, the action picks up and includes two class 3 drops in the last 0.3 mile. These last two drops can be avoided by taking out at the upper end of the campground on the left above the first class 3 drop.

Hazards

Expect The Slot to increase in difficulty substantially at flows of 1000–3000 cfs. The Slot is difficult to portage because it requires a carry of at least 0.5 mile around private homes and cliffs. You cannot portage from the area immediately adjacent to The Slot. The class 3 ledge and boulder drop at the end of the run can be scouted from the take-out by walking upstream through the campground.

Access

The 2020 Beachie Creek Fire burned the entire run; contact Marion County for access point status and road conditions.

Drive to Mehama. Go east on Oregon 22 and turn left at the flashing light 0.7 mile east of Mehama onto North Fork Road. The take-out is at the Elkhorn Valley Recreation Site, 8.3 miles up this road.

Continue upstream for 5.5 miles to the put-in at Salmon Falls County Park, which is on the right just below Salmon Falls.

Gauge

Little North Santiam near Mehama.

Steve Cramer, Arnie Adams, and WKCC Editors

113 ★ Little North Santiam River
Elkhorn Valley Recreation Site to Mehama

Class: 3(4) T	Length: 10 miles
Flow: 500–4000 cfs	Character: forested; canyon
Gradient: 30 fpm, PD	Season: rainy/snowmelt

The rapids on this run are varied, and the water is often crystal clear. The road appears only occasionally, and the upper parts of this run feel isolated, although there are many cabins along the lower section. Many good surfing waves are found at almost all flows. Waterfalls cascade into the river at numerous locations.

Before putting in at Elkhorn Valley Recreation Site, look at the two class 3 rapids visible from the campground road, a 0.3-mile walk above the gate. Then decide whether to put in above or below. Class 2 rapids continue downstream for about 3 miles to the concrete bridge.

Below the bridge 0.5 mile, the river narrows and drops to the right. Just below the drop, a large rock wall extends almost to the left bank, creating a large S turn. This is easy in low water, but formidable in flood.

Just downstream is the most difficult rapid on the run, Troll's Teeth, class 4. As the name suggests, this is a boulder garden with no clean route. At lower water levels it is very technical, and at flood it becomes a mass of holes and keepers to eat you. Approach cautiously and stop to scout on the left before the river disappears among several large rocks. At least one tree or log is usually caught in this rapid. Portage if necessary along the left bank and put in about 100 yards downstream in a large pool. The normal route enters on the right and goes far right behind the huge boulder and then to the left. Below Troll's Teeth is a steep, fast class 3 rapid.

The remaining rapids on this run are quite straightforward and can be scouted by boat. About a mile below Troll's Teeth, the trail from the alternative put-in (near milepost 3) meets the river. A particularly long and enjoyable section of rapids (class 2+) at North Fork Park is preceded by a large, curving undercut cliff on the left, followed by a nice play spot with a fast V, green waves, and generous eddies.

Downstream of the park you will pass under a bridge. At the next rapids, the river narrows to the left and drops sharply in an S turn rapid, named Slinky (class 3-). The large hole at the bottom usually can be punched. Slinky becomes more difficult at low water levels. The rest of this run bounces along pleasantly until meeting the North Santiam River, where nice surf waves occur just downstream. It is less than a half-mile to the take-out under the bridge in Mehama.

Hazards

Everyone, regardless of experience, should scout Troll's Teeth. Logs and debris from floods frequently plug the channels.

Access

The 2020 Beachie Creek Fire burned the entire run; contact Marion County for access point status and road conditions.

Drive to Mehama. The take-out boat ramp is located underneath the Lyons-Mehama bridge on the river left side of the North Santiam River.

To reach the put-in, cross the bridge and go east on Oregon 22. In 0.7 mile, at the flashing yellow light, turn left onto North Fork Road.

The uppermost put-in is at the Elkhorn Valley Recreation Site, which is 8.3 miles up from Oregon 22. Two alternative accesses, both below Troll's Teeth Rapid, are at North Fork Park (2 miles above Oregon 22) or the milepost 4 pull-out (4.2 miles above Oregon 22). Both require a short descent via forest trail.

Gauge

Little North Santiam River near Mehama. Optimal flows are 1000–2500 cfs.

Mick Evans and WKCC Editors

114★ North Santiam River
Pamelia Creek to Blowout Road

Class: 3(4); 3+(4)	Length: 11.3 miles
Flow: 800–1600 cfs; 1700–3000 cfs	Character: forested
Gradient: 62 fpm, C	Season: rainy/snowmelt

With its headwaters in the Mount Jefferson Wilderness, this upper stretch of the North Santiam River is usually runnable from first snowmelt (from early March to late April) through late spring. It may also be runnable after several days of hard rain during the fall or winter. It is not uncommon to tramp through snow at the put-in. In any season, the water is always very cold.

This run provides a continuous gradient with constant action throughout the run. Play spots are abundant. At flows below 1300 cfs, the river is technical, and eddies are numerous. From 1300 to 1700 cfs, eddies are fewer, and the river has more push to it. Waves and holes become much larger at flows above 2000 cfs, and eddies are scarce. On clear days, spectacular views of Mount Jefferson reward boaters who turn around and look upstream.

SECTION 1: PAMELIA CREEK TO BRUNO MOUNTAIN ROAD, 3.7 MILES, CLASS 3(3+)

This section of the river is sometimes combined with section 2 of this write-up for a longer run. It is more remote than the lower run because the road is rarely in sight. Climbing out of the river canyon to the road high above would be difficult if problems were to occur.

The first mile of the run has some short class 2+ drops followed by several class 3 drops, where logs commonly present issues. Be sure to scout for logs at the steeper drops. The gradient lessens a little during the middle of the run, enabling one to enjoy the scenery in this remote section of the run. However, stay alert for the last mile of the run. Whitewater Creek (the largest tributary) enters on the right, and the class 3+ rapid, Whitewater Mayhem, begins just below the confluence as the river bends left. This long rapid is best negotiated by starting on river left, then moving to the right toward the bottom. Look for the line in the center right to avoid some large holes.

One-half mile below Whitewater Mayhem, after a couple of class 2+ rapids, the Bruno Mountain Road bridge comes into view. Here, one may choose to exit the river or continue on to section 2.

SECTION 2: BRUNO MOUNTAIN ROAD TO BLOWOUT ROAD, 7.6 MILES, CLASS 3(4)

All the rapids on this section can be scouted from the river by eddy hopping if the flows are low to medium. The road is always nearby on river right, but it never seems obtrusive. Logs are occasionally a problem, so stay alert.

The first 0.7 mile offers a good warm-up of class 2 and 3 water. The major rapid, Ricochet, the most demanding of the run, begins on a sharp right bend. A steep hole on the left is followed by a long boulder garden below. It can be scouted near milepost 59 during the shuttle; check for wood. Some boaters prefer to put in below Ricochet Rapid at Whispering Falls Campground, another 0.3 mile downstream. The 3 miles of river below Whispering Falls are class 2+ to 3.

About halfway through the run, on a straight stretch of river, look upstream for views of Mount Jefferson. Stop in the left eddy (Mountain View Eddy) at the end of the straight stretch for the best view. Lunch Drop, a class 3 rapid, is runnable on either side of the island just below.

Having a look at Bodacious Rapid on the North Santiam River (Mark Scantlebury)

At the first bridge, use caution, because a fisheries trap is sometimes located there with cables attaching it to the bridge. Below this point, the river offers numerous class 3–3+ rapids with some significant drops and pushy water. Good rapids occur near the lumber mill in Idanha; the play waves along this stretch are so much fun that one barely notices the mill. About 0.5 mile below the second bridge, the single steepest drop, Bodacious (class 3+), is found on the left side of an island. Pick a path around and through the holes and waves scattered across the channel; middle to middle-right usually works best here. Good rapids continue to the take-out, where the superb play wave, Blowout Wave, is located.

Hazards

Difficulties include cold water, possible logs, the remoteness of section 1, and the class 4 rapid (Ricochet) in section 2.

Access

To reach the take-out for section 2, take Oregon 22 to Detroit. Continue east on Oregon 22 for 2.5 miles to Blowout Road and turn right. Follow the road left for 0.2 mile to the bridge for a free take-out on river left. Alternatively, go immediately right for the Santiam Flats USFS fee area (a take-out slightly downstream of the bridge).

To find the put-in, return to Oregon 22 and drive upstream 7 miles to Bruno Mountain Road, on the right. Put in under the bridge. This is also the take-out point for section 1. To reach the uppermost put-in, continue upstream on Oregon 22 for another 3.3 miles to a turnout just past Pamelia Creek where the road is near the river at milepost 63.

Warning: When the reservoir level is low, a steep class 5 rapid located between the take-out and the reservoir becomes exposed.

Gauge

North Santiam River below Boulder. Optimum level for a first descent is about 1200–1500 cfs. At the minimum flow of 800 cfs, Ricochet Rapid is very bony. (Section 1's minimum is 900 cfs.) At flows higher than 2000 cfs, the difficulty of the run increases.

Laurie Pavey

115 North Santiam River
Big Cliff Dam to Packsaddle County Park

Class: 3+(4–5) P	Length: 3.7 miles
Flow: 1000–3500 cfs	Character: forested
Gradient: 32 fpm, PD	Season: year-round

The North Santiam River in this stretch is regulated by the Detroit and Big Cliff Dams, above the town of Gates. The numerous class 2 rapids, along with several class 3 and 4 rapids, make this run, known as Niagara, a fun and exciting stretch of whitewater. The two named rapids in this stretch are The Narrows and Niagara.

The Narrows, class 4–5, is about 0.8 mile downstream from the put-in. It is preceded by a class 3 entry rapid with an eddy at the bottom on the right. The current continues on the left side and funnels into The Narrows, a 100-yard-long constriction with powerful hydraulics. The rapid begins with a large wave or hole, depending on water levels, followed by a diagonal hole, more turbulent water, and a good pool at the bottom. Be aware that at some flows, hazardous recirculating pockets are created along the left wall at the bottom of the rapid. At low discharges, portaging is recommended, although the entry hole can be avoided with a strong boof off the ledge on the far left. Scout before running it.

At flows over 3000 cfs, Niagara is a twisting class 4–5 drop at Niagara County Park. After a long class 3 lead-in, the river squeezes to a width of merely 5 feet. This is followed by a swirling pool that outflows into a turbulent snake of water leading into a huge, potentially dangerous boiling pool. The walls in Niagara are undercut in places, and several potholes create strange hydraulics. Be prepared for a difficult rescue if someone in your party swims. The boiling pool recirculates along a cliff and makes self-rescue almost impossible. At lower flows, Niagara is significantly easier, but wood in any part of the rapid could be very dangerous. Always scout Niagara.

Below Niagara, a couple of class 2–3 rapids offer good play spots at some discharges. Minto Hatchery Dam is 1.2 miles below Niagara. The 12-foot dam is used to divert salmon and steelhead for capture to supply eggs for fish hatcheries. The reversal at the bottom is dangerous and a portage is mandatory as reinforcing irons are embedded there. Portage on the right. The trail will lead you to the top of the hill near the highway. Follow the trail around the outside of the facility to a steep metal staircase that leads down to the river again and a rocky put-in area. Rafts would be difficult to portage down the staircase. Raft crews will mostly likely continue their portage up the hill to the highway for a vehicle portage (if continuing on downstream to the next run) or simply take out at the highway. Packsaddle County Park is just a couple of hundred yards below the dam on the right.

Hazards

The Narrows and Niagara are technically demanding rapids that should be scouted. Portage around Minto Hatchery Dam.

Access

From Interstate 5 near Salem, take Oregon 22 east past Mill City. The take-out at Packsaddle County Park is about 3 miles east of Gates on Oregon 22. The put-in is just below Big Cliff Dam, about 6 miles east of Gates on Oregon 22. Stop at Niagara County Park during the shuttle to scout Niagara. To scout The Narrows, stop about 1 mile east of Niagara where there is an abandoned gas station. The Narrows is down the steep bank near the sign "Little Sweden."

Gauge

North Santiam River at Niagara.

George Ice and WKCC Editors

116 ★ North Santiam River Packsaddle County Park to Mill City

Class: 2+(3); 3; 4	Length: 6.4 miles
Flow: 750 cfs; 1500 cfs; 4500+ cfs	Character: forested; residential
Gradient: 28 fpm, PD	Season: year-round

This run is one of the more popular boating trips in Oregon. Riffles immediately below the put-in can be used to warm up. Turning the corner, the riffles lead into a small rapid. Following a pool is a fun class 2 rapid that leads into a narrow chute. It has narrow eddies on both sides and can be very turbulent.

The next rapid finishes with an excellent play spot, referred to as The Swirlies, which is identified by rock formations on the left and a very large eddy on the right. The waves at this spot make excellent surfing. The runout is extremely turbulent, with small whirlpools and collapsing swirls. The Swirlies offer an excellent and challenging practice site for the ol' river roll.

About 0.5 mile after passing under the bridge at Gates, a series of bigger rapids begins. The last rapid in this series is Spencer's Hole (class 3 at low flows). Boaters generally choose between punching the hole on the right or sneaking on the left. At high flows, you will find several large waves and holes on the left. Current continues below this drop, but there are recovery eddies on both sides of the river.

About 0.2 mile below Spencer's Hole is Carnivore, hidden on the left side of an island. Jim Oliver named this small, twisting, frothy beast when it was hungry and "ate" him. Several mild rapids and play spots are found between Carnivore and Mill City.

Mill City Falls, a 4-foot ledge drop, is usually scouted by walking out on the road bridge before the trip begins. Otherwise, one can back-paddle while looking over the drop. The center-left of the drop usually has a clear chute, and a sneak slot is sometimes used on the far left. The take-out is at a path on the right below the bridge. Another take-out is at the boat ramp in Fishermen's Bend Park, 1.5 miles downstream, but it is closed in winter.

Hazards

Approach Spencer's Hole and Mill City Falls with caution. At lower flows, Spencer's Hole can be scouted from the right shore. This drop becomes much more difficult at high flows.

Access

Oregon 22 east of Salem follows the North Santiam River. The put-in is at Packsaddle County Park, about 3 miles east of Gates.

The usual take-out is at the small park (with changing rooms) in Mill City, at the north end of the bridge. The optional take-out is at Fishermen's Bend State Park, about 1.5 miles downstream from Mill City.

Gauge

North Santiam River at Niagara. At 10,000 cfs, the current and rapids on the river require expert paddling. Summer levels of about 1000 cfs are much less demanding. A flow of about 3000 cfs is optimal for playing, although Spencer's Hole is optimal between 900 and 1400 cfs.

George Ice and WKCC Editors

117 North Santiam River Mill City to Mehama

Class: 2; 3	Length: 8.4 miles
Flow: 1000 cfs; 3000+ cfs	Character: wooded; residential
Gradient: 22 fpm, PD	Season: year-round

This trip begins below the Mill City Falls. The rapids are less demanding than those upstream, but should still be respected. Maneuvering is required in some of the rapids, and some of the larger waves may swamp an open canoe. Flows below 1500 cfs are more technical in nature. The first rapid just downstream of the Mill City bridge is indicative of the difficulty of the rapids on this section.

Several rapids have standing waves that can be surfed, even at 1000 cfs. A favorite play spot is at North Santiam State Park, 2 miles below Fishermen's Bend Park. A small ledge provides boaters with a good place to practice surfing, S turns, and rolls. The ledge may be avoided by running far right. Novice paddlers have many opportunities to practice eddy turns, maneuvering, and ferrying in the rapids all along the run.

Near the end of the trip, John Neal Memorial Park is seen on the left, and the Little North Santiam River enters from the right. Excellent surfing waves develop along here at flows of 2000 cfs or more. The take-out is on the left under the Lyons-Mehama bridge, less than a half-mile below the confluence with the Little North Santiam River.

Hazards

The first rapid can be scouted from the lower bridge at Mill City. Downed trees and sweepers may occasionally block channels.

Access

Put in below the bridge in Mill City on river right. Alternative put-ins (featuring boat ramps) can be found at Fishermen's Bend Park or at North Santiam State Park, 1.5 and 3 miles downstream of Mill City, respectively.

The take-out is under the Oregon 226 bridge, between Lyons and Mehama. From the junction of Oregon 22 and 226, travel south on Oregon 226. After crossing the Lyons-Mehama bridge, turn right and then right again to the take-out under the bridge.

Gauge

North Santiam River at Mehama.

George Ice and WKCC Editors

118 North Santiam River
Mehama to Stayton

Class: 2- P	Length: 10.2 miles
Flow: 1000–2000 cfs	Character: agricultural
Gradient: 18 fpm, C	Season: year-round

The coniferous forests found along the upper reaches of the North Santiam gradually shift to foothill and farmland vegetation along this run. After about 0.2 mile of smooth water below the put-in, the river begins a series of mild rapids. Following these rapids is a nice play spot on the left known as Beginner's Hole. A particularly troublesome chute for beginners occurs just before a group of three powerlines comes into view. The chute flows from left to right directly into the bank and has a strong, swirling eddy on the inside of the turn. Another 0.2 mile below the powerline is the largest rapid on this run, which should be run on the far left. Below this drop is the traditional lunch stop on the right bank. In late summer, wild blackberries can be added to your lunch menu.

Below the lunch stop are a number of class 1 rapids and riffles. Following a mild rapid, farmland fringed by bird boxes can be seen on the left bank. Below the bird boxes, the river splits, and a dam sits in the left channel. The right channel looks inviting, but should not be taken, because it becomes an irrigation canal with very brushy banks and no take-outs. Take the left channel, and on the right side of this channel, catch the eddy, then use the drift-boat slide to bypass the dam. Salmon and steelhead can sometimes be seen jumping in the fish ladder or up the dam.

The rapids below the dam are rocky and swift. Beyond, the river becomes rockier and shallower. A few of the rapids have current moving into brush.

Hazards

The class 2 rapid below the powerline crossing is the most difficult.

Access

Take Oregon 22 east from Salem. The put-in is the boat landing located beneath the Lyons-Mehama bridge, just off Oregon 22 on Oregon 226.

To reach the take-out, take Oregon 22 to the Stayton turnoff and go south through Stayton. The take-out is at the boat ramp at the south end of the bridge that crosses the North Santiam in Stayton.

Gauge

North Santiam River at Mehama. Flows over 2000 cfs are not for beginners.

George Ice and WKCC Editors

119 North Santiam River Stayton to Jefferson

Class: 1+	Length: 19.4 miles
Flow: 1000–3000 cfs	Character: riparian forest; farmland
Gradient: 11 fpm, C	Season: year-round

Below Stayton, the North Santiam flattens as it winds through farmland and among stands of alders and cottonwoods. The scenery is very pleasant: wide gravel bars lined with trees, and almost no buildings in sight. At low water the banks could be characterized as class 1 with continuous lunch spots. There is little whitewater on this run, but a number of sharp turns, a few snags, and some turbulent water require boaters to pay attention. The relatively calm water and high frequency of eddies along the shore make this stretch excellent for beginning canoers and kayakers who can control their craft. This reach can be paddled all summer, and in the fall, the cottonwood colors are outstanding.

About 5 miles from the put-in, you pass the Buell Miller boat ramp on river left. About 7 miles below the put-in, the river splits and winds through many channels around a number of islands. This stretch has a well-earned reputation for becoming blocked by sweepers.

There is an alternative access to the river at Greens Bridge, 14 miles below the put-in. About halfway between Greens Bridge and the take-out, the South Santiam flows in from the left, and the river becomes the main stem of the Santiam. Soon, the continuous nature of the river ends and a flatwater pool extends to the take-out in Jefferson.

For a longer trip, you can put in at Mill City upstream on the North Santiam, with lively class 2 rapids, and paddle through Stayton and on to Buena Vista on the Willamette River—an extended class 2 overnight trip of 48 miles, with one low dam to negotiate via the drift-boat slide above Stayton (see North Santiam: Mehama to Stayton run).

Hazards

Be alert and scout for downed trees, root wads, and log jams that may require portages, especially below the Buell Miller boat ramp.

Access

All the accesses to the river on this run have well-developed boat ramps. To reach the take-out, take exit 238 off Interstate 5 and follow Jefferson Highway east for 2.5 miles to Jefferson. The take-out is about 100 yards downstream of the Jefferson bridge, on river right.

To reach the put-in, go back toward the Jefferson bridge and turn south on the road to Scio. About 2.5 miles east of Jefferson, this road crosses Greens Bridge, under which, on river left, is an alternative access to the river. Continue on this road to Scio and take the road north from Scio to Stayton. The put-in is at the boat ramp on the southwest side of the bridge just south of Stayton. (An alternative boat ramp, located about 5 miles downstream of Stayton, is at the Buell Miller boat ramp off Hess Road north of Scio.)

Gauge

North Santiam River at Mehama. The run begins to get a little bumpy at flows below 1,500 cfs. Winter flows can be very large and are not for beginners.

John Westall, Tim Palmer, and WKCC Editors

Opposite: *The gorge below Mama Bear Rapid, Molalla River* (Mark Scantlebury)

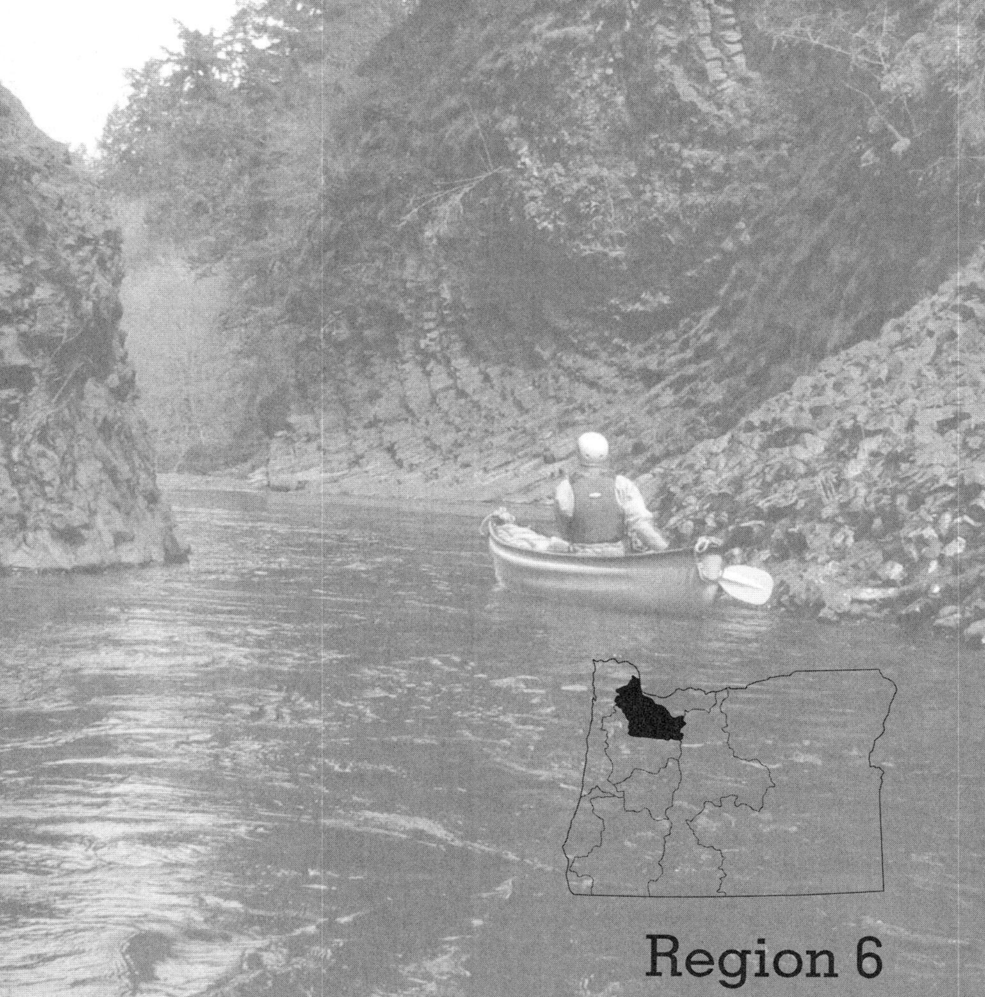

Lower Willamette
Valley and
Clackamas Rivers
Region 6

Silver Creek

120 Silver Creek
Silver Falls State Park to Silverton Reservoir

Class: 4(5)	Length: 10.1 miles
Flow: 300–500 cfs	Character: deep forested canyon
Gradient: 59 fpm, PD	Season: rainy

Silver Creek begins in the Cascade Foothills, flows through Silver Falls State Park and then northwest to Silverton. The many falls in the park drop over 15-million-year-old (Miocene) flood basalts from Eastern Oregon and Washington. Mountain building in the area has since raised the basalt higher than its original elevation. The run is characterized by falls, steep blind ledges, and gorges. It is mostly pool-drop with one rapid that is long and continuous. The put-in is a 1.1-mile downhill hike to the foot of Lower North Falls on the North Fork of Silver Creek.

From the base of Lower North Falls, there is 0.75 mile of pleasant small ledges and rapids before you reach the confluence with the South Fork. Obstructing logs may require you to portage in this section. The first large drop after the confluence is Crag Falls, a wide, diagonal 10-foot ledge drop preceded by a 150-foot-long shallow, ledgy slide on river left. Crag Falls can be scouted on the left from the slack water at its top.

Next comes Dobo Falls, a 15-foot plunge at a sharp right bend in the river. Dobo Falls is preceded by two river-wide ledges, with rollers that can be sneaked on the extreme left. Do not miss the eddy on river left just above the lip of the falls. The best line at Dobo is a boof on the left, but this line is complicated by the fact that most of the current flows perpendicularly to the lip of the falls and down into the ugly fold on the right side. Portage on the left.

Canyon Falls is an 8- to 10-foot slide just downstream from Dobo Falls. It is difficult to scout and could be a difficult portage because of the steep, slippery canyon walls. Run on the right as a double drop, with a 3-foot ledge 50 feet farther downstream. An old clear-cut on the left marks the park boundary 2.2 miles below the confluence of the North and South Forks. Once you leave the park, look for a green steel bridge over the creek. Just below this bridge is a 4-foot ledge that can develop a sticky hole on the right at some flows.

Dirty Falls, a 15-foot ledge with a short class 2 rapid just before the lip, appears in another 0.25 mile. From upstream, the falls appears like a dam. Scout from the left above the lead-in rapids. Below Dirty Falls, the creek gradually slows and the last 4 miles or so are mellow class 2 with one steep drop known as Murray's Slide. This fun drop has several parts and can be boat scouted at medium flows or bank scouted on either side if necessary. Below this ledge, it is 0.25 mile to the flatwater paddle across the reservoir and out.

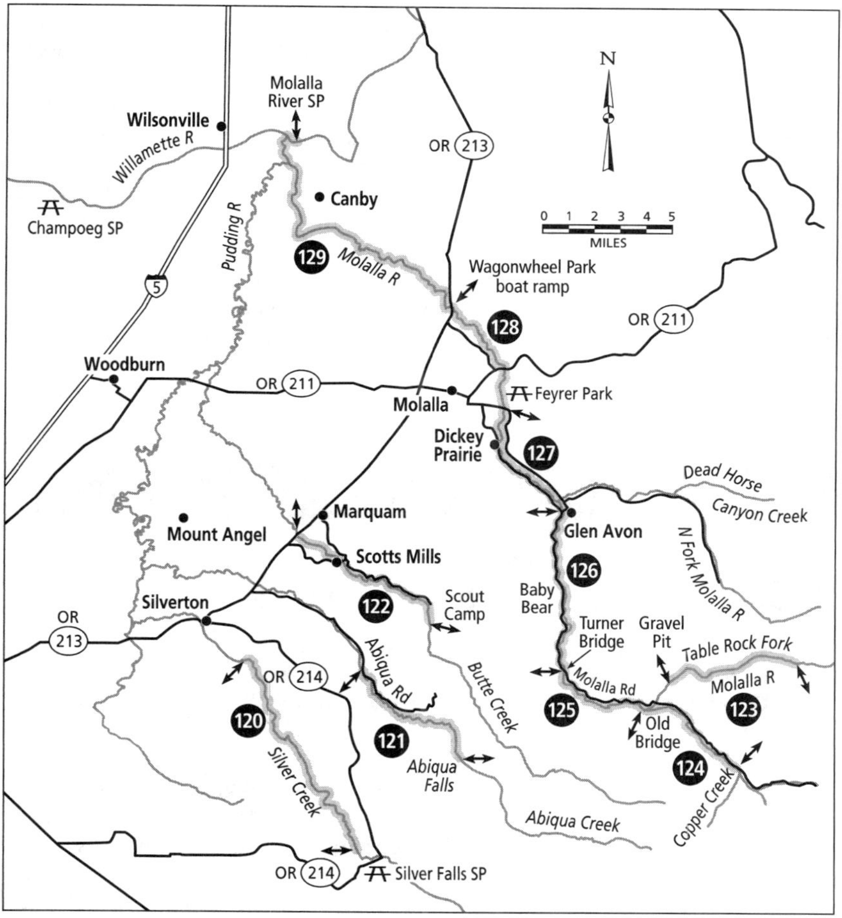

Hazards

Do not put in above Lower North Falls. Strict rules forbid ascending or descending the creek banks within the park—you may be cited by park staff if you are caught, so do not do it. The creek-side ecosystem is very delicate, so scout carefully and do not leave the creek once you are on it. Watch for wood blockages.

Access

From Silverton, follow the signs east on Oregon 214 (Silver Falls Highway) toward Silver Falls State Park. The take-out is at the Silverton Marine Park and Reservoir, a small park just outside the Silverton city limits on the south side of Oregon 214. There are parking fees and limited winter hours at the park.

For the put-in, drive about 12 miles southeast on Oregon 214 to the Winter Falls parking lot in Silver Falls State Park. (An Oregon State Parks parking pass is required.)

The put-in is a 1.1-mile downhill hike to the base of Lower North Falls. (The hike from North Falls Campground is about the same distance, but the campground may be closed in winter, and the trail is not marked.) From the parking lot, it is 0.5 mile down to the bridge over the North Fork, 0.2 mile to Middle North Falls, 0.2 mile to Drake Falls, and 0.2 mile to the base of Lower North Falls.

Gauge

Silver Creek at Silverton. Generally there is enough water after several days of rain. The Clackamas River (Clackamas River at Three Lynx gauge) should be at least 3500 cfs.

Hank Hays and WKCC Editors

Abiqua Creek

121 Abiqua Creek
Abiqua Falls to Abiqua Road

Class: 2+(3)	Length: 6 miles
Flow: 600–1500 cfs	Character: forested; residential
Gradient: 80 fpm, C	Season: rainy

Abiqua Creek is in the watershed between Butte Creek to the north and Silver Creek to the south. All are tributaries of the Pudding River, which flows into the Molalla just before the latter reaches the Willamette. Abiqua Creek's gradient and drainage area are similar to both sister streams, but it does not have as much action as either of them. The gradient is fairly constant, with some pool-drop action. Most rapids are rock gardens. Although the majority of rapids are class 2, the gradient and strainers make this a river of consequence. A solid roll is recommended, as swims can result in long boat chases or other issues.

Above the put-in, Abiqua Falls plunges over a 90-foot sheer drop into a pool. The first 1.5 miles of this run are class 2, with a few strategically placed sweepers to enliven the experience. These can generally be negotiated without scouting. Farther on, you will come to the first class 3, Hank's Mistake. Hank's has a large boulder near the bottom center. Most of the water pushes left, and there are a number of short drops/holes in quick succession at the end. The left line is generally advised, except perhaps at high water, since the right line is rocky.

A mile later comes Pink Bridge Rapid. This is a long boulder garden with a left bend and an eddy halfway through, about where the bridge comes into view. A quick scout for logs is prudent. The lower half of Pinky is quite steep and has some solid holes.

Next up is a 3- to 4-foot, river-wide ledge, marked by an obvious horizon line. Scout or run the left side, as the right side can be retentive at some flows.

Soon a steel grate bridge, a possible take-out, comes into view. Scout the section below it for strainers before the trip begins, if you plan to proceed. The next section contains more class 2 rapids, including Pumpkin Rapid (class 2+). A bit of rock dodging is required in this stretch. In a little more than a mile, you come to the concrete bridge take-out. Exit upstream left or downstream left, if you can't resist the last splashy water.

About 1.8 miles below the concrete bridge take-out (between miles 8 and 9) is an unrunnable low-head dam that would be difficult to portage, mainly because of steep banks with barbed-wire fences at the top. This is the water source for the town of Silverton.

Hazards

Hank's Mistake and Pink Bridge Rapid are the most difficult rapids, but strainers and a lack of eddies are the biggest danger on this stretch. The shuttle could also be a hazard to your vehicle. Four-wheel drive is recommended, especially in wet weather.

Access

From Oregon 99E in Salem, take Oregon 213 east to Silverton. About 3 miles north of Silverton on Oregon 213 is a blinking yellow light at Abiqua Road Northeast. Take Abiqua Road southeast about 6 miles to a concrete bridge over Abiqua Creek. Just upstream is a rocky turnout that makes a good parking spot for the concrete bridge take-out. To get to the upper (recommended) take-out, continue 1 mile and park on the right after crossing the steel grate bridge.

Because the previous (direct) route to the put-in is now gated, the shuttle involves some extra work; it's 24 miles, and about a 45-minute drive each way. Return to Oregon 213 on Abiqua Road and travel north 1.7 miles to the Mount Angel–Scotts Mills Road Northeast. Turn east and proceed 2.5 miles to the town of Scotts Mills. Turn right (south) on Crooked Finger Road Northeast. Continue 10.6 miles—it turns to gravel after about 9 miles—to a right turn at the sign reading "Crooked Finger ATV Staging Area." Follow the main road, which is quite rough at times, 2.5 miles down to a small pullout on the left, just above a gate blocking the road. Park here and head toward the river on the visible trail, but stay left at the start. (If you come to an open area, you took the right branch and need to return.) Head down the trail, which is steep at times, about 0.2 mile to the creek. To view Abiqua Falls from river level, hike upstream. At flows that allow paddling, this must be done along the hill rather than on the riverbank, which adds to the difficulty.

Gauge

Abiqua Creek at Silverton. Several days of rain are usually needed; flows drop quickly.

Hank Hays and Kevin Hill

Butte Creek

122 Butte Creek
Scout Camp to Oregon 213

Class: 3(4-) T, P	Length: 7.7 miles
Flow: 200–800 cfs	Character: forested
Gradient: 57 fpm, PD	Season: rainy

This run on Butte Creek flows through scenic forested mountain foothills that are an abrupt contrast to the rural countryside found near Mount Angel and Woodburn. It has considerable variety for a small stream: ledge drops, a few slots, S curves, rock gardens, a gorge, one slide, a couple of logs, and a dam/falls combination drop (which is sometimes runnable). The rapids are separated by long stretches of easier water. An alternative take-out at Scotts Mills County Park (above the dam) shortens the trip by 2 miles.

One mile below the put-in, at the first bridge, there is a 5-foot drop. It can be a nose cruncher at low water, but is less of a problem at higher water. Another mile below the first bridge is a difficult rapid (class 4-) that should be scouted from the right bank. The rock garden at the top leads into fast water that forms two large river-wide waves, funnels down to 20 feet wide, goes over a 4-foot drop, and bashes onto a rock on the right. The rock garden below is technical at low water. Boaters who choose to portage these two rapids should stay close to the river to avoid disturbing adjacent property owners.

After another mile, a tight S turn first curves to the left, and then right. A rock at the top of this rapid splits the river. It is difficult to scout this one from the river, but at least one member of the party should check it for wood. This drop is followed by a short, scenic gorge. After another 2 miles of fun rapids and ledges, the water slows behind a 3-foot concrete weir at Scotts Mills. The weir is immediately followed by the 10-foot Scotts Mills Falls. Although it is possible to portage the dam and falls and continue downriver, many people opt to take out at the park on the left next to the dam. Adventurous paddlers looking for an exciting finish can run the dam.

Immediately below the dam is a fun rapid with numerous holes and rocks to maneuver around. More class 2–2+ rapids and numerous surf waves continue to the take-out on the right at the Oregon 213 bridge.

Hazards

The 5-foot drop at the first bridge, the class 4- rapid 1 mile farther down, and the S-turn rapid should be scouted or portaged. Scout Scotts Mills Falls if you plan on running it.

Access

From Oregon 99E in Salem, take Oregon 213 east to Silverton. The take-out is on Oregon 213 5.2 miles northwest of Silverton at the Oregon 213 bridge. The

A class 3 drop on Butte Creek (Mark Scantlebury)

landowner does not want cars left at the take-out on river right; instead, leave cars at Butte Creek Elementary School, 0.3 mile east of the bridge.

Alternatively, to reach the upper take-out, drive 4.5 miles from Silverton and turn right onto Mount Angel–Scotts Mills Road. Proceed 2.5 miles to Scotts Mills, turn right onto Crooked Finger Road, and park at the Scotts Mills County Park. This take-out misses the final 2 miles of the run.

To reach the put-in from Scotts Mills, cross the Scotts Mills bridge, drive 0.1 mile north to Maple Grove Road, which runs east, and turn right. In 0.1 mile, turn right again onto Butte Creek Road. Follow it for 4.5 miles and turn right. This road crosses a brook and looks down on Butte Creek after 0.5 mile. The road is owned by the Boy Scouts, who prefer boaters use the parking lot at the end of the road rather than park on the shoulder. Put in just below the class 5 rapid adjacent to the parking lot. Local residents prefer that scouting be done from the creek rather than from the road. Please respect their wishes.

Gauge

Butte Creek at Monitor. Usually three days of rain fill the creek to a fair level. Optimal levels are 400–600 cfs.

Andreas Mueller and WKCC Editors

Molalla River and Tributaries

123 Table Rock Fork of the Molalla River
Second Bridge to Gravel Pit

Class: 3+(4) T	Length: 5.4 miles
Flow: 500–1500 cfs	Character: forested; roadside
Gradient: 134 fpm, C	Season: rainy

The upper section of the Table Rock Fork of the Molalla River is a great intermediate run for up-and-coming creekers. Although most of the drops are small, the continuous nature of the rapids keeps boaters busy. The road is always close, which allows for easy scouting during the shuttle and an escape route if the rapids are too demanding.

The first major rapid is The Pinch, class 4. It is about a mile below the put-in, immediately after a sharp left turn. It is recognized by steep rock walls on either side of the river and boulders that block much of the river. At most water levels, the river drops through a tight, undercut slot on the right and into a hole. The slot can be portaged on the right. Immediately after the slot is a narrow drop that could contain wood.

The remainder of the run offers continuous boulder gardens with the occasional larger rapid. Very few pools are present at most water levels, but eddies abound. There are a couple of rapids that are a bit harder than the rest of the run in the last mile before take-out. Scout and flag your take-out eddy.

Caution: Below the take-out and the next bridge is a 1-mile stretch of river that has class 5–5+ rapids. This extremely tight and technical gorge is recommended only to expert boaters after careful, but difficult, scouting.

Hazards

Scout The Pinch, about a mile below put-in. Scout the last mile during the shuttle. Potentially dangerous wood could be present anywhere throughout the run.

Access

To reach Turner Bridge, refer to the Molalla River: Turner Bridge to Glen Avon Bridge run. To reach the take-out, follow Molalla Road 4.4 miles past Turner Bridge and turn left just before crossing a bridge over Table Rock Fork. Continue on the Table Rock Road another 1.2 miles to a large gravel pit and parking area on your right.

To reach the put-in, drive upstream 5 miles to a spur road on the right. Put in at the bridge over the river on this spur road.

Gauge

Molalla River at Canby. This gauge is far downstream and does not always correspond well to flows in the upper river. In general, 3000–8000 cfs on the Canby gauge is good. Much of the run can be seen from the road, so take a look before you begin.

Pete Giordano and WKCC Editors

124 Molalla River
Copper Creek to Table Rock Confluence

Class: 3(4) T	Length: 4 miles
Flow: 600 cfs	Character: canyon; forested
Gradient: 82 fpm, PD	Season: rainy

This run offers a variety of rapids winding through a deep canyon with scenic views of a moss-laden forest. Being near the upper reaches of the Molalla, this run is runnable only after several days of heavy rain. Immediately below the put-in, where Copper Creek enters the main Molalla, is a small gorge that begins with a sharp, narrow class 3+ drop. This drop can be skipped by starting 0.75 mile downstream at the Copper Creek bridge over the Molalla. The drops in this beautiful gorge can be scouted from the road or the river.

The next major rapid, Dungeon (class 4), is about 2.75 miles from the Copper Creek bridge put-in. It consists of a boulder garden, several diagonal waves, and a tight S turn with several well-placed holes. Scout this rapid from the road at a point where the road bank drops off several hundred feet. The next major rapid is about 0.5 mile downstream. Lightning Lonnie, named in memory of a firefighter who loved the river, is a twisty 6-foot ledge. Stay far right or far left at the ledge since a middle run could cause a vertical pin.

The next part of the run consists of several small boulder gardens in another beautiful gorge. All of these drops can be boat-scouted by eddy hopping. Take out on the right 0.3 mile upstream of the confluence with the Table Rock Fork confluence. (There is no take-out at the confluence itself.) Boaters who desire a longer run can continue for 4.5–5 more miles and take out at Turner Bridge. For details, see the run Molalla River: Table Rock Fork Confluence to Turner Bridge.

Hazards

The narrow drop at the put-in can be avoided by starting just downstream. Scout Dungeon and Lightning Lonnie either from the road or the river.

Access

First go to Turner Bridge. (See the run Molalla River: Turner Bridge to Glen Avon for directions.) Two take-outs are possible. To reach either one, follow Molalla Forest Road 4.4 miles past Turner Bridge to the three-way intersection at the BLM river access site named "Old Bridge." Turn right and cross the bridge over the Table Rock Fork. From this bridge, drive another 0.3 mile to a pullout on the right and a short trail to the river. Another small pullout is 0.3 mile farther upstream. Scout both of these take-outs before putting on the river, as they are easy to miss if you are not paying attention.

To reach the put-in, continue upstream on the main road until you reach a locked gate blocking a bridge across the river, about 4.7 miles from Old Bridge. Park here, but do not block the gate. The lower put-in is at the Copper Creek bridge over the Molalla, approximately 0.75 mile downstream from the confluence of Copper Creek and the Molalla.

Gauge

Molalla River at Canby. The gauge is far downstream and does not always correspond well to flows in the upper river. In general, 1600 cfs on the Canby gauge is a good minimum if it is raining, but you may need more water if it has not rained for a couple of days.

Joe Gymkowski, Rick Kelley, and WKCC Editors

125★ Molalla River
Table Rock Fork Confluence to Turner Bridge

Class: 3(3+)	Length: 4.9 miles
Flow: 800–2500 cfs	Character: forested; canyon
Gradient: 60 fpm, PD	Season: rainy

This scenic and playful run on the Molalla River is mostly class 2, with several class 3 drops near the middle.

Two put-ins are possible. The more common put-in is on the Table Rock Fork of the Molalla 0.2 mile above the confluence with the main Molalla. The alternative put-in is on the main Molalla about 0.3 mile upstream of the confluence with the Table Rock Fork. The mile-long section past the confluence is a good class 2 warm-up with many surfing opportunities. At the end of this stretch is the first class 3 rapid. It is a read-and-run rapid, but watch out for the hole on the bottom left. Shortly below this rapid, boaters pass under Horse Creek bridge. Horse Creek enters the river as a beautiful falls on the left. About 0.2 mile downstream from the falls is Horse Creek Canyon, where the river narrows to a boat length in width. This class 3+ drop is clean but turbulent. It is a good idea to check for logs before committing to this drop. The flatwater runout gives paddlers a chance to enjoy the sheer and mossy canyon walls. Less than 1 mile downstream, be alert for logs where the river makes an S bend, first left and then right. The final couple of miles are class 2, with some nice play waves. Take out on the right above Turner Bridge where the road is next to the river. It is common to continue downriver through a portion of the Three Bears run and take out just below Baby Bear (see the Molalla River: Turner Bridge to Glen Avon Bridge run). This lengthens the trip to about 8 miles.

Hazards

Horse Creek Canyon is very narrow at the steepest part of the drop. Logs may be a problem, so be sure to scout.

Access

See the Molalla River: Turner Bridge to Glen Avon Bridge run for directions to Turner Bridge, the take-out for this run.

To reach the more common put-in, drive 4.4 miles upstream from Turner Bridge to a three-way intersection. On the right, just before the intersection, is the BLM river access area called Old Bridge. Park off the road, take the steep trail down to the river, and put in just downstream of the bridge. The alternative put-in can be reached by going right at the intersection, crossing the Table Rock Fork, and driving 0.3 mile to a small turnout on the right. Take the trail through the woods to the river.

Gauge

Molalla River at Canby. The gauge is far downstream. This stretch generally has about two-thirds of the flow at Canby. Optimal flows are 1500–3500 cfs on the Canby gauge. At higher flows, Horse Creek Canyon approaches class 4 and has serious hydraulics.

Laurie Pavey

126 ★ Molalla River
Turner Bridge to Glen Avon Bridge

Class: 3; 4	Length: 8.3 miles
Flow: 600–1000 cfs; 2000 cfs	Character: forested; canyon
Gradient: 50 fpm, C	Season: rainy

This run is known as the Three Bears Run. At the minimum flow of about 600 cfs, it is a technical class 3; at medium flows, it is a more enjoyable class 3; and at high water, it becomes a big class 4. Much of the river can be seen from the road on the way to the put-in. When running the rapids, some eddy hopping is necessary to pick the correct route. Many of the runouts are riffles leading to the next rapids.

Below the put-in, the water is fast but fairly straightforward for the first 0.7 mile. Papa Bear, the first major rapid, is identified by a large basalt cliff on river right. The rapid has two distinct parts. The top is usually run right to left, catching an eddy behind one of two large boulders. Be sure to avoid the far right undercut wall. The second half is often run middle to middle-right, threading through the boulders and holes. Papa Bear is best scouted from the road during the shuttle. Another mile down is the most difficult rapid on the run, Mama Bear, which can also be scouted from the road. The rapid starts with a boulder garden and some heavy water that leads into a fantastically picturesque gorge with moss-laden columnar basalt twisted into weird and wonderful shapes. The gorge is only 14 feet wide in places. The current slows near the end of the gorge. Class 2 and 3 rapids continue for another mile below Mama Bear and include Teen Bear and Head-Knocker.

Just below the bridge is the next major rapid, Baby Bear. The steepest (middle) part of this three-part rapid has a deceptively sticky hole just left of the large basalt boulder. The hole and the sheer right wall here can be problematic. Scout carefully. This middle part of the rapid can be avoided by taking an alternative route that leads around the right side of the large rock island; however, this route can be very shallow at low flows. In the half-mile below Baby Bear, there are several alternative access points using trails from the river to the road on the left.

Downstream of Three Bears, there are about 4 miles of easier water, but do not forget about Goldilocks, probably the most dangerous rapid. Goldilocks begins with fast water that is split by an island and can be run on either side. The left is easier, especially at low water. At the bottom is a blind turn to the right against an undercut rock that could entrap a boater. The final named rapid, Porridge Bowl, consists of an easier, short, fast drop where the river flows toward a headwall. A short distance below, Trout Creek enters from the right into a deep pool, followed by a house on the right. Take out on the right in 0.2 mile, where the road is close to the river. Glen Avon Bridge is 0.2 mile below the take-out.

Lower end of Mama Bear Rapid, Molalla River (Mark Scantlebury)

Hazards

Wood blockages can sometimes be a problem. The Three Bears should be scouted during the shuttle. Watch out for the undercut wall on the right in Papa Bear. Mama Bear, leading into the columnar basalt gorge, becomes solid class 4 at high water. Goldilocks cannot be seen from the road. It should be scouted on foot or by careful eddy hopping to check for logs and the undercut.

Access

Drive to the town of Molalla. Go east through downtown Molalla on Oregon 211 and take a right at the Y intersection. Follow signs to Feyrer Park, which is less than 2 miles from the Y, staying left at the first bend. From Feyrer Park, cross the river and turn right on Dickey Prairie Road. Go upriver and pass through the community of Dickey Prairie. Continuing upriver, Dickey Prairie Road crosses the North Fork Molalla, and after 0.2 mile, the Glen Avon Bridge is on the right, crossing the Molalla River. Without crossing the river on the Glen Avon Bridge, continue 0.2 mile to a wide area near river level, the take-out.

To reach the put-in, backtrack 0.2 mile and cross the Glen Avon Bridge. Continue upstream on the Molalla Forest Road for 9 miles to Turner Bridge. Cross the Molalla and continue a little farther up to a roadside pullout on the right.

Gauge

Molalla River at Canby. The recommended minimum flow at the Canby guage is 1000 cfs, which corresponds to about 600 cfs in this upper reach. At gauge flows over 3500 cfs, the rapids increase in difficulty, especially Mama Bear.

Rob Blickensderfer, Joe Gymkowski, and WKCC Editors

127 Molalla River
Glen Avon Bridge to Feyrer Park

Class: 2; 2+	Length: 6 miles
Flow: 650–2000 cfs; 3500+ cfs	Character: agricultural; rural
Gradient: 29 fpm, PD	Season: rainy

On this run, several straightforward class 2 rapids and good play spots alternate with class 1 stretches of fast water. The river is more interesting and not nearly as flat as it appears from the road on the way up to the put-in. At high flows, large roller-coaster waves appear in several stretches. Several houses are visible from the river. About 4 miles below the put-in, a private bridge crosses the river. The take-out is on the left at the next bridge at Feyrer Park. Depending upon the boater's skill and mood, this short run could be combined with the Molalla River: Turner Bridge to Glen Avon Bridge run or the Molalla River: Feyrer Park to Oregon 213 Bridge run.

Hazards

All of the largest rapids, class 2, occur in the upper half of the run. The waves can be relatively large, but the rapids are straightforward.

Access

See the Molalla River: Turner Bridge to Glen Avon Bridge run for directions to both the take-out and the put-in for this run. The take-out is at Feyrer Park, east of Molalla.

To reach the put-in from Feyrer Park, continue to Glen Avon and its bridge across the Molalla River. Without crossing the river, continue 0.2 mile to a wide area near river level, the put-in.

Gauge

Molalla River at Canby. Actual flows are about two-thirds of gauge flows. The recommended minimum flow at Canby is 1000 cfs. The river has been run at flows around 10,000 cfs; the river is very fast, and eddies are few at that flow.

Rob Blickensderfer and WKCC Editors

128 Molalla River
Feyrer Park to Oregon 213 Bridge

Class: 1+	Length: 6.7 miles
Flow: 600–2000 cfs	Character: rural
Gradient: 18 fpm, C	Season: rainy

This is an excellent run for a beginning kayaker's second river trip. It is relatively free of brush, and has numerous riffles and enough small rapids and speed to keep boaters interested. The first bridge, after 2 miles, is the Oregon 211 crossing. The second bridge, after an additional 6 miles, is the Oregon 213 crossing. Take out under the bridge on the left at Wagonwheel Park.

Hazards

There are no particular hazards, but keep an eye out for wood blockages.

Access

Drive to the town of Molalla. Go east through downtown Molalla on Oregon 211 and take a right at the Y intersection. Follow signs to Feyrer Park, which is less than 2 miles from the Y, staying left at the first bend in the road. The boat launch area is upstream of the bridge on river left.

To reach the take-out, return to Molalla and continue west on Oregon 211 to the intersection with Oregon 213. Go north on Oregon 213 for 3.5 miles. Turn right just before crossing the bridge over the Molalla into Wagonwheel Park, which has parking and a boat launch area.

Gauge

Molalla River at Canby. Actual flows are about two-thirds of gauge flows. The recommended minimum flow at Canby is 1000 cfs. The flow can be very high in the winter and is not suitable for beginners above 3000 cfs (gauge flow).

Rob Blickensderfer and WKCC Editors

129 Molalla River
Oregon 213 Bridge to Molalla River State Park on the Willamette River

Class: 1+(2)	Length: 15.3 miles
Flow: 1000–2000 cfs	Character: riparian forest; farmland
YGradient: 11 fpm, C	Season: rainy

The Molalla is the largest Willamette tributary with no dams affecting its flows, and this lower reach feels more remote than it is, offering a lovely example of a lowland cottonwood riparian corridor with gravel bars and a few backwater sloughs. The Pudding River joins the Molalla 1.5 miles above the confluence with the Willamette. The Molalla delta, at the mouth, is one of the Willamette's richest riparian forests. Take-out is just downstream of the confluence on river right.

Hazards

About 4 miles below the Oregon 213 bridge, avoid strong flows into an old railroad abutment.

Access

From Molalla, go north on Oregon 213 for 3.5 miles to the Wagonwheel access on the right before the bridge. For take-out, Molalla River State Park's ramp is on the Willamette 1 mile below the Molalla confluence; from US 99E at Canby, take Ivy northwest 1 mile, go left on Territorial for a block, and right on Holly Street to the state park.

Gauge

Molalla River at Canby. The flow can be very high in the winter and is not suitable for beginners above about 3000 cfs.

Tim Palmer

Clackamas River and Tributaries

130 Collawash River
Elk Lake Creek to Bridge
5.5 Miles from Mouth

Class: 4(5)	Length: 6.1 miles
Flow: 500–1000 cfs	Character: isolated canyon
Gradient: 78 fpm, PD	Season: rainy/snowmelt

This upper section of the Collawash River provides some great scenery and fun class 4–5 rapids set in a remote canyon. However, much of the first 4 miles of the run consists of class 2 rapids. Additionally, there is one monster logjam that must be portaged; it has existed for many years.

From the crystal-clear pool beneath the bridge at the put-in, the Collawash flows pleasantly through a rugged canyon with occasional class 2 and class 3 rapids. After about 4 miles of paddling, just above Happy Creek, you will encounter a huge logjam that blocks the entire river. There is not much current in this section, and the logjam is easy to walk on and around, so this portage is reasonable. The river remains flat below the logjam until the canyon narrows dramatically, and the river then drops over a distinct horizon line. Scout this fun class 4 rapid from the left, and be sure to look downstream. A big class 5 rapid, Big Dog, lurks just below. Scout Big Dog from the left, but portage on the right. The portage is a long climb over and around lots of big boulders and sharp rocks. After a steep boulder garden and a right turn, the river drops over several steep ledges that make up The Churn. The first ledge is runnable anywhere, but do not get pushed downstream, as the second ledge contains a nasty pin spot. At some flows, a good channel is available on the far left. The steep and challenging boulder garden in the final part of The Churn can change frequently due to active landslides in the area. Scout carefully. Below The Churn, the river has a couple of other fun rapids and possibly another log portage. More good class 4 rapids dot the remaining distance down to the take-out at the highway bridge.

Hazards

The difficult rapids on this run are formed by huge boulders deposited from landslides and can shift from year to year. In addition, there is potential for dangerous wood and pin spots in all the rapids. Scouting and portaging involve scrambling on unstable banks with sharp rocks. The canyon is very isolated, and hiking out is difficult.

Access

The take-out for this run is the put-in for the Collawash River: Bridge 5.5 Miles from Mouth to Two Rivers Picnic Area run.

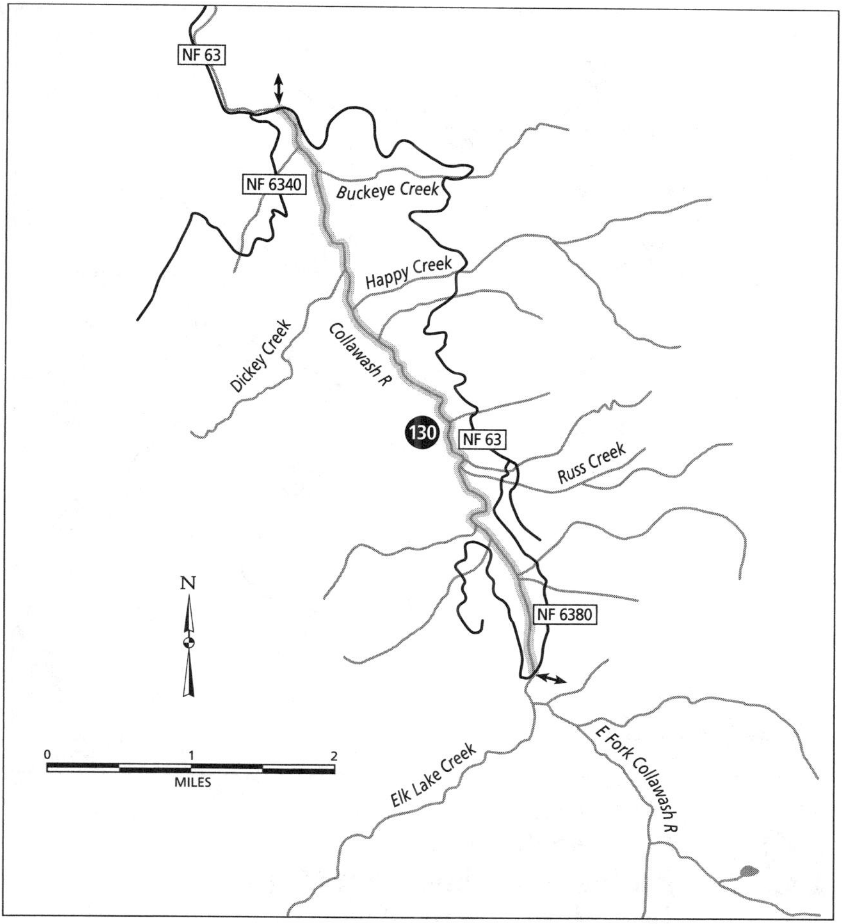

To reach the put-in, continue on NF 63 and NF 6380 for 8.6 miles to the bridge over the Collawash, staying right at major intersections after 2.75, 3.6 and 6.3 miles.

Gauge

Visual. The rapids visible from the take-out bridge are a good indicator of the flow on the upper river. It is generally runnable when the Clackamas River at Three Lynx gauge is over 2500 cfs.

Pete Giordano and WKCC Editors

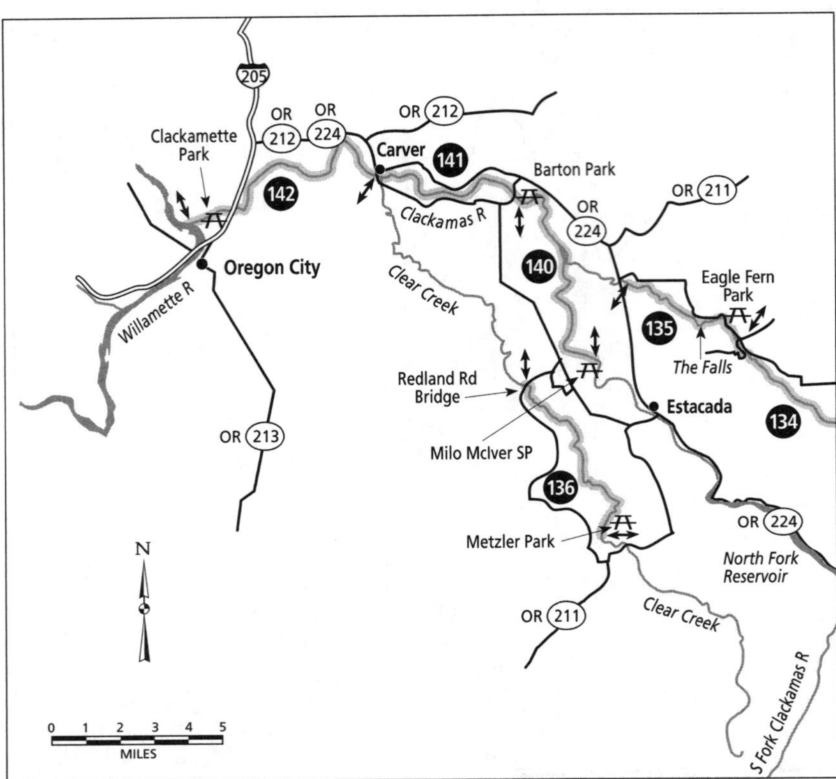

131 Collawash River
Bridge 5.5 Miles from Mouth to Two Rivers Picnic Area

Class: 3(4); 3+(5)	Length: 6.2 miles
Flow: 900 cfs; 2500 cfs	Character: wooded canyon
Gradient: 54 fpm, PD	Season: rainy/snowmelt

Enjoyable class 3 rapids and numerous play spots characterize most of this run, except for two difficult class 4–5 rapids. Both of these rapids are in the upper 2-mile section and can be avoided by using the lower put-in. From the bridge at the upper put-in, it is only about 0.25 mile to the first major rapid, Boulderdash, class 4, a 0.3-mile-long boulder garden complete with house rocks, narrow chutes, and a serious gradient. Scout the entire rapid from the roadside pullout 5.2 miles above the take-out. This involves some scrambling and peering through trees but is well worth the effort. From the river, scout Boulderdash from either bank. Most of the runnable slots are river left, with the exit near the center.

After 1.5 miles of class 2 rapids, the second class 4 rapid, Chute to Kill, is identified by the cliff on river right. Again, scout Chute to Kill on the way to the put-in from a roadside pullout 3.6 miles above the take-out. The run begins as a steep boulder garden followed by a large hole backed by a guard rock. A solid brace makes life more enjoyable here. A short pool leads into the last drop, a 5-foot plunge down a steep chute into a powerful hole on river left. A right chute deadends in a boulder jam, hence the name.

A quarter-mile below Chute to Kill, the Hot Springs Fork enters from river left. This optional put-in allows 1 mile of easy warm-up before entering the class 3 section with its many nice play waves and holes. The final class 3, Up Against the

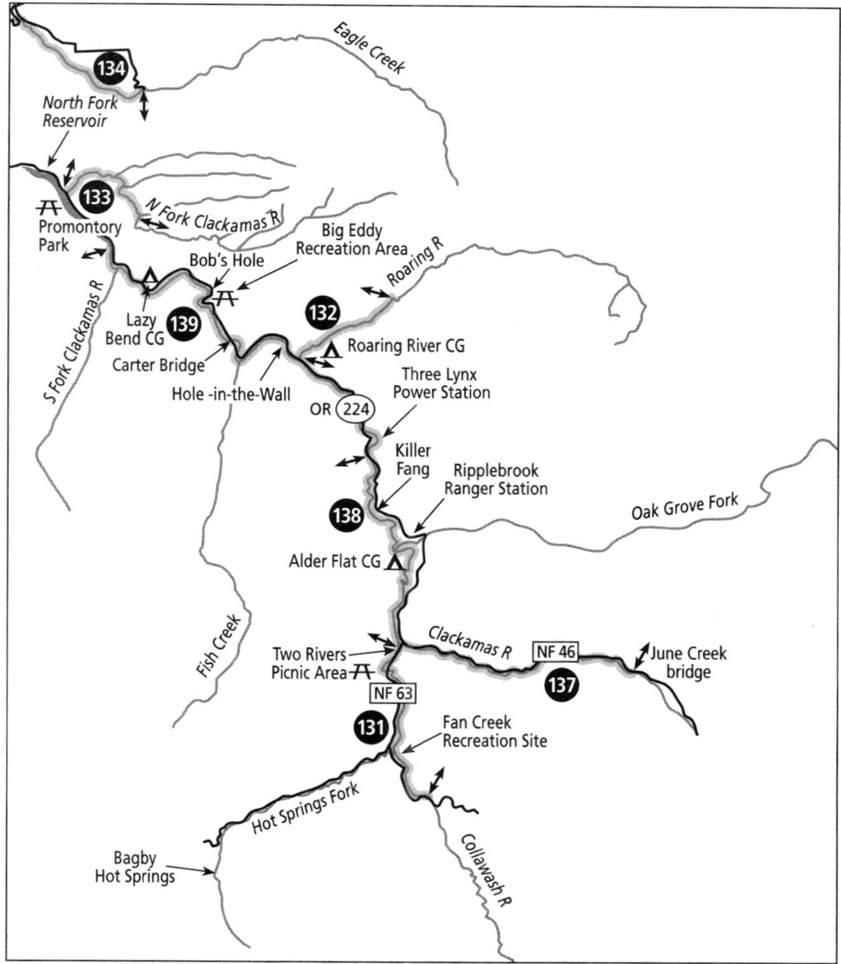

Wall, comes at a right bend in the river, just past the only bridge, and marks the end of good whitewater. Take out on the right just before the confluence with the Clackamas River.

Hazards

Boulderdash and Chute to Kill require skillful maneuvering and solid rolls at any flow. Scout both rapids on the way to the put-in; they are likely to become class 5 at higher flows. All the class 3 rapids are visible from the road except Up Against the Wall, but it is an easier rapid than those upstream. Logs and trees create some potential hazards and should be noted on the way to the put-in.

Access

From Interstate 205 southeast of Portland, take Oregon 212 east and then Oregon 224 south to Estacada. From Estacada, continue about 23 miles upstream to the Ripplebrook Ranger Station. Past Ripplebrook, turn right on NF 46, then turn right on NF 63, and continue for 0.1 mile to the confluence of the Collawash and the Clackamas. The take-out is at the Two Rivers Picnic Area, just upstream of the confluence, across the bridge on the right.

To reach the put-in, continue upstream on NF 63. The lower put-in for the class 3 run is 3.4 miles upstream at the Hot Springs Fork confluence at the Fan Creek Recreation Site. The upper put-in is another 2.1 miles upstream, where a bridge crosses the Collawash.

Gauge

None exists. Use the gauge Clackamas River above Three Lynx. The flow is about 40 percent of that at the Three Lynx gauge. The authors made the run between 900 and 1800 cfs (2300–4500 cfs at Three Lynx).

Jeff Bennett, Tonya Shrives, and WKCC Editors

132 Roaring River
3 Miles Above Clackamas River to Clackamas River

Class: 4 T	Length: 3 miles
Flow: 300–750 cfs	Character: isolated wooded canyon
Gradient: 207 fpm, C	Season: rainy/snowmelt

Roaring River is an interesting, short run for boaters looking to paddle in a designated wilderness area. The entire length of the run is a designated Wild and Scenic River, and the water and forest are pristine. Despite its steep gradient, Roaring River is mostly characterized by uniform boulder gardens with the exception of the last mile. Several fun ledges and pushy boulder gardens provide a great end to the run. Be prepared for multiple portages around logs, stumps, and other wood hazards. The steep gradient makes it difficult to see very far downstream, so judicious scouting is required. The run can take three–four hours the first time, so leave plenty of time to finish before dark.

Hazards

Wood shifts position every year, so be sure to scout often. The last mile of the run contains several ledges that develop sticky hydraulics at high flows. A notable one is a class 4+ to 5 keeper hole, named Gabe's Hole, which is often portaged. It is the third ledge in a series of three stair-step ledges. Scout on the left above this series of ledges. The scout eddy has a tricky entrance, but be sure to make the eddy.

Access

Access to this run can be blocked by snow much of the winter, creating a small boating window in the fall and spring.

To reach the take-out, go to Estacada. Drive upstream along the Clackamas River on Oregon 224 for 18 miles to Roaring River Campground. The take-out is at the bridge over Roaring River on Oregon 224, just downstream of the campground.

To reach the put-in, follow Oregon 224 downstream from the take-out for 12 miles and turn right across the highway from the Promontory Park entrance. Reset your odometer upon leaving Oregon 224. Immediately turn left onto NF 4610. At 4.3 miles, bear right (straight) where the road splits. At mile 7.3, go right onto NF 4611. Stay on the main road at all splits for the next mile. At mile 8.5, stay left at the fork. At mile 9.5, stay far right at the three-way intersection. At mile 10.7, stay right at the fork. Stay on the main road at all the splits for the next mile. At mile 12.1, the road begins to decline in quality. At about 14 miles, there are huge mud holes and trees, marking the end of the road.

Park and walk down the overgrown remains of the road, taking the middle road of the three. In a couple of hundred yards, watch for a small trail on the right. This is the Grouse Point Trail, which leads down to the river via switchbacks. The hike down takes about 45 minutes and is about 1.5 miles.

Gauge

Visual. If the rapid at the Oregon 224 bridge looks runnable, then the rest of the run should be fine. Generally, the Clackamas River at Three Lynx gauge should be at least 2500 cfs.

Pete Giordano and WKCC Editors

133 North Fork Clackamas River
3.75 Miles Above North Fork Reservoir to North Fork Reservoir

Class: 4–4+(5) P	Length: 3.8 miles
Flow: 250–500 cfs	Character: isolated canyon/gorge
Gradient: 193 fpm, PD, C	Season: rainy/snowmelt

The North Fork of the Clackamas River begins as a tiny stream in the foothills of the Cascades, gradually building in size and plunging through the basalt of the Clackamas River canyon to end in the backwaters of the North Fork Reservoir. The river is at the bottom of a steep and isolated canyon and is dotted with waterfalls, ledge drops, and that ever-present Northwest boater obstacle: wood.

Steep boulder gardens and small ledges characterize the first mile of the run. Most of these rapids can be scouted from a boat, but several are quite steep and should be scouted for wood by at least one member of the group. The first major obstacle is a short gorge with a river-wide ledge near the end. The lead-in to the ledge is swift with very small eddies, and the gorge has contained dangerous wood in the past. Scout early from the right bank.

Once past the gorge, be on the lookout for more fun rapids but also for a small overgrown road on the left bank. The road is just before a left turn with a series of small sliding ledges that end in a runnable 12-foot falls. Although the falls is fun, portaging the unrunnable 50-foot falls below it is much easier if you forgo the falls and hike up the road. Either way, portaging the falls requires hiking up the canyon wall, and lowering boats back down the steep canyon wall several hundred yards downstream. Almost immediately below the unrunnable falls and just downstream of a creek on river right is a steep class 5 waterfall, Stairway to Heaven. The waterfall totals about 20 feet and is a wild ride over two smaller ledges before the final 10-foot drop into a sticky hole. Scout or portage on the left.

The next 0.5 mile contains some class 3 boulder gardens before the river begins to drop through an amazing array of continuous, steep boulder gardens that only relent 0.5 mile from the reservoir. Many of these drops contain wood and numerous pin spots. At high water, eddies can become scarce. Scout often and be safe.

Hazards

The first gorge may become unscoutable at high water. The 50-foot waterfall must be portaged. Many of the hardest rapids contain wood that can shift from year to year. Pin spots abound throughout the whole run.

Access

From Estacada, follow Oregon 224 east about 5.2 miles and park in the small parking area on the left just before crossing the North Fork. This is the take-out.

To reach the put-in, return to Oregon 224 and continue east another 1.3 miles. Turn left and then left again. Follow this road, NF 4610, another 3.2 miles to a rough, gated road on the left leading down to the river. From here, it is an easy 0.7-mile hike down to the river.

Gauge

Visual. The North Fork usually has enough water when the Clackamas River at Three Lynx gauge is over 3000 cfs.

Pete Giordano

134 ★ Eagle Creek
Fish Hatchery to Snuffin Road

Class: 3(4+) T	Length: 5.4 miles
Flow: 300 cfs	Character: forested; cabins
Gradient: 69 fpm, PD	Season: rainy

Eagle Creek drains the Cascade foothills east of Estacada, and flows generally northwest into the Clackamas River about halfway between Estacada and Barton. It was named for the eagles that used to dip to catch the thousands of spawning salmon. The creek is small and anglers sometimes crowd the banks. Several bridges cross the creek, but paddlers catch only glimpses of the road, and then only in the vicinity of Eagle Fern Park.

At the put-in, the creek is narrow with overhanging shrubbery. If the water level is high, the current can be intimidating. Sweepers, logs, and blind turns make the upper part of this run quite interesting, although the rapids are usually not too complex, mostly class 2+. This upper section will likely have several logs or logjams that may require a portage.

A little more than halfway through the trip is a 15- to 18-foot waterfall. Watch for the 4-foot-high concrete fish ladder bypassing the falls. It is on the right bank past a sharp right bend. Take out on the right in the pool well before the concrete wall to scout and/or portage. An alternative portage begins in an easy eddy 30–50 yards above the falls on river left. It is considerably shorter, but the descent back to the river is steeper. The falls can be run down a tongue on the right or down the center-right. A large hydraulic can form at the base at high water. Portage on the trail or down the fish ladder.

It is about 1 mile from the base of the falls to Eagle Fern Camp—a large, open area on the left. The best action on this run comes in the mile between the camp and the take-out. The creek goes around a right bend and into an interesting boulder garden. It gets more challenging near the bottom, after a left bend. A short respite precedes some more fun boulder gardens and the bridge at the take-out. To scout the lower end of the final drop, park at the first pullout upstream of the bridge on Snuffin Road and walk through the woods a few yards.

Hazards

The falls, logs, possible logjams, brushy banks, and boulder gardens between the youth camp and the take-out are the difficulties on this run.

Access

From Interstate 205 southeast of Portland, take Oregon 212 east and Oregon 224 south to the community of Eagle Creek. Oregon 224/211 crosses Eagle Creek about 4.5 miles north of the stoplight in Estacada. Just north of the bridge, turn east onto Wildcat Mountain Drive, which is marked by a sign pointing to Eagle Fern Park. Keep right at an immediate Y and then cross Eagle Creek Road.

In 1.8 miles, veer right onto Eagle Fern Road. It is about 2.2 miles from here to the entrance to Eagle Fern Park. Snuffin Road comes in from the right about 0.8 mile south of the park entrance. Either the park or the Snuffin Road bridge can be used as a take-out. There's a $5-per-car park entrance fee year-round.

To reach the put-in, return to the junction of Snuffin and Eagle Fern roads, and find George Road, which starts at this intersection. (Eagle Road becomes George Road at Snuffin.) Follow George Road about 4.5 miles to a right turn onto Rainbow Road. A sign on the left points toward the fish hatchery, 2 miles away and 600 feet down. A marked parking lot is located next to a private bridge across the creek. Across the bridge is private property, too, so it is better to put in by the parking area.

Gauge

No online gauge exists. There is a stick gauge at the hatchery put-in. Runs between 0.5 and 1.5 on the stick gauge are usually good. Generally, upper Eagle Creek is runnable if the Clackamas River at Three Lynx is above 3000 cfs. The creek drops quickly after rains. The upper limit is reached when the stick gauge reads 1.9 feet (Clackamas at Three Lynx at 8400 cfs), and the creek runs slightly out of its banks; the run is solid class 4 at this level.

Hank Hays and WKCC Editors

135 Eagle Creek
Snuffin Road to Eagle Creek Road

Class: 3+(5) P	Length: 4.4 miles
Flow: 300–700 cfs	Character: forested; residential
Gradient: 59 fpm, C-PD	Season: rainy

The character of the lower run on Eagle Creek is similar to that of the upper run (see the Eagle Creek: Fish Hatchery to Snuffin Road run). About 0.5 mile below the put-in at the Snuffin Road bridge is a low-head dam (1–2 feet). A shallow slide in the center of the dam makes an easy run. A mile below the put-in, the North Fork Eagle Creek emerges on the right underneath a bridge at a left bend in the river. The Falls, a dangerous class 5 rapid, is 0.5 mile farther. Plenty of action can be had before the falls, and eddies get progressively smaller near the falls. Work toward the right as soon as you see the upstream end of a concrete fish ladder on the right bank, and take out at the upstream end of the fish-ladder retaining wall. If you decide to run the falls, stay far right, boofing off the end of the fish ladder. Most of the current pushes to the left and into a nasty undercut slot on the left bank. The portage trail is up the bank on the right and back down to the river about 100 yards downstream.

About 1.5 miles of boulder gardens await below The Falls. The first 0.5 mile drops at the rate of 125 fpm. There can be logs in the biggest rapids, so scout blind corners before attempting a run. The first hard right bend below The Falls may have logs. Scout left. About 0.5 mile below The Falls, a blind left bend around a small island may contain wood. Scout left, from the top of the island. Portaging would not be easy because the banks are sheer on both sides. Many more interesting drops and boulder gardens follow along the next mile.

The recommended take-out is the first concrete bridge, Eagle Creek Road. Land about 25 feet above it on the right for the easiest hike up to the road. The run could be continued down to the Dowty Road crossing, about 0.5 mile from the creek mouth, or even to Barton Park on the Clackamas.

Hazards

Difficulties include possible logjams, sweepers, The Falls, and the boulder gardens below The Falls. Many anglers are usually present in this section, so courteously avoid them. The Falls can be scouted by looking for a small pullout, yellow gate, and trail on the way to the put-in.

Access

For directions to a put-in at either Snuffin Road or Eagle Fern Park, see the Eagle Creek: Fish Hatchery to Snuffin Road run.

A vehicle can be dropped off at the take-out on Eagle Creek Road on the way in by taking a right onto Eagle Creek Road (the first crossroad after leaving Oregon 211) and parking in the pullout on the east side of the road before crossing the bridge.

Gauge

None exists. Generally, this stretch of Eagle Creek is runnable if the Clackamas River at Three Lynx gauge is about 2500 cfs. Creek flows fluctuate rapidly. 3000 cfs is often optimal. 7500 cfs would be high but runnable. Look at the water level from the Eagle Creek Road bridge at the take-out.

Hank Hays and WKCC Editors

136 Clear Creek
Metzler Park to Redland Road Bridge

Class: 2+(3) T	Length: 7.3 miles
Flow: 500 cfs	Character: forested; residential
Gradient: 41 fpm, C	Season: rainy

The main stem of Clear Creek drains the north face of Goat Mountain south of Estacada and flows into the Clackamas River at Carver. Because the stream is small and subject to logjams, check the blind bends in the river before proceeding. Flatwater with good current extends between drops. Most of the land along both banks is private except for two small sections of BLM land and Metzler Park.

From the very beginning the creek is fairly fast and continuous. Keep a sharp lookout for logs or downed trees in the creek. It could be difficult to land before getting into trouble. About 0.5 mile below the park is a good class 2+ rapid. About 4 miles into the run, a steel bridge spans the river. This marks the start of a half-mile steeper section consisting of three or four class 3 boulder drops. The last drop has a 3-foot pour-over at the bottom. The rest of the run flattens out to class 1. There may be a few logs to portage or pass under. A huge log jam existed in the slow water of this section in the past. Use caution. The take-out is on the right.

An alternative put-in is located down a steep bank where the Oregon 211 bridge crosses Clear Creek. This adds a mile to the trip, which will likely include wood.

Hazards

Logjams and logs spanning the river are the main hazards. It can be difficult to stop in the 0.5-mile steep section below the steel bridge. Logs could be very dangerous there.

Access

The put-in is about 25 miles southeast of Portland. From Estacada, take Oregon 211 south for about 4 miles. At the top of the hill, turn right (west) onto Tucker Road. Take the first left onto Metzler Park Road and drive 1.5 miles into the park, the put-in.

To reach the take-out, return to Tucker Road. Go straight (north) at the intersection; the road name changes to Springwater Road. Continue on Springwater Road for about 5 miles. Pass the entrance to Milo McIver State Park and at the next road on the left, turn left onto Redland Road. Proceed 1.5 miles to the bridge over Clear Creek, the take-out.

Gauge

None exists. Clear Creek rises and falls abruptly. It has been run when the Clackamas River at Three Lynx was at 4400–5400 cfs. Check the river level at the put-in and take-out bridges described above.

Hank Hays and WKCC Editors

137 ★ Clackamas River
June Creek Bridge to Collawash River

Class: 3+(4); 4	Length: 7.8 miles
Flow: 350–3500 cfs; 4000+ cfs	Character: forested; hot springs
Gradient: 74 fpm, C-PD	Season: rainy/snowmelt

The Clackamas River above the Collawash confluence contains nearly continuous, intermediate rapids, beautiful scenery, clear water, and a pleasant riverside hot springs. The rocky streambed and consistent gradient provide plenty of action for the first 5.5 miles. Two small, narrow gorges in this first section contain steeper drops and should be scouted from the road during the shuttle to check for wood. Austin Hot Springs, about 5.5 miles from the put-in, makes a nice spot to warm hands and feet. About 0.5 mile below the hot springs is a steep drop with a large rock in the middle of the river. The drop is preceded by 50 yards of waves and holes. Boaters generally run just to the right of the center rock, punch through a large wave, and keep left to avoid another rock on the right. A sneak route along the right bank is possible at some levels. The left side looks attractive but is dangerously undercut. A long boulder garden (class 3+ to 4) that contains some nice waves and holes, as well as large rocks, is 2 miles downstream. Scout the entire boulder garden from the road.

Hazards

This run collects a lot of wood in some years. Wood is constantly shifting position so it is important to scout all the more difficult rapids (and the rest of the river) from the road before starting the run. The significant rapids are 0.5 mile, 2.5 miles, and 4.4 road miles upstream of the take-out. In addition, steel cables left in the river from past stream habitat work could be hazardous.

Access

To reach the take-out area at the confluence of the Clackamas and the Collawash rivers (the Two Rivers Picnic Area), see the Clackamas River: Collawash River to Sandstone Road Bridge run. A good take-out is on the left immediately upstream of the NF 63 bridge over the Clackamas. Several other locations are also available.

To reach put-in, drive upstream on NF 46. Because the road follows the river for the entire run, any number of alternative put-ins and take-outs are possible. The uppermost put-in is at the June Creek bridge, about 7 miles above take-out.

Gauge

Clackamas River above Three Lynx. The flow on the June Creek section is roughly half of the flow at the Three Lynx gauge. Late-season runs as low as 700 cfs on the Three Lynx gauge are possible, with all sections runnable but very technical. Many boaters favor flows around 1500–3000 cfs on the gauge (which corresponds to about 750–1500 cfs in actual flow). When above 8000 cfs on the gauge, class 4 skills are necessary.

Pete Giordano and WKCC Editors

138 Clackamas River
Collawash River to Sandstone Road Bridge (Three Lynx)

Class: 4(5+) P	Length: 8.3 miles
Flow: 1000–4000 cfs	Character: forested; roadless
Gradient: 39 fpm, PD	Season: rainy/snowmelt

This secluded and scenic run on the Clackamas River, known locally as the Killer Fang run, can be dangerous and intimidating, particularly at high flows. A reliable roll, reliable equipment, and a competent leader make for a more enjoyable day.

Landslides and high water continually shape the rapids and landscape on this run. Logs commonly present problems.

After 1 mile of flatwater, the river leaves the road and boaters encounter some fun class 2 and 3 rapids. The rapids gradually increase in size before reaching Hole in the River rapid. At low flows, this rapid is a maze of rocks, but at high water, when the rocks become covered, several large holes appear in the left and middle of the rapid. Around the next bend is a steep rapid that slams into a huge undercut boulder. Move left immediately at the bottom of the rapid to avoid being pushed uncomfortably close to the boulder. Below this rapid are many fun class 3 rapids including Rocky's Rapid, where the river bends right after slamming into a wall. About 4.5 miles below the put-in, just below Rocky's Rapid, is Alder Flat Campground, a walk-in campground. This is the only take-out before the more difficult stuff begins downstream. From the trail on the right, it is a 1-mile hike up to the road; the trail ends just north of Ripplebrook Ranger Station.

Immediately below Alder Flat Campground is a pushy class 4 rapid called Drop Stopper, named for the large midstream boulder at the bottom. Twice in the next 0.5 mile, the river bends right after slamming into high rock walls. Prelude Rapid, two narrow slots, is just to the right of the second wall. Scouting Prelude from above is recommended because Killer Fang, class 5+, is 150 feet downstream and out of sight. After running Prelude, land on river right for the portage around Killer Fang. At most flows, the majority of water in Killer Fang flows into a dead-end sieve on the right. A small opening is on the left, but the left wall is undercut. Portage over the rocks and slide back into the river in the pool below the sieve. Water can be seen bubbling up from the exit of the sieve deep below the water's surface.

Do not relax after Killer Fang. The next mile has two class 4 rock gardens. The first, Sieve, is around the corner from Killer Fang. There's a pushy class 3 entrance rapid just above Sieve; make sure you catch the mandatory left eddy just below it in order to scout. At Sieve, the water slams into the middle of a rock jumble with several undercuts and sieves. The only clear passage is down a chute on the far left. At low water levels, wood occasionally blocks the exit of this chute. Scout and/ or portage Sieve on the left. Next comes River's Revenge, where some fancy eddy hopping is required to maneuver through the narrow slots between large rocks. Class 2 rapids continue for about a mile to the take-out.

Hazards

This section is very different from the more popular section immediately downstream from it (the Clackamas River: Three Lynx Power Station to North Fork Reservoir run). Landslides constantly deposit logs into the river and can change rapids from year to year. Logs pose a real threat on any of the rapids and can be difficult to see at river level. As always, scout if the bottom of a rapid is hidden from view. Definitely scout Drop Stopper, Prelude, and Sieve. Although it has been run, Killer Fang is almost always a mandatory portage at any water level.

Access

From the north: From Interstate 205 southeast of Portland, take Oregon 212 east and then Oregon 224 south to Estacada. From the south: From Interstate 5 exit 271, take Oregon 214 east through Woodburn, cross US 99 (stay straight at the traffic signal), and take Oregon 211 east to Estacada.

From Estacada, continue about 20 miles upstream on Oregon 224 to the Three Lynx Power Station. Go 0.25 mile past the power station to the bridge crossing the river. A good put-in/take-out area is located on river left just upstream of this bridge where Sandstone Road meets Oregon 224.

To reach the put-in, cross the Sandstone Road Bridge and continue up Oregon 224/NF 46 on river right. About 3 miles past the Ripplebrook Ranger Station, you reach the junction of NF 46 and NF 63. Here at the confluence of the Collawash and the Clackamas rivers, several put-ins are possible. Cross the NF 63 bridge for put-ins above or below the bridge on river left (by the Two Rivers Picnic Area). An alternative put-in, located 1 mile downstream at Riverside Campground, skips the beginning flatwater.

Gauge

Clackamas River above Three Lynx.

Roger Van Zandt, Hank Hays, and Pete Giordano

139★ Clackamas River
Three Lynx Power Station to
North Fork Reservoir

Class: 3(4)	Length: 13.1 miles
Flow: 700–10,000 cfs	Character: forested; popular area
Gradient: 37 fpm, PD	Season: year-round

This section of the Clackamas River is one of the most popular runs in Oregon. The beautiful canyon scenery, quality beginner-intermediate whitewater, and proximity to Portland entice boaters throughout the year. At high water levels, several of the rapids develop large waves and holes, while low water creates rocky, technical rapids followed by beautiful pools.

About 0.25 mile below the put-in is Powerhouse Rapid. This rapid can be quite challenging at some flows as the main current slams into the bank and splits. Aim for the large pool on the left as you negotiate the waves in the center. For the next several miles, the river moves through many fun class 2–3 rapids, including The Narrows, where the river is squeezed between beautiful basalt walls. Around the corner from Sunstrip Campground is Roaring River Rapid, a steep, rocky rapid that is generally run on the left. At low flows, the left wall at the bottom should be avoided because it is undercut and has sharp exposed rocks. The next

Taking a break below Carter Bridge Rapid, Clackamas River (Mark Scantlebury)

major rapid is Hole-in-the-Wall. At high water, this rapid develops a very dangerous recirculating pocket along the left wall. Avoid it by assertively moving hard right. It's good to scout Hole-in-the-Wall during the shuttle. Immediately past the next bridge is the Fish Creek boat ramp on the left, which provides good access for a shorter run.

About 0.5 mile below this bridge and past another bridge is one of the biggest rapids on the run, Carter Bridge. Scout on the left when a third bridge comes into view. The commonly run line is generally down the left, avoiding a ledge that extends across most of the river from the right bank. After a short section of easier water, the river plunges through Big Swirly or Slingshot. Run down the middle through the large waves and swirly water, or aim for the large eddy on the left. A boiling eddy forms along the wall on the right at the bottom of the rapid. Just below the large pool at Big Eddy is Rock 'n' Roll, a short plunge through some rocks on the right. At some flows, a great play hole develops in the wave train below the rapid. Toilet Bowl, class 3+ to 4, is just around the corner from Rock 'n' Roll and contains some huge waves at high water. Scout from the gravel bar on the right. Toilet Bowl is most easily portaged along the left. This is the last big rapid on the run, although several fun class 2 rapids lie ahead. Bob's Hole, a popular play hole, is just below Toilet Bowl. The section of river between Carter Falls and Bob's Hole is the site of an annual whitewater event, the Upper Clackamas Whitewater Festival, which has been held every May for the past several decades.

The remaining 4 miles to North Fork Reservoir are class 2 and generally easier than the rapids above. Inexperienced boaters may tend to get pushed into the bank in several places. All of this lower section can be seen from the road. Slack water begins just after the South Fork Clackamas enters from the left.

Hazards

Most of the major rapids can be scouted from the road. Be sure to scout Hole-in-the-Wall, as this rapid is very dangerous at medium and high water. A metal ladder is attached to the upstream rock wall of the pocket that can be used in rescue situations.

Access

For directions to Estacada, see the Clackamas River: Collawash River to Sandstone Road Bridge run. From Estacada, continue about 20 miles upstream on Oregon 224 to the Three Lynx Power Station.

The most common put-in is at the bridge 0.25 mile above the power station, the Sandstone Road bridge. This put-in has good raft access and is just above the bridge on river left. An alternative put-in spot is at the bridge below the Power Station on river left.

Other access points (from upstream to downstream) include: Sunstrip Campground, Hole-in-the-Wall, Fish Creek (raft-slide boat ramp located 0.3 mile from the highway), Carter Bridge, Big Eddy Day Use Area, a road pullout at Bob's Hole (at milepost 36.7), Moore Creek (milepost 35.3), Lazy Bend Campground, and Memaloose (good raft access at milepost 33.5). Below Memaloose, it's less than a mile to North Fork Reservoir, the final take-out. Since the road parallels the river, trips of between 3 and 13 miles can be made, depending on which access points are used. A common kayak play run is from Fish Creek to Bob's Hole.

Gauge

Clackamas River above Three Lynx. Optimal flows are 1000–3500 cfs. Between 700 and 900 cfs, the river is technical, and most paddlers use the Sunstrip Campground put-in. Flows over 5000 cfs demand big-water paddling skills.

Bill Ostrand, Hank Hays, Pete Giordano, and WKCC Editors

140 Clackamas River
Milo McIver State Park to Barton Park

Class: 2+	Length: 9.3 miles
Flow: 800–3000 cfs	Character: park; lowlands
Gradient: 16 fpm, PD	Season: year-round

This beautiful stretch of the Clackamas River may be run all year. The first 2.5 miles are located entirely within Milo McIver State Park; for a short trip, take out at the lower end of the park. If continuing downstream, it is another 6.8 miles to the take-out at Barton Park.

The put-in at the Milo McIver State Park boat ramp offers a view of the first and largest drop. A ledge across the river provides several good standing waves for surfing. The river twists through the park with more small rapids and goes into a rock garden. The rock garden is followed by a nice play spot with more standing waves and eddies on both sides. More bends and small rapids are encountered on the way to the optional take-out at Milo McIver State Park's lowest picnic area. From here to Barton Park are several more small rapids and play spots, and considerable flatwater with occasional class 1–2 rapids. Barton Park also has both a boat ramp (on river right just above the bridge) and a picnic area.

Hazards

In high water, the first drop should be checked for the boat-eating hole that develops. A headwall below the play spot mentioned above can circulate a swimmer at high water.

Access

Be prepared to pay an entrance fee at both parks. To reach the Barton Park take-out, from the Portland area take Oregon 212 east and then Oregon 224 southeast. The park, about 7 miles from Oregon 212, closes at dusk.

The put-in is reached by driving upstream on Oregon 224 to Milo McIver State Park. Once in the park, follow the road down the hill. The put-in is at the boat ramp.

The optional take-out for the short 2.5-mile run is reached by driving to the lowest parking lot (and picnic area) within Milo McIver State Park.

Gauge

Clackamas River at Estacada. This run is runnable most of the year. Rocky runs have been made at levels as low as 750 cfs.

Bob Collmer

141 Clackamas River
Barton Park to Carver

Class: 2	Length: 5.1 miles
Flow: 800–3000 cfs	Character: residential
Gradient: 14 fpm	Season: year-round

This stretch of the Clackamas River is an excellent training area for beginners. There are many small class 2 drops, usually with eddies close by. The rapids are clean and have good runouts. The scenery is uncluttered, even though some areas have housing on the river's edge. The river class rises to the 2+ level in the spring and drops to the 2- level in the summer. It is runnable all year and is often run in the evening, when daylight permits.

Hazards

The run presents no major problem areas, although several rapids pick up speed and provide some bouncy places.

Access

To reach the put-in at the boat ramp in Barton Park, which requires an entrance fee and closes at dusk, see the Clackamas River: Milo McIver State Park to Barton Park run.

To reach the take-out, return north on Oregon 224 to Carver. Cross the bridge and turn left into Carver Park. The boat ramp is on river left just upstream from the bridge.

Gauge

Clackamas River at Estacada (upstream of run). Clackamas River near Oregon City (downstream of run).

Bob Collmer

142 Clackamas River Carver to Clackamette Park

Class: 2	Length: 7.8 miles
Flow: 800–3000 cfs	Character: residential
Gradient: 8 fpm, C	Season: year-round

This stretch of river is a fine run for intermediate canoers and beginner kayakers. The rapids are characterized by turns with standing waves on the outside or in the middle of the channels, and nice, soft eddies on the insides of the turns. The most difficult rapids are a pair of right bends followed by a pair of left bends. The second pair has a central rock to avoid. High rocks and a trestle bridge are next. There is an easy riffle here, but several 17-foot aluminum canoes have wrapped around the bridge piers in the past. The run finishes with a nice moderate S turn. The waves here are irregular and can be fun. Clackamette Park is 0.8 mile farther down on the left. The Clackamas River then flows into the Willamette River.

Hazards

Canoers should know how to handle S turns with high standing waves.

Access

To reach the put-in, take Oregon 224 east from Interstate 205 for 4 miles to the town of Carver. At Carver, cross the bridge over the river and turn left into Carver Park. The boat ramp is just upstream of the bridge on river left.

To reach the take-out at Clackamette Park, go to the south end of the bridge in Carver and drive west on Clackamas River Road, which follows the south side of the river. When intersecting Oregon 213, continue straight onto Washington Street toward downtown Oregon City. Turn right at Fifteenth Street onto McLoughlin Boulevard. Continue north 0.2 mile to a left turn (past the hotel) at a sign for Clackamette Park. Turn right and go 300 yards north. The park is on the left. It has a good boat ramp. At good flow levels, a nice park-and-play wave develops at the ramp. Look for minus tides and flows of 900–1200 cfs.

Gauge

Clackamas River at Oregon City.

Kurt Renner and WKCC Editors

Opposite: *Columnar basalt on the upper Klickitat River* (Gary Adams)

Columbia
Gorge Rivers
Region 7

Sandy River and Tributaries

143 Salmon River
Wilderness Trailhead to US 26 Bridge

Class: 2+(3)	Length: 9.9 miles
Flow: 500–2000	Character: forested; cabins
Gradient: 54 fpm, C	Season: rainy

Upstream of this run on the Salmon, the river plunges through a beautiful gorge with several large waterfalls in the Salmon-Huckleberry Wilderness. However, this section, several miles below the gorge, provides an enjoyable day of fairly continuous, technical class 2+ rapids with great wilderness scenery. If you have time, some wonderful old-growth forests can be seen by hiking along the first mile of the trail into the wilderness upstream of the put-in.

The whitewater starts immediately as the river tumbles through small boulder gardens in a lush forested canyon. About 2 miles into the run, there is a long boulder garden that ends in a 3-foot ledge. This is the most difficult rapid on the run. After another mile, the canyon opens up, and cabins, which detract somewhat from the experience, begin to appear. For a short run, take out at the bridge at Arrah Wanna Road. The rapids continue for about 4 more miles amid forest and cabins before reaching the lower take-out, which is on the left at the US 26 bridge.

Hazards

Logs in places along the bank could be a problem at higher flows. Stay alert.

Access

To reach the lowest take-out, from Sandy travel east on US 26 for 12.5 miles to Brightwood. Just before crossing the Salmon River, turn right onto East Country Club Road and make an immediate left on East Country Club Loop. Park along this road before its first bend to the right. There's a path leading to a take-out spot underneath the US 26 bridge.

For a shorter run, stay on US 26 for 3 more miles past the bridge over the Salmon. Turn right onto Arrah Wanna Road (15.5 miles east of Sandy). Go 0.9 mile to the bridge over the river, an alternative take-out.

To reach the put-in, return to US 26, turn right (east) onto the highway, and travel 1.5 miles past Arrah Wanna Road to South Salmon River Road. Turn right and travel 5.0 miles to the bridge over the river. (A USFS pass is required to park here.)

Gauge

Visual. The Sandy River gauge (Sandy River near Marmot) can be used to estimate the flow on the Salmon. The flow on the Sandy should be a minimum of 2200 cfs.

Pete Giordano and Mark Scantlebury

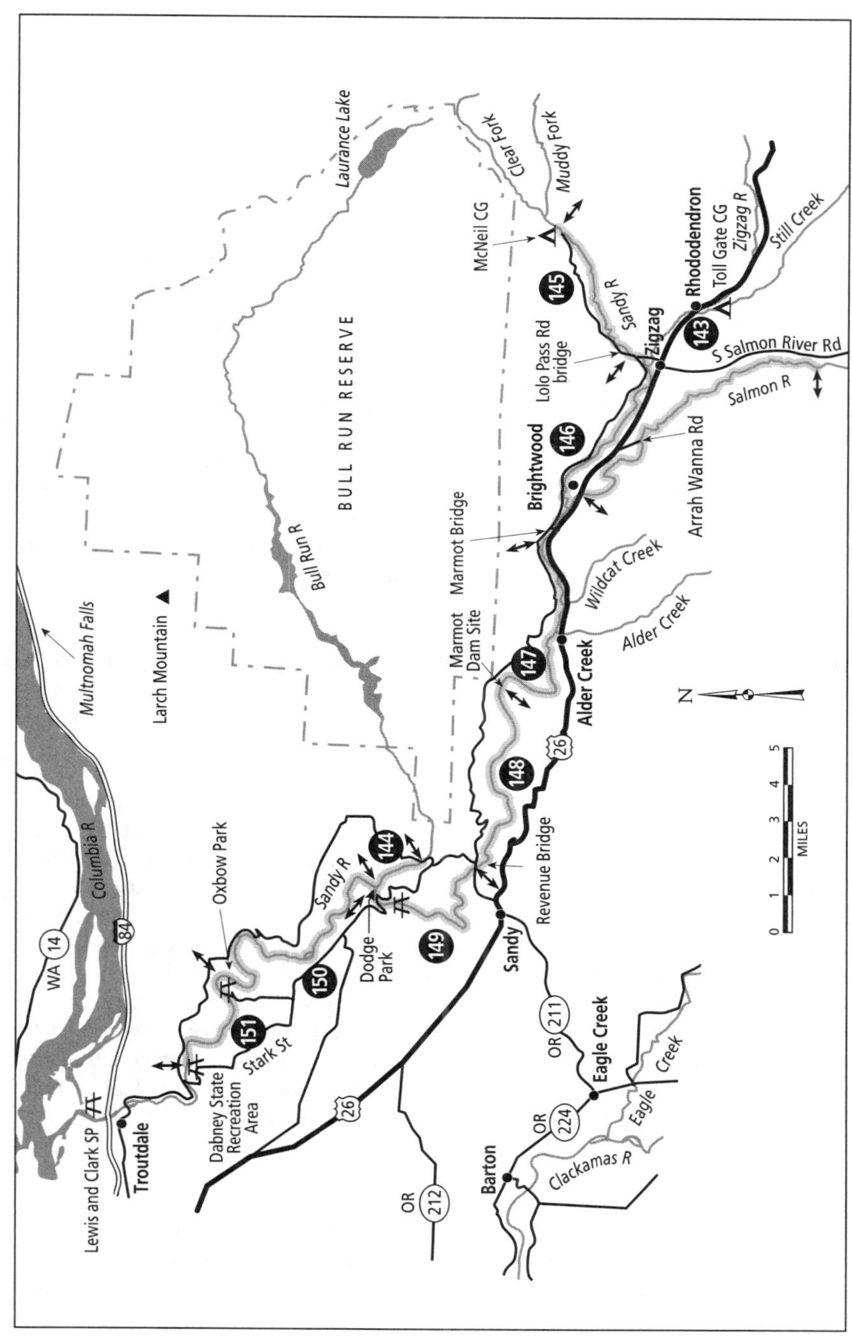

Laurance Lake
Clear Fork
Muddy Fork
McNeil CG
Rhododendron
Toll Gate CG
Zigzag R
Still Creek
145
Sandy R
Zigzag
143
S Salmon River Rd
Lolo Pass Rd bridge
Salmon R
BULL RUN RESERVE
Brightwood
146
Arrah Wanna Rd
Bull Run R
Marmot Bridge
Wildcat Creek
Alder Creek
Multnomah Falls
Larch Mountain
Marmot Dam Site
147
Alder Creek
26
148
Columbia R
Oxbow Park
144
Sandy R
Revenue Bridge
WA 14
84
150
Dodge Park
149
Sandy
OR 211
Eagle Creek
151
Stark St
Dabney State Recreation Area
26
OR 224
Eagle Creek
Lewis and Clark SP
Troutdale
Barton
Clackamas R
OR 212
N
0 1 2 3 4 5
MILES

144 Bull Run River
Bull Run Road Bridge to Dodge Park

Class: 3; 3+	Length: 1.5 miles
Flow: 400–2000 cfs; 2000–3000 cfs	Character: canyon
Gradient: 65 fpm, PD	Season: year-round

Portland's municipal water supply is drawn from the Bull Run River about 6 miles above the bridge at Bull Run Road. Consequently, the entire watershed is closed to public access. Only a 1.5-mile section from the Bull Run Road bridge to the confluence with the Sandy River can be run.

This brief run offers six class 3 drops beginning just below the bridge. The last of these drops is Swing-set, named for the cable and basket arrangement strung across the river just below the drop. At low water there's a rock in the central hole, so it's best to avoid it. The river mellows to class 2 for the final 0.3 mile to the confluence with the Sandy and the inviting take-out beach in Dodge Park, just above the confluence with the Sandy. A permanent slalom course at the put-in is a great destination for class 3 workouts, best at flows of 300–1300 cfs. At flows over 2000 cfs, the run is rated 3+ since the rapids are more continuous.

Hazards

None in particular, with the possible exception of the steep and often slippery put-in trail. The passages are narrow at lower flows, increasing the difficulty slightly. At higher flows, the run seems very short because it is continuous with large holes and waves.

Access

The take-out is at Dodge Park, east of Portland. Follow US 26 to the eastern city limits of Gresham. Turn left onto Palmquist Road. Turn right at the next stop sign, which is Southeast Orient Drive. Bear left after 2 miles onto Southeast Dodge Park Boulevard. Turn right after 4.8 miles onto Southeast Lusted Road and continue down the hill to the bridge over the Sandy River. Dodge Park is across the bridge on the left, on the point between the Sandy and the Bull Run rivers. The take-out beach on the Bull Run is at the back of the park.

To get to the put-in, take every paved road to the left after leaving the east end of Dodge Park bridge; the put-in bridge is within 3 miles. Specifically, turn left (east) out of the park onto Lusted Road. Proceed 1.6 miles, then turn left again on Southeast Ten Eyck Road toward Aims. After almost a mile, turn left on Bull Run Road and descend to the bridge. Park on the left just before the bridge; the trail to the river is at the downriver end of the parking lot.

Gauge

Bull Run River near Bull Run. Dam releases stair-step up and down several hundred cfs at a time, reflecting the number of generators operating. More water is usually released during local rainstorms and also during fall drawdown in preparation for the winter rains. The former diversions from the Little Sandy River ceased in 2009. Optimal levels for playing are 800–1200 cfs.

Thom Powell, Teresa Gryder, and WKCC Editors

145 Sandy River McNeil Campground to Lolo Pass Road Bridge

Class: 4+ T	Length: 4.3 miles
Flow: 100–800 cfs	Character: wooded
Gradient: 132 fpm, C	Season: rainy/snowmelt

This run on the Sandy takes you through only one rapid. It begins at the put-in at the McNeil Campground bridge and ends 4.3 miles later at the take-out at the next bridge. It begins as class 4, gets tougher around the middle (4+), and lets up a little toward the end. The run takes about 50 adrenaline-filled minutes to complete (barring unforeseen problems). The rather continuous gradient makes the drops fairly uniform in difficulty, but occasionally a steeper or narrower passage is encountered. The first trip down this run is an unforgettable experience.

This run has a remote feeling to it, but Lolo Pass Road is usually less than 0.3 mile through the woods on river right. The alders and underbrush are thick, but anyone who is experiencing early difficulty should opt for the nature walk, for the river gets tougher before it gets easier.

Near the bottom of the run are a couple of houses on river right. This is the start of a development called Zigzag village. Use the left channels in the vicinity of these houses, because one of the right channels may be completely blocked by a logjam.

Hazards

This run usually has many, many logs, and is likely to require multiple portages. As of early 2015, there was at least one portage in the first mile, and four in the last mile. At low or moderate flows the continuous bouldery whitewater makes rolling undesirable and rescue difficult. This run is extremely dangerous to boaters who do not know the locations of the logjams, or are lacking the skills to stop in continuous whitewater.

Access

To reach the take-out, take US 26 east from Portland and turn left (north) off US 26 at the Zigzag store onto Lolo Pass Road. The take-out is about 1 mile down Lolo Pass Road at the second bridge, or at the pullout on the right 0.1 mile past the bridge. (The first bridge crosses the Zigzag River.)

To get to the put-in, continue up Lolo Pass Road. After 3.3 miles, look for a sign that marks entry into Mount Hood National Forest. Just past this sign, turn right on NF 1825/Muddy Fork Road, which leads to Ramona Falls. Continue up this road for 0.7 mile, then take a right on NF 1825 to reach the put-in at the bridge just before the McNeil Campground.

Gauge

Sandy River at Marmot. Most of the time, there is not enough water to run this mountain stream. The gauge is 15 miles downstream and includes the flow of several tributaries. When the Sandy at Marmot is over 2000 cfs, McNeil may be running. The water in the McNeil section can also rise on hot summer days due to snowmelt, in which case the Marmot gauge could read less than 2000 cfs; however, McNeil has water because the pulse is coming from high on Mount Hood and may not have reached the gauge yet. Understanding runoff patterns in the area makes it possible to catch adequate flows, and the patience to let high water peaks pass by allows for boating at lower, more manageable flows.

Thom Powell, Teresa Gryder, and WKCC Editors

146 Sandy River Zigzag to Marmot Bridge

Class: 2 T; 3	Length: 7 miles
Flow: 700–2000 cfs; 2000+ cfs	Character: forested; residential
Gradient: 70 fpm, C	Season: rainy/snowmelt

The river flows through a broad valley with an almost constant gradient. The sandy bottom gives the river its name, and the boulders give the river its rapids. Areas without boulders form fast-moving pools. Individual rapids are not described here because each minor flood moves the rocks and may change the locations of deep channels and the best paddling routes. A major flood may completely rearrange the river.

The most difficult rapids are at the top of the run where the river is steepest. Farther downstream are more pools but still plenty of whitewater. After the confluence with the Salmon River (about 0.5 mile above the take-out at Marmot Bridge), the volume increases and more surfing waves develop. At all levels, even at the highest runnable flows just short of flood, the river does not form dangerous features, such as river-wide holes or exploding waves. The most difficult level is at medium-high flows, when the river is high enough to form holes behind the large boulders. When the river is so high that rocks and boulders can be heard crashing together on the bottom, consider another form of recreation for the day.

Hazards

No rapids stand out as significantly more difficult or dangerous than the general fast pace and rocky nature of the river. Occasionally, brush extending from the banks and logjams may cause problems.

Access

From the Portland area, take US 26 east to Zigzag. Turn left (north) onto Lolo Pass Road, just east of the Zigzag store. Continue to the put-in at the second river crossing. Another possible launch location is 0.1 mile farther upstream at a pullout on the right.

To reach the take-out, return to US 26 and turn right (west). After 6 miles, turn right (north) on Sleepy Hollow Road and proceed 0.3 mile to East Barlow Trail Road on the right. The bridge at the intersection is the Marmot Bridge, and the take-out.

Gauge

Sandy River near Marmot. This run is runnable most of the late fall, winter, and spring. Warm spring days during years of good snowpack may yield excellent run-off when many other rain-dependent rivers are low. If the river appears too low at the put-in, consider putting in farther downstream.

Bill Ostrand and Teresa Gryder

147 Sandy River
Marmot Bridge to Marmot Dam Site

Class: 3 (4)	Length: 7.4 miles
Flow: 700–3000 cfs	Character: forested; residential; gorge
Gradient: 41 fpm, C-PD	Season: rainy/snowmelt

This lovely intermediate run on the Sandy River is relatively unknown, because until 2007 it was blocked by a dam. It starts out class 2, has one large class 4 rapid and several rambunctious class 3s, and serves as a pleasant warm-up for the class 4 Sandy Gorge, which begins just below the former Marmot Dam site.

The first 3 miles of this section contain class 2 rapids. After another mile and immediately following a long series of waves and holes is Alder Creek Rapid, the only class 4. Recognize it by spotting the A-frame and other houses overlooking the rapids from the left bank. Stop early to scout or portage, because once you round the blind bend to the right, there is no way to stop.

Below Alder Creek Rapid are long class 2 and 3 rapids, gradually decreasing in difficulty. In the last 3 miles, the river carves into the same sheer volcanic ash deposits that form the Sandy Gorge, and begins to feel quite remote. The river bends north for 1.5 miles and then to the west again, as it winds through a series of small drops in the narrow section where the dam once was. You can ignore the warning signs about the Marmot Diversion Dam; it was removed in 2007.

Finally the river opens into a wider channel with class 2–3 rapids continuing to the take-out, which is located 1 mile after the river bends west again. Recognizing the primitive take-out trail is challenging, and prior scouting is advised, unless you plan to paddle another 6.5 miles down the class 4 Sandy Gorge. The last possible (and easiest to recognize) take-out before the gorge is up the ravine on the right just below the 1964 logjam. The easiest take-out is a small trail through the woods 0.25 mile upstream from this point.

"The Sandy River Water Trail Paddle Guide" also offers helpful information (see Appendix B).

Hazards

Alder Creek Rapid is a large, blind class 4 drop and may be more difficult at lower flows. Scout or portage on the right. The river becomes increasingly remote downstream from here. A major logjam marks the last possible exit from the river before the Sandy Gorge.

Access

From Portland, take US 26 east to the town of Sandy. The put-in is about 12 miles east of Sandy. Turn left (north) on Sleepy Hollow Road and drive to the intersection with East Barlow Trail Road. The bridge on Barlow Trail at this intersection is known as Marmot Bridge, and is the put-in.

To reach the take-out from US 26, see the Sandy River: Marmot Dam Site to Revenue Bridge run.

To reach the take-out from the put-in, cross Marmot Bridge on East Barlow Trail Road and take an immediate left onto Marmot Road, continuing for 7 miles. During a long, straight section of road, take a hard left onto a gravel road (it is called Big Sandy Dam Road, but the sign may be missing). Wind your way down the hill for 1.7 miles, passing one obvious pullout on the right, then a gate, to the pullout featuring large concrete blocks. Park here and walk down to scout your stopping point on the river. An old road goes about 200 yards downhill until it levels, then a small forest trail on the right goes 50 yards directly to the river.

Gauge

Sandy River near Marmot.

Bill Ostrand, Teresa Gryder, and WKCC Editors

148 ★ Sandy River
Below Marmot Dam Site to Revenue Bridge

Class: 4	Length: 5.4 miles
Flow: 700–5000 cfs	Character: forested; roadless canyon
Gradient: 42 fpm, PD	Season: rainy/snowmelt

This run is often known as the Sandy Gorge because it carves a sheer canyon through conglomerate rock made of volcanic ash. It is a favorite local run for advanced boaters because it is convenient to town and runnable at a wide range of

Magic light in the Sandy River Gorge (Mark Scantlebury)

flows in almost every season. The sculpted and overhanging walls of the canyon loom 100–150 feet overhead, framing a brilliant green summer forest that turns gold and scarlet in fall. Small waterfalls enter the gorge from both sides and freeze in winter to form striking ice formations. Maidenhair ferns and mosses trail from overhangs, and sunlight filters through, making it one of the most picturesque runs in Oregon.

Most people launch about 500 yards above the '64 Logjam Rapid, and most will opt to portage The Logjam on the right. For the next 3.5 miles, the rapids are mostly class 3. At about mile 2.5, a steeper set of rapids push class 3+. The last 2 miles of the run contain three class 4 rapids (Boulder Drop, Drain Hole, and Revenue), and one rapid that used to be class 4 but isn't any longer (Rasp Rock).

The character of this run changes dramatically with the flow. The gorge is easiest at low water (700–1200 cfs) and clean, but pushy at higher (2500–5000) flows. It's most challenging at medium flows (1200–2400 cfs) because the holes are fully developed. At 2500 cfs and higher, many fantastic play waves and holes develop, which are rarely appreciated. It has been run at summertime base flows and at flood.

About 3.5 miles into the run, the gorge narrows and bends to the right, revealing a house-size boulder in the middle of the river. This is Boulder Drop. It is usually run in the left channel, driving left to make the best slot for the bottom drop. There is a sieve under the central boulder. The right channel is runnable, but it is narrower, blinder, and more often clogged with wood. It is possible to portage the top of the left channel by floating downstream along the left cliff into a rock pile, then portaging over the rocks to an eddy from which you can run the bottom portion. Once you have landed on the far left, you no longer have the option of running the top drop.

A couple of smaller rapids are interspersed between Boulder Drop and Rasp Rock—which is less steep and often unrecognized until reaching the bottom of the rapid. Rasp Rock converges gradually with a few holes, ending in a narrow channel. The drop in the narrow channel used to form a sticky hole at higher flows because it is backed up by rocks. The right side of the slot is where you could sneak past the hole at any flow; however, the rapid has changed, and this massive hole is rarely, if ever, seen. At medium and lower flows, the left side is also good if there is no new wood in there. If you are not sure, scout from either side of the river.

There is one more class 3 before you arrive at the horizon line at Drain Hole. In this class 4, the river accelerates dramatically down the left side of the river-bed into a line of three mega-boulders and slams into the left boulder, which is dangerously undercut. The flow then diverts to the right across the line of boulders, pushing into the slots between them, which often catch logs. The chute that is farthest to the right is usually clear of wood, and there is an eddy above it. Scout on the right to see the far right sneak, and verify that the right channel is clear. Portage on the right. For those gutsy enough to consider running the meat, a scout from the left reveals more information about the main line, which is an aggressive left-to-right drive.

Revenue Rapid becomes obvious when you see Revenue Bridge high above the river. The rapid has two parts, starting rocky and finishing powerful. It is possible to scout from both sides of the river and still have no idea where to go. This is because you can't see the entry lines from either shore. The top part of the rapid is a convoluted jumble of rocks with many small jets of water rumbling through. The best way to find your entry is to follow someone who knows. There are three known entries: the dogleg, the straight shot, and the far right. The dogleg works at the lowest flows, and involves starting center and driving right to catch a hesitation eddy and then finding the channel from there. The straight shot needs more water and goes over/through shallow rocks to enter the same channel. The far right entry may be easiest, but ends right against the wall. All of the channels converge and flow toward a cliff on the right. Then there is a brief pool before the river plunges into the bottom part, which ends with a stout hole on the right. The portage is on the left.

Take out on the left about 50 yards upstream or immediately downstream from Revenue Bridge, climbing up rocks to the bridge, where you can quietly follow the trail past some homes. Do not park on Dusty Lane, and be diplomatic, as relations with the landowners have been strained. Carry your boats up the hill to the parking area at the intersection of Southeast Ten Eyck and Kubitz roads.

"The Sandy River Water Trail Paddle Guide" also offers helpful information (see Appendix B).

Hazards

It is rare to complete this run without portages. The Sandy Gorge is a dynamic river environment where the riverbed changes every year, and large logs float in to obstruct channels that were not clogged a day earlier. The major rapids are most likely to contain wood and deserve regular scouting. Undercut rocks and sieves are common. Escape from the gorge and rescue are limited by sheer and overhanging walls.

Access

To reach the take-out from Portland, head east on US 26 to the town of Sandy. In town, the highway divides for nine blocks and then converges again. At the light immediately after the opposing lanes converge, turn left onto Southeast Ten Eyck Road (Wolf Road comes in from the right). At 0.6 mile, keep left at the steep hairpin turn to stay on Ten Eyck. Continue 1.1 miles to a parking area at the intersection with Kubitz Road, before you reach Revenue Bridge.

To get to the put-in, go north on Ten Eyck Road across Revenue Bridge, taking a look upstream at the final class 4 rapid as you pass. The road name changes to Marmot Road, without turns. In 1.7 miles, go right at the hairpin to stay on Marmot. Continue for a total of 3.6 miles up a series of switchbacks to a long straightaway. Hidden on the right is a turn onto the gravel Big Sandy Dam Road. Wind your way down the hill for 1.7 miles. Continue past a gate to park at the second pullout with large concrete blocks preventing further vehicular travel. Carry your boats about 200 yards down the abandoned road. After the road levels, look for a small trail to the right and follow it about 50 yards through the forest and down a sand bank to the river. The logjam is about a quarter-mile downstream.

Gauge

Sandy River near Marmot. Sediments are still shifting after the removal of the Marmot Diversion Dam in 2007, so gauge readings may not be reliable after a high water event. Use other data points in your calculations; for example, by subtracting the Bull Run flow (Bull Run near Bull Run) from the Sandy River below Bull Run flow. One may also make a visual estimation of the flow based on the appearance of Revenue Rapid from the bridge, or from a rock midway between the rapid and the bridge. If the water is forming a pour-over at this rock, the water level is good.

Hank Hays, Rod Kiel, Teresa Gryder, and WKCC Editors

149 Sandy River
Revenue Bridge to Dodge Park

Class: 2+ to 3	Length: 5 miles
Flow: 1200–4000 cfs	Character: residential
Gradient: 40 fpm, C	Season: rainy/snowmelt

This is a great run for boaters making the transition from beginner to intermediate. The run starts at Revenue Bridge with a climb down the sloping rock to the river. The upper part of the run is class 2 with many small rapids. The ride picks up where a long slide area is visible on the left. Below here drops are steeper, more frequent, and sometimes rocky. The hardest rapid is a winding slot through a ledge on the left side of an island, and can be missed entirely by going right of the island. Scout this drop from the left bank, if desired. This is a pretty run, but a little more open and populated than the next runs. Ample play opportunities appear at flows of 2500 cfs or more.

"The Sandy River Water Trail Paddle Guide" also offers helpful information (see Appendix B).

Hazards

Run the lower drops with caution. Follow the main current and be careful of rocks in the drops. At very high water, the water runs through trees and shrubs along the bank, and stopping is much more difficult. Logs may be present in the river at high water.

Access

The take-out is at Dodge Park (see the Bull Run River: Bull Run Road Bridge to Dodge Park run).

To reach the put-in from Dodge Park, head east on Southeast Lusted Road for 1.6 miles, then turn left onto Southeast Ten Eyck Road. Continue 2.3 miles until you cross Revenue Bridge and go up the hill a short distance to the parking area at the intersection with Kubitz Road. Carry your boat down the hill along the road and take trails to the river on either side of the bridge. Be diplomatic with the locals and do not park on Dusty Lane.

Gauge

Sandy River below Bull Run.

Bob Collmer and Teresa Gryder

150 ★ Sandy River
Dodge Park to Oxbow Park

Class: 2+(3)	Length: 6.8 miles
Flow: 1200–4000 cfs	Character: forested; roadless
Gradient: 25 fpm, PD	Season: rainy/snowmelt

The Sandy River is very beautiful in this area. The forested canyon contains several stands of old-growth trees, and beautiful calm pools separate fun rapids. This stretch is designated as a Wild and Scenic River.

The river is quite isolated for most of this section, which adds to its appeal. It is a popular stretch, with people fishing both from the banks and from drift boats. The whitewater is pool-drop, with most of the drops clean and with surfing waves scattered along the way. Pipeline Rapid, a rocky class 3, is the first rapid downstream from the put-in. Scout by stopping on the left above the visible pipe across the river. Just around the corner is High Cliff Rapid. After the next calm stretch, you will encounter a long boulder garden, Blue Hole, which ends with several large waves. At medium water, a large hole develops at the end of the waves. Work right to avoid the hole. After Blue Hole there are several more fun rapids separated by slow-moving water.

This run can be boated at extremely high water levels without too many dangerous features developing. At 8000 cfs, most features are washed out.

"The Sandy River Water Trail Paddle Guide" also offers helpful information (see Appendix B).

Hazards

Scout Pipeline. Beware of floating and snagged trees at higher flows. Watch for fishing lines and hooks when near the shores.

Access

The put-in is reached by driving to Dodge Park (see the Bull Run River: Bull Run Road Bridge to Dodge Park run).

The take-out is the boat ramp at the upstream end of Oxbow Park, which has an entrance fee. After leaving Dodge Park on Dodge Park Boulevard, go 4.4 miles to Hosner Road. Turn right (north) and proceed about 2 miles to the Oxbow Park entrance. After entering the park, continue to the boat launch farthest upstream.

Gauge

Sandy River at Bull Run.

Bob Collmer, Pete Giordano, and Teresa Gryder

151 ★ Sandy River
Oxbow Park to Dabney State Recreation Area

Class: 1(2)	Length: 6.2 miles
Flow: 700+ cfs	Character: wooded canyon; roadless; residential
Gradient: 7 fpm	Season: year-round

The Sandy River from Oxbow Park to Dabney Recreation Area is popular with beginning kayakers, family rafters, sports fishers, and others looking for a scenic float close to Portland. Small gravel-bar-type rapids are sprinkled throughout this section, and plenty of eddy lines are available for practicing boating skills. Opportunities abound to view wildlife, including salmon, ospreys, bald eagles, and great blue herons. This section of the Sandy is a designated Wild and Scenic River.

"The Sandy River Water Trail Paddle Guide" contains much useful information and a map (see Appendix B).

Note: The 3.5 miles below Dabney is heavily used by summer inner tubers and is less appealing due to the noise from the roads nearby.

Hazards

Large logs along the banks and on the outsides of turns are quite dangerous to boaters without good boat control. Flows higher than 2000 cfs can be very pushy and are not recommended for beginners.

Access

To reach the take-out at Dabney State Recreation Area (a fee area), follow Interstate 84 out of Portland and take exit 18 after crossing the Sandy. Turn left off the ramp onto Crown Point Highway, which changes names to Historic Columbia River Highway, and continue 3.3 miles to Dabney State Recreation Area. Boaters who desire to avoid the entrance fee at Dabney can leave a vehicle at Lewis and Clark State Recreation Site (just 0.2 miles from exit 18 off Interstate 84) and brave the tubers and road noise for an extended run of 10 total miles.

To reach the put-in at Oxbow from Dabney, turn left onto the highway and backtrack 0.4 mile to cross the Sandy on the Stark Street bridge. Go 0.6 mile and turn left on Southeast Kerslake Road, continuing 0.8 mile to a right bend onto Southeast 302nd for a mile. Next, turn left on Southeast Oxbow Drive and follow the obvious signs to the park. This involves turning left at 2.5 miles and driving 1.4 miles down the steep hill to the park entrance. Pay to enter, then drive another 1.6 miles to the boat ramp and beach at the end of the park road.

Gauge

Sandy River below Bull Run.

Sarah Ostrand, Pete Giordano, and Teresa Gryder

Hood River and Tributaries

152 ★ West Fork Hood River
Lake Branch Fork to East Fork Hood River

Class: 4(5) P	Length: 5.6 miles
Flow: 800–2000 cfs	Character: forested
Gradient: 84 fpm, PD	Season: rainy/snowmelt

The West Fork of Hood River is one of the finest class 4 runs in Oregon. Beautiful basalt gorges, nearly continuous rapids, and an isolated canyon make this a run a classic. The run is a solid class 4 at normal flows, and as flows increase, the pools between rapids push through faster, increasing the difficulty of rescue.

The first 2 miles of the run contain many fun class 3–3+ rapids and two scenic basalt gorges that at higher flows contain powerful holes and funny water. About 2.5 miles downriver from the put-in is a river-wide fish ladder with dangerous hydraulics. Portage on the left.

Below the fish ladder, the difficulty increases with higher gradient and long, continuous boulder gardens that contain large holes. When the river sweeps left and then bends right again, a very long boulder garden presents itself, which builds in intensity for a quarter of a mile. Boaters generally begin center and work right to avoid large holes in the middle of the river at the bottom of the rapid. It can be scouted on the right bank.

The whitewater remains intense for a mile, eases to class 3 for a mile, and then the river enters another gorge. When Green Point Creek cascades in from the left, you are two drops above a serious hole that occupies the left half of the river. This final gorge section has a long series of steep class 3+ and 4 rapids, interspersed with fast-moving pools. In general, the rapids have clean lines that become evident as you go over the horizon; however, new wood could be an unwelcome surprise.

It is helpful to scout the final rapid from the take-out bridge before launching. It is one of the steepest; however, its gradient cannot be appreciated from the bridge. The line is generally center right and not difficult, but the total drop is considerable. It is important to remain in control below this rapid because the take-out above Punchbowl Falls is at a small eddy on river right against a steep, grassy basalt slope. Missing this eddy means you must deal with Punchbowl Falls, which has an extremely deep and retentive hydraulic. When the water is low enough, it is possible to land on the concrete slab on the left side of the falls to scout or portage from there.

If you choose to run Punchbowl, boof hard left into the boiling eddy at the base of the falls. It is another 0.25 mile to the confluence with the East Fork of Hood River. The trail back up to the parking area is on the right gravel bar just above the confluence.

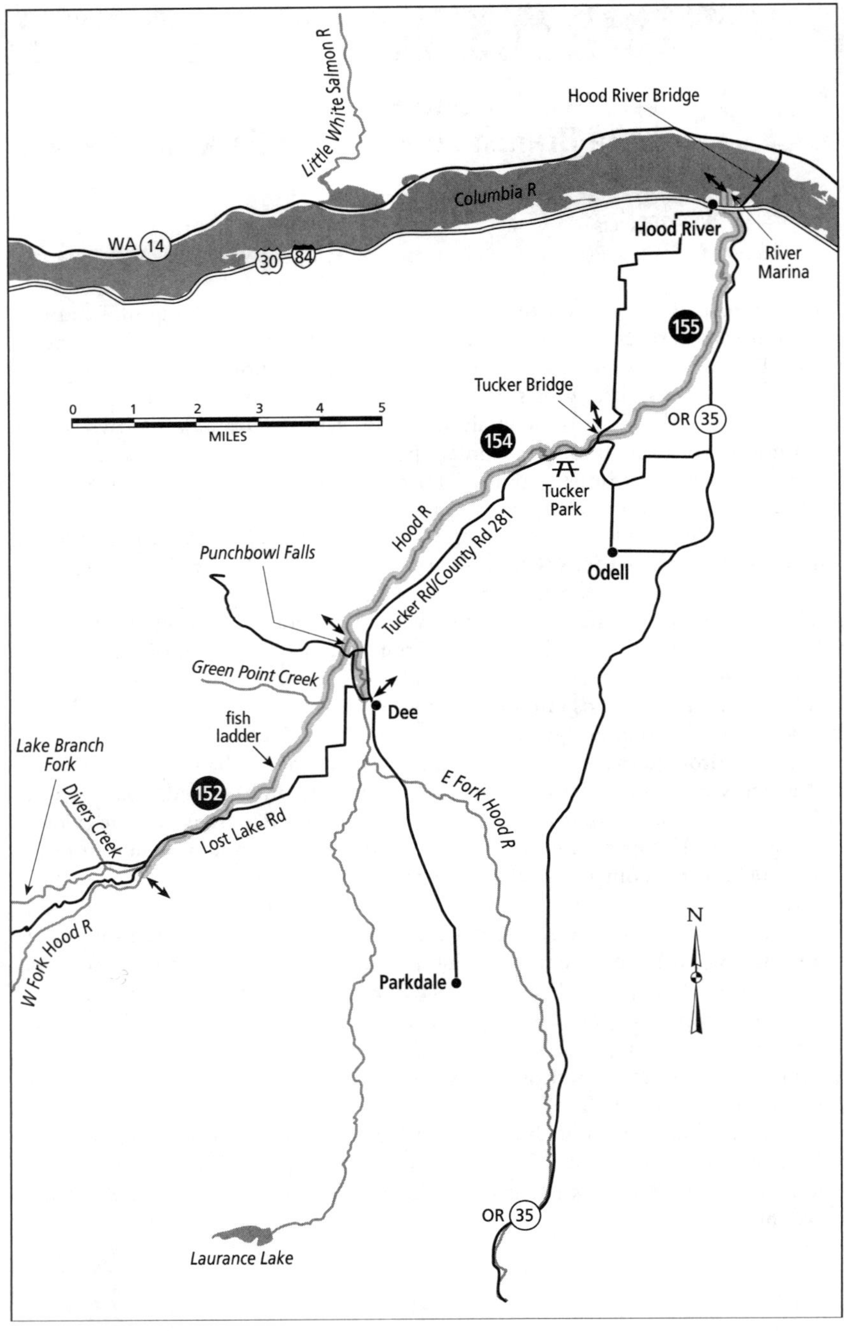
Little White Salmon R
Hood River Bridge
Columbia R
WA 14
30 84
Hood River
River Marina
155
Tucker Bridge
OR 35
154
Hood R
Tucker Park
Tucker Rd/County Rd 281
Odell
Punchbowl Falls
Green Point Creek
fish ladder
Dee
Lake Branch Fork
Divers Creek
E Fork Hood R
152
Lost Lake Rd
W Fork Hood R
N
Parkdale
OR 35
Laurance Lake
0 1 2 3 4 5
MILES

Hazards

Long, continuous whitewater, dangerous hydraulics, and gorges with difficult access are hazards. Beware of the fish ladder (portage left). Punchbowl Falls is a large, powerful drop. Before you put in, scout the final rapid, Punchbowl Falls, and your take-out eddy and trail.

Access

For directions to the take-out at Dee, located near the East Fork Hood confluence, see the run East Fork Hood: Dee to Tucker Bridge. The bridge over the East Fork Hood in Dee is located 11.4 miles south of the city of Hood River. As soon as you cross the bridge over the East Fork Hood, turn right onto Punchbowl Falls Road and go 1.2 miles to an old gated road just before the bridge over the West Fork Hood River. Park here and scout your take-out, the falls, and the final rapid above the falls.

To get to the put-in, backtrack to the three-way intersection near the bridge over the East Fork Hood River at Dee and veer right (south) at the split. The road name changes to Lost Lake Road, which you follow around a right bend, left turn, and a right turn. About 4.6 miles from the take-out, the road crosses the West Fork again, and in 1.1 miles, it crosses the Lake Branch Fork. Park on the left immediately after this bridge and carry your boat downstream on an old road to the confluence put-in.

Gauge

West Fork Hood River near Dee. This gauge is located just above take-out. If this gauge is unavailable, use the Hood River at Tucker Bridge gauge. Two-thirds of the flow at Tucker is a good estimate of the flow on the West Fork, if the source is rainfall. During summer snowmelt, the flow at Tucker may be disproportionately affected from the higher elevation East Fork and this proportion would not apply. A reading of about 1500 cfs at Tucker is optimum.

John Karafotias, Teresa Gryder, and WKCC Editors

153 East Fork Hood River Sherwood Campground to Oregon 35 Bridge

Class: 4+ to 5	Length: 6 miles
Flow: 200–800 cfs	Character: roadside
Gradient: 155 fpm, C	Season: rainy/snowmelt

Also known as the Upper Upper East Fork Hood, this is a very fast river with nonstop action for the suitably skilled boater. At medium and high water, the whole run is essentially one long rapid. Lacking in eddies, pools, and large drops, this narrow river offers plenty of waves, holes, and wood obstacles to maneuver around. Several sections are steeper than others, and several blind corners can contain wood. If the rapids look big from the road, do not attempt the run. Alternative launch spots are available downstream from the put-in.

Out of a total of about 6 miles of runnable whitewater alongside the road, there is usually a 2–3 mile stretch that is passable in any given year. When there is water, the locals will find the clearest section and run laps on it, so check with local sources before launching. The riverbed changes with every high flow, so it is pointless to describe individual rapids.

The run can be great when it's raining in February or during those few days each June when the temperatures peg 90 degrees. On those hot early summer days, the solar-powered increase in snowmelt makes it possible to do a first lap at low water, a second at medium water, and a third lap with some juice.

Hazards

Steep, continuous rapids, potential wood, and an absence of eddies combine to make the entire run hazardous. Rescue is difficult. Lost boats go a long way, even at low water. Be sure to scout before committing to the run.

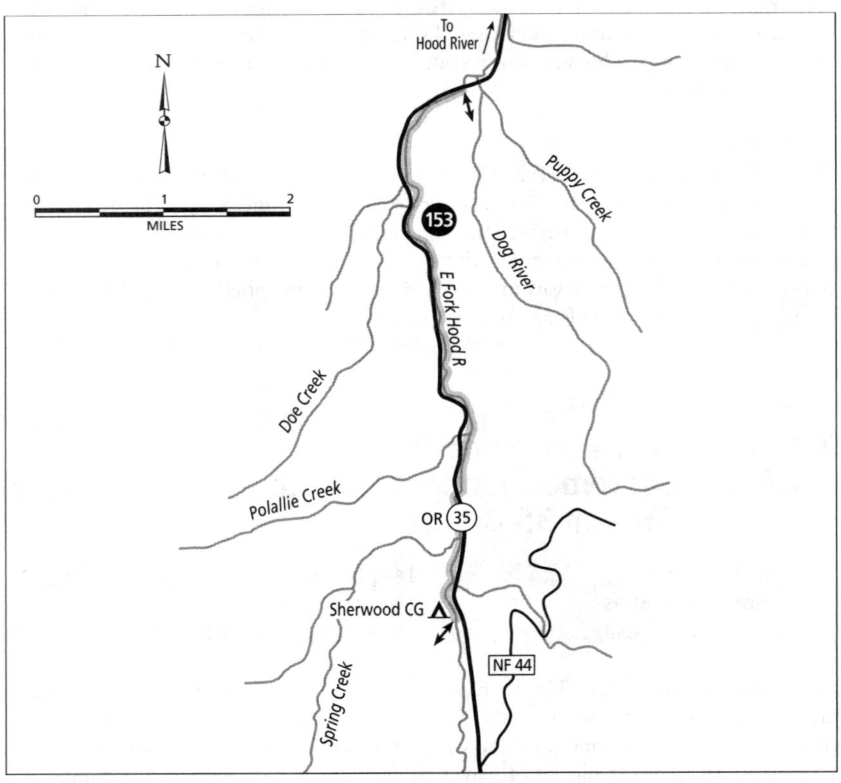

Access

From Hood River, go south on Oregon 35 for 18.5 miles, where the lowest take-out is at the bridge over the river.

To reach the put-in, continue to drive south on Oregon 35 to a pullout on the right just below Sherwood Campground. If wood is present as one scouts from the highway curves, use alternative access points along the road. One alternative access point is at the highway bridge 1 mile below the put-in; another is at the Polallie Creek trailhead below there.

Gauge

Hood River at Tucker Bridge. The level at Tucker Bridge should be at least 5.5 feet in the winter, but 4.5 feet is the rough equivalent in June when it hits 85 degrees in Hood River.

Pete Giordano, Ron Reynier, and Teresa Gryder

154 ★ East Fork Hood River/Hood River Dee to Tucker Bridge

Class: 3(4); 4	Length: 7.5 miles
Flow: 700 cfs; 2500+ cfs	Character: forested; residential
Gradient: 66 fpm, PD-C	Season: rainy/snowmelt

This run is a very popular intermediate run with beautiful scenery, challenging rapids, and good play spots. The first mile is on the East Fork, which is pool-drop and runs through a beautiful narrow canyon punctuated by several technical class 3 rapids.

The first big rapid on the run is at an island, where most paddlers follow the major flow of the river to the right of the island. The top right has a ledge drop followed by a powerful wave train and some holes. At the end of the first mile, Cyclops (class 4) is encountered right at the confluence with the West Fork. Stop early on the left if you wish to scout (or to check for wood). Most paddlers go hard left to avoid the stout hole that forms against the cliff wall on the right.

The water volume nearly doubles at the confluence, and the gradient lessens and becomes more uniform. After a scenic class 2 section, the action picks up again for the last 2 miles. A bridge with an overhead aqueduct marks the beginning of a long run with complex boulder gardens. Island Rapid, class 4, is immediately below the bridge. Most of the river runs right of the island. If desired, scout from the island. Class 3–3+ rapids continue past Tucker County Park to the take-out, which is on the right at Tucker Bridge. At higher flows, most of this run becomes continuous class 4.

Hazards

Cyclops and Island rapids, both class 4, deserve respect. Keep a watch for wood.

Access

From the Portland area, drive east on Interstate 84 to Hood River and take the first exit (No. 62). Go 1.2 miles and turn right on Thirteenth Street, which becomes Tucker Road (County Road 281) as you travel south. Follow signs to stay on this road and, after several turns, cross the historic Tucker Bridge over the Hood River, where the take-out is on river right, under the bridge.

To reach the put-in, continue driving on County Road 281 (also called Dee Highway) up the river past Tucker County Park. For the alternative, lower put-in on Iowa Drive, turn right at 5.7 miles and park at the end of the road (limited parking here; do not block access for neighbors). The steep trail to the water is downstream from the guardrail; use a rope for lowering boats to the river. Launch here to avoid Cyclops if it has wood.

To reach the traditional put-in at Dee, continue upstream another 0.9 mile and stay right at the road split. Park on the left after crossing the river. The put-in is about 50 yards downriver, down a steep bank on river left. Please heed any nearby "No Trespassing" signs.

Gauge

Hood River at Tucker Bridge. Flows of 1000–2400 cfs are ideal. Minimum flows are around 700 cfs.

Stan Jacobs, Jay Nigra, Ron Reynier, Teresa Gryder, and WKCC Editors

155 Hood River
Tucker Bridge to Hood River Marina

Class: 3; 4-	Length: 5 miles
Flow: 750–3000 cfs; 3500 cfs	Character: forested
Gradient: 60 fpm, C	Season: rainy/snowmelt

Powerdale Dam was removed in 2011, and the very successful Hood River restoration project has provided boaters with new paddling opportunities. The river in this stretch is scenic and has abundant class 3 rapids that are very rocky at low water and become continuous class 4- at higher flows.

The first mile is class 2+. Soon thereafter, the river steepens with solid class 3 rapids as one goes right of an island and through a long, sweeping S turn. The whitewater becomes nearly continuous, and in two places there are sticky holes on the left at the bottom of steeper sections. As the river bends to the right, it drops into Dam Rapid, which is located at the old dam site. It can be scouted from the right bank. Here, a technical entrance is followed by a steep runout with several holes and a long class 3 rapid immediately downstream.

The action continues with class 2+ boulder gardens and occasional islands until one sees a slatted wooden sluiceway on the left. The next rapid forms some pushy water at the bottom, especially at high water. A railroad bridge passes overhead, and most paddlers stay right, although other options vary year to year. The remainder of the run is class 2 as it winds toward the Columbia. The best take-out is at the footbridge located at the west end of the Hood River Marina near the museum.

Hazards

The rapids below the first mile become class 3+ to 4- and are quite continuous at higher water. Watch out for rebar and other dangerous debris near, and downstream of, the wooden sluiceway on the left.

Access

From Interstate 84 in the city of Hood River, take exit 63 for Hood River/White Salmon. Turn north from the ramp and proceed toward the Columbia River and the marina. Go right on Riverside Drive and make an immediate right onto First Avenue. Continue past the gas station to park near the footbridge. The short take-out trail is on river left, just upstream of the footbridge.

To reach the put-in, reverse your route to cross Interstate 84, turn left on Oak Street, and follow it as it becomes Oregon 35 south. After 5 miles, turn right on Dethman Ridge Road toward Odell and follow it for 2 miles. Go right at the stop sign. In 1.3 miles, after a hairpin right turn, continue straight/right onto County Road 281 and proceed 0.1 mile to Tucker Bridge.

Alternatively, head south through the Heights in Hood River where Twelfth Street turns into Tucker Road. Follow Tucker Road south, jogging right and left a couple of times. In about 4 miles, it crosses the river at the put-in bridge.

Gauge

Hood River at Tucker Bridge. Levels of 750–2900 cfs (4–6.5 feet) are ideal, but higher runs are common.

Jeff Bennett, Ron Reynier, and Teresa Gryder

Klickitat River, Washington

156 ★ Klickitat River
Yakama Indian Reservation to Klickitat Salmon Hatchery

Class: 3; 4	Length: 11.6 miles
Flow: 800 cfs; 1800+ cfs	Character: canyon; forested
Gradient: 57 fpm, C	Season: snowmelt

This remote upper run begins near Mount Adams. The highest put-in is by the Yakama Indian Reservation boundary. Nonnatives are prohibited beyond here. The put-in is east of the road, 100 yards down a steep, rocky, forested slope. Most paddlers use a short line to lower a boat, because a runaway boat may not stop

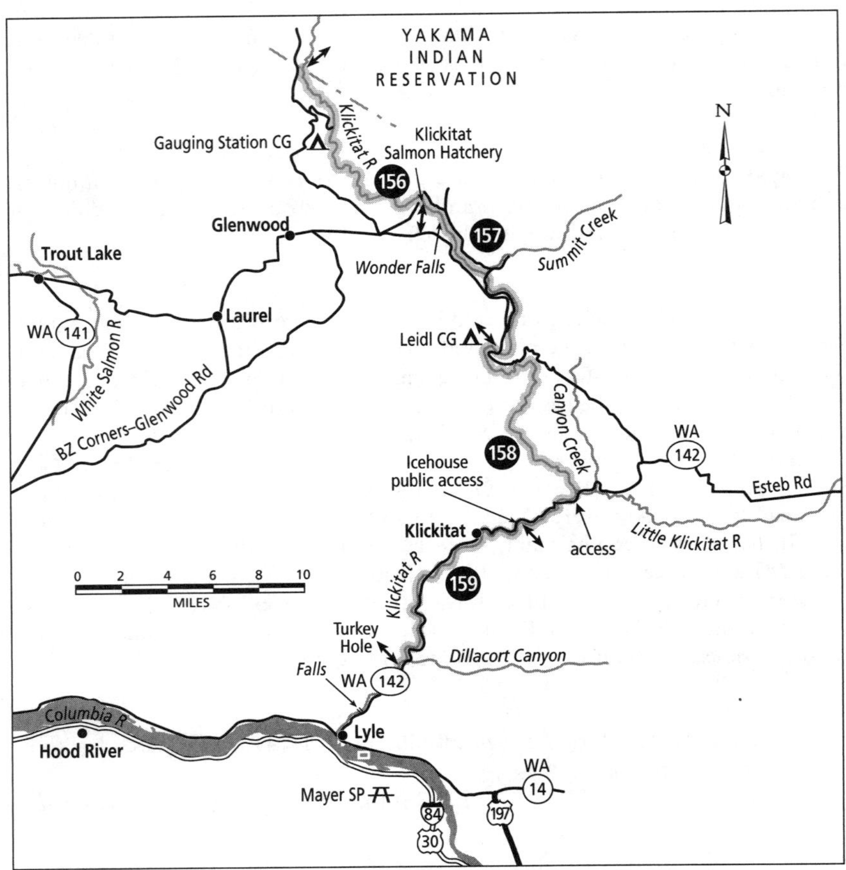

until reaching the bottom or may crush a companion. At river level, the put-in is just below Big Muddy Creek. An alternative put-in, preferred by rafters and many kayakers, is located 3 miles downriver at the gauging station primitive campground. There is no easy way out from the upper canyon once on the river.

The upper 3 miles move very quickly. There are occasional eddies, but the whitewater is continuous class 3. Most paddlers agree that class 4 boating skills are needed, even at moderate levels. When the flows exceed 1800 cfs, the water speed increases, and rescue becomes difficult. Sweepers and logjams are often present throughout this run, and occasionally the water runs headlong into a wall. The gradient lets up a bit at the gauging station, but the current remains fast below there, and pools are rare.

The middle third of the river is highlighted by immense vertical walls of columnar basalt. The river crashes into these walls, then runs alongside the gray cliffs, drawing dwarfed boaters' wide-eyed gazes upward. Many of these walls form long S turns. The bottom third of the river is lesser in gradient. About a mile above take-out, powerlines overhead signal the last of the more difficult rapids. Take out at the eddy river right and upstream of the Klickitat salmon hatchery. A trail leads up the hill to the parking area. Do not continue downstream; a dangerous weir with a serious reversal is directly below the take-out eddy.

If you plan on continuing downstream to the next run, carry your craft up the hill and ask for permission to launch in the area below the fish ponds at the downstream end of the salmon hatchery. Usually permission to launch will be given by the workers there. Follow any instructions they give you, and please be respectful at this facility.

Hazards

The upper put-in is tough because of its steepness, loose rocks, and fallen logs. The upper river is continuous at all flows, and the uppermost section becomes nonstop class 4 at high water, making swims dangerous. Watch for big holes at high water and for strainers at all flows.

Wood is always a problem on this run. The best option is to inquire with local rafting companies prior to your launch about the current location of logjams. Many logjam locations change nearly every year and sometimes daily during high water.

The weir at the fish hatchery should be avoided; take out above it.

Basalt walls and river wood on the upper Klickitat River (Mark Scantlebury)

Access

From Oregon, cross the Columbia River at Portland or Hood River and take Washington 14 to Washington 141 near the town of White Salmon. Go north on Washington 141 for 10 miles to the community of BZ Corner. Then take the BZ-Glenwood Highway east and north for about 19 miles to the community of Glenwood. Continue east 3.5 miles beyond Glenwood and watch for the sign on the left for the "Klickitat Salmon Hatchery." Make the shallow left turn and follow the gravel road for 2.8 miles down to the hatchery. Park at the bottom of the hill, upstream of the buildings in the visitor parking area. The trail at the far end of the lot leads to the river, the take-out.

To reach the put-in, return to the pavement and go back toward Glenwood about 300 feet, and then turn right on the first road to the right. There will be a cattle grate to cross at the start of this well-maintained gravel road, which leads north and northwest. The lower put-in is reached by going 7.9 miles up this road, without turning off onto any side roads, to road K1400, which splits off to the right; take this road for 0.6 mile, then turn right onto K1410. (These road signs are small and almost concealed or perhaps missing; however, the route is well traveled.) Proceed downhill about a mile to the gauging station primitive campground, the lower put-in. This put-in is about 0.5 mile downstream of Dairy Creek. To reach the upper put-in, return up the hill to the intersection of the main road and side road K1400. Reset your odometer and travel upstream 2.8 miles to a large pullout on the right. A side road meets the main road at this parking spot. This is the put-in, high above the river. The sign for the Yakama Indian Reservation is just ahead in 75 yards (the sign may be missing). Do not go past the sign. Parking or driving beyond this sign is illegal. Begin the arduous lowering of boats.

Gauge

Klickitat River near Pitt.

Frank Furlong, Bill Ostrand, Jon Ferguson, Teresa Gryder, and WKCC Editors

157 ★ Klickitat River
Klickitat Salmon Hatchery to Leidl Campground

Class: 3	Length: 10 miles
Flow: 700–3000 cfs	Character: forested
Gradient: 36 fpm, C	Season: snowmelt

This is a popular class 3 run that is commonly paddled during the late spring and early summer months. In the early spring, the road to the put-in is often blocked by snow.

The initial 5 miles below the hatchery consist of fast-moving and challenging technical rapids. At flows around 3000 cfs, the rapids wash out, and the run involves missing a few big holes and riding big waves. Scenic 30-foot Wonder Falls, a spring-fed cascade on the right, is 2 miles downstream from the put-in. About 1 mile below Wonder Falls is a difficult rapid that cannot be seen from the road. A long, rocky class 2 rapid occurs 1.5 miles below Summit Creek bridge. This is followed by some big boulders and two headwalls, with a deceptively vicious eddy on the right of the second wall. The lower 5 miles offer relatively easier paddling.

Flows on the Klickitat will rise with local rainfall, but are generally stable and drop slowly during the summer. Good camping in the area's open ponderosa forests make this river an excellent destination for a long weekend.

Hazards

The fast water gives boaters very little time to react to river-wide logjams. The weir next to the hatchery has reinforcing rods in the water. Do not run the weir; launch below it.

Access

For the put-in, see the directions for getting to the take-out for the Klickitat River: Yakama Indian Reservation to Klickitat Salmon Hatchery run.

The visitor parking area at the fish hatchery is at the far upstream end of the site. However, the put-in spot for launching is at the downstream end of the hatchery, near the fish ponds. This launch area is below the dangerous weir, which should not be run. Be sure to ask permission before launching. The workers will usually say yes to those who want to launch, but may give specific instructions to you, especially concerning where to leave your vehicle. Be respectful at this Yakama Nation facility.

To reach the take-out from the fish hatchery, return up the hill to the Glenwood Highway and turn left. Go 9.5 miles to Leidl Campground. At Leidl Campground, turn right (west) for the boat ramp take-out or left into the upper part of the campground, where there is a sandy beach at the end of the road. A Discover Pass is needed for parking at Leidl.

Gauge

Klickitat River near Pitt.

Ernie Carpenter, Teresa Gryder, and WKCC Editors

158 ★ Klickitat River
Leidl Campground to
Icehouse Public Access

Class: 2	Length: 17 miles
Flow: 500–3500 cfs	Character: wooded canyon
Gradient: 24 fpm, C	Season: year-round

This is a run for those who want to see beautiful basalt cliffs and ponderosa pines, not for those who want wild whitewater. The river moves along through the scenery, with many class 1 rapids and a few class 2s toward the end of the run, making it an excellent playground for open canoers and beginning kayakers. The canyon at this point is nearly 2 miles wide and 1500 feet deep. The first 12 miles are on Washington state land, but from 1 mile above the Little Klickitat confluence on down is private land. Because plenty of logs are on this river, practice log recognition and log dodging elsewhere before attempting this run.

The put-in is at Leidl Campground, river mile 33, at the boat ramp below the bridge, or at a sandy beach 0.3 mile upstream of the bridge. The river is braided with many channels for the first 7 miles. Stinson Flats, an alternative river access point, is about 2.5 miles from put-in on the left. At river mile 28, an abandoned homestead is on a bench to the west. At river mile 24.5, a four-wheel-drive road comes down to the river. About 5 miles downstream is a series of waves and holes that can be avoided by staying left.

At river mile 19.5, the Little Klickitat River enters from the left. Some paddlers may opt to take out 0.2 mile below the confluence at the river access on the left. The more difficult class 2 rapids are located below this access in the next 3.5 miles.

A class 2 rapid, identified by a cliff on the left and boulders on the right, is 0.2 mile downstream of the access. At river mile 17, 2 miles farther, is the most difficult rapid on this section. It is the second rapid below the second bridge, class 2. Scout right, if desired. It has a pointed rock in the middle. It is usually run left of the pointed rock. The take-out at river mile 16 is preceded by an old historic icehouse on the right, which was used to store dry ice made from carbon dioxide produced from local wells. Take out on the right at the concrete boat ramp.

Hazards

Ever-present logs and possible logjams are the greatest danger. Scout if in doubt. The class 2 rapid at river mile 17 is the most difficult.

Access

From Oregon, cross the Columbia River at Portland or Hood River and take Washington 14 east along the Columbia River to Lyle and then Washington 142 north to the town of Klickitat. Continue 2 miles on Washington 142, cross the abandoned railroad tracks, turn right, pass the old icehouse, and go to the public boat ramp, the take-out.

To reach the put-in, follow Washington 142 east; in 3.5 miles you'll pass the alternative river access on the left. The road then continues north along the Little Klickitat River toward Goldendale. After the road leaves the river and reaches a flat summit, turn left on the road to Glenwood. Before reaching Glenwood, cross the Klickitat at Leidl Campground and turn left (west) to the boat ramp or, alternatively, turn right to a sandy put-in at the end of the road. A Discover Pass is needed at Leidl, Stinson Flats, and Icehouse accesses.

Gauge

Klickitat River near Pitt.

Ernie Carpenter

159 Klickitat River Icehouse Public Access to Turkey Hole Access

Class: 2+; 3	Length: 11 miles
Flow: 500–1000 cfs; 1500+ cfs	Character: forested; roaded; residential
Gradient: 20 fpm, PD	Season: year-round

Fun rapids and good surfing waves are found on this run. The river is pool-drop with some long rock gardens that can be seen from the road. The last 5.5 miles of the run are in the Columbia River Gorge National Scenic Area. Some of the land is private and posted.

The run begins with some easy class 1 and 2 paddling. Soon one passes by the town of Klickitat. The Pitt bridge follows in a couple of miles, with an alternative access point on river left just below the bridge. About halfway through the run is a fun set of rapids located about 1 mile below the Pitt bridge. The most difficult rapid of the run (class 2+) is located 0.3 mile above the take-out. It can be scouted on the right or from the road during the shuttle. Take out just below the rapid on the left at the access point. The class 6 Klickitat Falls and Narrows are only 2.5 miles downstream, with no easy access between this final take-out and the falls—so be sure to take out here.

Hazards

Logs are not as common as they are on upstream sections, but keep an eye out for the possibility. The rapids in this run get more difficult at higher water. Beware of the class 6 Klickitat Falls and Narrows 2.5 miles below the take-out.

Access

From Oregon, cross the Columbia River at Portland or Hood River and take Washington 14 east to Lyle; at Lyle, turn north on Washington 142 and proceed 5 miles upstream along the river to the take-out, Turkey Hole public access, on the left. There's no boat ramp, but it's an easy walk up from the river.

To reach the put-in, continue upstream about 8 miles to the town of Klickitat. The Icehouse public access put-in is on the right, about 2 miles past Klickitat (see the Klickitat River: Leidl Campground to Icehouse Public Access run). For a longer run, follow the road for another 2 miles upstream to the access point just below the Little Klickitat River on river left. An alternative take-out (or put-in) is at the downstream left side of the Pitt bridge. A Discover Pass is required at Icehouse and Turkey Hole accesses.

Gauge

Klickitat River near Pitt.

Ernie Carpenter and WKCC Editors

White Salmon River, Washington

160 ★ White Salmon River
Warner Road Bridge to Green Truss Bridge

Class: 4(5)	Length: 5.1 miles
Flow: 800–1500 cfs	Character: forested canyon
Gradient: 60 fpm, PD	Season: snowmelt

Nicknamed Farmlands, this run is hidden in a gorge through an otherwise pastoral valley below Mount Adams. It contains numerous class 3 and 4 rapids and some sharp ledge drops of 5–15 feet. Since the river is so narrow, a small change in flow creates big changes in the river's speed and power. When flows exceed 1400 cfs, the run contains continuous whitewater and powerful hydraulics; below 1000 cfs, it becomes an enjoyable pool-drop run with recovery pools. It can be run in any season, but has the most water during spring runoff, and is the lowest in late summer. When Farmlands is too low, local paddlers shift to the run below here (Green Truss Run 161), which has more water because of underground springs.

After 0.5 mile of warm-up, the river descends into a steep-walled canyon and drops 200 feet in the next 2 miles. It first drops over two 4-foot ledges and enters a narrow 100-yard-long chute with turbulent hydraulics. The second ledge, Sidewinder, can force kayakers uncomfortably close to an undercut ledge on river left at medium flows. Scout or portage one or both of these ledges on the left. An alternative put-in is available by doing a seal launch into the gorge below Sidewinder.

Almost a mile downstream, Lava Dam, the biggest single drop on the run, is at the end of a quiet pool. Scout or portage right. The runnable tongue in the center is fine if you keep your bow up, but avoid getting stuck in the hydraulic, because it can stuff boats and boaters behind the falls, where they may not emerge in a timely fashion.

Lava Dam is followed by 0.5 mile of pool-drop rapids that are pushy at high water. The canyon then opens up, and the gradient tapers off. The next 2 miles are mostly class 2 rapids with an occasional class 3. At low flows, this section is shallow and rocky.

Around mile 4, the second major rapid, Off Ramp, is signaled by a distinct horizon line. Eddy left to scout or portage. A portage here requires climbing and teamwork. It may be easier to attempt the marginally runnable 12-foot ledge or the far right side of the ledge. The lead-in is trickier than it looks. The last narrow canyon has a bad pin slot on river left. The run ends just below the green truss bridge. Save some energy for the strenuous rock-climbing take-out, or put in early and continue all the way to BZ Corner.

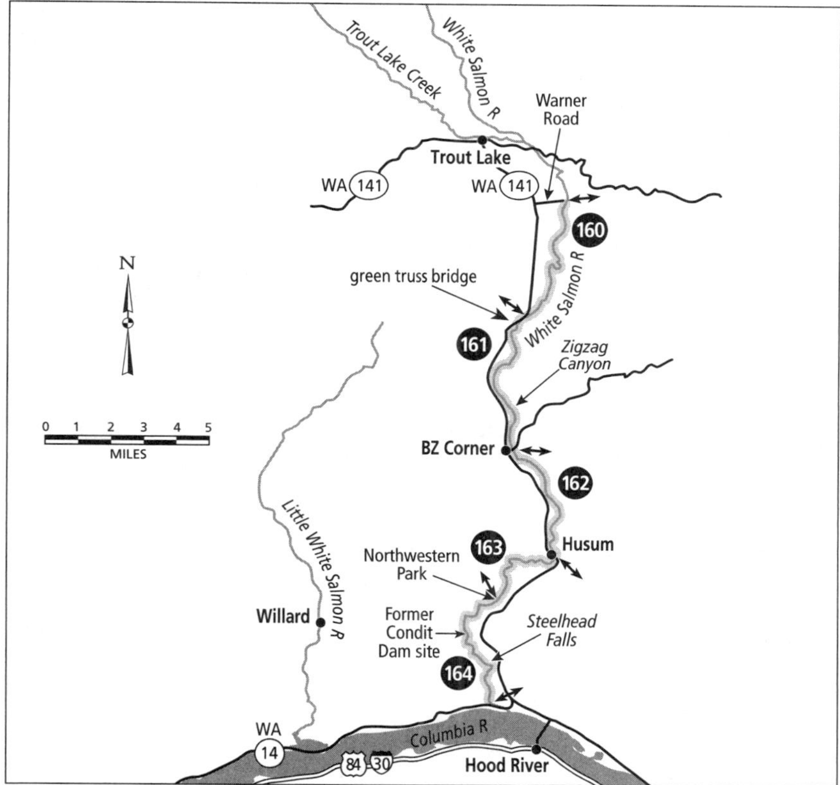

Hazards

Wood must be avoided. Lava Dam has a serious hydraulic and an undercut ledge, where many boats have been lost. The first 2.5 miles become very powerful and nearly continuous above 1400 cfs. At low flows, the middle section is shallow and rocky. The take-out requires a throw rope for hoisting kayaks up the cliff.

Access

This run is upstream of BZ Corner. For general directions to BZ Corner, see the White Salmon River, Washington: BZ Corner to Husum run.

To reach the take-out, drive north from BZ Corner on Washington 141 for 4.5 miles and turn right on Winegartner Road. Park vehicles in sight of the highway for security. At trip's end, you can drive closer to the green truss bridge, 150 yards from the highway, for loading after hauling the boats up the cliff.

For the put-in, drive up Washington 141 until you are 8.3 miles past BZ Corner. Turn right on Warner Road. (Road signs point toward Glenwood and Conboy Lake National Wildlife Refuge.) Follow Warner Road about 1 mile to the first bridge. The put-in is on the northeast side of the bridge.

An alternative route allows boaters to scout two major drops during the shuttle: Go north of BZ Corner 6.6 miles and turn right off Washington 141 onto Sunnyside Road. Lava Dam is beneath an alder stand 0.6 mile up this road (find a small ledge to peer into the canyon), and Sidewinder is found at a wide spot an additional 0.9 mile upstream. Continue upstream and turn right at the T intersection for the put-in bridge.

Gauge

White Salmon River near Underwood. Flows listed in this description are gauge flows. Actual flows on the river may be 40 percent lower than at the gauge.

Jeff Bennett, Doc Loomis, Curt Knight, Ron Reynier,
Teresa Gryder, and WKCC Editors

161 ★ White Salmon River
Green Truss Bridge to BZ Corner

Class: 4+ T; 5	Length: 5 miles
Flow: 400 cfs; 1000 cfs	Character: forested canyon
Gradient: 119 fpm, PD	Season: rainy/snowmelt

The Green Truss section of the White Salmon is a Northwest classic. This run almost always has enough water to run, making this stretch a world-class destination for expert paddlers in the late spring and early summer. The spectacular basalt gorges on this section are unforgettable, but you probably will not notice the scenery your first time down.

The run starts with a marginal climb down into the canyon, which gets worse every year as erosion takes its toll on the cliff face. (If it is snowing, you will have to rappel to reach the river.) This run is pool-drop with a capital D, and the action begins immediately below the put-in with a fun series of class 3 and 4 drops that gradually get bigger as you head downstream.

The first major rapid is The Meatball. Here the river drops to the left over an 8-foot diagonal ledge into a small, turbulent pool. A large boulder (The Meatball) blocks the exit of the pool. This drop requires a leap of faith through the right side slot, but if you haven't run the drop recently, be sure to scout on the left for wood.

Just below the Meatball is Bob's Falls, a sloping 10-foot, river-wide ledge that contains the first of the many menacing holes for which this run is known. At higher flows, Bob's begins to resemble a low-head dam and has sent many paddlers swimming; run left with momentum or portage on the left.

Below Bob's a couple of class 3 drops lead to a pool above 25-foot-tall Big Brother. This drop is deceptively difficult as the current flows from right to left across the lip of the falls, which makes hitting the crucial 3-foot-wide boof flake difficult. A missed line here often has severe consequences because of the undercut cave on the right and the piton rocks on the left at the bottom. Scout and portage on the left side.

Just below Big Brother is Little Brother, a forgiving 15-foot falls that is often run on the left, boofing right. A short distance below Little Brother is Double Drop, an 18-foot double falls that is rarely run with style. This falls has a rapid leading right to a left eddy above the lip of the drop, so stay alert. If you get out to scout, keep in mind that the portage is on the left. The line is aggressively right down the middle. The bottom hole is deep and powerful, but there is a good pool to roll in.

Below Double Drop, the difficulty eases, and paddlers are treated to the spectacular scenery for which the White Salmon is famous. Cold springs cascade in from the base of the canyon walls, adding to both the scenery and the flow.

The next major rapid is signaled by a funky basalt outcropping on river left. This is the Cheese Grater, which is generally run center, moving away from the nearly invisible undercut in the river-right wall. Scout or portage on the right.

The walls begin to close in again at Zigzag Canyon, which contains two of the most intense gorge-type rapids on the river. Scout Upper Zigzag on the right, and pick your lines carefully. One short pool separates Upper from Lower Zigzag, which is scouted on the left side. To run Lower Zigzag, follow the water as it piles into a mid-river boulder and then pours left. Cut the insides of the bends to avoid the walls as the river slams back and forth across the chasm while racing downhill. Be cautious throughout the run as logjams form in narrow spots like this.

It is possible to put in below Lower Zigzag by hiking down the bed of Wieberg Creek. The run from here to BZ Corner is sometimes called the Orletta run, and is runnable at base summer flows.

The rapids below Lower Zigzag continue in pool-drop style for about a mile until The Flume, a steep drop signaled by a set of pumps on river left. Just below The Flume is the final pool above 14-foot BZ Falls. Eddy right and scout. The next rapid leads into the falls, with only a few small eddies on the river-right side just above the lip.

BZ Falls is one of the most dangerous drops on the White Salmon, but lots of paddlers run it anyway. There is a piton rock at the foot of the drop, and expert boaters who hit it once will commonly begin to portage after that experience. If this drop is not to your liking, you can seal launch down the rock slope on the right immediately below the falls, or hike down on the river-right side and rock-climb down to the water a hundred yards downstream. The take-out at BZ Corner is a short float downstream.

Hazards

This run contains many steep, powerful drops that can develop extremely powerful hydraulics. If boaters get into trouble in several of the large rapids, opportunities for other boaters to help are limited.

Access

To reach the take-out from the Portland area, take Interstate 84 east to Hood River. Cross the Columbia River at the Hood River Bridge, turn left onto Washington 14, then turn right onto Washington 141 just before crossing the mouth of the White Salmon River. Follow Washington 141 north, following the signs to

Husum. Continue north on Washington 141 past Husum to BZ Corner. Go past the town about 0.2 mile and turn right at the sign indicating the take-out.

To reach the put-in, continue north on Washington 141 for 4.7 miles to a dirt road on the right, Weingartner Road. The put-in is down the steep cliff below the bridge on river right. Parking is available along the main highway or a little way up the highway to a road on the left.

Gauge

White Salmon River near Underwood. There is also a stick gauge near Husum.

Jason Rackley and Teresa Gryder

162 ★ White Salmon River BZ Corner to Husum

Class: 3+(4)	Length: 5 miles
Flow: 900–2000 cfs	Character: forested canyon
Gradient: 76 fpm, C	Season: year-round

Known as the Middle White Salmon, this is a run on which a great many kayakers have cut their class 3 teeth. On a hot afternoon, the cold, clear water, nice lunch spots, and good play spots draw rafters and kayakers to this scenic canyon. The rapids are fairly continuous, especially during the first few miles. The river is very narrow, and one must use technical skills to maneuver across strong currents and avoid rocks while staying away from the walls. Most of the rapids are of the rock garden and wave train variety, with an occasional small ledge. Be aware of Husum Falls at the end of the run.

The put-in trail leads to a rapid called Maytag, class 4, one of the more intimidating rapids on the run. If boaters choose to run Maytag, they should take the short trail upstream and put in at the pool immediately above the rapid. The right trail leads to a put-in on the rock shelf below the rapid.

Below Maytag there is a long series of class 2–3 rapids. Be careful near the undercut cave on the right about 0.5 mile from the put-in. Several bigger rapids appear in the first half of the run. At most flows, they are fairly straightforward. At low flows, they get quite rocky. Scout if you are unsure of your line.

The last drop, Husum Falls (class 4–4+), is a 10-foot vertical drop generally run right of center. One can scout Husum Falls from the bridge near the take-out in Husum. To avoid the plunge, take out 150 feet before the falls on river right. A portage on the left immediately above the falls is also possible. Rafters often line their boats on the left of the falls if continuing downstream.

Hazards

Maytag and Husum Falls are the most intense, and scouting is advisable. Logs and snags line the banks, making landing difficult in some places. Fast, continuous current and cold water make swimming to shore difficult.

Access

To reach the take-out from the Portland area, take Interstate 84 east to Hood River. Cross the Columbia River at the Hood River Bridge, turn left onto Washington 14, then turn right onto Washington Alternate 141 just before crossing the mouth of the White Salmon River. Drive north, following the signs to Husum. The take-out is on Washington 141 at Husum, either 500 feet below the falls on river left or 150 feet above the falls on river right.

To get to the put-in, continue north on Washington 141 to BZ Corner, go past the town about 0.2 mile, and turn right at the sign indicating the put-in.

Gauge

White Salmon River near Underwood. Gauge readings can also be seen on a stick gauge at Husum, which is on river right and visible from the side road bridge downstream of the highway bridge.

John Karafotias, Ron Reynier, and Teresa Gryder

163 White Salmon River
Husum to Northwestern Park

Class: 2+	Length: 3 miles
Flow: 900–2000 cfs	Character: shallow canyon
Gradient: 25 fpm, PD	Season: year-round

The scenic lower run on the White Salmon winds its way through a shallow, wooded canyon. It is short, but playful and enjoyable for novices and intermediates. Boaters doing the sections above and below this one often add on this section for the Cave Wave, which is an excellent surfing wave at almost every flow.

For the beginner, the run starts out a little scary, with an abrupt 3-foot drop into a hole at Rattlesnake. A pool below the drop makes rescue easy. Rattlesnake can be scouted and portaged on either side of the river. After a class 1+ section, there is a class 2 S-turn rapid with a sharp turn to the right; watch for wood here. Around the next left bend is a long class 2 section with some steeper parts. The rest of the run is easier. Cave Wave is about halfway down the run.

The river wanders through rich forests and class 2- shoals into the section that was formerly inundated by Northwestern Lake before the removal of Condit Dam. Recognize the take-out by the massive bridge overhead and a final class 2 rapid that is immediately above the concrete boat ramp on the right. If you miss the right eddy or the boat ramp, just around the corner is another trail up to Northwestern Park.

Hazards

The cold water and longer rapids in the top mile are challenging for beginners. Watch carefully for strainers. At high water, expect class 3 character.

Access

For directions to the put-in at Husum, see the White Salmon River: BZ Corner to Husum run.

The take-out is about 2 miles south of Husum, off Washington 141. Follow the signs to Northwestern Park. Go over the bridge and turn left into the park.

Gauge

See the White Salmon River: BZ Corner to Husum run.

Bob Collmer, Ron Reynier, and Teresa Gryder

164 White Salmon River
Northwestern Park to the Columbia River

Class: 3 (4,5)	Length: 5 miles
Flow: 300–1000 cfs	Character: steep canyon; gorges
Gradient: 55 fpm, PD	Season: year-round

This gem was rarely attempted until after the removal of Condit Dam in 2011, liberating a section that had been impounded for 100 years, thus making access easier. Nicknamed the Bottom White Salmon, it contains mostly intermediate whitewater in a setting of sheer basalt gorges. Like most runs on the White Salmon, it has areas where rescue and access are difficult, in addition to a tendency to develop large logjams. The run is best explored during the dry summer months when water levels are low and unlikely to rise, and when there have been no recent floods to introduce wood. It should be considered only after a thorough investigation of current conditions. The whitewater exceeds class 3 in one section, and that section can be unforgiving to the uninformed.

The run begins in open terrain with class 2 and 3 whitewater that used to be underneath Northwestern Lake. The slopes have been planted with alder, and the waterline is festooned with cabled log bundles for fish shelter. The first class 3 is Sweet Pea, on a right bend with a log pile on the left bank. On the next left bend, a cliff rises overhead on the river, followed by a long, open class 3 rapid called Land of Oz, and a shorter rapid called Jaws, which feeds into the first gorge. The old dam site is in this chasm, just downstream from the waterfall entering on the right.

After the dam site, the rapids ease up, but the riverbed is narrow, and at higher flows, strong eddy lines and boils form there. The second short gorge also contains class 2–3 whitewater, then there is a brief open section before the river enters the third and longest gorge, where you will find Steelhead Falls (class 4–5, depending on flow).

The approach to Steelhead can be recognized by powerlines overhead. Where the river sweeps right and steepens, conservative boaters stop on the left to scout or portage the entrance rapid. More aggressive boaters may run the entrance and catch an eddy on the left before the blind left bend, which leads into the falls itself. With enough water, this entrance rapid develops large holes and can be run on the left. Below this, the current rushes headlong around a blind left bend and drops over Steelhead Falls.

The final confirmation that you have reached Steelhead is the safety rope anchored to the left wall, leading around the corner. There is one more eddy on the outside of the bend on the right, but there is no portage from there. This eddy is often caught in the process of running the drop.

Scouting or portaging Steelhead Falls involves wading in fast water along the left wall to the point where you can climb up onto a bedrock shelf that provides a platform for setting safety. At higher flows, this portage route closes off, and it becomes necessary to rock climb across the cliff. There is a trail escaping the gorge on river left, back upstream by two bends.

Steelhead Falls is a river-wide ledge that forms a powerful hydraulic. The line over the ledge at most flows follows a tongue down the far left; however, this line is complicated by a rock that diverts paddlers toward the hydraulic, which drags swimmers and equipment toward the sheer wall on river right. A strong rope throw can reach a swimmer on the right wall from the left bank, and by walking downstream, one may pull them out of the hole. A swimmer who is lucky enough to go for a deep swim in the hydraulic may surface in the current headed into the sheer gorge below. There are small eddies along the left, where one might land a roped-in swimmer.

Below the falls, the sheer gorge enters a sharp right bend, after which the water slows and winds through some broken logjams. This bend has captured major logjams in the past and will do so again. Check with local paddlers regarding the wood situation before you launch, because there is no reasonable portage.

Where the narrow stretch widens out, there is an island and then a fun rapid called Baby Bear, which has a good surfing wave and a large eddy on the right. You will pass a powerhouse, the dilapidated Bootlegger's Bridge, and an old fish hatchery. Then the river bends to the right and drops through The Maze, a rocky final class 3 that lives up to its name. In the last half-mile to the take-out, the river flattens and braids into gravel bars, and toward the end, you can expect a headwind feeding in from the Columbia Gorge. A spectacular view of Mount Hood and the antics of the kite boarders on the Columbia keep this short flat-water stretch amusing.

Hazards

Logjams, inaccessible gorges, scouting difficulties, keeper hydraulic.

Access

To reach the take-out from Hood River, take Interstate 84, exit 64 and cross the Columbia River on the Hood River Bridge. Take a left on Washington 14 and go 1.5 miles, then turn right onto Washington Alternate 141. The take-out is at the first pullout on the left. There is a steep angler's trail to the water. The docks and land on river right are private property; don't trespass.

To reach the put-in, continue up Alternate 141 for 2.2 miles to the stop sign, turn left, then drive another 1.9 miles to a left turn onto Northwestern Lake Road. Drive 0.4 mile down the hill, cross the bridge, and take a left into the park, which no longer has a lake. A popular alternative launch site is at Husum Falls, 2.1 miles farther up Washington 141, adding 2.5 miles of class 2 warm-up and the Cave Wave to the run. (See White Salmon: Husum to Northwestern Park for details.)

Gauge

White Salmon River at Underwood. This gauge is located downstream from the removed dam, and its readings continue to shift with the sediments. Locals tend to trust the stick gauge at Husum, where a reading of 1.2–3 feet is good, with the portage around Steelhead being the limiting factor at high water. Commercial rafting companies do not attempt it over 2.5 feet on the Husum stick gauge. Exact cfs for this limit is unknown at this time.

Teresa Gryder

Wind River, Washington

165 ★ Wind River
Stabler to High Bridge

Class: 4+; 5	Length: 6 miles
Flow: 300–1500 cfs; 2500 cfs	Character: forested gorge
Gradient: 90 fpm, PD	Season: rainy/snowmelt

The Upper Wind is a winter favorite for advanced boaters because of its consistent flows and nonstop technical whitewater in a wild, forested gorge. Even though the run feels quite remote, the road is a short, steep hike up the river-left side of the gorge for the first half. For a class 5 boater, this run is almost entirely read and run. For the class 3 boater who has run a few class 4 rapids, it would be a mistake to launch. There is no way to scout, portage, or sneak all the big ones: The whole river is hard. It is possible to put together class 5 moves in nearly every rapid, making this an excellent training ground for the solid class 4 boater looking to progress. With the right skill set, this run is a playground of boofs, slots, eddies, and holes.

The Wind has a long season, starting with the fall rains and continuing through the winter into late May or June. The easiest levels are in the medium-low range. It is more difficult when very low, because there are more rocks in the lines, and more dangerous when high, because there are huge holes everywhere and no way to stop the ride. When flows are adequate for this section, the river is too high for the waterfall run downstream of High Bridge.

Put in at Stabler and enjoy almost a mile of technical class 3- warm-up. An optional put-in is on Trout Creek for 0.6 mile of very technical water before reaching

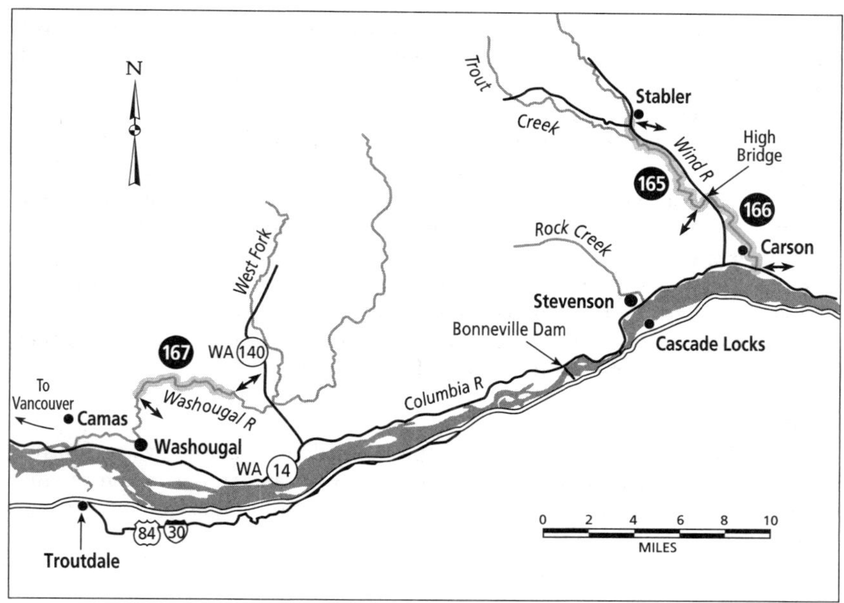

the Wind River. The biggest rapids on the Wind are in the first third of the trip and are connected by long, continuous class 3 sections.

The first big rapid is Initiation, which begins immediately after Trout Creek enters on the right. It is rarely scouted, because it is hard to see much of the rapid from the scout point and because it is not really more difficult than the rest of the section. First-timers usually opt for a rocky far right sneak so they can boat-scout the congested first ledge below. There are eddies below this ledge, but no pool. The river continues to drop with only brief slowdowns for the next 2 miles.

The next named rapid follows a rapid in a gorge that has an actual pool at the bottom. The river at this point bends to the right and enters Balls to the Wall Right, which can be run in the right channel by punching two holes, or by cutting from the right to the center and boofing small ledges. When the river bends left again, one is entering Balls to the Wall Left, which is generally run on the left, where laterals smack you away from the wall. Below here, steep and rocky whitewater continues right up to the edge of Ram's Horn, where a large eddy on the left allows boaters to catch their breath. The standard line through Ram's Horn is to first run the far left ramp, then reposition in the brief slow water for a drive to the left edge of the breaking wave/hole (known as Whoop-de-woo).

The rapids downstream from Ram's Horn are class 3 until you reach Climax, which is the blindest ledge on the run. Scouting is possible from both sides, and there is a good eddy on river left above the drop. At low water, the easiest line is on the left side of the center left channel, where a boof flake becomes visible after you've gone over the horizon. At higher levels, this same line can capture boats and swimmers in a retentive corner pocket hole. The far left "helicopter move" is a challenging double boof to the left. The center right channel has a peak boof that avoids the hole as water levels rise. The far right has a kayak sneak, and it is also possible to portage on the right.

Do not relax yet. The very next rapid below Climax is the final class 4. It is comprised of two rows of boulders with many slots. The easiest line is to catch or spin in an eddy on the left below the first boulder fence, from which you can see an easy channel. The far right line is amusing until the holes get too big.

From here down, the rapids top out at strong class 3 and have a bounty of interesting boofs and play spots. A scenic waterfall streams in from river right. A few log obstacles have been in place for years, while others shift around. After a couple of miles of class 3, the river tapers down to mostly class 2 before reaching the take-out on the right, upstream from High Bridge.

Hazards

Initiation, Ram's Horn, and Climax are the most difficult and are all within the first third of the trip. This run has more mandatory moves per mile than many rivers have in 10 miles. Several large logs are fixtures in the middle third of the run, and new wood can lodge anywhere at any time.

Access

The Wind River is near the town of Carson, Washington, which is off Washington 14 about 5.6 miles east of Stevenson. From Carson, drive north on Wind River Highway. To get to the take-out, turn left onto High Bridge Road about 2 miles outside of Carson. From High Bridge Road, make the first right onto Old Detour Road and follow this dirt road down to the river and the take-out. Please drive slowly past the houses and warehouse to avoid disrupting fragile relations with locals.

To reach the put-in, return to Wind River Highway, turn left, and continue north another 5.3 miles to Hemlock Road. Make a left onto Hemlock Road and immediately cross the Wind River. Put in at the first pullout on the right after this bridge, or make the first right and then bear right for an alternative put-in.

To get to the Trout Creek put-in, continue west on Hemlock Road from Stabler and turn at the first left, which is Trout Creek Road. Follow this road south until it crosses Trout Creek. (Alternatively, continue on Hemlock Road and put in about 1 mile higher on Trout Creek. No significant rapids are found along this mile.)

Gauge

Wind River at Stabler. The gauge is located at the put-in on river left. Readings on the stick gauge correspond with the online readings for the gauge. A minimal flow on the stick gauge is 4.7 or so, easiest first-timer flows are 4.9–5.2, and the river becomes a big water run around 6 feet.

Harvey Lee Shapiro, Teresa Gryder, and WKCC Editors

166 ★ Wind River
High Bridge to Saint Martin Road

Class: 4-(5); 5	Length: 5 miles
Flow: 90–130 cfs; 140–200 cfs	Character: forested gorge
Gradient: 61 fpm, PD	Season: summer, post rainy season

Commonly known as the Lower Wind, this gem is a technical playground with a few difficult rapids, a set of waterfalls near the end, and a hot spring before the take-out. At appropriate flows, it is easier than the section upstream and is commonly used as a training ground for aspiring creek boaters. It is usually run during summertime low water when it is class 3 and 4 with one portage. The river will look very low at the put-in, but the waterfalls are only runnable at low flows. Side streams that are spring-fed enhance the flow during the run.

The half-mile of warm-up rapids are technical class 2 water. When High Bridge comes into view, the first major rapid begins with a long, convoluted rock garden, which finishes in a gorge. At normal (low) water, there is at least one clean line through each obstruction here. Lateral moves and boofs are required to avoid pinning, and while you can scout from river right, the best way to explore this run is to follow someone who knows it. If this rapid is too much, hike back up on river right and run shuttle.

Class 3 rapids continue for less than a mile before a distinct horizon line signals you to stop and scout on the right. This is The Flume, arguably the most difficult and dangerous rapid on the run. At low flows, when the rest of the run is class 4 or less, The Flume is rocky and unforgiving, and is commonly portaged on the right. If you are going to run it, there are three possible entries that all lead into a sinuous hole-punching sluice down the left side of the gorge, ending in a good pool.

Beyond The Flume, the next big rapid is Beyond Limits, a 5-foot sliding drop that creates a nasty hole at medium and higher flows. It can be portaged along the fish ladder on the left. At lower flows there are two lines, a straight shot down the middle and a far right boof. Your goal is to get well past the hole.

After a mile or so of easier rapids, the river bends to the left, and there is a steep rapid ending at the concrete bulkhead of a fish ladder on the left. Avoid the intake of the fish ladder. Suspended over the water downstream is a cable footbridge that is accessible by trail from the old Hotel Saint Martin. This marks the infamous Shipherd Falls, which contains four distinct drops, including two waterfalls, one bony slide, and one weir. If uncertain, or if you know the flows are too high for running the falls, eddy out high on the left to scout and portage on top of the fish ladder. There are two portage options: You can throw your boat off the 30-foot drop at the end of the fish ladder and jump in after it, or you can carry your boat along the even higher cliff trail until you reach a reasonable launch spot.

If the flows are suitable for running the falls (90–130 cfs), avoid the fish ladder intake on the left and eddy out on the right above the first falls, a drop of 10–12 feet. The normal line is a far left auto-boof. A right boof opens up at the upper end of the runnable range. Dropping over the center at this falls results in a very deep "experience," and immediately below it there is a short gorge and then the tallest falls.

The tallest falls is about 18 vertical feet. It is usually run in the main right channel with a center-left delayed straight boof, or by boofing the right edge. At higher flows, the left channel is best. There are eddies on both sides below the drop. From the left eddy, one can climb onto the fish ladder and portage back upstream to do laps on the falls.

The next drop is a bony slide, run right of center. There are eddies below, but scant time for rescues between this drop and the next, which is a 10-foot-high weir. Run the weir on the right side of the left channel, boofing right. The eddy on the left below this drop collects wood and may contain metal.

Downstream from Shipherd Falls, eddy out and enjoy the view. A soak in the lovely natural hot springs on river left, still within sight of the falls, is a treat. The take-out is on river right, a short half-mile of bony class 1–2 rapids downstream from the hot springs.

Hazards

Never cross a horizon line without scouting or having trustworthy guidance. The Flume is class 5 at low water, Beyond Limits is class 5 at high water, and Shipherd Falls is class 6 at high water. Scout and portage accordingly.

Access

In Oregon, take Interstate 84 to Bridge of the Gods at Cascade Locks. Cross the Columbia River and turn right (north and east) onto Washington 14. Go 5.9 miles and turn left at the blinking yellow light toward Carson. In Carson, turn right at the four-way stop onto Hot Springs Avenue, and go 0.9 mile to a left turn toward the old Saint Martin Hotel hot springs resort. Go past the entrance to the new resort and take the small dirt road on the right, signed "St. Martin Road." Drive down steep switchbacks to the take-out.

To reach the put-in, backtrack to the four-way stop in Carson and take a right going north on Wind River Highway 2 miles to a hard left turn onto Old Detour Road. Take the first right and continue respectfully past houses and a warehouse into the forest and down to the river.

Gauge

Wind River at Stabler. Optimal flows are 90–130 cfs in the summer. Only class 5 paddlers should attempt the run at higher flows.

Teresa Gryder

Washougal River, Washington

167 ★ Washougal River
Public Fishing Road to Milepost 3

Class: 3(4); 4	Length: 5 miles
Flow: 300–2000 cfs; 2500–6000 cfs	Character: forested; residential; agricultural
Gradient: 33 fpm, C	Season: rainy

This pleasant run is close to Portland and Vancouver, and it contains class 2 and 3 rapids and one class 4 boulder garden. The rapid types vary from wide shoals and rock gardens that are technical at low water to narrower channels with concentrated current and big water features at higher flows.

Be sure to launch downstream from the fish control weir at the public fishing access. The first two rapids are class 2–3 shoals and boulder gardens. Soon after these is Big Eddy Rapid, the only class 4, recognized by the giant calm pool above it. Scout or portage on the right, or catch the last eddy on the left to boat scout. (The "No Trespassing" signs along the right shore are not meant to discourage paddlers; the current owner is a paddler.) At flows above 6.5 feet on the Hathaway gauge, it is possible to run far right from the top and miss the largest features.

The first rapid below Big Eddy is a steep class 3 with a large hole midstream. Below this point the class 2–3 pattern resumes with small ledges, holes, boulder gardens, and surfing spots interspersed with pools. For most of the run, the easiest lines on ledges are on the left.

About 3 miles into the run, the river swings right and drops into Cougar Creek Rapid, which is visible from the road. Most paddlers go left of the island at the head of the rapid, with the main flow. Below the island there is an eddy on the right, and then a narrow channel with a series of large waves and a waterfall entering on the right.

After 1.5 miles of long class 2 shoals, the final class 3, called Island Rapid, is also recognized by an island. The standard line is on the right of the island, but on the left side of the right channel. A successful run requires crossing a strong eddy line to hug the left bank.

Hazards

Big Eddy, the class 4 boulder garden, can be scouted from the road 4.7 miles above the take-out.

Access

Cross the Columbia River in Portland and take Washington 14 east to the town of Washougal. Take a left at the light onto Washougal River Road and continue upstream to the take-out at milepost 3. A Discover Pass is required to park near the unimproved trail to the river. Note the waterfall across the river from the take-out trail. An alternative take-out is in the town of Washougal at Hathaway Park's boat launch. This adds another 2.2 miles of class 1 and 2 river travel.

To reach the put-in, drive upstream for 5.5 additional miles to a right turn onto a road marked simply "Public Fishing." This launch is at mile 8.5 on Washougal River Road. An alternative, informal launch at milepost 5 allows paddlers to skip the biggest rapids.

Gauge

For Washougal River at Washougal, see Pat Welch's flow page. For Washougal River at Hathaway Park, see Washington State Department of Ecology website (Appendix A). A flow of 1500 cfs is excellent and occurs when the Twin Rocks in Big Eddy are barely exposed.

Stan Jacobs, Jay Nigra, and Teresa Gryder

Opposite: *Geology in action on the Deschutes* (Kathy Shelby)

Central
Oregon Rivers

Region 8

Metolius River

168 ★ Metolius River
Source to Lake Billy Chinook

Class: 3(4-)	Length: 27 miles
Flow: 1300–2000 cfs	Character: forested; fishing
Gradient: 36 fpm, C	Season: year-round

This very unusual river originates in the Cascades beneath Black Butte. Within several hundred feet, the river wells up from the ground and becomes 30 feet wide. Within 0.5 mile, the river swells to an average flow of 1500 cfs, from which it deviates little throughout the year. Because the water comes from underground, it is always frigid. The river level fluctuates so little that the banks are overgrown with heavy vegetation. At the first bridge in the community of Camp Sherman, visitors may pause to look for the huge trout. In the autumn months, bald eagles gather in great numbers along the river corridor. The character of the Metolius can be divided into two sections.

SECTION 1A: SOURCE TO LOWER BRIDGE CAMPGROUND, 10 MILES, CLASS 3

This section has a resort atmosphere with private camps, forest campgrounds, and picnic areas. The river's source is open for public viewing. The river flows through meadowlands for the first few miles, and put-ins are along the road. The bridge at the resort community of Camp Sherman, about 3 miles downstream, provides access, as do the improved campgrounds farther downstream. From the source to several miles below Camp Sherman, the river is swift and replete with snags and several low bridges, but has no significant whitewater.

The tempo increases below Gorge Campground, which is 3 miles below Camp Sherman and 6 miles below the source. The Gorge has two fast class 3 rapids beginning 1 mile below Gorge Campground. Along the right bank of The Gorge, a group of springs gush forth into the river. Several low bridges may require portage. Kayakers sometimes do a limbo move to get under them. Just above a low bridge to Wizard Falls fish hatchery, a narrow, turbulent channel cuts through lava bedrock. The 3 miles from Wizard Falls to Lower Bridge Campground are class 1. Because this section has been designated for fly-fishing only, it is a favorite area for anglers, so respect their space.

SECTION 1B: LOWER BRIDGE TO CANDLE CREEK CAMPGROUND, 1.7 MILES, CLASS 3

In the past a river-wide log blocked the lower end of the long class 3 drop in this section. It has been cleared and a portage is no longer required. However, paddlers must always be cautious of logs on the Metolius, since many logs are being placed in the river to improve fish habitat.

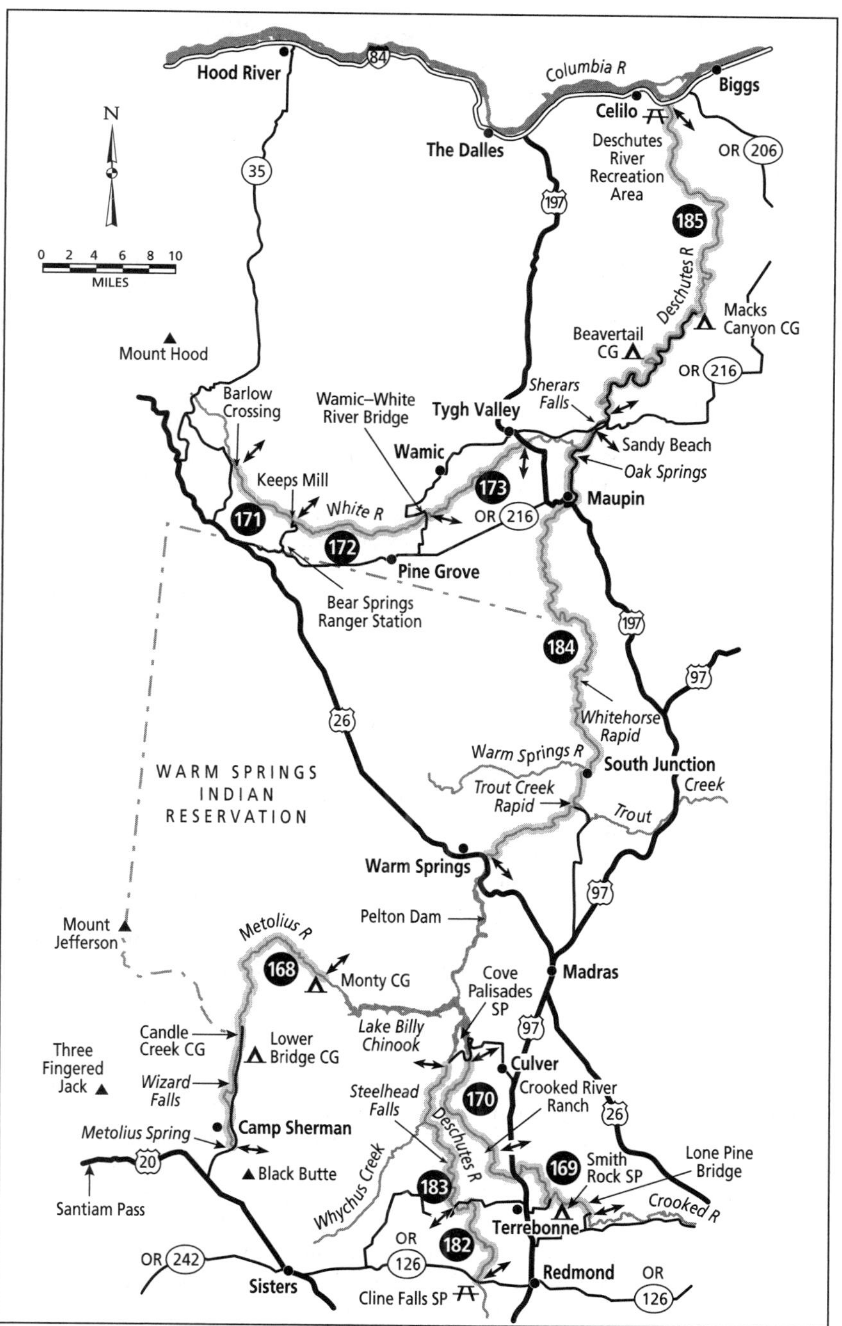
N
0 2 4 6 8 10
MILES
Hood River
84
Columbia R
Biggs
Celilo
The Dalles
Deschutes River Recreation Area
OR 206
185
35
197
Deschutes R
Macks Canyon CG
Mount Hood
Barlow Crossing
Wamic–White River Bridge
Tygh Valley
Sherars Falls
Beavertail CG
OR 216
Keeps Mill
Wamic
Sandy Beach
Oak Springs
173
Maupin
171
White R
OR 216
172
Pine Grove
Bear Springs Ranger Station
197
184
97
26
Whitehorse Rapid
WARM SPRINGS INDIAN RESERVATION
Warm Springs R
South Junction
Creek
Trout Creek Rapid
Trout
Warm Springs
97
Pelton Dam
Mount Jefferson
Metolius R
168
Monty CG
Cove Palisades SP
Madras
97
Candle Creek CG
Lower Bridge CG
Lake Billy Chinook
Culver
Crooked River Ranch
26
Three Fingered Jack
Wizard Falls
Steelhead Falls
Deschutes R
170
169
Smith Rock SP
Lone Pine Bridge
Metolius Spring
Camp Sherman
20
Whychus Creek
Crooked R
Santiam Pass
Black Butte
183
Terrebonne
OR 242
OR 126
182
Redmond
OR 126
Sisters
Cline Falls SP

SECTION 2: CANDLE CREEK CAMPGROUND TO LAKE BILLY CHINOOK, 15.3 MILES, CLASS 3(4-)

This section contains premier crystal-clear whitewater in a primitive setting. The swiftness and uniform gradient of the water and the thick vegetation make eddies and landing spots hard to find. A swimming boater may float a long way before finding a landing spot. Because of the river's swiftness, these 15 miles can easily be run in a day.

The left bank, below Candle Creek Campground, is private property owned by the Confederated Tribes of Warm Springs; please respect the no-trespassing rule on native lands. Much of the river has no road nearby, although a gravel road does extend up from the take-out for a few miles on river right.

Starting at the downstream end of Candle Creek Campground, there are numerous long class 2 and 3 rapids with truly beautiful whitewater. At 10.5 miles downstream of Candle Creek, after Whitewater River enters on the left, the tempo picks up. A class 3 rapid is followed by a mellower stretch of water for about 0.2 mile, and then the most difficult rapid of the run, the class 4- rapid, begins. There are sketchy and difficult-to-see logs coming in from both sides of the river as you enter the rapids. Logs often need portaging here. The crux of the rapid is a shelf that extends from river left. Take the narrow channel just to the right of the shelf while maneuvering to avoid the few holes on the right.

The river continues at a fast pace to Lake Billy Chinook, where the change to flatwater is like a gentle awakening from a pleasant dream. Take out on the right at Monty Campground along the river above the lake.

Hazards

The greatest danger is the existence of large ponderosa pines completely blocking the river. At least five such blockages exist currently (2015) with dangerous, hard-to-spot logs occurring in many locations. The potential for large buildups of wood in the river is real, due to the lack of high water. The Forest Service no longer removes dangerous wood from the river, so be very cautious. Forest Service fish habitat restoration work is ongoing. Numerous logs have been added to the river channel between Riverside Campground and Bridge 99 (Lower Bridge). Be sure to read the signs posted at put-ins and take-outs describing the changes in wood management and be very careful. The Gorge is relatively fast and requires rock dodging. Be prepared for very cold water year-round, about 43 degrees Fahrenheit.

Access

From the west, take US 20 or Oregon 22 east across Santiam Pass, or from the east, take Oregon 22 west from Sisters toward Santiam Pass. The turnoff to the Metolius is 5.5 miles east of Suttle Lake. Follow the signs to "Head of the Metolius." This unusual sight is well worth seeing. The paved road from the Head of the Metolius essentially parallels the river on the east side to Lower Bridge Campground.

Put-ins are available at any of the campgrounds along the road to Lower Bridge Campground. If you put in at Gorge Campground or Wizard Falls, for example, the take-out can be at any of the unimproved camps below Lower Bridge Campground

Below Camp Sherman on the Metolius River (Tim Palmer)

or at the end of the dirt road. If the take-out is at one of the unimproved camps, be sure to find a good landmark, because this region all looks the same from the river. Most paddlers of the lower stretch of river put in at the lower end of Candle Creek Campground, river left below Bridge 99, to avoid a portage of the river-wide log located in the rapid just upstream of Candle Creek Campground. From Lower Bridge, go west on NF 12 for about 0.5 mile, then northeast on NF 1200-980 for about 1.5 mile to Candle Creek Campground, the end of the road. Put in by the creek.

The shuttle to the Lake Billy Chinook take-out is about 35 miles, mostly over gravel roads. From Lower Bridge Campground, go upstream about 0.5 mile on Oregon 14. Turn left onto NF 1490 and climb Green Ridge. At the junction with NF 1140 (Prairie Farm Road), head east on 1140. Farther east, Prairie Farm Road continues as NF 1180 and then 1170 to its end at a blacktop road, Oregon 64, near the lake. Turn left, pass Perry South Campground, and continue another 4.5 miles to Monty Campground on the lower Metolius, about 0.5 mile above lake water.

Gauge

Flow information is unnecessary because discharges range from 1250 to 2500 cfs, with a 58-year mean of 1500 cfs.

T. R. Torgersen, Rob Blickensderfer, Trevor Groves, and Karen Daniels

Crooked River

169 Crooked River
Lone Pine Bridge to Crooked River Ranch

Class 4 (4+ to 5)	Length: 16.2 miles
Flow: 1400–4500 cfs	Character: inaccessible desert gorge
Gradient: 31 fpm PD	Season: dam-controlled (very limited releases)

The Crooked River, a designated Wild and Scenic River, has many big rapids and runs through a spectacular gorge. This hair-raising run for advanced to expert boaters offers few good places to put in or take out. Lots of equipment has been lost in the Crooked River gorge. It is important to know your abilities before entering the river due to the difficulty of hiking out past Smith Rock State Park (especially if using a raft). If you choose to run only the upper stretch and plan to hike out at Hollywood Road up to the Crooked River Ranch, be aware of the strenuous 1-mile trail hike up that begins with a demanding 100-yard, semi-vertical climb without trail.

The only "legal" put-in for this run is 4 miles above Smith Rock State Park at Lone Pine Bridge, where it crosses over the Crooked River following Lone Pine Road. The access is on the edge of a ranch, so please be courteous and tidy while launching. About 2.5 miles below the bridge and directly below the aqueduct crossing overhead, the flatwater comes to a halt and the continuous class 4 rapids begin. This first group of rapids is followed by a long, meandering stretch of very slow water leading into and finally exiting Smith Rock State Park. Rock climbers flock to this area year-round for some of the best climbing in Oregon and the Northwest.

About a mile downstream of the park is Number One (class 4), the first rapid in a series. Number One is a very steep, short drop with a boulder the size of a Volkswagen bug in the center, and smaller boulders and medium holes on the left. Cut down behind the large boulder obstructing the drop, making your way back to center below. Scout/portage right. Almost a mile lower is Number Two, which may be run left or right of the lava island. This drop has a difficult approach and should be scouted from the left.

The next rapid is a series of waves called The Bumps, class 3+ to 4, located about 0.25 mile below Number Two. The Bumps are a prelude to Wap-te-doodle, class 4+ to 5-, a very long drop with powerful hydraulics and two large back-to-back holes at the bottom center. Scout from the left. A couple of lesser rapids lie between here and the US 97 bridge crossing high above.

After the bridge, the river is a busy class 3–4 leading to the most difficult rapid of the upper section, No Name, class 4+ to 5. No Name is a long, rough rapid scattered with boulders and holes, finally dropping into the very large, culminating bottom hole that tends to be fairly sticky. Scout on the right. Several easier and shorter rapids follow.

The next major rapid, China Dam, class 4+ to 5, is located at the end of a stretch of flatwater along sheer cliffs just below the upper take-out. The rapid is situated at an old dam site built years ago for mining operations. The river broke through the dam, leaving sharp rocks and a shallow riverbed to the center and the left.

You can either take out just above and scramble up 100 yards to Hollywood Road, or run the rapid and hope to make the eddy on bottom river left. Unless you are running the whole stretch to Lake Billy Chinook, plan on taking out above, especially if in a raft. You definitely want to avoid missing the bottom eddy and being swept past the take-out. Scout. China Dam can be very difficult at lower levels.

Hazards

This stretch is runnable for only a short time each year, usually in late April. It presents many difficulties that demand special attention. Retreat from the river due to equipment loss or injury is very difficult in most of the canyon. The take-out at Hollywood Road is very difficult.

Access

The put-in is 6 miles east of US 97 between Redmond and Madras. From US 97 at Terrebonne, go east for 4.9 miles on Smith Rock Way to Lone Pine Bridge, the put-in. The take-out is at Crooked River Ranch. The roads to the ranch are public. From US 97 north of Terrebonne, follow the signs to Crooked River Ranch and the clubhouse. Drive past the clubhouse and turn right just below the little white church. Park in the gravel lot. Hollywood Road is a difficult access, so expect a strenuous 1-mile hike up from the river and plan accordingly.

Gauge

Crooked River below Osborne Canyon. In years of low snowfall, no water may be released. For information on planned releases, contact the Oregon Department of Water Resources watermaster in Bend (541-388-6669) or the Ochoco Irrigation District in Prineville (541-447-6449). Optimal flows are 2000–3400 cfs.

Ron Mattson, Scott Russell, Yann Crist-Evans, and WKCC Editors

170 Crooked River
Crooked River Ranch to Lake Billy Chinook

Class: 3(4) P	Length: 10.2 miles
Flow: 1000–5000 cfs	Character: inaccessible desert gorge
Gradient: 30 fpm, PD	Season: year-round

This part of the Crooked River is not quite as intense, and only half as long, as the previous run. Still, some of the rapids are challenging, and boaters are a long way from help. It is a 1-mile steep hike down the old Hollywood Road to the put-in. Most rafters choose to put in above this run at the Lone Pine Bridge, 16 miles upstream.

The minimum release flow is only 100 cfs at the Prineville Dam many miles upstream, but numerous springs along this run increase the flow to 1000 cfs, making the river runnable year-round. At the river, boaters may opt to put in either above China Dam, 4+ to 5, or about 200 yards downstream. At normal summer flows (low), China Dam is not runnable. Put in below it.

One mile past China Dam is The Wave (class 4), which, at flows above 3500 cfs, has a steep V wave that envelops boaters with water converging overhead. An old rockfall from the left at the top of the rapid makes low-water runs more difficult. The Wave is steep; at really low water, the left looks most promising, but it may not be runnable. It is rocky on the top left and even worse on the bottom right. At higher water, center to right is best.

Opal Springs Dam is 4 miles ahead, where the river disappears into a power tunnel that is recognizable by a concrete structure on the left. Portage right for 0.2 mile (beware of sharp and slippery rocks) and put in at the generator tailwater. Below Opal Springs Dam is Opal Springs itself, followed by a gauge; both are on the right. Several easy rapids follow. The last class 4 rapid before Lake Billy Chinook is long, with heavy whitewater and big holes. It is very likely to contain logs or trees. Scouting is highly recommended. The main chutes force boaters left where logs are most likely to be lurking. The recommended route is to work right as soon as possible and stay there. About 3 miles of reservoir paddling brings boaters to the take-out at the bridge over the Crooked River arm of the reservoir.

Hazards

The Wave, 1 mile below China Dam, is steep. Opal Springs Dam must be portaged. The last rapid has big water. Logs or trees in the river may block channels at any time.

Access

For the put-in at Crooked River Ranch, see the take-out for the Crooked River: Lone Pine Bridge to Crooked River Ranch run.

The take-out bridge crosses the Crooked River arm of Lake Billy Chinook several miles west of US 97 near Culver, between Madras and Redmond. From US 97 south of Madras, go west a few miles to Culver. Follow signs to The Cove Palisades State Park, about 6 miles west of Culver. The take-out bridge is the first one encountered over the reservoir. (The second bridge is the Deschutes arm of the reservoir.)

Gauge

Crooked River below Opal Springs. Crooked River near Culver.

Scott Russell and Hank Hays

171 White River
Barlow Crossing to Keeps Mill

Class: 3+(4)	Length: 6.8 miles
Flow: 400–1400 cfs	Character: forested
Gradient: 63 fpm	Season: snowmelt

The magnificent White River starts on the east side of Mount Hood among the trees and often in snow, continues through a wilderness gorge, and ends in a desert. The change in scenery en route is spectacular. This upper run is seldom done because the next run, starting at Keeps Mill, is long, interesting, and spectacular enough to keep most paddlers content. This upper run has accumulated many logs in recent years. Check with local paddlers about the current log situation before launching.

The put-in is at Barlow Crossing, where the pioneers crossed the White River while traveling Barlow Road. The first 2.5 miles below Barlow Crossing are class 1+. The river gradient then increases, with many blind turns. The first significant drop is 3 miles below Barlow Crossing. It consists of two big ledges, class 4, which should be scouted on river left. From here to Keeps Mill is fast-flowing continuous class 3+ with lots of maneuvering required. A Mount Hood National Forest map, which shows the entire river and all shuttle roads, is indispensable.

Hazards

The numerous logs in the river make the run especially hazardous.

Access

From Portland, take US 26 east; from Eastern Oregon, take US 26 west from Madras. On the shoulders of Mount Hood, turn north onto Oregon 35. After a few miles, turn right on NF 43, just past the White River bridge. Go 8.9 miles and turn right. Go 500 feet to a bridge, which crosses the White River at Barlow Crossing, the put-in.

To get to the Keeps Mill take-out, return to US 26 and follow the instructions for the put-in for the White River: Keeps Mill to Wamic–White River Bridge run.

Gauge

None exists. For a close estimate of the White River's flow farther downstream see Pat Welch's flow page: White River below Tygh Valley.

Harvey Lee Shapiro

172 White River
Keeps Mill to Wamic–White River Bridge

Class: 3+(4); 4-(4+)	Length: 12.2 miles
Flow: 400 cfs; 1400 cfs	Character: forested
Gradient: 79 fpm, C	Season: snowmelt

The water here is always cold, but from January to March the air temperature is also cold within the deep canyon. Winter runs are, therefore, uncomfortably cold and not recommended. In May and June, the air temperature is warmer and the steep canyon rocks radiate heat, resulting in very warm or hot air, especially in the lower half of this run. The character of the run is very similar to what you see at the put-in: continuous fast-moving whitewater over rocks, a few boulders, and an occasional logjam. The river is a continuous class 3+ with a beautiful rhythm all its own. There is one class 4 rapid. At medium levels, eddies and play spots are abundant. All drops are runnable, except for the occasional logjam. Most drops can be scouted by eddy hopping.

The most difficult rapid on the river is about 1.5 miles below Keeps Mill. It can be recognized by the high cliffs located on river left one or two drops above the rapid. It should be scouted by first-time paddlers. Problems in this rapid could be unpleasant and might result in an extremely long and difficult day in this wild canyon. Scout on the right from above before starting the easy lead-in because you will find no easy eddy immediately above the drop. Normally, this rapid is approached on river left and run right of center. About 8 miles below the put-in, a wire crosses the river, with hanging metal gates on each shore and several others in the river. These mark the Mount Hood National Forest boundary. A short distance below here, the river gains more volume and, at higher water levels, becomes pushy and more memorable.

Hazards

Logjams that require portaging are likely. Some paddlers might underestimate the speed of the current, which could result in dangerous encounters with logjams. Scout the class 4 rapid located 1.5 miles below Keeps Mill.

Access

From the Portland area, take US 26 east; from Central and Eastern Oregon, take US 26 west from Madras. At Oregon 216, turn east toward Maupin. After 3 miles, look for a small green sign to Keeps Mill/White River on the right side just as the road takes a long curve to the right. (If you see a sign for Bear Springs Ranger Station, you have gone 0.3 mile too far.) Turn left and continue on the main road for 3.5 miles down to the river. Follow signs to Keeps Mill. The road for the last 1.5 miles is dirt with rock slides. It is slow but passable and arrives at a primitive campground.

To reach the take-out, go back to Oregon 216, turn left (east) toward Maupin, and continue past Bear Springs Ranger Station to Pine Grove. About 2.4 miles past Pine Grove is a small green sign on the right that reads, "Victor Road, Wamic, White River." Turn left onto this dirt road and follow it as it jogs right and then left. Shortly after it turns right again, take the first road to the left (a sign to Wamic is on the right side, if someone has not knocked it over). After turning left, note the sign about the road being extremely hazardous, especially in winter. Have faith and continue to the river and the take-out at Wamic–White River Bridge on river left.

Gauge

None exists. For a close estimate of the White River's flow farther downstream, see Pat Welch's flow page: White River below Tygh Valley.

Harvey Lee Shapiro and WKCC Editors

173 ★ White River
Wamic–White River Bridge to Tygh Valley

Class: 3(3+ to 4-)	Length: 11.1 miles
Flow: 400–2000 cfs	Character: forested canyon
Gradient: 42 fpm, PD	Season: snowmelt

This is a beautiful run through some of the most delightful canyons in Oregon. Do not do this run just for the whitewater. Do it for the scenery and the possibility of seeing hawks, eagles, lynx, ouzels, vultures, mergansers, grouse, deer, deer flies, and butterflies. The river passes springs, caves, beaches, and creeks and, most of all, it has a wonderful sense of isolation. The first half of this remote run has the easiest whitewater and the best scenery, where rock walls rise right out of the river. In the run's second half, the steep canyon walls are farther from the river and the difficulty of the rapids increases. At low levels, the run is very technical, especially the last two rapids. At higher flows, the first 9 miles provide fast-moving class 2+ rapids. The last two rapids are more open and have more lines, but also have bigger waves and are significantly pushier.

The run starts with a rocky or bouncy rapid, class 2+ to 3-, just below the put-in. If you have trouble here, return to your vehicle, because the rapids on the lower part are significantly more difficult. About halfway through the run, an eroding multihued ash-and-dirt bank on river right signals the start of the more challenging whitewater. Scout on the right because logs frequently complicate this class 3+ to 4- rapid, and all the other rapids as well, so be prepared to dodge, duck, or portage at any time.

About three-quarters of the way down the run, note where the river splits around an island and the powerlines are high overhead. This marks the start of about 0.75 mile of class 3–3+ rapids. These are the most difficult of the run; two steep rapids with a short break between them. They start quickly, so pay careful attention and eddy out before entering these rapids, and possibly scout. After these rapids, the river mellows to class 2 and 1+ for the final 1.5 miles to the take-out on the left at the Tygh Valley Road bridge.

Warning: Three miles below Tygh Valley, there is a 90-foot unrunnable waterfall. It can be viewed from White River State Park.

Hazards

Throughout this run, watch constantly for logjams and use extreme care when approaching them. Be sure to leave room to stop for logjams. Do not underestimate the speed of the current. Consider scouting the last two rapids.

Access

To reach the put-in, follow directions to the take-out for the White River: Keeps Mill to Wamic–White River Bridge run.

To reach take-out, return the way you arrived at the put-in (via Victor Road), to Oregon 216. Turn left (east) and go 10.7 miles to a T intersection. Turn left (north) on US 197 toward Tygh Valley. Go 5.3 miles and turn left on Tygh Valley Road. The take-out bridge is just ahead in 0.8 mile.

Gauge

None exists. For a close estimate of the flow see Pat Welch's flow page: White River below Tygh Valley. A warm day on Mount Hood will increase the flows. If the first rapid below the put-in is runnable, probably the entire run is runnable.

Harvey Lee Shapiro, Linda Starr, and WKCC Editors

Deschutes River

174 ★ Deschutes River Tenino Boat Launch to Pringle Falls Campground

Class: 1(4)	Length: 9.2 miles
Flow: 500–1600 cfs	Character: forested; ospreys
Gradient: 9 fpm, C	Season: dam-controlled

This is one of the author's favorite class 1 runs in Oregon. Many features combine to create a stimulating and often exhilarating experience: high mountain air, clear blue water, ponderosa pines, abundant camping sites, and great fishing are but a few. Perhaps the strongest asset of this region is the dense population of ospreys. The sound of an osprey calling and the sight of a vertical dive to pull a 12-inch trout from the water near your canoe are experiences not soon forgotten.

Pringle Falls (class 4) at the very end of this run is an optional rapid. Most paddlers choose to run only section 1 of this run.

"The Deschutes Paddle Trail River Guide" also offers helpful information (see Appendix B).

SECTION 1: TENINO BOAT LAUNCH TO WYETH CAMPGROUND, 8 MILES, CLASS 1

The usual launch spot is at the Tenino boat launch, which is the designated put-in for the Deschutes Paddle Trail. It is located 0.5 mile below Wickiup Dam on river right. From here, the river meanders through the pine forest; the paddling is easy as the current is usually slow. Some paddlers opt to take out at Bull Bend Campground, located 6.6 miles downstream from the put-in on river left. Many continue on for another 1.8 miles to the take-out at Wyeth Campground boat ramp on the left. (Note: For years, a chunk of concrete has been missing from the Wyeth Campground ramp. It poses no real hazard for those hand-carrying their craft to or from the water; however, use caution near the ramp.)

At Wyeth Campground, there are signs warning of upcoming Pringle Falls, class 4, which lies just below here. Only advanced paddlers should consider this drop, and only after scouting. Take out at Wyeth unless you are skilled at class 4 rapids. It is not possible to hand-carry boats around this falls since the land is private on both sides of the river. For class 1 paddlers who wish to continue downstream without running the falls, a short vehicular portage of this section of the Deschutes is necessary.

SECTION 2: WYETH CAMPGROUND TO PRINGLE FALLS CAMPGROUND, 1.2 MILES, CLASS 4

The Pringle Falls run starts just below Wyeth Campground with 200 yards of class 2- whitewater. After passing under the NF 43 bridge, the next 100 yards of class 3+ water lead into a class 4 drop with a potential keeper hole just above a footbridge. The remaining 200 yards are a bouncy class 3. The take-out at Pringle Falls Campground is on the right in 0.5 mile.

Hazards

Keep an eye out for logs that occasionally block the river. Do not accidentally go over Pringle Falls.

Access

Most people reach this river section from US 97 between La Pine and Bend. About 2 miles north of La Pine, or about 4.5 miles south of the entrance to the La Pine State Park, turn west onto NF 43 at a sign to Wickiup Reservoir. In 7.5 miles, NF 43 crosses the Deschutes River just above Pringle Falls. The first left after the bridge, NF 4370, leads to Wyeth Campground, the take-out, with a boat ramp. Continuing up this road another 1.3 mile leads to the side road to Bull Bend Campground, an alternative access point.

To reach the put-in at the Tenino boat launch, return to the bridge over the Deschutes near Pringle Falls. Cross the bridge, go 0.2 mile, and turn right onto NF 44 (East Deschutes Road). Travel up this road along the south side of the river for a total of 5 miles and turn right onto Old Wickiup Road. Go 1.4 miles and look for the short road on the right leading to the Tenino boat launch.

For a portage by vehicle around Pringle Falls from Wyeth Campground, return

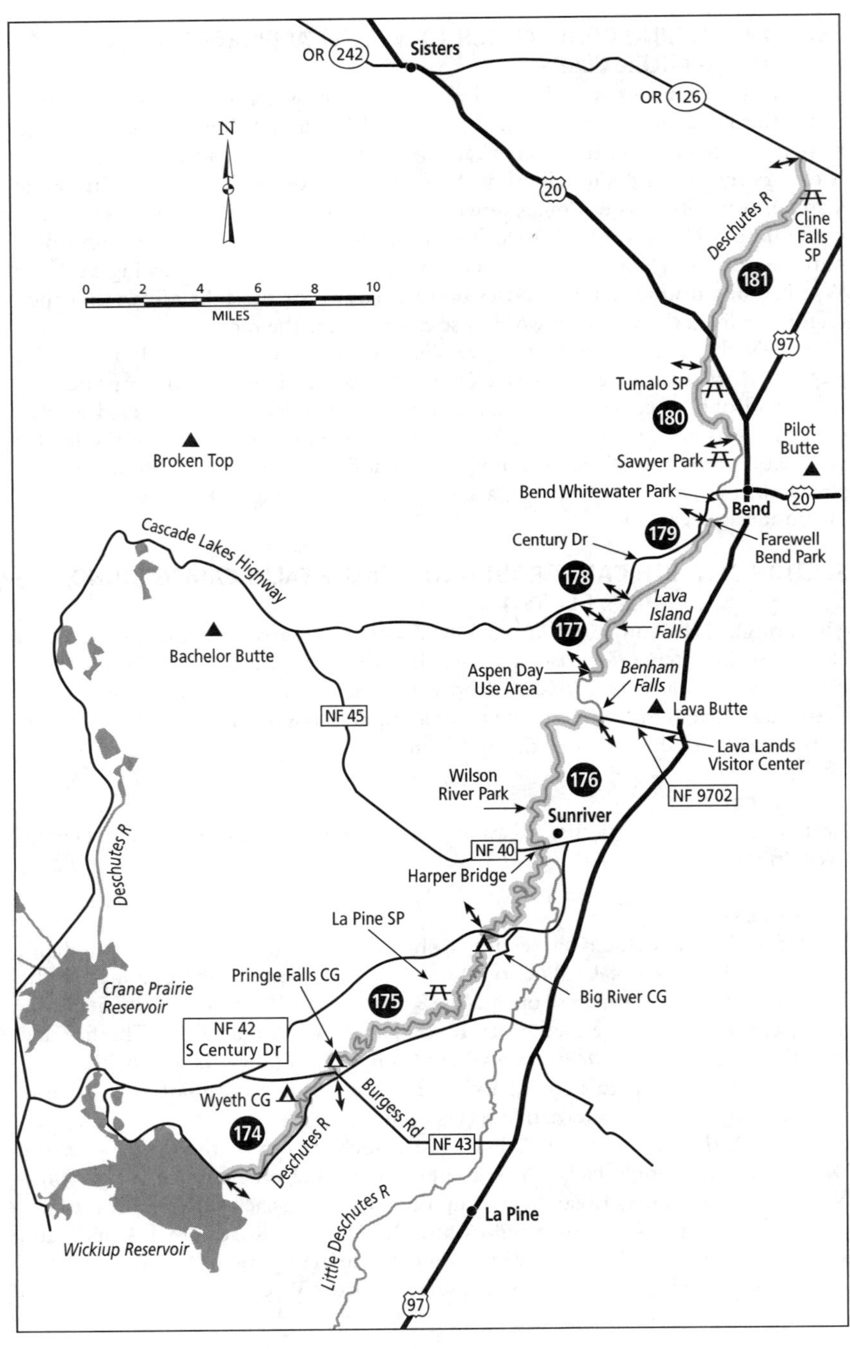

OR 242
Sisters
OR 126
20
Deschutes R
Cline Falls SP
97
N
0 2 4 6 8 10
MILES
Tumalo SP
180
Pilot Butte
Sawyer Park
Bend Whitewater Park
Bend
20
Broken Top
Century Dr
179
Farewell Bend Park
Cascade Lakes Highway
178
Lava Island Falls
177
Benham Falls
Bachelor Butte
Aspen Day Use Area
Lava Butte
NF 45
Lava Lands Visitor Center
Wilson River Park
176
NF 9702
Deschutes R
Sunriver
NF 40
Harper Bridge
La Pine SP
Crane Prairie Reservoir
Pringle Falls CG
Big River CG
175
NF 42
S Century Dr
Wyeth CG
Burgess Rd
174
NF 43
Deschutes R
Little Deschutes R
La Pine
Wickiup Reservoir
97

to the bridge over the Deschutes and cross the river. Continue east about 0.2 mile to the second road on the left and follow it to Pringle Falls Campground.

Gauge

Deschutes below Wickiup. Deschutes near La Pine. Flow is regulated at Wickiup Dam. From late spring until early fall, the flow is generally consistent at 1200–1600 cfs. At other times, the flow can be severely and abruptly reduced. For information on water release from Wickiup Dam, contact the Oregon Department of Water Resources watermaster for the Bend region (541-388-6669).

Carl Landsness and WKCC Editors

175 Deschutes River
Pringle Falls Campground to Big River Campground

Class: 1(2) P	Length: 17.3 miles
Flow: 500–1000 cfs	Character: forested; marsh grass; waterfowl haven
Gradient: 2.3 fpm, C	Season: dam-controlled

SECTION 1: PRINGLE FALLS CAMPGROUND TO LA PINE STATE PARK, 7.9 MILES, CLASS 1(2) P

The first 7 miles of this run are similar to the pine-forested run upstream. The Tethrow Logjam completely blocks the river 3.6 miles below Pringle Falls. Several signs warn of its presence. The mandatory portage is an easy 250-yard walk along the left bank. The take-out eddy for this walk is on the left, just above a right bend. (One could also do a right bank portage just after the bend; however, this puts one dangerously close to the logjam and is not recommended.)

It's another 4 miles to La Pine State Park, where one can take out at the campground, the picnic area, or at the boat launch at the bridge.

"The Deschutes Paddle Trail River Guide" also offers helpful information for both sections (see Appendix B).

SECTION 2: LA PINE STATE PARK TO BIG RIVER CAMPGROUND, 9.4 MILES, CLASS 1

Below the park, the river begins to slowly meander through wide-open areas of marsh grass. In 4 miles, Fall River enters on the left just above the Deschutes River Land Trust wildlife preserve. (Please stay in your boat for the next mile or so to avoid disturbing the wildlife in this area.) The serenity is occasionally interrupted by the sounds of fish and waterfowl. Views of the nearby hills and distant mountains further enhance this enchanting run. Take out at the downstream right end of the bridge.

Hazards

Tethrow Logjam is a mandatory portage. Watch for logs in other areas of the run.

Access

Put in at Pringle Falls Campground, below Pringle Falls on river right (see the Deschutes River: Tenino Boat Launch to Pringle Falls run).

To reach the Big River Campground take-out from the put-in at Pringle Falls, return to the bridge above the falls, drive west on NF 43 for 0.4 mile, and then go right on NF 4350 for 2 miles. Turn right onto NF 42 and follow it 8 miles to Big River Campground, which is on the left just after crossing the General Patch Bridge.

To reach Big River Campground from US 97, drive 2 miles south of Sunriver, turn right onto Vandevert Road, and go 1 mile. Turn left onto NF 42/South Century Drive. In a mile, go right and continue another 2.7 miles to the Big River Campground on the right just before crossing the General Patch Bridge.

To reach the La Pine State Park access, turn off US 97 6 miles north of La Pine and follow the signs to the park. The launch is on the right, just downstream of the bridge over the Deschutes.

Gauge

See the Deschutes River: Tenino Boat Launch to Pringle Falls run.

Carl Landsness and WKCC Editors

176 Deschutes River
Big River Campground to Benham Falls

Class: 1	Length: 17.2 miles
Flow: 1000–3000 cfs	Character: forested; residential; resort country
Gradient: 1 fpm, PD	Season: dam-controlled

The first 7 miles to Harper Bridge wander very slowly, with houses lining the banks for most of the length. The next 6-mile section passes Sunriver with a noticeably stronger current and a large contingent of leisurely drifters. Below Sunriver, the Deschutes makes a rather dramatic geological transition as it passes around and over the many lava flows of this region. After miles of mirror-like water, the river is suddenly and violently churned into a frenzy at Benham Falls, a spectacular series of class 5+ ledges, holes, and froth, cascading more than 100 feet in 0.5 mile. Do not miss the take-out above the falls. It is on river right at the Benham Falls boat ramp, just above a footbridge over an impassable logjam.

"The Deschutes Paddle Trail River Guide" also offers helpful information (see Appendix B).

Hazards

Do not get into the logjam just below the take-out ramp. Keep an eye out for wood all along the run.

Access

Put in at Big River Campground, on river right, by the NF 42 bridge (see the Deschutes River: Pringle Falls to Big River Campground run).

Reach the take-out at Benham Falls from US 97 just south of the Lava Lands Visitor Center. Take NF 9702 west for 4 miles to Benham Falls East Day Use Area. Alternative access points are at Harper Bridge (river right) and Besson boat ramp (river left), near the middle of the run. Refer to the Deschutes National Forest map for roads and campgrounds.

Gauge

Deschutes River at Benham Falls.

Carl Landsness and WKCC Editors

177 Deschutes River
Aspen Day Use Area to Lava Island Falls

Class: 2(3)	Length: 1.9 miles
Flow: 1000–3000 cfs	Character: forested; rafting freeway
Gradient: 23 fpm, PD	Season: dam-controlled

This is the famous Big Eddy run. The nearby resorts run an incredible number of visitors down this whitewater mini-run in the summer. One curler here has undoubtedly captured more rafts on film than any other in Oregon.

The first mile offers a few class 2 rapids before the river makes a sharp right turn through a quiet pool above Big Eddy. Big Eddy (class 3) consists of several curlers. These can be great play spots or potential keepers, depending on the flow. Scouting is advised (left bank). A hundred yards farther downstream is a class 2+ drop with a nice play wave at the top. To play here, catch the small eddy on river right. For the ambitious, it is an easy 300-yard carry back upstream to do Big Eddy again.

The take-out is on river left immediately above Lava Island Falls. It is clearly marked with warning signs. Lava Island Falls is 0.5 mile of class 4–6 rapids, where several drownings have occurred.

"The Deschutes Paddle Trail River Guide" also offers helpful information (see Appendix B).

Hazards

Scout Big Eddy Rapid. Take out above Lava Island Falls; do not run Lava Island Falls unless you are a class 5 boater.

Access

To reach the take-out from US 97 in Bend, drive west on Century Drive toward Mount Bachelor; turn south on NF 41. Turn left at the sign to Lava Island Falls. Refer to the Deschutes National Forest map for details.

To reach the put-in, return to NF 41, turn left, and travel just over a mile. Turn left, following the signs to Aspen Day Use Area.

Gauge

Deschutes River at Benham Falls.

Carl Landsness

178 Deschutes River Lava Island Falls to Meadow Camp Day Use Area

Class: 4+ to 5; 5- to 5+	Length: 1.4 miles
Flow: 350–1200 cfs; 1400–2200	Character: forested; lava canyon
Gradient: 63 fpm, C	Season: year-round

Known locally as Lava, this section of the Deschutes should only be run by experienced boaters (kayak or raft). Because of the difficulty of scouting throughout this section, first-timers are urged to go with someone who knows the run. Portage or scout from the right; however, do not use the irrigation canal walkway as locals have been working hard to keep a balance between the boating world and the privatized right bank.

The run features two difficult class 5 drops: Lava 1 and Lava 2. Both are long rapids, full of holes, ledge drops, waves, and large boulders. These are separated by the class 4 rapid called Cut 'Em Up (appropriately named for those who went for a swim in Lava 1).

"The Deschutes Paddle Trail River Guide" also offers helpful information (see Appendix B).

Hazards

The higher the water level, the more dangerous this run becomes. At high water, it is a serious class 5+. Logjams are often found along the run; inquire locally concerning the current status of log placement. The rocks are extremely sharp in this run. A swim could result in injury, loss of equipment, or worse.

Access

To reach the take-out from US 97 in Bend, drive west toward Mount Bachelor on Century Drive; turn left at the Meadow Camp Day Use Area sign. Park near the river.

To reach the put-in, return to Century Drive and turn left. Just past the Inn of the Seventh Mountain, turn left on Conklin Road (NF 41). Go 0.4 mile, turn left. Follow NF 4120 to the Lava Island Falls shelter sign. Turn left and go to the end of the road. Put in at Lava Island Falls.

Snowstorms may affect access during wintertime.

Gauge

Deschutes River at Benham Falls. In winter, the flows are usually around 500–1000 cfs. In summer, the peak release flows are usually between 1700 and 2200 cfs.

Morgan William Smith, Yann Crist-Evans, and WKCC Editors

179 ★ Deschutes River
Meadow Camp Day Use Area to Farewell Bend Park

Class: 4(4+)	Length: 4.1 miles
Flow: 800–2200 cfs	Character: forested; canyon
Gradient: 54 fpm, C	Season: dam-controlled; summer

Meadow Camp (or "MC") is an excellent summer town run with lots of action. Most of the riverbank is private property with no public access, so once on the river, stay on it. The run starts with a 1-mile flatwater warm-up. This is followed by Play Time (class 3+) with more than a quarter-mile of continuous eddy hopping and some great play spots. Play Time is not a friendly place to swim as Dammit (class 4+), an old dam site, lies directly below. In the calm water just above the diversion dam, get out and scout left (portage right). At the entry, about half the flow is diverted into a canal that parallels the right side of the river, a possible hazard. Dammit is entered center-right, driving through the right side of the rapid without hitting the large boulder near the bottom. Also, unique to this rapid is a pipe on river right near the middle of the rapid that pumps out a juicy flow directly into the river. It can catch one off guard if not prepared for it. The river slows and deepens briefly below Dammit as it flows through some technical class 3 before reaching the entrance to Amazing (class 4). A handicapped-accessible fishing dock on river right signals that Amazing is coming up.

Amazing is a long rapid that starts off with a tight boulder garden, where most of the water pushes to the right. Remain in the main channel, avoiding the sleepers in the middle, and be aware of two logs on river right above the main drop. The first is large but barely rises above the waterline, while the other log, 50 yards down, spans the right channel just below the waterline. In a raft, a log boof here sets you up clean for the steepest and final drop of Amazing.

Once past the boulder guarding the second log jamming the right channel, 90 percent of the flow pushes through the right side of the river. At this point, Amazing has an impressive gradient drop through a shallow garden of large, submerged boulders. A swim here will likely leave a paddler beat-up and bruised. The main drop consists of a succession of five holes. A sizable boulder between the fourth and the fifth hole is best run down the right side.

The river widens and grows more shallow immediately above the next drop, Marioland (4-). The entrance to this rapid is marked by a middle island with logs jammed above it that divide the flow of the river. The recommended line is down the right channel, around the house-size boulder, and then a tight move to either side around a protruding boulder (it's best to run right in a raft).

Below a pedestrian bridge, the river becomes tame, leading up to 100 Percent (4+), the final rapid in the set. Stay on river right leading up to the entrance drop of 100 Percent. Enter right of center. The steepest section features holes, waves, and a beautiful lateral hole at the bottom that pushes to the right. So square up and charge it! About 50 yards down river at the final bend and the exit of 100 Percent, there is a very large hole on river right. If you must punch it, try to hit the left corner, as it lines you up nicely for the turn. The rapid tapers off around a few more turns, and the Deschutes becomes meandering flatwater through the town of Bend.

The first take-out is on river right just past the only boulder sticking out of the water and well before the bridge. There is a faint trail leading up to a small parking lot in the trees. You may choose to continue down river and take out at any number of places below on either side of the river. The large, grassy area below the bridge on the right is the main part of Farewell Bend Park.

Another option is to paddle downstream 1.5 miles to the Bend Whitewater Park for some park and play.

"The Deschutes Paddle Trail River Guide" also offers helpful information (see Appendix B).

Hazards

Logs are the biggest problem on this run. A couple of continuous class 4+ drops need scouting. A swim in this stretch could result in injury and loss of equipment.

Access

To reach the take-out, take Reed Market Road west from US 97. Farewell Bend Park is in 1 mile. Park alongside the grassy area in the larger part of the park. For the uppermost take-out spot, take Alderwood Circle to Ashwood Drive to Cedarwood Road. A small neighborhood park with limited parking is there.

To reach the put-in, follow Reed Market Road west from the park for 0.5 mile. Turn left at Century Drive. Go 3.2 miles and turn left at the sign to the Meadow Camp Day Use Area. Park near the river.

Gauge

Deschutes River at Benham Falls. Flows are usually good April–October, depending on the release schedule.

Morgan William Smith and Yann Crist-Evans

180 ★ Deschutes River
Sawyer Park to Tumalo State Park

Class: 4; 4(4+)	Length: 4.6 miles
Flow: 600–900; 1000–1700 cfs	Character: canyon; residential
Gradient: 66 fpm, C	Season: rainy/winter release

Beginning at Sawyer Park on the north end of Bend, the "Riverhouse run" is a classic Oregon creeking run when you can catch it. Unfortunately, the Deschutes in this section is managed as an irrigation ditch with all but a trickle of water removed through a canal system. The exception is during winter when a "guaranteed release" occurs and the river flows usually increase to runnable levels. Paddlers may feel conspicuous in Bend with kayaks on their rig while others drive about with snowboards, yet occasional warm days during the winter can provide better boating than skiing. The continuous nature of this run at higher flows can connect rapids and keep you paddling the whole time.

The put-in is under the pedestrian bridge at Sawyer Park, where the run begins immediately with a fun class 2 rapid. The first of two long class 3 rapids starts directly upstream of the Archie Briggs Road bridge. Just around the bend from the rapids is the second long class 3 rapid, which begins just above the low footbridge. Once under the bridge, keep right to punch a sizable hole and avoid a nasty curler on river left that spills into a boulder just below.

The third drop, at river mile 1, comes up just around the corner. The Wright Stuff (class 4) is a tricky ledge drop at lower flows and fills in when higher to open up more lines. At low to moderate flows, the line is on the left, running just right of the large boulder at the bottom. About 50 yards downstream, an island splits the river just above the Flumes of Doom (class 4+). Both channels are runnable, but the classic line is down the left side of the island. As the channels are narrow, complex and long, a scout should be considered. There are some definite pinning spots to be avoided.

The river stays very active with class 3 and 4 drops for the next 3 miles with a gradient of 80 fpm. At about river mile 2.0 of the run, following a class 3 rapid with a narrow slot entrance, the river bends right and enters a rapid known as T-Rex (class 4). The lower end of this long rapid is guarded by a boulder fence best run on the far right. At high flows, this becomes an ugly river-wide hole.

The next 0.8 mile is a succession of twisting drops leading blindly into The Ogre (class 4). To scout, pull out on the right near the big log on shore. A house-size boulder at the bottom, just as you plunge over the main drop, makes things interesting. Swimmers should be aware of some ledges below.

The remainder of the run maintains a continuous nature all the way to the take-out on river left, just below the vehicle bridge across from Tumalo State Park. There is an alternative take-out on the green lawn of Tumalo State Park day-use area (fee area) on river right above the vehicle bridge.

"The Deschutes Paddle Trail River Guide" also offers helpful information (see Appendix B).

Hazards

The named rapids should all be scouted. The narrow technical nature of the run always makes logs a threat. During rare high flows of 1500 cfs and higher, it is one continuous rapid from Archie Briggs Bridge to below The Ogre. Be prepared for cold conditions.

Access

The put-in is at Sawyer Park, just north of the Riverhouse Motel in Bend. The 5-mile shuttle to the take-out at Tumalo State Park is along O. B. Riley Road, which enters Business US 97 on the north side of the Riverhouse Motel. A bicycle shuttle is quite easy.

Gauge

Deschutes River below Bend. Optimum flow is 800–1200 cfs.

Carl Landsness, Jon Ferguson, and Yann Crist-Evans

181 Deschutes River
Tumalo State Park to Cline Falls State Park

Class: 3 (P)	Length: 13.2 miles
Flow: 600–2000 cfs	Character: rural; canyon
Gradient: 26 fpm, PD	Season: rainy or annual winter release

This run offers the intermediate paddler one long trip that includes a very scenic canyon or several short sections. Since most of the river is diverted for irrigation in the summer, this run is usually only available from mid-October through mid-April. Because of the length of the run and the short days of winter, an early start is recommended to avoid taking out in the dark. The sun rarely penetrates the lower canyon in midwinter, so be prepared for cold temperatures. Still, on nice fall, winter, and spring days, this can be a wonderful run. If the weather is not favorable for paddling the entire trip, the easier upper sections can provide a fix for die-hard winter boaters.

From the put-in to just beyond the community of Tumalo, the river is class 1 with one class 2 rapid at the lower end of Tumalo State Park, with some nice, small surf waves to play on. Below this section, the river slows as it goes under the US 20 bridge and through the community of Tumalo. Beware of wire fences in some of the side channels. Access at this point (2 miles below Tumalo State Park) is on river left, on the downstream side of the Tumalo Road Bridge.

Below the bridge, the river meanders for about a mile before coming to a class 2+ rapid as the river enters a small canyon. The character of this canyon is only a preview of the much deeper canyon yet to come. Below this rapid, the river again mellows as it passes though typical Central Oregon ranch land. Three miles below the bridge (5 miles below Tumalo State Park) is Twin Bridges. Take the main channel on the right as the left channel takes you into a wire fence and culvert. This is the last public access before entering the lower canyon, so if you had any difficulties with the upper canyon, consider taking out at Twin Bridges. The best access is on river right, just upstream of the bridge.

About 0.5 mile below Twin Bridges, you will pass under a bridge at the resort of Deschutes River Ranch, followed by a short rapid, Pot Holes, class 2+. Pot

Holes is a low ledge dropping into some swirly water below. Over the next mile, the river gradually picks up speed, as it approaches Awbrey Falls (2 miles below Twin Bridges). The portage is on the right, and boaters should move toward the right when the river opens up with a horizon line ahead, as it becomes increasingly more difficult to get out of the channelized main current the closer you get to the falls. (Do not get too close on your first trip.) The portage involves boating (or walking, depending upon the level) through a maze of small channels, constantly moving toward the right shore, before carrying the boats a short distance around the falls. This is approximately the halfway point and makes a great lunch spot. The river enters a beautiful canyon for the remainder of the trip.

Immediately below Awbrey Falls is the White Mile, a long class 3–3+ rapid that tends to become more difficult (technical) with lower flows. This rapid is typical of, though longer than, most of the rapids yet to come. Below here, the river alternates between long mellow sections, along which you can gaze up at the canyon walls with houses perched on top, and class 2+ to 3 rapids.

The condominiums at Eagle Crest resort, on the top of the river-left cliffs, and the lowering of the canyon walls signal that you are approaching the take-out at Cline Falls State Park on river right. Over the last several years, the Oregon Parks and Recreation Department has been attempting to keep the road into Cline Falls State Park open year-round. If it is closed, you will need to make a long carry up the access road to Oregon 126.

"The Deschutes Paddle Trail River Guide" also offers helpful information (see Appendix B).

Hazards

Awbrey Falls is a mandatory portage on the right. Beware of wire and wood fences, willows and other streamside brush. A long trip, in often cold weather, makes having proper equipment and clothing mandatory. Emergency exit below Awbrey Falls is difficult.

Access

The put-in at Tumalo State Park is the take-out for the Deschutes River: Sawyer Park to Tumalo State Park run. To get there, drive west from Bend on US 20 toward Tumalo. Shortly after crossing the river, turn left on O. B. Riley Road and follow it to the park. A fee is charged to park here.

For the lower access points and the Cline Falls take-out, turn left out of the park and drive downstream on O. B. Riley Road. Cross US 20 and continue north through Tumalo on Cook Avenue. The Tumalo Road bridge access will be at the junction of Cook Avenue, Tumalo Road, and Cline Falls Highway. For the Cline Falls take-out, continue north on the Cline Falls Highway about 10 miles to Oregon 126. Turn east (toward Redmond), cross the river, and turn right into Cline Falls State Park. Should you wish to access the river at Twin Bridges, continue north on the Cline Falls Highway from the Tumalo Road Bridge for 2.8 miles to the White Rock Loop. Turn right and go 0.5 mile to Twin Bridges Road. Turn right again and follow this road 0.6 mile to the bridge over the river.

Gauge

Deschutes River below Bend. A nice flow is between 600 and 2000 cfs. Tumalo Creek, which enters the Deschutes just upstream of the put-in, adds an additional 50–150 cfs to the gauge reading.

Steve and Holly Engquist, and WKCC Editors

182 Deschutes River
Cline Falls State Park to Lower Bridge

Class: 3 (P)	Length: 11.9 miles
Flow: 400–1500 cfs	Character: rural; canyon
Gradient: 26 fpm, PD	Season: rainy

This Central Oregon run offers the intermediate paddler a nice trip through two very scenic canyons with the option of a midway access point. Since most of the river is diverted for irrigation in the summer, this run is usually only available from mid-October through mid-April. Unlike the preceding section upstream, these canyons seem to get more sun exposure, making cool temperatures a bit more tolerable.

Starting at Cline Falls State Park, the river flows through a shallow area as it approaches Cline Falls, about 0.5 mile below the park. The Cline Falls Dam, previously operated by Pacific Power, was once located just upstream of the falls. The no longer operational wood and concrete dam was demolished in 2017 to allow safe passage for fish. Eddy out on river left just past the highway bridge and above the braided channels of the river. Portage Cline Falls is on the left. Alternatively, boaters can put in at the base of the falls just downstream of the power station.

Immediately below the falls is a straightforward class 3 rapid as the river enters the first canyon. Another short drop, class 2+, soon follows. Below this rapid, the river mellows to a playful class 1+ for about 3 miles. The scenery is beautiful, with only occasional houses on the rimrock high above.

As the canyon opens up, the river slows, allowing for a maze of brush "islands" that need to be negotiated with care. More homes become visible, and soon the river passes under the low bridge at Tetherow Crossing (3.75 miles below Cline Falls State Park). Tetherow Crossing has been used for centuries, first by local Indians and then later by early Oregon settlers headed for the Willamette Valley, as a place to cross the Deschutes River. An old stage stop and ferry building remain, on river right, just a short walk up the road.

Below Tetherow Crossing, the brush islands continue for another mile until Odin Falls. This class 4+ falls can be identified, not only by the sound, but by a large home, river left, situated on the very edge of the canyon rim. If you choose to run this drop, beware of the remnants of a broken irrigation dam at the top of the falls. An easy portage can be made on river right. After the falls, the river enters its second canyon.

A few hundred feet downstream of Odin Falls is a simple class 2+ plunge before the river slows considerably to a leisurely pace, allowing lots of time to gaze at the spectacular canyon walls. This slow area lasts for about 0.5 mile before the pace picks up with several pool-drop class 2–3 rapids over the next 3 miles.

The final 3 miles are once again punctuated by numerous brush islands as the river winds past interesting rock outcroppings. The westerly trend of the river in this area allows for frequent views of Mount Jefferson. The take-out is on river left, at Lower Bridge (the put-in for the Deschutes River: Lower Bridge to Lake Billy Chinook run).

"The Deschutes Paddle Trail River Guide" also offers helpful information (see Appendix B).

Hazards

Cline Falls is a mandatory portage on the left. Scout and possibly portage Odin Falls on the right. Beware of in-stream and side-stream vegetation.

Access

Put in either at Cline Falls State Park or 0.5 mile downstream on river left. Cline Falls State Park is located about 4.5 miles west of Redmond, along Oregon 126, on the south side of the road. To get to the alternative put-in below Cline Falls, go west a short distance from the park, cross the river, and turn right (north) on Seventy-Fourth Street. Travel about 0.5 mile downstream to a gated access road leading down to the power station. Park along the main road and hike down to the river.

To reach the take-out, travel west from Cline Falls State Park on Oregon 126 for 4 miles. Turn right (north) on Buckhorn Road and continue for 4.3 miles to Lower Bridge Road. Turn right (east) and drive 1.5 miles to Lower Bridge. Good parking is on river left.

To reach the alternative access point at Tetherow Crossing, follow the directions above to the alternative put-in below Cline Falls. Continue north on Seventy-Fourth Street, which will eventually become Tetherow Road as it winds down into the canyon before crossing the river.

Gauge

Deschutes River below Bend gauge. Tumalo Creek (about 16 miles upstream) adds 50–150 cfs to the gauge reading. The level can also be obtained from the watermaster's office in Bend (541-388-6669).

Steve and Holly Engquist

183 Deschutes River
Lower Bridge to Lake Billy Chinook

Class: 4–4+ P	Length: 15.7 miles
Flow: 900–2000 cfs	Character: inaccessible desert gorge
Gradient: 36 fpm, PD	Season: dam-controlled, rainy or winter release

This extraordinary run has been overlooked because of its short season, inaccessible gorge, and long paddle out. Magnificent canyon scenery, bountiful wildlife, and challenging whitewater await those who attempt this usually cold-weather run. The river is class 3 for the first 4 miles as it winds through brushy shallows and braided channels. At mile 1.5, an obvious horizon line marks Big Falls, an 18-foot drop that can be portaged from either side.

Four miles below Lower Bridge is Steelhead Falls, a river-wide vertical 15-foot runnable waterfall. (If using the alternative put-in at the Steelhead Falls parking lot, the falls are about 0.7 mile below the put-in.) Portage on either side using the trail on river right, or on the left near the left side lip. Run the left side to avoid a nasty horseshoe-shaped pocket in the middle. The falls are marked by a class 3 entrance rapid, a steepening of the canyon, and a stone wall at the brink of the falls on river right. For 2 miles below Steelhead Falls, the river meanders through class 1–2 rapids as the canyon walls steepen. Gradually the gradient increases, and some long class 4 boulder gardens present the first real challenges. The first major rapid below Steelhead Falls is called Leslie's Bailout (class 4). The move is a simple but mandatory big left-to-right ferry. After Whychus Creek enters from a huge canyon on the left, the flow increases, and class 4 rapids line up in quick succession. Great whitewater and breathtaking scenery combine for the last few miles above Lake Billy Chinook. The final 2 miles to the take-out bridge at the reservoir are flatwater.

Hazards

If you choose to put in at the Lower Bridge, Big Falls, at mile 1.5, must be portaged. Putting in at Lower Bridge is generally not recommended due to the strenuous first portage of Big Falls. This portage can be avoided by putting in just above Steelhead Falls downstream. Doing so avoids the extra aerobics and shortens the already long run by a few miles without missing much up top. Steelhead Falls can be scouted (or portaged) from the right or left banks. Thick brush along the river can make scouting and rescue difficult in several places. Other difficulties include the shallows and brush in the first few miles below Lower Bridge.

Access

To find the put-in, drive to Terrebonne, on US 97 15 miles north of Redmond or 17.3 miles south of Madras. Just north of Terrebonne, turn west on Lower Bridge Road (marked by a Crooked River Ranch sign) and proceed 6 miles to the river. Put in at Lower Bridge. To reach the alternative put-in at the Steelhead Falls parking lot, from US 97, take Lower Bridge Road west for 2.1 miles toward Crooked River Ranch. Take a right on Northwest Forty-third Street and go 1.8 miles. At the T junction, go left onto Chinook Drive and proceed 1.1 mile. Turn left on Badger, go 1.8 mile to its end. Turn right on Quail and go 1.2 miles. Turn left onto River Road and go 1 mile to the Steelhead Falls trailhead. The camp area is just south of the trailhead. Park there and carry about 300 yards to the river.

The take-out is reached by turning west from US 97 toward the Cove Palisades State Park, 24 miles north of Redmond or 7.2 miles south of Madras; follow signs to the park. Once at the park, continue south and west to the Upper Deschutes

Day Use Area and cross the bridge. A pullout and an informal trail lead to the reservoir at the west end of the bridge.

Gauge

Deschutes River at Culver. Optimal flow is about 1500 cfs or a bit higher. Annual winter release is usually from October to April.

Jeff Bennett, Yann Crist-Evans, and WKCC Editors

184 ★ Deschutes River
US 26 Bridge to Sherars Falls

Class: 3	Length: 52.6 miles
Flow: 3000–8000 cfs	Character: popular desert canyon
Gradient: 12 fpm, PD	Season: year-round

The lower Deschutes runs through a large desert canyon with an active railroad along the river. Rattlesnakes, chukars, and deer live here. The bottom of the canyon can become oppressively hot in the summer. Stiff up-canyon winds are normal in the afternoon. This stretch is a designated Scenic Waterway. The river has numerous class 2 play spots, good sharp eddies, and several big-volume class 3 rapids. The water is clear, fishing is usually good, and campsites are plentiful—but watch out for poison ivy. The Confederated Tribes of Warm Springs own the land along the left in the upper part of the run. The section from Harpham Flat (just above Maupin) to Sandy Beach (just above Sherars Falls) is a popular day trip of 10.4 miles. The fast tempo on this particular section explains why it one of the most popular summer rafting runs in Oregon.

The put-in is just below the US 26 bridge at Warm Springs boat launch (river mile or RM 98). At river mile 94 pass through a gorge of dark basalt. At RM 89 is a large island and the whitewater begins. The Trout Creek campground and boat launch are on river right at RM 88.4. Trout Creek Rapid, class 2, begins just below the launch as the river bends left. The next 8 miles are open valley with dirt access roads on both sides. South Junction is on the right at RM 84. Riverside camping is allowed at South Junction, but no boat launching. The Warm Springs River enters on left.

The entrance to Whitehorse Rapid (RM 77), class 3+, is identified by a sharp pinnacle on the right and a steep bank leading up to the railroad on the right. A stretch of slack water ends in a short plunge. Land below here on the right to scout Whitehorse. The rapid begins on a sweeping right bend. A mile later, take the left channel because the right channel runs onto rocks. The water is enjoyable through here. From North Junction, where the railroad crosses to the left bank (RM 73), little whitewater appears for the next 10 miles. The river passes through the very scenic Mutton Mountains, with wind-eroded windows through the cliffs of colored stone. At RM 69, the Warm Springs Indian Reservation boundary is passed; campsites now become available on river left.

At RM 64, Buckskin Mary Falls is run straight down the middle for a fine roller-coaster ride. The next 3 miles offer good whitewater. The Harpham Flat launch site is passed at RM 55.8. Upper Wapinitia Rapid (RM 55) can be spotted after a left bend where a steel railroad bridge on the left crosses Wapinitia Creek. The rapid begins there on a right turn. Run right. A mile later, the class 3 Boxcar, also called Lower Wapinitia Rapid, begins with an abrupt left turn, then curves right with a very fast current over a ledge across the entire river, with a big hole on the left and a 4-foot drop on the right. Scout the first time through from either bank.

At Maupin, a possible take-out (for a fee) is available at the bridge at the city park on the right (RM 52). Fine whitewater follows from here to Sherars Falls. The big waves of Surf City (RM 48) provide popular surfing for many boaters. Oak Springs Rapid (RM 47.5), class 3+, can cause problems. Look for green growth on the left side of the canyon and the mossy tanks of the Oak Springs fish hatchery. Scout on the right. Whitewater begins 200 yards above the hatchery. The lower rapid is made difficult by the two ribs of basalt that divide the river into three channels. At high water, the left channel can be run easily; at low water, the middle channel is often run. The big hole next to the rock, on the right, flips many boaters. The run-out is shallow and rocky.

In 0.5 mile, the White River enters on the left with nice waves, followed in 0.3 mile by Upper Elevator. The Elevator (RM 46) provides a great wave train with good surfing. A long, narrow eddy elevates boaters back up to the top. In 0.5 mile, Sandy Beach (RM 45.4) on the right marks the take-out. The 1.5 mile of river below Sandy Beach to just above Sherars Falls is no longer accessible to boaters, because the BLM has closed the take-out immediately above Sherars Falls.

"The Deschutes River Boater's Guide" also offers helpful information (see Appendix B).

Hazards

Watch for overheating in hot weather, and beware of poison ivy. Several rapids present difficulties. Whitehorse Rapid, class 3, drops 25 feet in 300 yards. Upper Wapinitia Rapid has probably the fastest chute on this run. Boxcar Rapid (where a boxcar fell into the river in the late 1940s), class 3, requires going over a 2- to 4-foot ledge and maneuvering around some large boulders. Oak Springs Rapid is a class 3 that becomes more difficult (up to class 4) as the water drops and rocks become exposed. It is considered the most difficult drop on this run.

Access

From US 97 in Madras, take US 26 northwest 11 miles. The uppermost put-in at Warm Springs boat launch is located at the upstream east end of the bridge where US 26 crosses the Deschutes. Trout Creek is an optional launch point—go north from Madras 2.5 miles on US 97, then left and 8 miles to Gateway. Cross the railroad tracks and continue 4 miles. Many put-ins and take-outs can be found upstream of Maupin and can be reached by following the road out of Maupin on the east side of the river. A common day's run is from Harpham Flats to Sandy Beach.

The take-out farthest downstream is at Sandy Beach, downstream of Maupin and about a mile above Sherars Falls. To reach the take-out from Tygh Valley, take Oregon 216 north and then east out of Tygh Valley for 8 miles. Cross the bridge, turn right at the first road, and proceed upstream 1.8 miles to the take-out. If coming from US 97 in Grass Valley, take Oregon 216 west to Sherars Falls. An alternative shuttle route is a paved road that follows the east bank from Maupin to Sherars Falls.

Note: A boater's pass is required to float on the Deschutes River anywhere between the US 26 bridge and the Columbia River. Contact the BLM office in Prineville (541-416-6700) for more information or purchase a pass online at www. boaterpass.com. Maps and other helpful information about this run can also be found at this website.

Gauge

Deschutes River near Madras (upstream gauge). Deschutes River at Moody (downstream gauge).

Rob Blickensderfer and WKCC Editors

185 ★ Deschutes River
Sherars Falls to Columbia River

Class: 3	Length: 42.8 miles
Flow: 3000–8000 cfs	Character: popular desert canyon
Gradient: 12 fpm, PD	Season: year-round

This run has more horseshoe bends and fewer rapids than the Deschutes River: US 26 Bridge to Sherars Falls run, but the current is brisk. Allow from three to four days to run this portion of the Deschutes River. From early times, the Native Americans had a bridge across the narrow gorge below the falls. Today, they have treaty rights to fish for salmon at the base of Sherars Falls. During the spring and fall, they stand on scaffolding to dip salmon from the maelstrom below.

The put-in is 1 mile below Sherars Falls on river right at the Buck Hollow launch site at RM 42.8. (RM is river-mile.) (The river-right road continues for about 23 river miles to Macks Canyon, an alternative access point and campground.)

Wreck Rapid (RM 39.5) is the first major rapid. In this class 3+ drop, the extreme right is clean; the center is runnable but has some concealed rocks. No major rapids appear for the next 30 miles, but the river moves at 5 miles per hour, and many small rapids are present.

Beavertail Campground (an alternative launch site) is passed at RM 31.4. Cedar Island is just below, and a dramatic basalt cliff is seen near the end of a large horseshoe bend. Sinamox Island and the abandoned buildings of Hill's Ranch on both sides of the river are followed in a mile by Ferry Canyon (RM 25.6) on river left. A railroad bridge crosses this side canyon. Macks Canyon Campground on river right (RM 23.9) is an alternative access point and the end of the road.

At RM 20, note two islands after a right bend in the river. Harris Canyon (RM 12) and an old water tank are seen on the right near tall, overhanging reddish basalt cliffs. At RM 7.5, stop on the left near the powerlines overhead to scout Washout Rapid (class 3), usually run on the left to avoid a large hole. This rapid was formed in 1995 from a blowout coming down Stecker Canyon (Mud Springs Canyon) on the left. Freebridge, with old piers remaining, and Kloan, a railroad shed, are seen on the left at RM 7.2.

At RM 5.7, Gordon Ridge Rapid, class 3, occurs after the river makes an abrupt right turn and drops over a 3-foot shelf, followed by heavy whitewater for 0.5 mile. Colorado Rapid (RM 3.9), class 3, is a long series of large standing and breaking waves. Small rafts sometimes capsize here. In another mile, the Green Narrows (or Knock Knock) Rapid is a maze of rock ridges covered with grass that divides the river into numerous channels; the right side is deepest. This leads directly to Rattlesnake Rapid (RM 2.6), class 3, which can be scouted from either bank. This is the most powerful rapid on this run. Most of the river flows over a very narrow upper ledge. The fierce hole below must be avoided. It is normally run on the left. In 2 more miles, Moody Rapid, class 2, consists of standing waves, where the fast Deschutes encounters the pool caused by The Dalles Dam. Take out in 0.5 mile on the left at Heritage Landing boat ramp.

"The Deschutes River Boater's Guide" also offers helpful information (see Appendix B).

Hazards

Five class 3 rapids are hazards: Wreck Rapid, near the beginning of the run; and four other major rapids—Washout, Gordon Ridge, Colorado, and Rattlesnake—that come within the last 8 miles.

Access

To get to the put-in, see the directions to the Sherars Falls bridge as described in the run Deschutes River: US 26 Bridge to Sherars Falls. From the bridge over the falls, travel east for 0.5 mile, turn left (north), and go 0.5 mile to the Buck Hollow launch site (RM 42.8). This dirt road parallels the river on the right for approximately 18 miles with alternative launch sites at Pine Tree (in 3 miles), Beavertail (in 10 miles), and Macks Canyon (in about 17 miles), where the road ends.

To reach the take-out, take exit 97 from Interstate 84 (between The Dalles and Biggs) and follow the frontage road east 2.5 miles to the Heritage Landing boat ramp, at the Deschutes River State Recreation Area.

Note: A boater's pass (permit) is required. (See the Note in the previous run: Deschutes River: US 26 Bridge to Sherars Falls.)

Gauge

Deschutes River at Moody.

Rob Blickensderfer and WKCC Editors

Klamath River and Tributaries

186 ★ Wood River
Jackson F. Kimball State Park
to Loosely Road

Class: 1 B, (P)	Length: 10.8 miles
Flow: 180–220 cfs	Character: mixed woodland; pastoral
Gradient: 4 fpm	Season: year-round

This class 1 paddle, which originates at the headwaters of the Wood River, is one of the favorites of both local paddlers and savvy visitors to the Klamath Basin. Crystal-clear, spring-fed water, spectacular scenery with views of the Cascade peaks to the west and the "back door" of Crater Lake National Park, as well as outstanding fishing and birding opportunities are just a few of the reasons people love this river. Wildflowers dot the river banks in springtime and summer, replaced by fiery aspen in the fall.

The river is spring-fed and maintains a relatively constant flow year-round. Agricultural diversion below Dixon Road may reduce flow in the summer, but the river is generally still boatable. However, late-spring runoff can create problems with clearance on the bridge crossings on county roads. Check bridge clearance at Fort Klamath and Loosely Road during springtime shuttles.

Although the river has no whitewater, it does require some basic maneuvering skills, as the channel is extremely sinuous and ox-bowed, with tight turns and occasional woody debris.

SECTION 1: JACKSON F. KIMBALL STATE PARK TO WOOD RIVER ACCESS AREA, 4.9 MILES, CLASS 1 (P)

At the put-in, the crystal-clear, spring-fed water burbles to the surface and flows into a pond before entering the main channel itself. Your first glimpse of the water here will undoubtedly be an "oh, wow" moment. The white sandy bottom reflects the sky through the pristine water.

Once under way, watch for woody debris that can sometimes accumulate here. Soon the watercourse opens up, and the real rewards of paddling this section of river become obvious as you travel through a pastoral landscape at eye level with the surrounding meadows, kept green year-round by artesian springs.

As you paddle downriver, pay careful attention to where the deep-water channel actually is. The river is very oxbowed, and the surrounding geology of this area means that the fastest, deepest channel will not always be on the outside bend of the curve. After Annie Creek enters at river mile 2.6, the Wood becomes narrower, and lots of tight 180-degree turns require quick maneuvering.

At mile 4.6, a picnic table visible on the river left bank with a fence coming down to the river signals the beginning of Forest Service property. You can take out here or continue on for 0.3 mile around a long oxbow to the actual parking area for the Wood River access. Use caution near the take-out. A fallen tree may be blocking the left side of the river near there.

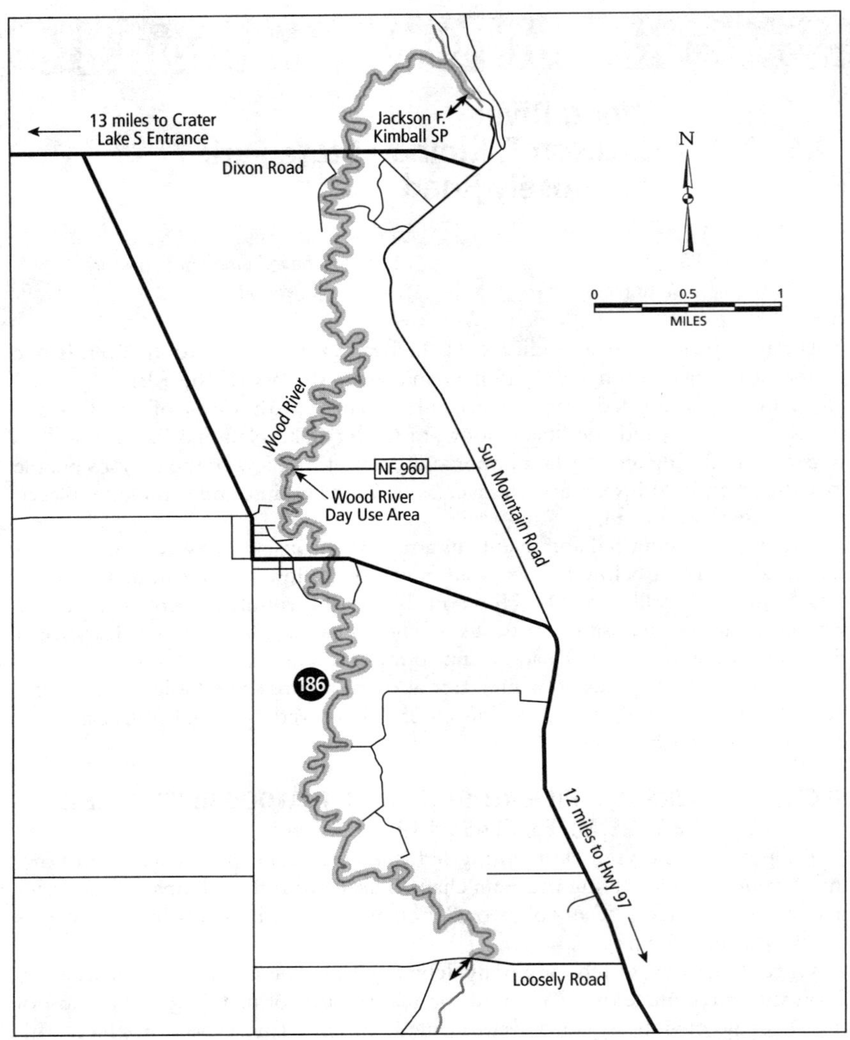

SECTION 2: WOOD RIVER ACCESS TO LOOSELY ROAD, 5.9 MILES, CLASS 1

Although most people opt to take out at the Wood River access, those who desire a longer run can continue downriver to Loosely Road. The gradient here slows a bit, and the countryside becomes more pastoral and less treed. A few snags are encountered in the last mile, but the current is slow, and the snags can easily be avoided. Take-out is easiest on river right on either the upstream or downstream side of the bridge on the county road right-of-way, between the fenced private land and the road.

Clear water and classic mountain views on Wood River (Marianne Musitelli)

Hazards

Watch for naturally occurring snags and woody debris intentionally placed for fish habitat. Most have passage around them, and the current is generally slow moving, so these obstacles usually can be easily avoided. There is a low private bridge at river mile 2.0, which canoeists will have to duck under. A weir at river mile 2.6 may require portaging. Scout before running.

Access

From Klamath Falls, drive north on US 97. Cross over the Williamson River, and look for the turnoff for Oregon 62 and Crater Lake. Turn left and drive 12.1 miles. Shortly after you pass the Fort Klamath Historical Monument, the road makes a sharp left bend and heads northwest. Look for Sun Mountain Road entering there on the right. Turn right on Sun Mountain Road and follow the signs to Jackson F. Kimball State Park, 2.9 miles. At the park entrance, turn left and drive to the end of the road. Park in one of the designated day-use spots and walk east through the picnic area to the pond. You can launch from the sandy bank anywhere.

To reach the take-out for section 1, from Jackson F. Kimball Park, backtrack down Sun Mountain Road. Drive approximately 2 miles and turn right at the entrance to the Wood River Day Use Area, NF spur road 960. Drive to the end of the road and park in the paved parking area.

To reach the take-out for section 2, from Jackson F. Kimball Park, backtrack down Sun Mountain Road to Oregon 62. Turn left and drive 1.9 miles. Turn right on Loosely Road and drive 0.5 mile to where the road crosses the river. Parking is limited here.

Gauge

Oregon Water Resources Department gauge: Wood River at Dixon Road (see Appendix A).

Marianne Musitelli

187 Sprague River
Williamson River Road Bridge to Chiloquin County Park

Class: 2	Length: 10.5 miles
Flow: 850–2000 cfs	Character: rural; high desert
Gradient: 9 fpm	Season: snowmelt

With removal of the Chiloquin Dam in 2008, this "new" section of river became available to boaters for the first time. This section of the Sprague passes through a striking volcanic canyon in a high-desert landscape. History, scenery, and wildlife-watching opportunities provide interesting diversions in the slower sections, and a handful of class 2 rapids provide some excitement.

For the first 2 miles, the river is very slow moving, and in the spring, the water is chocolate brown, carrying a large sediment load from the Sycan Marsh at its headwaters. Beavers and muskrats are often seen here.

At approximately river mile 2.3, the Chiloquin Narrows begins. At flows above 1400 cfs, this is a fairly continuous 1-mile-long rapid. Enter the main drop right of center on a fairly pronounced tongue and then move left. A half-mile-long boulder garden follows. There are multiple routes through, but watch for submerged rocks, which can be hard to see in the dark brown water.

At river mile 4, a bridge crosses the river at Chiloquin Ridge Road across from a Pacific Power substation. Tribal trust lands, managed by the US Forest Service, begin at approximately mile 6.4 and continue for about 2 miles. In this stretch, the river flows south around a large bend and then back north. Although passage floating on the river is allowed, the surrounding banks should be considered private property. In this area, the river offers a wilder character due to the rugged canyon walls created by an old lava flow. Mink, otters, and peregrine falcons are sometimes spotted here.

At river mile 7.6, the river picks up gradient again, and three easier class 2–2- rapids are found farther downriver: one in the vicinity of Water Cave Rock (8.7 miles), one at and immediately below the old dam site (9.1 miles), and a third below the confluence with the Williamson (10.1 miles).

Between the old dam site and the take-out, watch for so-called "sinker logs." The Sprague had been used historically to raft logs downstream to the sawmills in Chiloquin, and when the dam was built, those logs that remained became waterlogged and sank to the bottom of the pond above the dam. With removal of the dam in 2008, the logs temporarily resurfaced, posing a threat to swimmers. Most of the sinkers have either washed downstream and resubmerged or have been removed. Still, caution is warranted when paddling downstream of the old dam site. The take-out at Chiloquin County Park is on river right.

Hazards

Appropriate cold-water gear is recommended. The Chiloquin Narrows is a very long, rocky rapid and requires solid class 2 skills and an appropriate whitewater

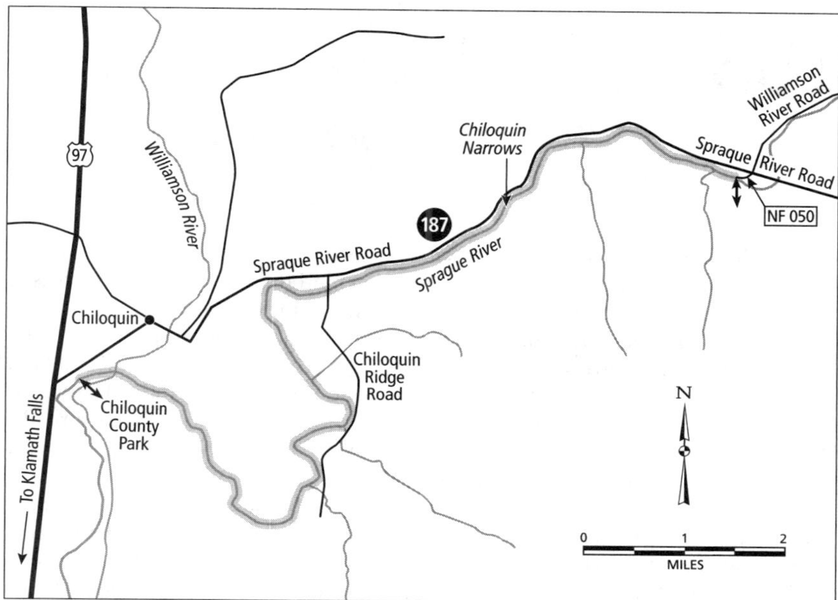

boat with flotation. It can be scouted from the highway on the drive to the put-in. Sinker logs may be present in the last mile and a half of the run, from the old dam site (mile 9) to the take-out.

Access

From Klamath Falls, drive north on US 97 about 23.5 miles to Klamath Lake Boulevard in Chiloquin. (The signs will point you to Chiloquin and tribal headquarters.) Turn right and drive less than 0.25 mile to Chiloquin County Park, the take-out.

To reach the put-in, return to Klamath Lake Boulevard, turn right, and drive an additional 0.7 mile. At the intersection, veer right onto Chocktoot Street and drive an additional 0.3 mile crossing the Williamson River bridge and the railroad tracks. At the next intersection, turn left onto North First Avenue (which shortly becomes Sprague River Highway) and drive 5.3 miles to the intersection of Sprague River Highway and Williamson River Road. At this intersection, turn right onto unmarked NF 050, which will turn back to the west, running parallel to the highway you just traveled on. It continues for approximately a mile in this direction on a level bench adjacent to the river. There are many suitable hand-launch sites here. Find one that suits your taste and unload your gear.

Gauge

Sprague River near Chiloquin Oregon. During most years, the river level is good from mid-March to mid-June.

Marianne Musitelli

188 Klamath River
Keno Dam to John C. Boyle Reservoir

Class: 3+	Length: 5.2–6.6 miles
Flow: 1000–2000 cfs	Character: forested; remote
Gradient: 50 fpm, C/PD	Season: rainy; dam-controlled

After gathering in the lakes of the Klamath Basin, the Klamath River enters the Cascade Mountains where, after being slowed behind the Keno Dam, it is released for a lively 6-mile run down to the pool above the John C. Boyle Dam.

Although the water is murky (due to agricultural runoff from above), the rugged canyon, numerous rapids, and proximity to Klamath Falls and Ashland make this run worth the effort. Once on the river, the rapids are difficult to scout from the bank, and the canyon is inaccessible except from a few logging roads. Oregon 66 is high above and distant from the river. This stretch is often rocky and shallow—not recommended for kayak practice rolls.

The first 2 miles consists of short, busy rapids. Some of the best play spots (including the "Keno Wave") are in the rapids immediately below the dam. Then an easier section culminates in a rapid with a sharp drop at the bottom. The next notable rapid has waves that pile up on a wall at the bottom. This is followed by a rocky, pebbly section of river that is more open. The water then gathers together again for one last rapid, and a good play spot, before flowing into the reservoir. Take out on the right or paddle another 1.4 mile on flatwater to a take-out on the left before the bridge.

Hazards

Scout the final rapid, with difficulty, if desired. Check for toxic algae alerts before paddling.

Access

To reach the put-in from the US 97/Oregon 66 junction south of Klamath Falls, drive 8.6 miles on Oregon 66 west to Keno. At the Oregon 66/Clover Creek Road junction (Y) just outside Keno, stay right on Clover Creek Road for 0.1 mile and then turn left on Puckett Road (which parallels Oregon 66). Immediately after going under the overpass, turn right on Riveredge Road and follow this rock road 1.1 miles to Old Wagon Road. Turn left and in 50 yards pass through an open Pacific Power property gate. Old Wagon is a very rough road requiring a high-clearance vehicle. If you cannot pass over the rocks at the gate, the remaining mile to the put-in will be very difficult. The road follows the shore of the pool above the Keno Dam and ends along the river at a nice turnaround, the put-in.

To reach the put-in from Ashland, take Oregon 66 to Keno, cross the Klamath River, and bear left on Puckett Road, turning left on Riveredge Road, then follow the directions given above.

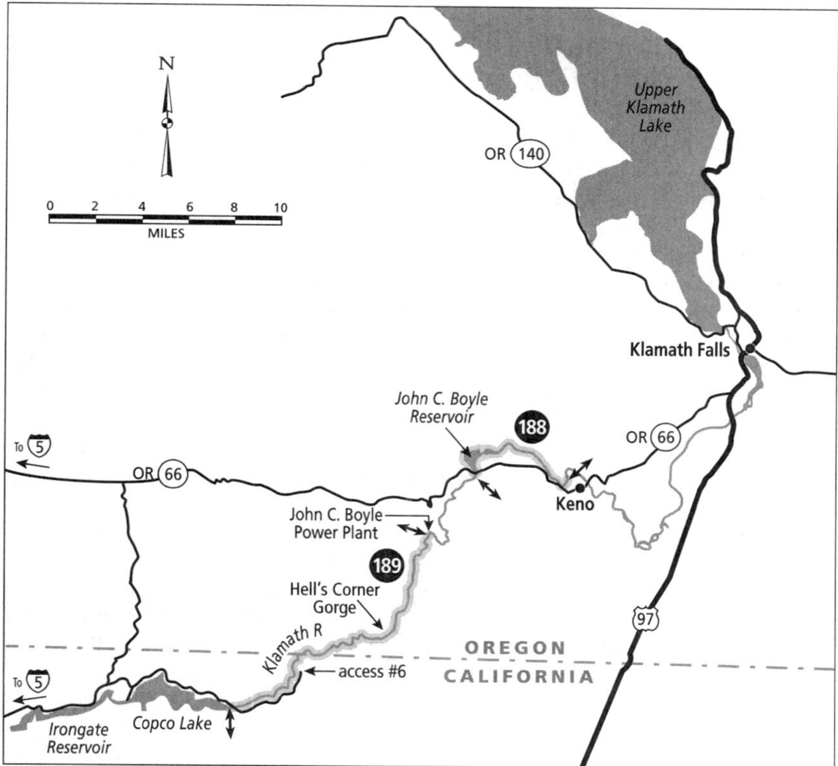

To get to the take-out, return to the Riveredge road junction with Puckett Road and Oregon 66, and drive west through Keno for 6.8 miles. Just after crossing the John C. Boyle Reservoir, turn right onto Keno Road. Follow Keno Road for 0.9 mile and then take a right onto a wide forest road. Continue 1.7 miles, and while in a curve to the right, turn right onto a single-track four-wheel-drive road and continue 0.5 mile to the river. The last part of this road has a fairly steep pitch, but this road is much better than the last mile of the put-in road. The take-out is a short carry, on river right just below the last rapid at the mouth of the canyon, ending with the Boyle pool. Alternatively, one could take out at the wayside area on the left at the Oregon 66 bridge. To reach the take-out from Ashland, look for Keno Road on the left at milepost 44, and proceed as directed above.

Gauge

Klamath River at Keno. The "Keno Wave" play spot just below the dam is best between 1200 and 1400 cfs.

Karen Lewis, Kevin Buck, and Marianne Musitelli

189 ★ Klamath River
John C. Boyle Power Plant to Copco Lake

Class 4(5); 5	Length: 16.6 miles
Flow: 1750 cfs (one turbine); 3000 cfs (two turbines)	Character: mostly roadless
Gradient: 42 fpm (75 fpm though Hells Corner), PD	Season: year-round

The proposed removal of four out of five dams on the upper stretches of the Klamath River will be the largest dam removal in history and is scheduled to commence in 2020 if it receives congressional approval. If authorized, the Klamath could flow freely for more than 200 miles to the Pacific Ocean, the first time in more than a century. This huge undertaking will likely leave us with a very different river than we have come to know and enjoy for such a long time. If dam removal occurs, this run will probably only be available during spring runoff and during heavy rainstorms. On the other hand, some sections of the river currently inundated by the dams may once again be runnable and may possibly open up new boating opportunities.

This stretch of the Klamath is known as the Upper Klamath or the Hell's Corner run. It may be the most exciting day trip in Oregon, especially in the summer when other rivers usually have declining flows. The canyon is nearly inaccessible and remote, and contains several steep, long, powerful rapids. The rapids demand respect and focus, and boaters should be self-reliant and capable of handling class 4–5 water. The water is never clear, and the rock tends to erode to sharp edges. Other than the Columbia, the Klamath is the only other Northwest river that cuts through the Cascade Mountains to the ocean.

Flows are regulated by releases from one or two turbines below the John C. Boyle Dam, normally starting at about 9:00 AM and ending at about 2:00 PM each day, but are dependent on electrical demands and the amount of water entering the river system upstream. The normal daily release from one turbine is 1250 cfs, which, combined with the minimum flows, creates 1650–1750 cfs by midmorning. With two turbine releases, the river climbs to over 3000 cfs, increasing most rapids by a class.

It may be helpful to think of the run in three sections: the initial 5-mile "warm-up"; the 4-mile Hell's Corner Gorge; and the final 8 miles of class 3 and 2 rapids ending at the lowest take-out. The overall gradient of the river is 42 feet per mile, but the 5 miles from Caldera to Salt Caves is 75 feet per mile.

The action starts immediately with a class 2 drop and continues with three more class 2's in the first mile, followed by the first class 3, Osprey (take the left channel around the island). The river widens and slows with class 1–2 rapids for the next 4.5 miles. Camping is available at several spots along the river under mature ponderosa pine trees.

The beginning of Hell's Corner Gorge follows a big, sweeping bend and pool with the old Frain Ranch on both sides of the river. As you approach a right bend, the canyon narrows dramatically, and you see the horizon line and hear the roar that signals you are at the top of Caldera, class 5. Eddy out left and walk up to scout the rapid: a 200-yard chaos of whitewater, holes, and rocks. There are two huge boulders in the upper part of the channel, and one must choose to run either left or right of the initial midstream menace, called Mushroom Rock. Most oar rafts seem to go right and then cut back left of a second boulder, riding out the rest of the rapid by pushing hard and keeping the boat midstream. Paddle rafts tend to take the left side, blasting through a huge trough-like hole and running between the left bank cliff and Mushroom Rock. Eddy out on the right at the bottom, catch your breath, and get ready for another 5 miles of challenging whitewater.

The next mile below Caldera includes four class 3 rapids, ending with a 2+. A few hundred yards later, the intensity returns with Satan's Gate, class 4. This long, steep, chaotic rapid bends right about halfway down. Stay in the middle of the river, as the current will otherwise push you left into dangerous rocks. There is no pool below Satan's Gate, but if you want to and can, immediately eddy left to stop and scout what can be a very difficult rapid, Hell's Corner, class 5. The rapid begins with a sharp cut to the left, but stay right of center to avoid sharp, unseen, submerged rocks. The river first sweeps to the left, then back to the right. It is important to stay right or centered to avoid getting swept left into the rocks, but not so far right that you get caught in the shallows of the inside of the curve. As you approach what appears to be the bottom, stay right of center to avoid the Ego Bruiser, a hidden rock that catches many a boat. Grab the big eddy on the right for a breather, or stay in the current for the final big drop, a 90-degree left turn into The Dragon, class 4. Two large boulders (the teeth of the dragon) lurk at the bottom. Eddy out right for a nice lunch spot.

The action continues almost immediately with two class 3+ rapids, then widens into a shallow rock-dodger rapid called Dance Hall. Stay left of the island and to the inside of the curve, but not too far right, as the river cuts hard right and drops into Ambush, class 4. Stay left of center into this steep, powerful drop. Eddy left in the pool below for another nice lunch spot, or line up for Bushwhacker, class 3. This rapid is clean and has a huge wave mid-rapid. Pool and drop class 2 rapids continue past Salt Caves (once the site of a proposed dam that would have flooded the canyon back to Caldera).

The next mile continues with nice pools and class 2–3 drops, followed by Snag Island, class 3+. Stay in the main, right channel around the island, which is long, swift, and choppy. As the island ends, there is a midstream rock, and the channel bends sharply back to the left. It is important to make this tight corner or you will be washed onto rocks on the outside of the bend—usually not a hazard, but a bit embarrassing. As you enter the pool, a look upstream reveals the tail of the falls coming off the top of the left side of the island. This marks the end of the gorge section; however, four class 3 rapids remain, including State Line Falls, about 1.5 miles downstream. As you approach State Line Falls, which doesn't look like much from the top, stay left. The falls is a sharp vertical drop and surprisingly strong and retentive. The first primitive access point is just below the falls on the left (the BLM Stateline Campground is up on the hill), with another, larger access area 0.7 mile below there (PacifiCorps access no. 6). However, many boaters continue another 5 or more miles to Copco Lake (access no. 1).

The lower section of the river below access 6 is a pleasant float with class 1–2+ rapids among woodlands and pastures. Minor challenges include running some natural rock irrigation dams. This section is sometimes done as a run by itself; be sure to start at noon or later to have sufficient water.

Just below Shovel Creek, which enters on the left, is the old town site of Beswick. Klamath Hot Springs are still there, which can make for a nice stop over on a cool day.

The final take-out is at Copco Lake on the left; the last half-mile is flatwater.

Hazards

Caldera, Satan's Gate, and Hell's Corner (which includes The Dragon) are long, steep, difficult rapids, which should be approached with caution, a high degree of respect for the river, and solid boat-handling skills. Ambush, Bushwhacker, Snag Island, and Stateline Falls are less intense than the others, but still require focus, and good river reading and boat handling. Given the steep gradient, most holes are not keepers as long as you keep your boat straight and provide forward momentum.

Access

Starting from the US 97/Oregon 66 junction in Klamath Falls, drive west on Oregon 66 for 17.3 miles, passing through the town of Keno and going past the J. C. Boyle Reservoir. Between mileposts 42 and 43, you will see a sign for the Klamath Wild and Scenic River and John C. Boyle Power Station. Turn left (south) and follow this well-maintained road a few miles as it descends into the canyon, past the flume carrying water to the power plant. The road is less maintained beyond this point, but continue another mile or so and you will see the acute-angle turnoff and the sign for the put-in. Continue a couple of hundred yards, make the sharp turn, and descend to the put-in, which is paved and features pit toilets.

To reach the take-out, only 17 miles downstream, return to Oregon 66 and continue west to Interstate 5, then south on the interstate to the Hornbrook, California, exit. Drive east 3 miles, and cross the river. Go 3.5 miles past the bridge on Ager Road, then turn left onto Ager-Beswick Road for another 16 miles to the top of Copco Lake and the lower take-out. It is a 5-mile drive to the uppermost PacifiCorps access no. 6, but this is a nice section to float. This 80-mile drive takes 2.5 hours, and is best arranged by local shuttle drivers (shuttle drivers normally stay with vehicles for the return trip). Unfortunately, the former alternative route near milepost 24 on Oregon 66 to Copco crosses private property, and although it cuts the time by fifty percent and 55 miles, as of this writing (2015), the owner prohibits access.

Gauge

Klamath River below John C. Boyle Power Plant. Normal release is the flow from one turbine (1500–1800 cfs). An occasional release from two turbines makes it a respectable class 5 challenge. When the flow exceeds 3400 cfs, it is extremely dangerous to run.

Lance Stein, Dan Valens, Mike Hale, Noah Hague,
Yann Crist-Evans, and Kevin Buck

Opposite: *Hoodoos on the banks of the Owyhee River below Three Forks* (Gary Adams)

Eastern
Oregon Rivers
Region 9

John Day River and Tributaries

190 Middle Fork John Day River
Above US 395 Bridge to Confluence with North Fork John Day

Class: 2(3)	Length: 10–53 miles
Flow: 400–1200 cfs	Character: pine savanna; private ranches
Gradient: 27 fpm, C	Season: rainy/snowmelt

The upper two sections of the river pass through cattle ranches among hills. The lower section is less inhabited and provides fine views of basalt buttes. All three sections run through private land. Please respect private property. Look out for possible fences across the river. The flow exceeds 2000 cfs less than once a year, on average, and then for only a short time.

SECTION 1: ABOVE US 395 BRIDGE, 10 MILES, CLASS 2

This fairly continuous section has pleasant class 1 and 2 rapids and a small road alongside it. Put in and take out at any of the accesses found along the road upstream from the US 395 bridge. A nice pullout found 10 miles above the bridge makes a good starting point for a pleasant one-day outing.

SECTION 2: US 395 BRIDGE TO RITTER, 10 MILES, CLASS 2(2+ TO 3)

Put in along the road at an access 0.4 mile above the US 395 bridge. The flow is fairly continuous, as the river follows the road all the way to Ritter. Look out for possible fences across the river. About 2 miles below the US 395 bridge is a half-mile class 2+ rapid (class 3 above 800 cfs). This is the biggest rapid on these three sections. The gauge is at Ritter. The fish traps in the river, above and below the gauge, may require a portage. Take out in or near Ritter.

SECTION 3: RITTER TO MOUTH, 16 MILES (PLUS 9–17 MILES ON NORTH FORK), CLASS 2

The put-in is the take-out for section 2. Note: There is no take-out at the mouth of the river. Below Ritter, the canyon becomes more rugged after the last house is passed (near mile 3) and the road leaves the canyon. The basalt buttes are beautiful. The river continues, with a few class 2 rapids, to the confluence with the North Fork John Day. Boaters must continue on down the North Fork another 9.4 miles to a take-out at Wall Creek boat ramp, or 7.8 miles beyond that to the Monument boat ramp. There are camping areas along the North Fork; however, the North Fork is regulated by the BLM, which requires permits year-round. For details, see: North Fork John Day River, Dale to Monument run.

Hazards

A barbed-wire fence across the river is likely and may be difficult to see. It could present an extreme hazard. During the spring, one or two fish traps are normally in the river above and below the gauge at Ritter; a portage may be required.

Access

From Ukiah, take US 395 south, through Dale, to the bridge over the Middle Fork. From Long Creek, take US 395 north to the bridge over the Middle Fork. Follow the road upstream or downstream, depending upon the section desired.

Gauge

Middle Fork John Day River at Ritter.

Rob Blickensderfer and Murray Johnson

191 ★ North Fork John Day River Dale to Monument

Class: 2+; 3	Length: 45 miles
Flow: 800–2500 cfs; 4000+ cfs	Character: forested canyon
Gradient: 19 fpm, C	Season: snowmelt

On this run, boaters will experience the transition from the forested foothills of the Blue Mountains to the more open country of Eastern Oregon. The north-facing slopes are moderately steep and forested, while the opposite bank features grassy slopes nestled between giant stairsteps of basalt. Abundant spring wildflowers make walks into the hills above camp quite worthwhile. The trip is usually done with two nights of camping. Most of the land on both sides of the river is under BLM management, but remains of old fences may be seen on the right. From about 2500 to 3500 cfs, the four named rapids are class 3–3+, and there are at least twenty class 2 rapids. Below about 2500 cfs, the four named rapids are class 2+. At any water level, the North Fork is definitely more difficult and much faster than the sections downstream.

A common put-in is at Tollbridge Campground, river mile (RM) 60.5, where Desolation Creek enters the river. (See Access below for other put-in options.) The US 395 bridge is just downstream at RM 59.8. The highway is on river right for the next 3 miles of class 1 and 2 water. At RM 56.8, Camas Creek enters from the right. Here, US 395 leaves the river corridor. A dirt road follows the river on the right for much of the way downstream to Monument.

Grandstand Rapid, class 2+ to 3, begins at RM 54. To scout, land on the right and walk along the road. The rapids begin in a wide curve to the left. The main drop ends with a curve to the right as the water rolls off the cliff on the left.

Look for Surprise Rapid, class 2+ to 3, where Sulphur Gulch enters on the left at RM 51.5. The approach for this relatively short rapid is not obvious and it is difficult to scout. The hole along the left wall and the boils in the large eddy on the right of the main chute have surprised many boaters with a capsize.

Chainsaw Rapid is located at RM 49.5. This class 2–3 rapid has an upper section with large standing waves between narrow banks. The middle section has a large class 1 eddy, which empties into a 400-foot-long rapid with big waves. Class 2+ to 3+ Zipper Rapid is next at RM 48.1. The rapid in this large S curve begins gently and continues to build. At low flows, it features a rock garden at the bottom. Zipper can be scouted on either side.

Zion Scope, a symmetrical mountain ahead on the right, is visible at RM 47. Stony Creek enters on the right at RM 45, and in a mile, Devils Backbone is the prominent mountain on the right. Upper Bridge Rapid is followed by Lower Bridge Rapid, both class 2-, starting at RM 43. The concrete bridge at RM 38

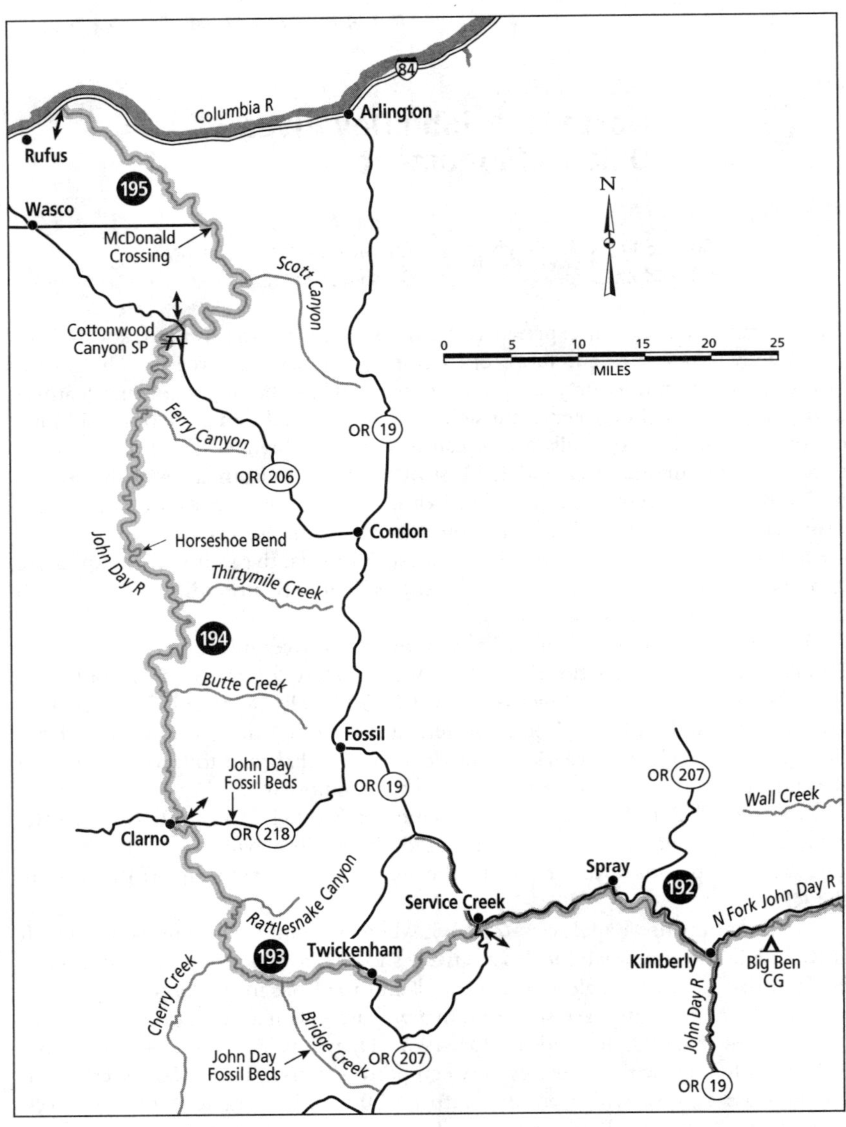

has a road that goes to Ritter, leading up Wrightman Canyon on the left. Mallory Creek is soon passed on the right.

The Middle Fork John Day River enters from the left just below an island at RM 32.2. There are some nice camps below here in the next few miles. In another 4 miles, Johnny Cake Mountain is the conspicuous feature on the right. Wall Creek, a major tributary, enters on the right at RM 22.8. There is public road access to the river at Wall Creek, but a better take-out is 6 miles farther at Monument. About a half-mile past the Monument bridge, look among the willows on the right for the BLM boat ramp. This take-out is at RM 15.

Hazards

This run is fairly remote. The water comes from snowmelt and is quite cold. Weather conditions can change quickly, with frosty nights or snow flurries possible through May.

Access

Several put-ins are in the vicinity of Dale, which is on US 395 and can be reached from the north via Ukiah or from the south via Mount Vernon. From Ukiah, US 395 follows Camas Creek southward to the North Fork John Day River. A common launch site is at Camas Landing—go 0.7 mile downstream from the Camas Creek US 395 bridge using the side road. Several unimproved launch sites may be found along the 2.8 miles of highway upstream of this bridge. A gravel road, NF 55, continues upriver to an access launch point on Desolation Creek. When the highway turns south, drive 0.5 mile up the gravel road, turn right, cross the river and turn into Tollbridge Campground. Other access points are available farther upstream along NF 55; inquire locally.

To reach the take-out, follow US 395 south from Dale 26 miles to the town

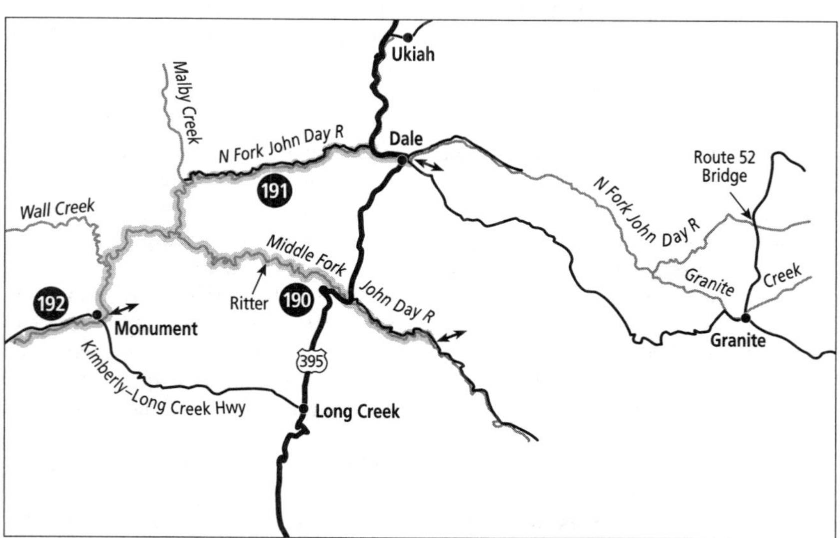

of Long Creek, turn west onto the Kimberly–Long Creek Highway and proceed 21 miles to Monument. After crossing the river, drive downstream 0.5 mile to the boat ramp take-out at the BLM park. Shuttles are available at the Boyer's Cash Store in Monument and the store in Dale.

Gauge

North Fork John Day River at Monument. During the snowmelt season, the North Fork contributes two-thirds or more of the total flow at Monument, with the Middle Fork contributing the other third. However, after heavy rain, the proportion of water coming from the Middle Fork may increase significantly. It's often helpful to check the gauge: Middle Fork John Day River at Ritter.

Rob Blickensderfer and WKCC Editors

192 North Fork John Day River/John Day River
Monument to Service Creek

Class: 1+ to 2-	Length: 43.4 miles
Flow: 1000–3000 cfs	Character: farmland; desert canyon
Gradient: 7 fpm	Season: snowmelt

This trip follows the North Fork of the John Day River downstream for 15 miles from Monument to the its confluence with the main John Day River near Kimberly. The river then continues as the main stem John Day to the communities of Spray and Service Creek. Oregon 19 and the Kimberly–Long Creek Highway follow the river closely for the entire distance. The river valley alternates between broad farmland terraces and steep canyons. Campsites are rare, with little public land along the river. Numerous launch points and class 1+ rapids make this an ideal stretch for beginning boaters looking for a day trip.

Cross the river in Monument and drive downstream about 0.5 mile to the BLM park and boat ramp on river right. The put-in is at RM 15. (RM refers to river mile.) Immediately below the put-in, the river flows into a short, isolated, and beautiful canyon. At about RM 13.3, keep an eye out for a low concrete dam spanning the river around a left bend. It can be scouted and portaged on either side, with the least effort on river right. Because the dam face is angled, it can be run, except possibly at low flows. Immediately below the dam is a class 2- rapid that leads into class 1+ riffles and rocks for another 0.25 mile. The river then opens into farmland. At RM 10 is a broken concrete weir immediately upstream of a bright blue bridge. Keep far left to avoid turbulence near the weir. Two small BLM campgrounds, Big Bend and Lone Pine, are located on river right at RM 3.2 and RM 2.1, respectively. Both are accessible from the road and could be alternative launch points.

Another launch point is at the Oregon 19 bridge near Kimberly, RM 0.1. Below this bridge, the main John Day enters from the left, increasing the total flow by about one-half. Now on the John Day River, with a different mileage system, the river mile is 185 at Kimberly. About 1.5 miles downstream from the confluence is an island on a left bend with a rapid (class 2-) on both sides. It is the most difficult rapid of the run. The left side is easiest to scout. The Shady Grove rest area on Oregon 19 is on river right at RM 178.2. It has toilets and picnic tables, but no camping, and is another place that can be used for launching. Spray is at RM 171, and the town has a park with camping and a boat ramp on river right. The 13.8-mile segment between Spray and Service Creek offers the most enjoyable canyon scenery and a nice sequence of class 1+ rapids. Alternative launch points found in this segment are just upstream of a small bridge at Wooden Bridge boat launch (RM 162) and at Mule Shoe Campground (RM 159.2). The Service Creek boat launch is on river right at RM 157.2.

An essential paddling resource is the helpful BLM guide and map: "John Day River Recreation Guide: Kimberly to Tumwater Falls" (see Appendix B).

Hazards

The concrete dam 2 miles below the BLM park put-in near Monument should be scouted. The broken concrete weir at 6.5 miles below the put-in should be approached with caution and avoided.

Access

Numerous access points are described above. Boats could access the river at Monument, Kimberly, Spray, Wooden Bridge, and Mule Shoe Campground. For directions to Monument, see the North Fork John Day River: Dale to Monument run. For directions to Service Creek, see the John Day River: Service Creek to Clarno run.

Gauge

North Fork John Day River at Monument. John Day River at Service Creek. The gauge at Monument gives flows on the North Fork. The Service Creek gauge gives flows below the confluence at Kimberly. The suggested flows listed above are for the Service Creek gauge.

John Van Sickle and WKCC Editors

193 ★ John Day River
Service Creek to Clarno

Class: 1+(2)	Length: 47.8 miles
Flow: 1200–6000 cfs	Character: desert canyon
Gradient: 7 fpm, PD	Season: snowmelt

This stretch of the John Day is a favorite for open canoers, drift boaters, and beginning kayakers who want a fine desert wilderness experience. Although a number of ranches and cultivated fields are located at several places along the river, other sections are uninhabited and cut off from civilization by the towering walls of the canyon. Below the put-in at Service Creek, boaters float several easy class 1 rapids and riffles while they feel themselves slipping away from civilization. Nature's sculpting of the twisted basalt canyons presents forms never before imagined. The most beautiful stretch has been designated a scenic river. The other stretches have seen ever-increasing pressures of humanity's relentless efforts to cultivate any land that has water available. Thus the many irrigation pumps flooding alfalfa fields leave boaters with the uneasy feeling that the river may be pumped dry before they reach the take-out.

Campsites are quite plentiful, often with sandy beaches at water level and juniper trees higher up. No campsites are found near the ranching area of Twickenham or along the last 8 miles to Clarno. The trip is normally done with two or three nights of camping on the river.

The put-in at Service Creek is at river mile (or RM) 157. About 7 miles after the put-in, the boater encounters Russo Rapid, class 2, at RM 150.3. The approach is at a curve to the left. The rapid is straight, with a cliff at bottom left. In a mile is another easier rapid, followed by a campsite on the left. Just below there, the land is private all the way to Twickenham. Do not camp along that stretch. The Twickenham bridge, an alternative launch site, is at RM 144.2. Four miles below the bridge some campsites are available. At RM 138.9 is Wreck Rapid, class 2, with a side-breaking wave off the cliff on the right at the lower end. The approach is a slight curve to the right. Boaters can land on river left to scout or portage. Pass the Priest Hole access, a mile below, at RM 137.6. Burnt Ranch Rapid (or Schuss Rapid) is in another 5 miles, at RM 132.4. At levels below 3000 cfs, a large rock sits in the center at the head of the rapids. Boaters can scout from left or right. A boat launch with rough access, at Lower Burnt Ranch, is available just downstream of the rapid on river left, RM 131.7

Around RM 130, there are several camps on the left and the right, followed by Cherry Creek on the left. In another 2 miles, at RM 127.5, one enters the Big Bend region. Here, the river makes several sweeping bends in a beautiful, deep canyon with fine beaches and campsites, and numerous class 1 rapids. Upon leaving the Big Bend region, one can see Rattlesnake Canyon on the right (RM 122); a back road leads up the canyon from here. Between RM 120 and 119 one finds the last cluster of campsites available before the take-out. A secondary road on the right begins around RM 117, with mostly private land downstream. It is 8 more miles to the Clarno bridge. The take-out is on the right, just past the bridge, at RM 109.1.

An essential paddling resource is the helpful BLM guide and map: "John Day River Recreation Guide: Kimberly to Tumwater Falls" (see Appendix B).

Hazards

Open canoers are encouraged to scout the three class 2 rapids in this run; kayakers with class 2 experience will likely not have difficulty. In places, the river drives headlong into cliff walls. At high water, the waves rolling off the cliff, as well as the eddy on the inside of the bend, can give the unwary boater problems. Afternoon up-canyon winds are normal with occasional strong, erratic side gusts. Rattlesnakes and scorpions are present but seldom seen.

Access

The take-out is at Clarno where Oregon 218 crosses the river. Parking and a boat landing are located at the east end of the bridge. Oregon 218 is located between US 97 at Shaniko and Oregon 19 at Fossil. (Oregon 19 can be reached from the north from Interstate 84 at Arlington or from the south from US 26 near Dayville.)

The put-in is near Service Creek, about an hour's drive from Clarno. From Clarno, take Oregon 218 east to the town of Fossil. Then go south on Oregon 19 to Service Creek, which features a general store. The Service Creek Stage Stop (www.servicecreek.com) can shuttle cars to Clarno. Service Creek is at the junction of Oregon 207 and Oregon 19. For the put-in, go south from Service Creek on Oregon 207 for 0.2 mile toward Mitchell. The put-in is on river right 100 yards upstream from the bridge.

Note: Permits are required to float this stretch of river. Visit www.blm.gov/or/permit for more information and to obtain a permit.

Gauge

John Day River at Service Creek.

Rob Blickensderfer and WKCC Editors

194 ★ John Day River
Clarno to Cottonwood Bridge

Class: 2(3)	Length: 69 miles
Flow: 1200–6000 cfs	Character: desert canyon
Gradient: 11 fpm, C	Season: snowmelt

This run on the John Day is a favorite for many, including open canoers, drift boaters, and kayakers. Because the gradient here is steeper than in the preceding run, the river moves faster and has more wave action. The presence of fewer ranches makes boaters feel more isolated along this stretch, which has been designated a Natural River Area under the Oregon Scenic Waterways Act. Many magnificent canyon walls exist, unseen by all but river runners. Allow at least four nights of camping on the river. A very relaxed trip with swimming and side-canyon hiking may last from six to seven days.

Put in on the right at the Clarno bridge at RM 109.1 (RM is river-mile). In 3.5 miles, boaters encounter a large riffle with big holes in the middle at high water and rocks at low water. In less than 1 mile, Clarno Rapid (RM 104.5) is marked by an island ahead of the rapid; take the left channel. A bank scout is available on the left from an eddy located about mid-island, just past some trees. Portage trails are visible above this eddy. Clarno Rapid is a long, complicated class 3 rapid. It is class 4 above 6000 cfs, and a capsize could have significant consequences. Heavy, fast water, class 2, leads around a left curve and into the main drop about 300 feet downstream. The portage for Clarno Rapid is a carry of about 150 yards up and over the rise. The rapid can also be lined, with difficulty, on the left. Lower Clarno, class 2, continues for 0.3 mile. It is rocky at low water.

Studying the canyon walls below Clarno, John Day River (Mark Scantlebury)

On the right below Clarno Rapid is Mulberry Camp (RM 103.7). In about 6 miles, powerlines cross the river, followed by ranch buildings that signal 0.3 mile of class 1+ to 2- rapids. Butte Creek enters on the right at RM 97.3, following a 90-degree left bend.

Basalt Rapid, class 2 (RM 93), is another long rapid. It is class 3 above 6000 cfs and has some meaty pour-overs and holes at this level. It is replete with basalt boulders. The approach is not obvious, but can be identified by fast water leading around a slight curve to the right, with juniper trees on the right. Land right to scout. Below 3000 cfs, the rounded black basalt rocks are exposed in the rapids, and some maneuvering is required. The main rapid is fairly short and curves to the left. Lower Basalt Rapid, with large black basalt boulders in the river, continues for 0.5 mile, with some dodging of holes and rocks. Good campgrounds can be found here and for the next 4 miles, into Great Basalt Canyon. Arch Rocks (RM 91.1) is a large camp on the right.

Thirtymile Creek enters on the right at RM 83.9; a privately owned access road is nearby. Near RM 76, the river begins a sweep to the right. The Saddle, ahead, is only 300 feet wide. It is followed by Horseshoe Bend, a 320-degree, 2-mile-turn to the left. A few miles downstream, near RM 71.4, two springs emerge from the vegetation on the hillside on the left. This area is identified by a dirt bank on river left and distorted columnar basalt near the river on river right. In about 4 miles, pass The Palisades cliffs on river left. A couple of camps in this area have stunning views.

Southbound Rapid (RM 64.1), a straightforward class 1+, occurs where the river heads due south, with a large gravel bar on the left. A couple of distinctive landmarks are visible in about 4 miles. Near RM 60, Hoot Owl Rock, a 6-foot-high "owl," is seen against the skyline about 200 feet above the river; a gravel bar is on the left. Citadel Rock, a fairy-tale fortress of a rock formation, dominates the view downstream. The river makes a sharp 180-degree turn to the right around Hoot Owl Rock.

In 0.6 mile, Doomsday Wall is on the left at RM 58.4; the river seems to disappear under the wall. A good ferry is required here. Campsites are less numerous and less desirable from here on. In 3 miles, Little Ferry Canyon comes in on the left at RM 55.4; two flat islands can be seen just downstream, and the red bluffs ahead on the left are The Gooseneck. The river first curves sharply right, then makes a long 200-degree curve left around The Gooseneck. At the apex of the curve, Ferry Canyon Rapid (class 1+) is found just downstream of Ferry Canyon (RM 53.6), entering on the right.

Near RM 49, powerlines first become visible on a distant ridge. Watch for bighorn sheep in this vicinity. Very few campsites can be found below here, and those that are found are somewhat marginal for larger groups. It is another 9 miles to the take-out at Cottonwood Bridge (RM 39.7). The boat ramp is just below the bridge on the right.

An essential paddling resource is the helpful BLM guide and map: "John Day River Recreation Guide: Kimberly to Tumwater Falls" (see Appendix B).

Hazards

In addition to the rapids described above, the terrain provides difficulties. Spring weather can range from snow flurries to sunny with temperatures above 100 degrees Fahrenheit within a few days. Beware of rattlesnakes, strong up-canyon winds in the afternoons, and the lack of potable water. Scouting Clarno and Basalt rapids can easily involve long hikes because of the length of the rapids.

Access

The put-in is at the bridge in Clarno where Oregon 218 crosses the river. Parking and a boat landing are located at the east end of the bridge. Oregon 218 is located between US 97 at Shaniko and Oregon 19 at Fossil. (Oregon 19 can be reached from the north from Interstate 84 at Arlington, or from the south from US 26 near Dayville.)

The take-out is at Cottonwood Bridge where Oregon 206 crosses the river. To get from Clarno to Cottonwood, follow Oregon 218 east to Fossil, then take Oregon 19 north to Condon, and from there, take Oregon 206 north to Cottonwood.

Note: Permits are required to float this stretch of river. See previous run (John Day: Service Creek to Clarno) for more information about the permits.

Gauge

John Day River at Service Creek.

Rob Blickensderfer and WKCC Editors

195   John Day River
Cottonwood Bridge to Columbia River

Class: 2(5+), P	Length: 39.7 miles
Flow: 700–6000 cfs	Character: desert canyon
Gradient: 6 fpm	Season: snowmelt

This stretch of the John Day can be divided into three sections of very different character: the float from Cottonwood Bridge to Tumwater Falls, Tumwater Falls followed by the 0.4-mile Narrows, and Lake Umatilla as part of the Columbia River/John Day reservoir. This description is based on a late-season run at 700 cfs in an inflatable kayak.

Put in river right at Cottonwood Bridge, RM 39.7 (RM is river-mile). The first 25 miles are comparable to the last few miles of the John Day River: Clarno to Cottonwood run. The river meanders through relatively open desert canyons, occasionally passing basalt cliffs, and past a few ranches. Stretches with jeep trail access alternate with stretches that have no road access. None of the few rapids in the first 25 miles exceed class 1+. At low water, gravel bars near islands may be a problem. Take the narrower channels that drop just before the island; the other channels often end in shallow gravel bars. Despite a few fences and "No Trespassing" signs, opportunities to camp are plentiful. The McDonald Crossing of the Barlow Cutoff of the Oregon Trail crosses the river at an angle at RM 20.7 (left) to RM 20.5 (right). An Oregon Trail monument can be visited a quarter-mile up the dirt road on river left. Although the falls are more than 10 miles away, this is the last option to take out before Tumwater Falls. Anglers and boaters with larger craft often use this take-out. There is access on river left and on river right. (See Access for details.)

The river picks up speed at around river mile 17, and in 2 more miles, numerous boulder gardens provide a welcome change of pace. All the action is well within class 2 levels at low water, but narrow passages and the more technical character may create challenges for some.

The river makes a 90-degree turn from north to west at about river mile 11, continuing west for another 0.5 mile before it turns northwest. This northwest turn indicates the upcoming Tumwater Falls. The noise, a continuous cliff river right, a black basalt island in the middle (at low to medium water levels), and a series of cliffs on river left all provide a clear warning of Tumwater Falls just ahead. Take out river right, climb up a 50-foot slope to a trail that parallels The Narrows. The trail is fairly level and an easy walk for several people, but not for larger groups carrying boats. Use this trail (and DO NOT stray from it) for the 0.5-mile portage leading to the beginning of Lake Umatilla, the John Day arm of the Columbia River Reservoir. The lower half of The Narrows is a popular area for smallmouth bass fishing.

Competent class 5 boaters interested in running parts of The Narrows need the following information: Tumwater Falls is the beginning of The Narrows, a series of cascading falls. The Narrows extends over 0.4 mile for a total drop of about 30 feet. A 30- to 50-foot vertical cliff river right makes access to the river impossible. On river left, a 20- to 30-foot cliff is broken at several places and allows for scrambles down to the river. At low water levels, several 5-foot drops are located down deep between the cliffs and are separated by pools.

Below Tumwater Falls the river is impounded by the John Day Dam on the Columbia. The flatwater is now shared with anglers in powerboats. Camping is available at Albert Philippi Park, at about river mile 3.5. Otherwise, undeveloped campsites are on both shores, but very few trees provide shade. The final take-out is on the left at LePage Park, near river mile 0.

An essential paddling resource is the helpful BLM guide and map: "John Day River Recreation Guide: Kimberly to Tumwater Falls" (see Appendix B).

Hazards

In addition to Tumwater Falls and The Narrows, the remoteness of the terrain, heat, and wind pose challenges. Upriver winds on this stretch can be very strong. Rattlesnakes, scorpions, and poison ivy share the riverbank with boaters.

Access

To reach the take-out, take exit 114 on Interstate 84 and go to LePage Park at the mouth of the John Day. Check with camp host about fees and parking.

To reach the put-in, go west on Interstate 84, take exit 109, and go through Rufus and south on Scott Canyon Road to Oregon 206. Go southeast on Oregon 206 to Cottonwood Bridge.

Boaters who wish to take out before Tumwater Falls, at the McDonald Crossing, have two options. The right take-out, on BLM land, is the recommended take-out. For directions and road condition reports about this gravel road access, contact the BLM office in Prineville. The left access is reached from Klondike Road off Oregon 206. Park your car up at the BLM's John Day Crossing Monument a quarter-mile up the road and not at the river (which is private land). The gas station in Rufus can be consulted for shuttle service.

Note: Permits are required to float this stretch of river. For information, see www.blm.gov/or/permit.

Gauge

John Day River at McDonald Ferry, or John Day River at Service Creek (upstream of run).

Horst Lueck

Malheur River

196 Malheur River
Riverside to Irrigation Dam Above Juntura

Class: 2	Length: 18 miles
Flow: 300–600 cfs	Character: desert; ranchland
Gradient: 16 fpm, C	Season: dam-controlled; summer irrigation release

Unlike the lower Malheur's severely diverted, weedy remains seen along US 20 between Juntura and Vale, this surprising hidden nugget above Juntura is often boatable all summer, a rarity in Eastern Oregon. Warm Springs Dam, just above the put-in, often releases 500 cfs during the irrigation season, and none of it is diverted until the end of this reach. The run includes good desert scenery, striking black basalt peaks, and ranchland, with an abandoned railroad on the left and then the right. However, there are some fence hazards (see below).

The Malheur here can have surprisingly good trout fishing, and some anglers believe that with more attention to dam releases, this productive stream could become a trophy trout fishery and economic boon to the area.

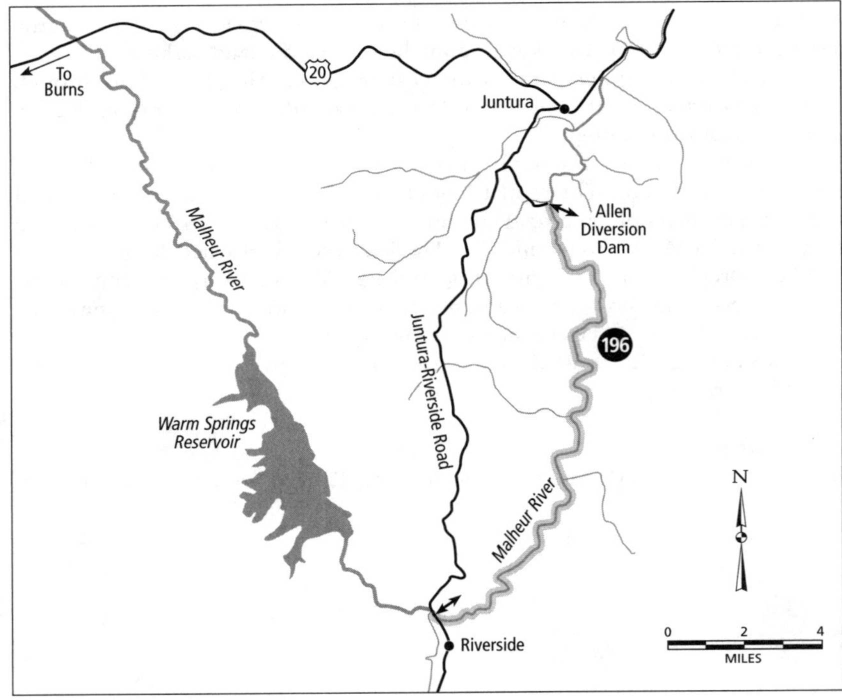

Hazards

Definitely be on the lookout for barbed-wire fences. At last count, two crossed this reach: one about 11 miles below the put-in (above Little Mosquito Creek), and the second one between two houses a mile above the take-out. Canoeing over the top of these sagging fences is possible, but the wire is almost impossible to see until the last instant, and in other flows or with other fence rigging, the height of the wire could be troublesome. Take-out is just above a diversion dam of sharp rock; worse fences are encountered downstream.

Access

To reach the put-in, take US 20 to Juntura, go south on the gravel Juntura-Riverside Road for 17 miles. Cross the Malheur River, go 0.1 mile, and turn left on a short dirt road that leads to a put-in spot.

The take-out is at Allen Diversion Dam. To get there from Juntura, drive south on Juntura-Riverside Road for 2.2 miles and go left on a rough two-track lane for 2 miles to the rock dam. For shuttles, call the Oasis Cafe in Juntura.

Gauge

Malheur River below Warm Springs Reservoir.

Tim Palmer

Donner und Blitzen River

197 Donner und Blitzen River
Blitzen Crossing to Page Springs

Class: 3(3+) T	Length: 17.3 miles
Flow: 500–800 cfs	Character: remote high desert canyon
Gradient: 49 fpm, PD	Season: snowmelt

The Donner und Blitzen is a National Wild and Scenic River and a superb fly-fishing stream. The river drains the magnificent Steens Mountain, an uplift fault block in the parched southeast Oregon desert region of the Basin and Range Province, and flows into Malheur Lake. The waters of the river and the lake create a region of exceptional wildlife and biological diversity. The river flows 17.3 miles and drops more than 800 feet from Blitzen Crossing to Page Springs through a deep, remote basalt canyon. Major tributaries are Indian Creek, Little Blitzen River, and Fish Creek, all flowing out of high glacially carved gorges on the west side of Steens Mountain. The river is demanding, the action is continuous, the scenery and setting are spectacular, and the river is remote, yet it can be run as a (long) day trip.

The paddling is technical, and the action is nonstop class 2+ and 3 for 11.6 miles, then it tapers off to 1+ and 2- for the last 5.7 miles. The river demands excellent boat control and respect for the remote nature of the run. The banks on

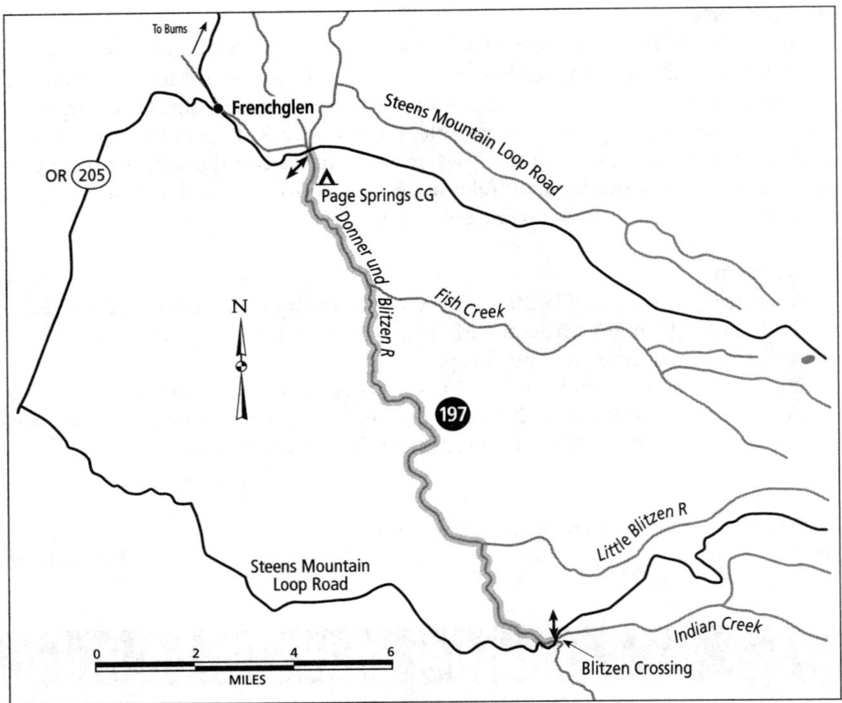

the South Fork are choked with alder and dogwood. These trees and their roots create continuous obstacles for hundreds of feet along the bank. The South Fork starts out 10–20 feet wide; the Donner und Blitzen at Page Springs is 50–70 feet wide. Near the end of the run is a 4-foot-high dam that separates the lower river from the upper river and its native population of redband trout.

The river has three distinct sections: from the South Fork at Blitzen Crossing to Little Blitzen, from Little Blitzen to Fish Creek, and from Fish Creek to Page Springs. Because of the limited access, you must paddle all three. The Little Blitzen increases the flow of the South Fork by about 60 percent; Fish Creek adds approximately the same amount. Total paddling and scouting time is about six hours.

SECTION 1: SOUTH FORK AT BLITZEN CROSSING TO LITTLE BLITZEN, 3.7 MILES, CLASS 3

This is a narrow, technical stream crowded by brush on both banks, particularly in the first mile. At mile 2.3, in a sharp left bend, is a class 3+ drop beginning a

1-mile section at 75 fpm. The confluence on the right with the Little Blitzen has a broad, grassy delta with a very old jeep trail coming down from the Riddle Brothers Ranch. The canyon walls rise from 75 feet near the put-in to more than 150 feet at the confluence.

SECTION 2: LITTLE BLITZEN TO FISH CREEK, 7.9 MILES, CLASS 3

The river widens substantially at the Little Blitzen. Two 70–75 fpm sections are each roughly 1 mile long. They begin about 2 miles and 4 miles downstream from the Little Blitzen. The canyon walls rise more than 400 feet above the river. Very steep side canyons offer some interesting hikes to the rim; in particular, Tombstone Canyon is on the left 2 miles below the Little Blitzen.

SECTION 3: FISH CREEK TO PAGE SPRINGS, 5.7 MILES, CLASS 2-

This section actually starts about 1.8 miles above Fish Creek. Bottomland begins here and gradually expands downstream toward Page Springs. The canyon walls are lower but still 200 feet above the river. Beware of the low dam at the gauging station 1 mile above Page Springs and of the fence across the river at Page Springs.

Hazards

The 3+ drop at 2.3 miles below the put-in will catch you by surprise on a sharp left bend. The canyon is remote, so prepare for emergencies, injuries, and any need for a layover in the canyon. Cell phones do not count (and will not work).

Access

From the west, take US 20 east to Burns. Proceed southeast on Oregon 78 for about 1.5 miles, then go south on Oregon 205 for about 55 miles to Frenchglen and Steens Mountain. Follow the Steens Mountain Loop east for 3 miles to the BLM Page Springs Campground, the take-out.

The put-in is reached by continuing south from Frenchglen on Oregon 205 for 10 miles to the south entrance to the Steens Mountain Loop. Turn left onto the loop road and continue 16 miles to Blitzen Crossing. This is the steel bridge where the loop road crosses the South Fork Donner und Blitzen, the put-in. The loop road has four gates. Gate 4, the South Gate, is opened by the BLM in May and provides access to Blitzen Crossing. Gate 3, east of Blitzen Crossing, is opened later, depending upon the snowpack on Steens Mountain. It is possible to arrange some form of shuttle to Blitzen Crossing at the Steens Mountain Resort near Frenchglen.

Gauge

Donner und Blitzen River near Frenchglen.

Steve Cramer and Larry Hodges

Powder River

198 Powder River
Bacher Creek to Canyon Creek

Class: 3(4)T	Length: 11 miles
Flow: 450–900 cfs	Character: desert canyon
Gradient: 29 fpm, PD	Season: snowmelt

The Powder River starts in the Elkhorn Range above the mining town of Sumpter, and flows east through Baker City and into the Snake River at the town of Richland. This run is 20 miles downstream of Baker City, beginning at the eastern end of the Lower Powder Valley and ending just before Eagle Valley. The run is described in two sections separated by the half-mile-long Slide Lake, created by a major landslide in 1984. Adequate flows usually occur from March into June, created by snowmelt. The average river width is less than 20 feet.

SECTION 1: BACHER CREEK TO DRY GULCH, 6 MILES, CLASS 2–3
The canyon begins just 0.2 mile downstream from the put-in. The first 3.5 miles are mostly class 2 with rocky drops rarely more than 3 feet high. Continuous rocky class 3 rapids with numerous narrow chutes begin about 3.5 miles from put-in. An optional take-out is at Dry Gulch, a mile above the bridge, where the road is close to the river. This avoids Slide Lake, a 0.5-mile flatwater paddle, and the class 4 water below it.

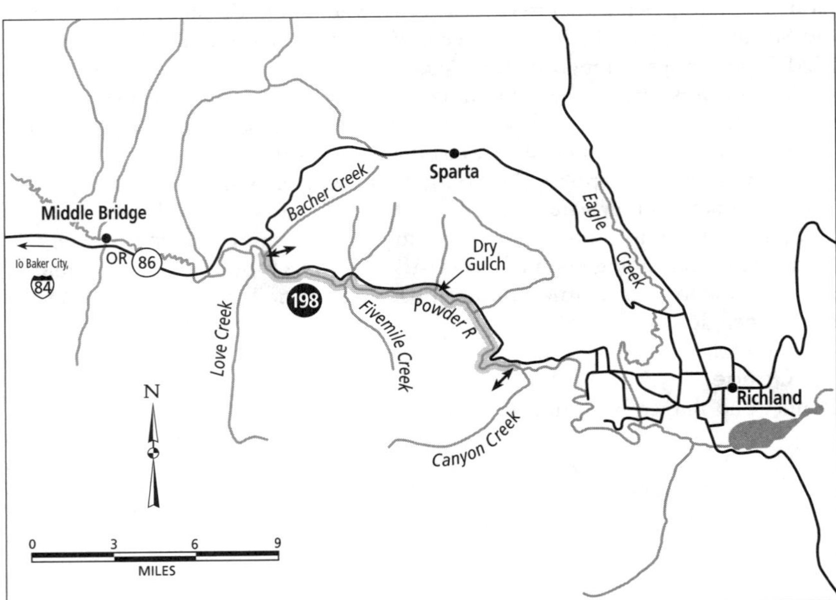

SECTION 2: DRY GULCH TO CANYON CREEK, 5 MILES, CLASS 3(4)

Past Dry Gulch the rapids continue for about a mile, until coming to an abrupt halt at Slide Lake. After a half-mile flatwater paddle, the more adventurous boater might consider boating the outflow of the lake, a 30-foot drop over a distance of 100 feet. Scout left for a vantage point of the rapids. (A steep, rocky 0.2-mile portage trail on the left is also an option.) The river below Slide Lake is similar to the continuous class 3 portion of section 1.

Hazards

The rapids at the outflow of Slide Lake are class 4. Below the take-out at milepost 34, numerous barbed-wire fences cross the river.

Access

From Interstate 84 near Baker City, take exit 302 onto Oregon 86 and drive east to milepost 23.3. The put-in is at a pullout near the river, just downstream from Sparta Lane. The section 1 take-out is at Dry Gulch, a pullout located at milepost 29.1. The section 2 take-out is at milepost 34, near the gauging station cable tram. To view the landslide (and the class 4 outflow rapids) up close, go to milepost 32.4 and take the abandoned highway road upstream; it will dead-end in 0.8 mile at the landslide. A viewing trail leads upstream.

Gauge

Powder River near Richland. The gauge is at the milepost 34 take-out. Irrigation diversions occur upstream of the gauge. A visual check of the flow is best.

Alan Jones and WKCC Editors

Jarbidge and Bruneau Rivers, Idaho

199 ★ Jarbidge River/Bruneau River Murphy Hot Springs to 8 Miles South of Bruneau

Class 4(6) P	Length: 72 miles
Flow: 600–2000 cfs	Character: desert canyon
Gradient: 35 fpm, PD	Season: spring runoff

The Jarbidge and the Bruneau carry you through a remote wilderness, on a ribbon of spectacular whitewater, in the scenic desert canyons where Idaho meets Nevada. Like the nearby Owyhee, some stretches are characterized by sheer vertical walls adorned with hoodoos dropping to the river. Some hiking is possible. Because of the whitewater challenges and remoteness, the trip requires solid class 4 paddling skills, good judgment, and thorough preparation. Given the portages, five nights out is a comfortable time to allocate. While there is little competition for campsites, some stretches have few suitable sites.

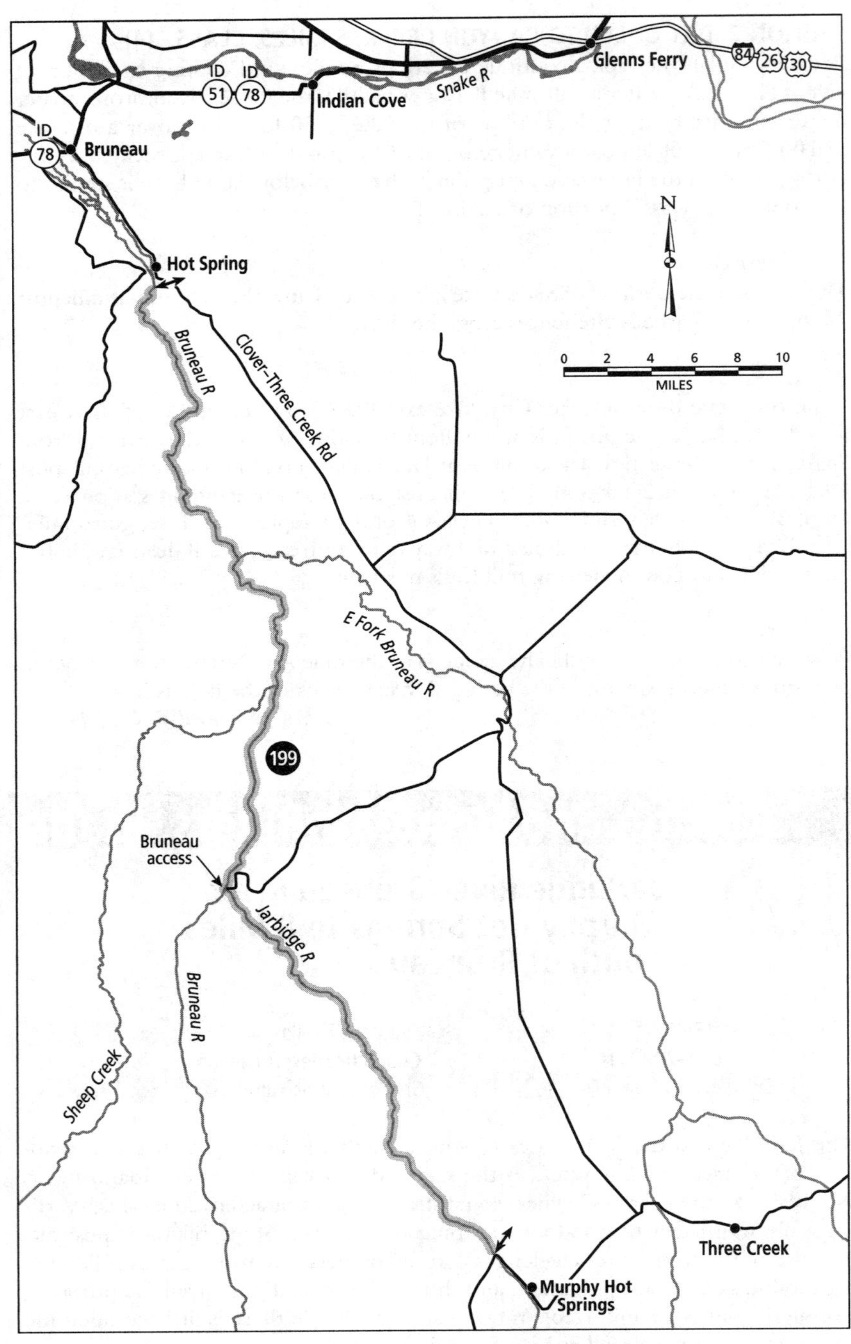

ID 51
ID 78
Indian Cove
Snake R
Glenns Ferry
84 26 30
ID 78
Bruneau
Hot Spring
Bruneau R
Clover–Three Creek Rd
N
0 2 4 6 8 10
MILES
E Fork Bruneau R
199
Bruneau access
Jarbidge R
Bruneau R
Sheep Creek
Three Creek
Murphy Hot Springs

From the put-in, the Jarbidge starts as continuous class 2–2+, with a few class 3 rapids to keep you alert. This pace continues for 10 miles. The river lets up a little, and then Castle Greyskull Rapid, class 5, appears around mile 18. This new rapid was created following the 2009 landslide that totally blocked the river. Sevy Falls is now gone. Castle Greyskull (also known as Tonsmeire Falls or Barker Falls) is portaged on the left on a narrow, rocky trail that is not recommended for wide loads. Wally's Wallow, class 4, appears after 21 miles and can be scouted and portaged on the left over a boulder jumble. The river difficulty now picks up with a series of challenging rapids. First comes The Maze at mile 25.5, a good place to practice eddy hopping. Right around the corner is John's Jollies, a long class 4. About a mile below John's Jollies is Jarbidge Falls, class 5. It is portaged by nearly everyone. This long portage is on the left over large boulders and is extremely difficult for rafts. Below Jarbidge Falls, the river lets up and soon joins the West Fork to form the main Bruneau River. A very hot hot spring is near the confluence. The alternative put-in, commonly used by rafters, is on the right at mile 31, just below the confluence.

Easier water continues for miles on the Bruneau, with an occasional class 3 drop, until Five-Mile Rapid, which begins at about mile 61. This rapid, truly 5 miles in length, comprises nearly continuous intermixed class 3 and class 4 rapids. The first 3 miles are most difficult, making them a good place to put those eddy-hopping skills to the test. At mile 68.8 is class 4 Wild Burro. The take-out is on the right, immediately above a dangerous low-head dam, near mile 72.

Contact the BLM office in Vale, Oregon, or Boise, Idaho, for maps (the BLM publishes an excellent one) and information about access, river conditions, and regulations on river use. Self-issue permits (available at put-in) are required to run this river. An excellent resource written by the BLM is also found online: the "Owyhee, Bruneau and Jarbidge Wild and Scenic Rivers Boating Guide." It includes the BLM's requirements for paddling the river and useful maps.

Hazards

Difficulties include: the mandatory portages at Jarbidge Falls and Castle Greyskull, Wally's Wallow Rapid, and the section known as Five-Mile Rapid. Wood blockages and logjams are possibilities. This canyon is one of the most remote areas in the lower 48 states. Overland rescue would be difficult, but could be made easier with a map of the primitive roads in the area. Cell phones don't work here. Watch out for poison ivy, particularly at the Jarbidge Falls portage. Purify water and watch for rattlesnakes. The river is dangerous above 2000 cfs.

Access

To reach the take-out from Mountain Home, Idaho, turn south onto US 51 and continue 22 miles to Bruneau. From Bruneau, drive south on Hot Springs Road for 8.2 miles, turn right onto a gravel road, go 0.6 mile, and turn right again to the take-out area just above the Harris low-head dam. It is private property, but the current landowner is okay with leaving rigs here.

To reach the put-in, return 0.7 mile to the main road and turn right. This road is known as the Clover–Three Creek Road. Drive south on this gravel and dirt road for about 60 miles. Turn right at the T junction at the end of the road, Three Creek Road. Go about 10 miles to Murphy Hot Springs. Drive downstream along the East Fork Jarbidge River for 2.5 miles to where it meets the West Fork Jarbidge, the put-in.

An intermediate access can be found at the confluence of the Jarbidge and the West Fork Bruneau. Access to this point is via a long, steep, bad road requiring a rugged, highly capable four-wheel-drive rig. The turnoff for this access road is about 32 miles south of Bruneau, off the Clover–Three Creek Road. Just after crossing Clover Creek (and a steep switchback), look for a road to the right about 1.4 miles past the creek. Take this road for about 15 miles, generally heading south and west at each intersection. The last 1.5 miles are extremely bad road.

The best trip is doing the Jarbidge and the Bruneau together. The Jarbidge section is not recommended for rafts due to the strenuous portages. Rafts would do better on the Bruneau only, although the road to the put-in there is class 5 in nature. Shuttle services are available from drivers in the town of Bruneau.

Gauge

Bruneau River near Hot Spring. The gauge is located just above the take-out. For an enjoyable run, catch the river as it drops through about 1200 cfs. This may occur as early as the last week in May or as late as the last week in June. It will run at about 1200 cfs for as long as two weeks. As the flow drops below 800 cfs, kayaks and small rafts will be okay, but open canoes (with flotation) are better suited. The river is dangerous above 2000 cfs. Care should be exercised in scheduling a trip. Patience must be exercised if the river rises during a trip. The best thing to do is to wait for the water to drop.

Dick Sisson and WKCC Editors

Grande Ronde River and Tributaries

200 Grande Ronde River
Red Bridge State Park to
Hilgard Junction State Park

Class: 2; 2+	Length: 8.6 miles
Flow: 850 cfs; 5000 cfs	Character: forested
Gradient: 21 fpm, C	Season: snowmelt

The river canyon broadens considerably on this run and is bounded by open forest and some rangeland. A modest gradient and easy riffles make this a fine float for competent beginners in almost any craft.

Note: It is possible to put in another 5.5 miles upstream near Starkey Station for a class 2 stretch of river. Above Starkey, numerous wood blockages are present, some natural and some that are placed in the river for fish habitat.

Hazards

Rapids constitute little hazard on this run, but beware of barbed-wire fences across the river. A rifle club shooting range is situated on the river about 4.2 miles below Red Bridge State Park. A sign indicating "Danger–Rifle Range, Entering Impact Area," hanging on a wire crossing the river, warns boaters of the potential hazard. Make your presence known to any shooters who may be at this spot.

Access

Four miles west of La Grande, take exit 252 on Interstate 84. Go south on Oregon 244 for 0.1 mile. The take-out is on river left at Hilgard Junction State Park, either above or below the bridge. Proceed 7.5 miles west on Oregon 244 to Red Bridge State Park, the put-in.

Gauge

Grande Ronde River near Perry. The gauge is near the take-out.

T. R. Torgersen

201 Grande Ronde River Hilgard Junction State Park to Riverside City Park

Class: 2(3+); 3(4)	Length: 8.9 miles
Flow: 1500–6000 cfs; 7000 cfs	Character: road
Gradient: 25 fpm, PD	Season: rainy/snowmelt

This is a favorite conditioning and play run for local boaters. The river is wide and gentle at first. After a few miles of warm-up, a ledge called Snoose Falls nearly spans the river to form a good surfing wave. It also marks the beginning of intermittent rapids. The first significant rapids begin when the tall Interstate 84 bridge comes into view. Below the bridge is a series of splendid standing waves as the river veers to the right. Two bridges beyond is Vortex Rapid, a fine play spot and well-known spectator vantage for watching rafters and others get "eaten" in the curl. The last rapid, Riverside Rapid, is the most difficult on this run. Take out on the left immediately below the rapids. To avoid Riverside Rapid, take out just before the Spruce Street bridge.

Hazards

Vortex, below the third bridge, can flip a raft. Riverside Rapid, known by kayakers as Baum's Swimmin' Hole, should be scouted when parking the shuttle vehicle before the run. On the river, the sound of the rapids and the presence of the Spruce Street bridge forewarn of the two closely spaced drops and the large curl at the bottom on river right.

Access

The put-in is at Hilgard Junction State Park, Interstate 84, exit 252, west of La Grande. The take-out is in La Grande at Riverside City Park. Take Interstate 84 to exit 261 in La Grande. Proceed southwest. Turn right before the railroad underpass at the five-way intersection regulated by a traffic signal. Travel one block and take another right onto Spruce Street. Continue for about 1 mile to Riverside City Park.

Gauge

Grand Ronde River near Perry.

T. R. Torgersen

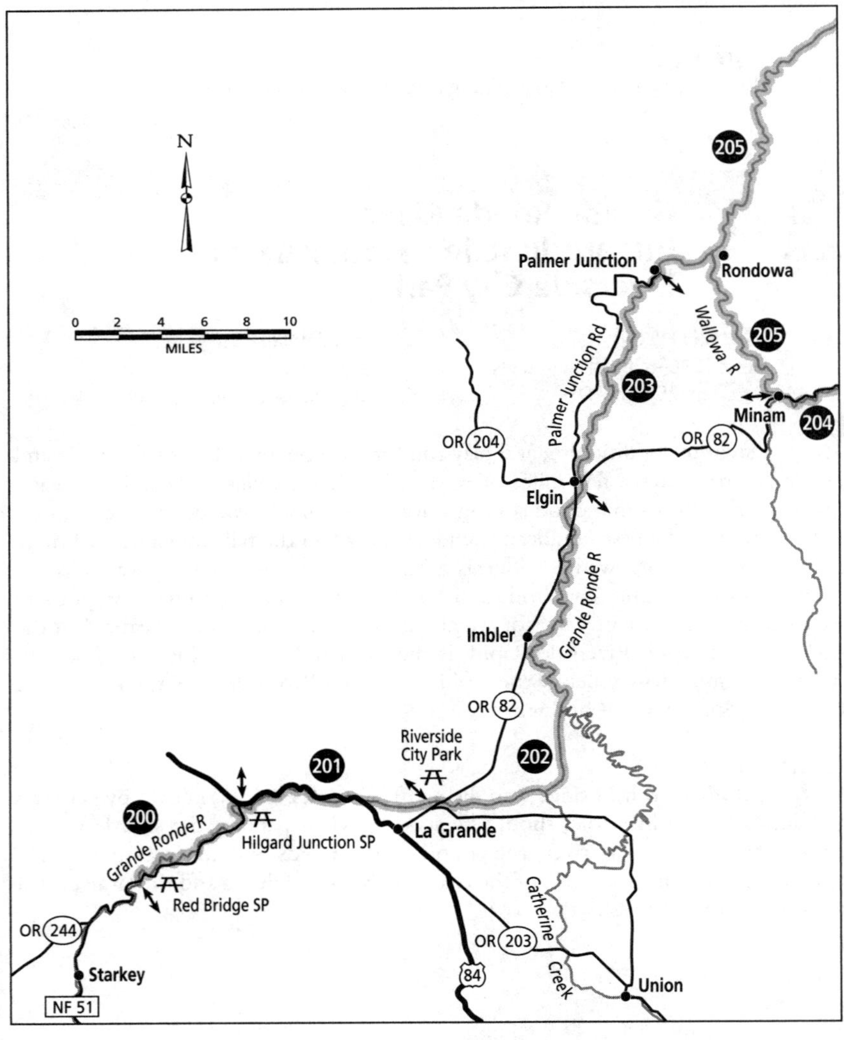

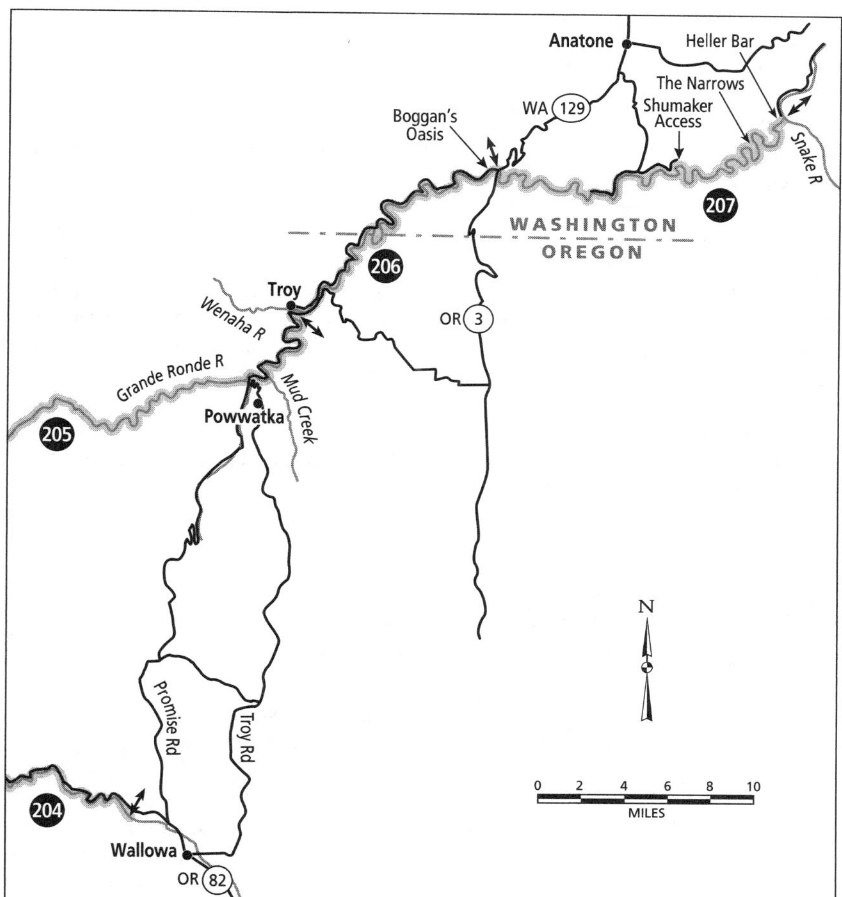

202 Grande Ronde River
Riverside City Park to Elgin

Class: 1	Length: 32 miles
Flow: 600–5000 cfs	Character: agricultural
Gradient: 4 fpm, C	Season: rainy/snowmelt

This gentle, slowly flowing stretch has appeal for leisurely day outings. The borders of the river abound with wildlife, including small mammals, waterfowl, and songbirds. In its meandering course through the broad, fertile Grande Ronde floodplain, the river is crossed intermittently by numerous county roads and lanes that grid the valley. This abundance of crossings permits an almost limitless variety of trip lengths.

Hazards

Be on the lookout for obstructing debris and barbed wire.

Access

To reach the put-in at Riverside City Park from Interstate 84, take exit 261 and proceed southwest, toward town. Turn right at a five-way intersection, go one block, and turn right on Spruce Street. Riverside City Park is about 1 mile farther on Spruce Street. The put-in is also accessible from Oregon 82 via either of the Interstate 84 exits in La Grande.

To reach the take-out in Elgin, take Oregon 82 north from Interstate 84 in La Grande. In Elgin, take Cedar Street east to Hu-Na-Ha City Park. The Wallowa-Whitman National Forest map shows road details for alternative put-ins and take-outs along this run in the Grande Ronde Valley.

Gauge

Grande Ronde River near Perry. Flows for this run may be difficult to estimate because of water diversions for agriculture.

T. R. Torgersen

203 Grande Ronde River Elgin to Palmer Junction

Class: 2(3); 2(4)	Length: 14.1 miles
Flow: 2000–5000 cfs; 8000 cfs	Character: agricultural; hilly
Gradient: 19 fpm, PD	Season: rainy/snowmelt

This run initially retains the agricultural and rangeland character of the Grand Ronde River: Riverside City Park to Elgin run. Within 5 miles of Elgin, the river descends into a deeper, narrower, V-shaped valley that characterizes the river's course for much of its remaining length to the Snake River. For a much longer trip, boaters may continue 3 miles to the confluence with the Wallowa River at Rondowa and from there, another 36 miles to Troy (see the Wallowa and Grande Ronde Rivers: Minam to Troy run). The former access point at Rondowa is on private property and is not available.

Hazards

Andy's Rapid occurs 4 miles from Elgin, just past a sharp S turn; scout it. Portage or line on the left, or run the normal route on the right.

Access

To reach the put-in from Interstate 84 in La Grande (at exit 261), take Oregon 82 north to Elgin. Take Cedar Street east at the south end of town to get to Hu-Na-Ha City Park.

For take-out, return to Oregon 82 (Eighth Avenue), go north to Division, west to Twelfth Avenue, north to Hartford Lane, then east on Hartford, which becomes Palmer Junction Road as it bends north. Follow Palmer Junction Road north for 12 miles to its end. Turn right on Moses Creek Lane, and go 2.6 miles. The take-out is at the primitive campsite on river left.

Gauge

Grande Ronde River near Perry. Use the gauge to estimate flows; it is far upstream. Also the flow is affected by agricultural diversions below the gauge. Visually check the levels at the put-in.

T. R. Torgersen

204 Wallowa River
Lower Diamond Lane to Minam

Class: 1–2	Length: 10.2 miles
Flow: 300–1000 cfs	Character: forest; road
Gradient: 27 fpm, C	Season: rainy/snowmelt

This run offers one of few possibilities for paddling in Eastern Oregon in early summer. The canyon is a scenic mix of ponderosa pines and grasslands. Here, the river riffles quickly, as can be seen from Oregon 82, which follows alongside much of the way. This reach can be added to the classic Minam–Troy overnight trip on the Wallowa and Grande Ronde, pushing the distance up to 57 miles to Troy and up to 101 miles if you continue on to Heller Bar on the Snake.

Hazards

Watch for barbed-wire fences, although none were there at last count.

Access

For the highest put-in without likely fence problems, take Oregon 82 west from the town of Wallowa for 3 miles, turn south on Lower Diamond Lane, and go 0.3 miles to the bridge, with informal access on upper river right. Two roadside-rest pulloffs are also good between there and Minam. Take out on the left just below the Oregon 82 bridge at Minam.

Gauge

Minam River at Minam. The Wallowa River above the Minam confluence should be comparable. Flows are usually boatable into early July.

Tim Palmer

205 ★ Wallowa River/Grande Ronde River Minam to Troy

Class: 2; 3	Length: 46.3 miles
Flow: 1000–3800 cfs; 5000–12,000 cfs	Character: forested canyon
Gradient: 21 fpm, C	Season: year-round

This is the popular wilderness run of the Wallowa/Grande Ronde. Boaters often spend two or three nights camping on the river. This section is a designated Wild and Scenic River and is administered jointly by the BLM, Oregon Parks and Recreation Department, and US Forest Service.

Use the link www.tinyurl.com/clmy9ze or use your Internet browser to search for "Wallowa and Grande Ronde Wild and Scenic Rivers Details" to obtain information about the river, regulations, permits, and other details. A self-issue permit station is located at Minam. You can obtain an excellent waterproof map and boater's guide from the BLM office in Baker City (see Appendix B). The BLM patrols the river from Minam to the Snake.

Campsites are pleasant and abundant, except on Memorial Day and Fourth of July weekends, when hundreds of boaters appear. This description is dedicated to Tu-eka-kas and Hin-mah-too-yah-lat-kekt, who, along with other Nez Percé tribal members, respected the land and had the wisdom never to abuse a river or to wish that they could stop it from flowing. They called the Wallowa/Grande Ronde rivers Welleweah—"River that Flows into the Far Beyond."

A rolling plateau makes up the canyon rim. The canyon walls present tiers of horizontal lava flows that occurred during the Miocene epoch. These stratified formations are the oldest exposed rocks in the canyon and contain pillars, spires, window holes, and caves. Abstruse dikes and columnar basalts add to the geological variety.

Except at high flows, this stretch is reasonably well-suited to intermediate boaters. It usually has enough water for rafts until August, and sometimes all year. The month of May normally has the highest mean flows, while September sees the lowest flows. In very low water (700–1000 cfs), anticipate encounters with rocks. Rafters and drift boaters should be prepared to do a lot of pushing and tugging. Flows of about 2000 cfs are optimum for open canoes. Kayakers find flows of about 5000 cfs optimum. From 10,000 to 15,000 cfs, eddies become rare, the current is fast, and large standing waves develop into great rides for dories, rafts, kayaks, and expertly handled canoes. At these volumes, swimmers would experience a long, cold endeavor to gain shore or re-enter a craft. The trip is normally done with two nights of camping on the river, but at flows above 5000 cfs, this run can be a day trip.

The weather begins to warm up in June, but snow and rain are possible in late May and early June. December, January, and February are very cold. The river can freeze during these months, but they are good times for observing winter populations of bald eagles and big game animals. In summer, shorebirds such as sandpipers and killdeer nest in the same areas that people use for camping. Be on the lookout for nests to avoid destroying them. Bear Creek seems to have the highest incidence of rattlesnake sightings, and occasionally scorpions are seen. Treat or boil drinking water. These lower river sections receive heavy use. The carry-out method for solid human waste is required. Also, fire pans are required.

The put-in at Minam is at the confluence of the Minam River with the Wallowa River. The first 10 miles of the run are on the Wallowa River, which merges with the Grande Ronde River at Rondowa. The initial 6 miles below Minam contain nearly continuous rapids with few eddies. Below the put-in 1.5 miles is the Minam Roller. The roller develops at about 3000 cfs and becomes a great surfing hole at about 5000 cfs. Beyond this volume, the roller becomes a boat eater and thrasher because of the pronounced backwash. This hole consumes swimmers, who may not surface until 30 feet downstream. This rapid is located on the first major right bend in the river and is recognized by several large basalt rocks on river left. At flows exceeding 5000 cfs, open boats should avoid the Minam Roller by holding to the right bank.

Minam State Recreation Area is 2 miles from the put-in. Because of its campground, this is a popular alternative put-in. A mile farther down is Red Rock Rapid (or House Rock Drop). The chute is to the left of a house-size boulder that fell into the river during construction of the railroad. Stay close to the left side of the rock to avoid the large hole farther left.

At 5 miles from the put-in, Blind Falls (also called Vincent Falls), class 2–3, may surprise many boaters. A rock garden leads into a ledge featuring a hole that is difficult to see. Look for it 0.5 mile below railroad marker 42, after catching a glimpse of a powerline; it's just after a left bend. A railroad bridge is located at the confluence of the Wallowa with the Grande Ronde. The confluence is at RM 81.5 on the Grande Ronde River. (RM is river mile.) Many nice campsites exist for many miles below here. Sheep Creek Rapid occurs at RM 79.5. At RM 69.6, there's a long boulder garden rapid known as Martin's Misery.

Many other rapids, some of which lead into headwalls, occur between here and Wildcat Creek at RM 53.4. Just below Wildcat Creek, the unpaved road from Troy crosses the river on the Powwatka bridge. Two unimproved take-outs are available on the right, above and below the bridge. An alternative take-out, with a ramp and sanitary facilities, is found 0.5 mile downstream from the bridge on the left opposite Mud Creek at river mile 52. The 8 miles to Troy are somewhat slower than the upstream miles. The unimproved take-out is on the right at the green bridge (foot traffic only) at Troy, RM 45.4.

Hazards

The Minam Roller can swamp or flip boats at high water. Blind Falls (Vincent Falls) is difficult to see when it's being approached. It develops a keeper hole at low water. It and Sheep Creek Rapid should be approached with caution or scouted. Most of the rapids require more maneuvering at lower water.

Access

To reach the put-in from Interstate 84 in La Grande, take Oregon 82 north to Minam. The put-ins are near the store on the south (left) side of the river bridge at Minam. One of the put-ins is an Oregon Parks and Recreation site; the put-in at the store is private, for shuttle patrons only. An alternative put-in is at Minam State Recreation Area about 2 miles downstream; however, it has no boat ramp. This recreation area, with a campground, is at the end of a gravel road along the left bank of the river.

There are three or more routes to the take-outs. Go east on Oregon 82 to Enterprise, then take Oregon 3 north for 32 miles. Turn left at the Flora–Troy junction and follow the signs to Troy (about 2.5 hours driving time). The unpaved part of this route gets rough in spring and summer, slick when wet, and snow-covered with the onset of colder weather. A longer, three-hour, mostly paved route goes similarly via Enterprise to Oregon 3 and Washington 129 to the bridge crossing the Grande Ronde at Boggan's Oasis café. Go upriver on Troy Road to Troy, the Mud Creek recreation site, or the Powwatka bridge. A third, mostly unpaved route to the Powwatka bridge is via the Wildcat Creek road, which can be rough, dusty, or muddy and slow; ask the locals what they know. Shuttle service is available; call the Minam Store (541-437-1111).

Gauge
Grande Ronde River at Troy.

Gary Lane and T. R. Torgersen

206 Grande Ronde River
Troy to Boggan's Oasis

Class: 2; 2+(3)	Length: 19.2 miles
Flow: 1400–3500 cfs; 5000–12,000 cfs	Character: canyon; roaded
Gradient: 17 fpm, C	Season: year-round

Below the put-in at Troy, at RM 45.4 (RM is river-mile), the lines of trees spilling over the canyon rim begin to withdraw from the more arid side slopes, and the canyon becomes progressively steeper and drier. The brushy draws and grassy rimrocks are frequented by mule deer instead of the elk that are dominant upriver. A few ranches are established along the river, connected by a road that parallels the run for the entire distance. Campsites are fewer. At RM 38.7, one passes into Washington state. A café (with great milkshakes) and a small park (with outhouses and a boat ramp) greet boaters at Boggan's Oasis at RM 26.2.

"The Wallowa and Grande Ronde Rivers Boater's Guide" offers helpful information (see Appendix B).

Hazards
High flows create some powerful wave trains and strong headwall crosscurrents. Such places are accompanied by surging boils and large whirlpools that may require some heavy stroking to avoid.

Access

To reach the put-in, and for shuttle services and other river-running details, see the Wallowa and Grande Ronde Rivers: Minam to Troy run.

The take-out is at Boggan's Oasis café and lodge on Washington 129/Oregon 3 between Enterprise, Oregon, and Lewiston, Idaho. The highway winds steeply down to the bridge that crosses the Grande Ronde at the café. The infamous Rattlesnake Grade claws its way tortuously north out of the river canyon from here. A good all-weather route that follows the river's left bank to Troy and the Powwatka bridge is found immediately off the northeast end of the bridge.

Gauge

Grande Ronde River at Troy.

Gary Lane and T. R. Torgersen

207 Grande Ronde River
Boggan's Oasis to Snake River (Heller Bar)

Class: 2(4); 3(4)	Length: 26.6 miles
Flow: 1400–3500 cfs; 5000–12,000 cfs	Character: valley desert
Gradient: 15 fpm, PD	Season: year-round

Below Boggan's Oasis, the canyon becomes increasingly arid and devoid of coniferous forest. Semidesert vegetation, characterized by hackberry trees and prickly pear cactus, becomes common. This river run is not known for its inviting campsites. Overnighters in the canyon could encounter a rattlesnake, scorpion, or black widow spider.

The put-in is at RM 26.2 (RM is river-mile). Some of the better campsites are found within the first 10 miles. At low water, a few class 2 rapids occur. At high water, several class 2 and 3 rapids accompany some very large, powerful eddies. The Narrows, class 4, is toward the end of the run and is considerably more difficult than the other rapids.

Slippery Creek, at RM 10, is a major tributary that enters from the left. It's about 5 more miles to The Narrows, the most difficult rapid on this stretch. The approach is marked by a big natural X-like erosion of soil on the left, one bend above the rapids. Some imagination must be used to see the X. Look a little above eye level on an open hillside near the apex of the horseshoe bend. The appearance of powerlines as the river bends right warns of The Narrows below.

Irregular ledges and volcanic debris that contort the river as it flows through a cut in solid basalt create the rapids in The Narrows. The Narrows normally has two sections. The upper section, at RM 4.6, is a long set of irregular waves and holes. The second section is about 100–150 yards farther downstream, where most of the river funnels left to form a large, cresting, back-curling wave. The size of this curler varies widely with water level, but it has eaten many a craft. At flows above 10,000 cfs or so, additional cresting waves develop immediately below the curler. These waves can become the nastiest part of The Narrows. Farther on, a turbulent class 2+ to 3 drop, Bridge Rapid (RM 3), is found just above the bridge. The take-out is at Heller Bar on the Snake River, 0.3 mile below the confluence with the Grande Ronde.

Use the link www.tinyurl.com/clmy9ze or use your Internet browser to search for "Wallowa and Grande Ronde Wild and Scenic Rivers Details" to obtain information about the river, regulations, permits, and other details. You can obtain an excellent waterproof map and boater's guide from the BLM office at Baker City (see Appendix B). The BLM patrols the river from Minam to the Snake.

Hazards

The Narrows, class 4, is considerably more difficult than the other rapids. Scout from either bank. Be on the alert for rattlesnakes when scouting.

Access

The put-in, with its self-issue permit station, is at Boggan's Oasis, where Washington 129 crosses the Grande Ronde (see the Grande Ronde River: Troy to Boggan's Oasis run). This put-in is a partially improved Washington Department of Fish and Wildlife recreation site. An alternative put-in is at Shumaker Access, about 8 miles downstream from Boggan's Oasis. Obtain local knowledge to get to the steep, rough road that will get you to Shumaker from the top of the north side of the canyon.

To reach the take-out, drive north on Washington 129 through Anatone to the town of Asotin, then upstream along the Snake River to the Heller Bar boat ramp. Shuttles can be arranged through Boggan's Oasis (509-256-3372).

Gauge

Grand Ronde River at Troy.

Gary Lane

Snake River

208 ★ Snake River
Hells Canyon Dam to Heller Bar

Class: 3(5)	Length: 79.2 miles
Flow: 6000–60,000 cfs	Character: desert canyon; roadless
Gradient: 8 fpm, PD	Season: year-round

Multiday river trips on the Snake feature large sandy beaches, hiking opportunities with good trails, and more than 200 archaeological sites to visit. The Snake is typically a pool-drop river, so there is usually plenty of time to retrieve flipped boats and swimmers below the major rapids, if the water flows are between 6000

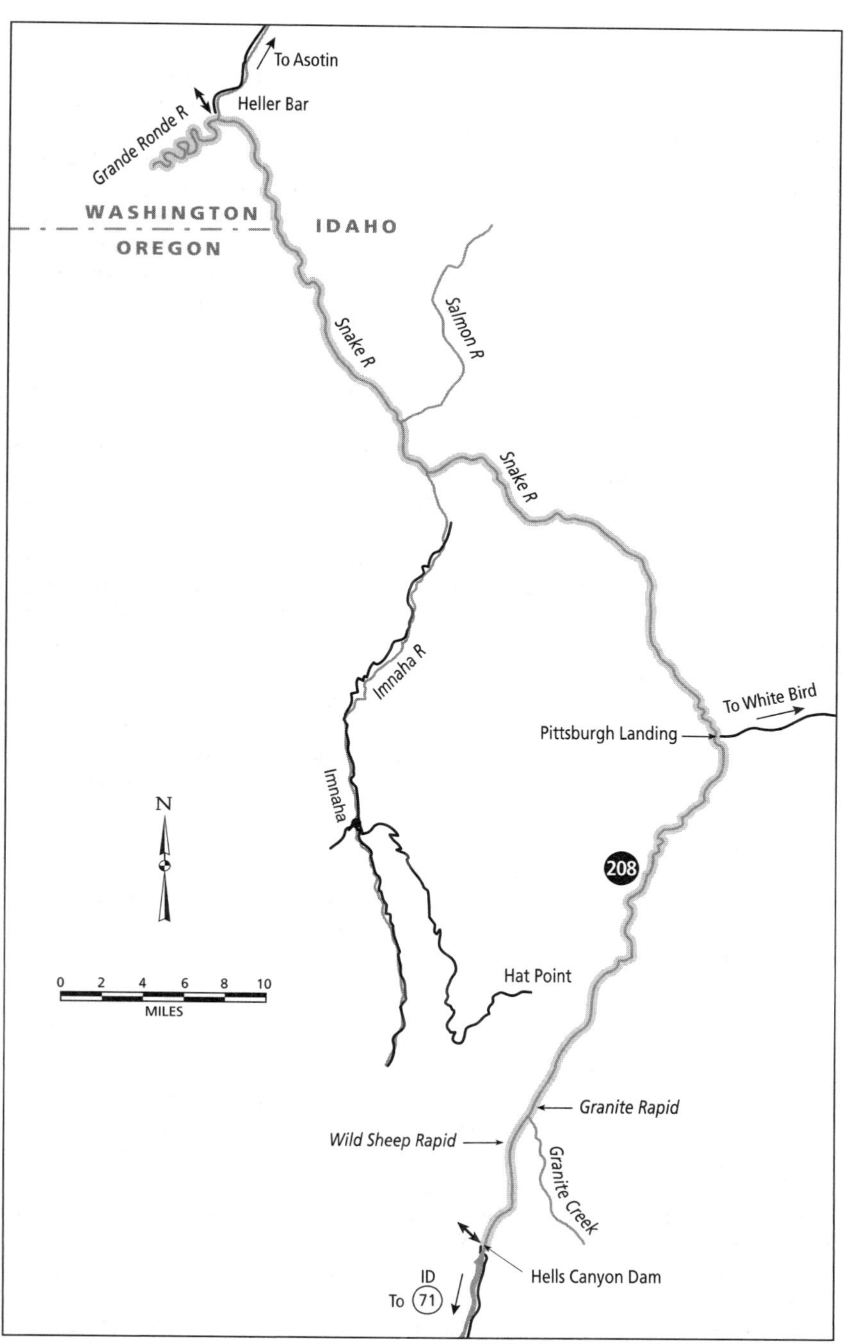
To Asotin
Heller Bar
Grande Ronde R
WASHINGTON
OREGON
IDAHO
Snake R
Salmon R
Snake R
Imnaha R
Imnaha
To White Bird
Pittsburgh Landing
208
N
Hat Point
0 2 4 6 8 10
MILES
Granite Rapid
Wild Sheep Rapid
Granite Creek
Hells Canyon Dam
ID
To 71

and 8000 cfs. Skilled river runners find tremendous challenge as the water level increases and the big drops become bigger, the water pushier, and the flow much faster. The biggest water is encountered at about 20,000 cfs; above this level, the rapids begin to wash out slightly while strong eddy lines and currents begin to develop. Flows in the spring and early summer can easily reach 60,000 cfs at the put-in and may double after the Salmon enters at 61 miles from the put-in.

Late-spring trips are a real treat; the canyon is still green, the weather is usually pleasant. Summer is paradise: hot days and 70-degree water. Into late September and early October, the weather remains pleasant, the water cools a bit, and quick squalls can pop up. Year-round upstream winds can be encountered; it is best to boat in the morning to avoid them.

The two major rapids on the Snake can be run by intermediate boaters with a little guidance from skilled boaters. The first rapid is Wild Sheep, located not quite 6 miles from the put-in. Look for a large, lone pine tree on the left and take out. A trail located up the left bank leads to a good scouting point. At low water, work either left or right of exposed rocks at the top before working to the center of the river for the final drop. The large, diagonal waves from the left at the bottom can easily flip an 18-foot raft if not hit straight on.

Downstream about 2 miles is Granite Rapid. The best scouting is from river right, where boaters can see the favored route: a tongue just right of center. Optional routes depend upon skill and size of boat. After Granite Rapid, Waterspout and Rush Creek are other major rapids. Many miles of river with class 2–3 rapids, towering canyon walls, and possible wildlife sightings lie ahead.

Permits are required year-round. An excellent map and boater's guide is published by the BLM (see Appendix B). Other useful information about the river and the permitting process can be found at the Wallowa-Whitman National Forest website. Search online for "Wild and Scenic Snake River Private Floatboat Reservations."

Hazards

Wild Sheep and Granite rapids have big waves and holes that can flip a large raft. Scout both. Beware of jet boats on the river, especially during the fall hunting season. Flows can fluctuate steeply every day due to power generation releases; watch your gear so that it doesn't float away.

Access

The put-in is located just below the Hells Canyon Dam, where a BLM ranger checks permits. The BLM can supply permit holders with a list of people who run vehicle shuttles, or you can run your own. From Interstate 84 in Eastern Oregon, between Huntington and Ontario, take any of several exits to US 95 in Western Idaho, and proceed north to Weiser. From Weiser, drive 31 miles north on US 95 to Cambridge, then turn left onto Idaho 71 and continue 29 miles to the dam.

To reach the Heller Bar take-out, return to US 95 and go north to Lewiston; cross the Snake River to Clarkston, Washington. Go south on Washington 129 to Asotin, Washington. Go straight through town and continue upriver along the Snake for 21 miles to Heller Bar. The take-out is a very convenient concrete ramp. An alternative to running the lower section of the Snake is to take out at Pittsburgh Landing, 31.5 miles downstream from Hells Canyon Dam.

To reach the Pittsburgh Landing take-out, return to US 95 and go north to White Bird. Cross the Salmon River and continue west on Deer Creek Road for about 18 steep, curvy miles to Pittsburgh Landing.

Gauge

Snake River below Hells Canyon Dam. The combined flow of the Snake and Salmon rivers is given by the gauge: Snake River near Anatone, Washington.

Ron Mattson

Owyhee River and Tributaries

209 East Fork Owyhee River
Garat Crossing to Three Forks

Class: 3+(4)(6) P	Length: 75 miles
Flow: 600–6000 cfs	Character: remote desert canyon
Gradient: 11 fpm, PD	Season: snowmelt

The East Fork Owyhee takes you on a trip through history and geology in the remote desert canyons where Oregon, Idaho, and Nevada meet. There are mile-long stretches where sheer vertical walls adorned with hoodoos drop to the river. There are historic sites to visit and side canyons to explore. Bald Mountain Canyon is a superb hike. In some areas, it is possible to hike up to the canyon rim for spectacular vistas of the Owyhee Mountains. Birds abound, but boaters are unlikely to see other humans. Because of the challenges and the remoteness, the trip requires solid class 3 paddling skills and thorough preparation for wilderness expeditions. There is a lot of flatwater, particularly in the Bald Mountain reach and below the West Little Owyhee. Given the portages, six nights out is a comfortable time to allocate. While there is little or no competition for campsites, some stretches have few usable sites.

Most of the rapids are easy class 1 and 2 whitewater, with a few class 3 rapids. Owyhee Falls, class 6, about 33 miles into the trip, is a mandatory portage. Portage right at lower water, through the boulders, and put in just above a class 3 drop. At higher water, the more difficult left portage must be used. Be aware that 2 miles farther, there is a 3+ drop just above Thread-the-Needle. Thread-the-Needle is a boulder choke that is rated class 4 when the water goes over it, but at lower levels, it is a sieve. It will likely require a portage. Cabin Rapid, located about 12 miles below the confluence with the South Fork, is a long class 4 drop. Scout from the house-size rocks on river right. Cable Rapid, 2 miles below Cabin, is class 4, with the most difficult part at the very bottom. Again, scout right. On the left, 7 miles downstream, is the abandoned Five-Bar Ranch.

The crowning glory is Tudor Warm Springs, located about 2 miles upstream of the take-out. It is truly a world-class spa. Don't miss it, you will have earned it. A gravel bar on the left provides a good camp 0.2 mile above the warm spring.

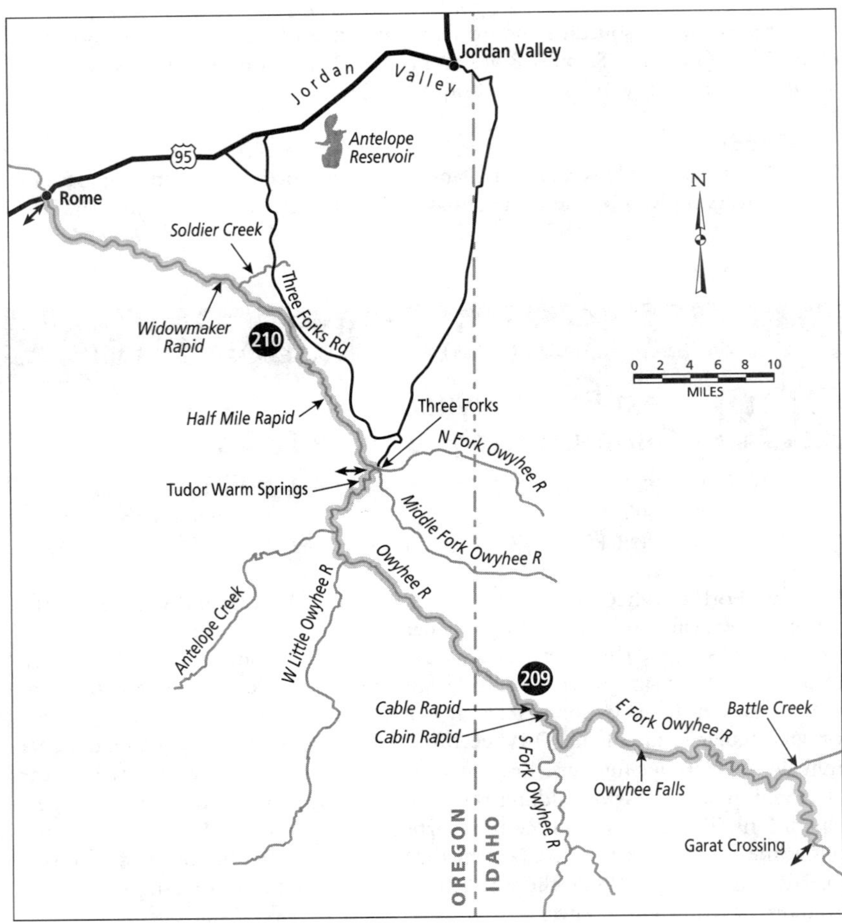

There is more to know about this remarkable wilderness river than can be reported here. While planning, contact the BLM office in Boise, Idaho (208-384-3300), for maps and information about access, river conditions, and regulations on river use. Self-issue permits are required. An excellent resource written by the BLM is also found online: the "Owyhee, Bruneau and Jarbidge Wild and Scenic Rivers Boating Guide." It includes the BLM's requirements for paddling the river and useful maps.

Hazards

The two mandatory portages and two probable portages (Cable and Cabin rapids) present difficulties. Use extreme care approaching the portage of Owyhee Falls; the water is fast, and the entry is on a blind left turn. The canyon is in very remote desert country, some of the most remote in the Great Basin. Overland rescue would be difficult, but it would be made easier with use of a detailed map of the primitive roads in the area. Purify water and watch for rattlesnakes.

Access

On some maps, the river is labeled as the East Fork of the Owyhee, and on other maps it is simply the Owyhee. Same river, same trip. Trips are likely to start in Jordan Valley, Oregon, the town nearest Garat Crossing and one providing a glimpse of Basque culture. Take Interstate 84 east into Idaho, turn south onto US 95, and continue 80 miles. Jordan Valley can also be reached from Central Oregon via US 20 or US 395 to Burns. From Burns, take Oregon 78 southeast to US 95, turn left onto US 95, and continue 46 miles to Jordan Valley.

To reach the take-out from Jordan Valley (where some boaters set up a shuttle or meet a driver), drive 2 miles east, turn right onto a secondary road, and proceed 37 miles south to Three Forks. (Alternatively, access Three Forks Road leading south from US 95 about 16 miles east of Rome.) The final 2-mile pitch down into the canyon is steep and rough. The take-out is possible without four-wheel drive, unless it rains.

To reach the put-in at Garat Crossing, from Jordan Valley, drive north on US 95 about 45 miles, go east to Marsing, then turn south on Idaho 78, and then south again onto Idaho 51 to Riddle. South of Riddle, you enter the Duck Valley Indian Reservation. Stop and request permission to drive on backroads crossing tribal land. Soon you enter the state of Nevada; turn right 0.8 mile past the state line. Proceed 6 miles, turn left, then go about 20 miles more to Garat Crossing, Idaho. Garat Crossing is a gas pipeline crossing. Either slide your boats down from the rim or take one of the two possible tracks down to the river. A highly capable four-wheel-drive rig is recommended for this part of the trip.

For more information on road conditions or to arrange a shuttle, inquire with Jordan Valley or Caldwell, Idaho, shuttle drivers.

Gauge

Owyhee River at Rome. The flow on the run itself is lower than the flow at the gauge, which is far downstream. All the cfs numbers listed here are gauge numbers. For a most enjoyable run, catch the river as it drops through about 1500 cfs. However, even 600 cfs is not too low to make this run. Optimum flows may occur as early as the first week of May or as late as the third week of June.

Dick Sisson, Paul Norman, and Alex McNeily

210 ★ Owyhee River
Three Forks to Rome

Class: 4(5)	Length: 36.5 miles
Flow: 1200–8000 cfs	Character: inaccessible gorge; desert
Gradient: 15 fpm, PD	Season: snowmelt

The canyon of the Owyhee River in this section can be as deep as 3000 feet from river to rim. In many places, the first layer of sheer basalt cliffs may tower 1000 feet directly upward from the river's surface. The arid countryside has little vegetation and no human inhabitants. There are no access roads or trails between the put-in and take-out, although in a few places a person could climb out of the canyon in an emergency. The canyon has one of the densest rattlesnake populations in Oregon. Camping areas are not nearly as plentiful here as on the Owyhee River: Rome to Leslie Gulch run or on most other Eastern Oregon rivers. Plan plenty of time for the necessary scouting of rapids and for savoring the isolated river canyon. The normal trip entails two or three overnights.

While it's likely the weather conditions will be dry and hot during April and May, when this stretch is high enough to run, the changeable nature of weather in this region may yield quick transitions to rain, cold, and even snow. Be prepared.

Three Forks, the put-in, is a slow-flowing pool. As the canyon narrows about 1.5 miles from the put-in, the rapids pick up to class 2, and The Ledge, class 4, is approached. The Ledge consists of several narrow chutes between boulders. Land near the base of large rocks on left to scout. About 400 yards of class 4 boulder garden follow. A mile below The Ledge, a warm spring is downstream of the site of an abandoned sheepherder's cabin on the right, and a hot spring is on river left 100 yards farther down. Several class 2 rapids appear in another 2.5 miles.

At RM 8.5 (RM is river-mile), after several class 2–3 rapids, look for a bend to the right. Stop before the bend and scout Half Mile Rapid, class 4+. This rapid has an upper section and a lower section, with a short class 2 pool in between. Scout from the right initially. At low water, the lower section becomes extremely rocky. About 100 feet upstream from the bottom of this rapid at the river's edge on the right bank is a large boulder (among many large boulders) with petroglyphs exposed on its top surface.

It is only 100 yards to the next major rapids, Raft Flip Drop (river mile 9.8). Raft Flip Drop, class 3–4, can be sneaked by kayaks on the left through the small left channel at high water levels, but there is a deceptively powerful roller at the bottom of the main chute that can flip a raft. Several class 3- rapids are found in the next 5 miles. Subtle Hole (RM 14), class 3+, is longer than Raft Flip Drop. It leads into Bombshelter Drop, class 3, at RM 14.5. A large cave on the left, just above river level, is a possible campsite. A mile later is Shark's Tooth Rapid (RM 16), class 3. This is followed 1 mile later by several class 2 rapids. Soldier Creek, at RM 18, enters from the right, with an extensive gravel bar.

The next mile brings springs on the right and several class 3 rapids among boulders in a steep canyon located 100 yards above Widowmaker, class 5 (RM 19.8). The approach to Widowmaker is identified by a 200-yard stretch of straight, narrow canyon. Ahead, the river seems to disappear among large boulders. At flows below 2000 cfs, competent boaters may run the class 3 lead-in rapid before stopping to scout Widowmaker, but all others should land on the right above this class 3 rapid. Although at levels below 1800 cfs, Widowmaker looks very tempting to kayakers, a portage is highly recommended. The portage is difficult on either side, but is usually done on the right. The drop from the class 3 rapid to the bottom of Widowmaker is about 20 feet, with Widowmaker itself having about a 10-foot drop.

Numerous class 2 and some class 3 rapids characterize the next 8 miles. Small beaches occasionally dot the river banks. At RM 26.5 are class 2+ rapids; beyond, the canyon begins to open up. Several camping beaches and flatwater can be found for the next 2 miles. The last rapid (RM 31), class 2, is followed by riffles and flatwater, as the canyon rim fades away. The Rome boat ramp is on the right at RM 36.5.

Maps, access information, permit requirements, and other important information can be found online. Search for "Owyhee, Bruneau and Jarbidge Wild and Scenic Rivers Boating Guide." It includes the BLM's requirements for paddling the river, history, geology and useful maps.

Hazards

This pool-drop river is much more difficult than the gradient of 22 fpm implies. A number of class 4 rapids of varying length and one class 5 rapid await the boater. Because of the remoteness of the canyon and the extreme difficulty of hiking out, river travelers must be conservative on this run. The road to the put-in becomes impassable after a rain. When scouting along the riverbank, be alert for rattlesnakes.

Access

From Burns in Central Oregon, take Oregon 78 southeast to US 95, turn left onto US 95, and continue 13 miles to Rome. The take-out is located about 0.2 mile upstream from the Rome bridge off US 95 on the east bank. A large parking area, boat ramp, and toilets are there. Shuttle service can be obtained from local drivers in either Jordan Valley or Caldwell, Idaho.

To reach the put-in from Rome, drive 16 miles east on US 95 to a dirt road marked "Three Forks Road." Head south 35 miles, then descend to the river. The dirt road, especially the steep final mile, can be muddy and impassable during wet weather.

Gauge

Owyhee River at Rome. Although 1200 cfs is the normal minimum runnable flow, it has been run, with steep, rock-scraping drops, as low as 400 cfs.

Rob Blickensderfer and WKCC Editors

211 ★ Owyhee River
Rome to Leslie Gulch

Class: 3(4)		Length: 67.2 miles	
Flow: 1000–4000 cfs		Character: roadless; desert	
Gradient: 11 fpm, PD		Season: snowmelt	

This run on the Owyhee has an interestingly diverse landscape. The canyon, in general, is broad and shallow, although several stretches are narrow and steep-walled. The predominant basalts found in the upper canyon are interbedded with rhyolitic ash and sediments, which add various shades of white, red, green, and black to the canyon walls. Lambert Rocks are colorful badlands eroded from these sediments.

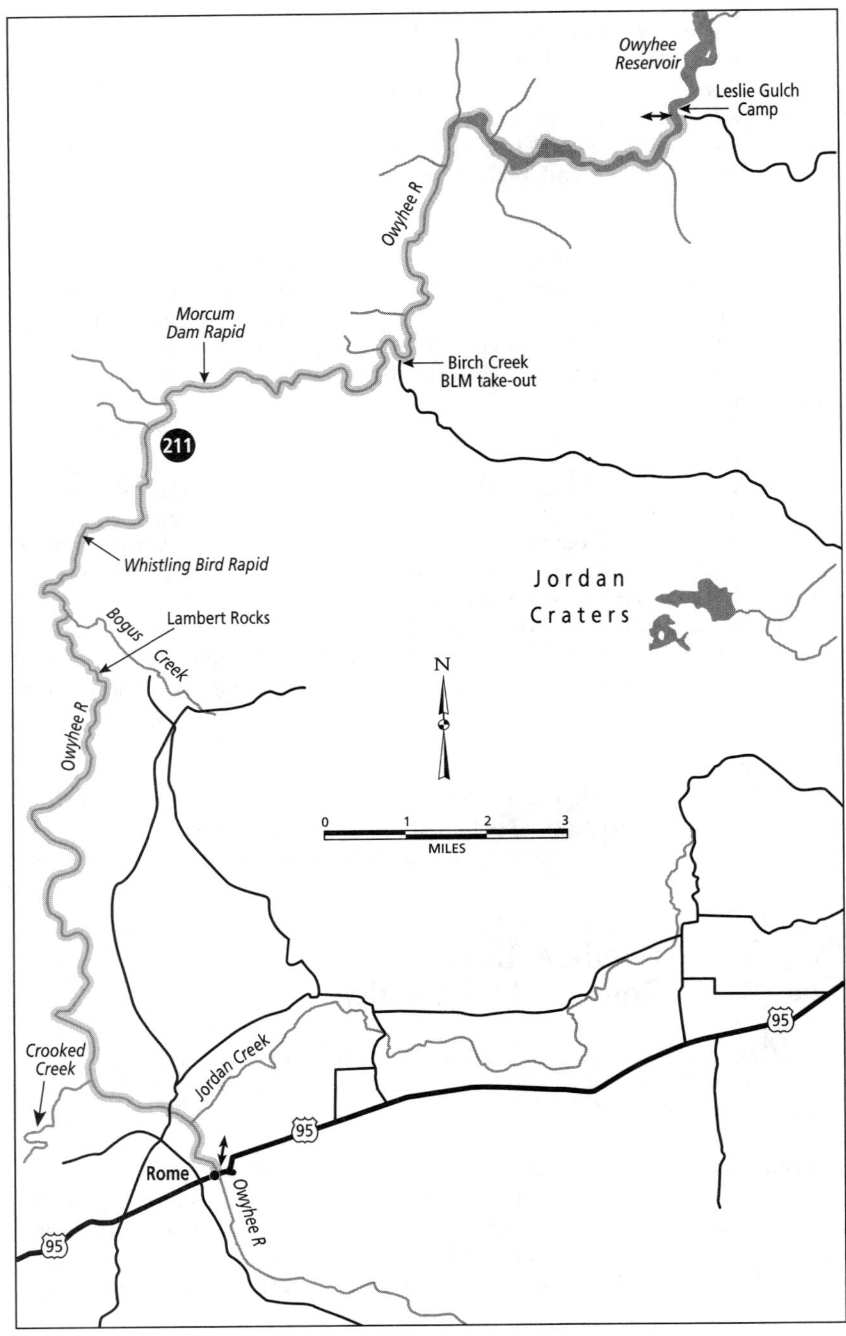

Owyhee Reservoir
Leslie Gulch Camp
Owyhee R
Morcum Dam Rapid
Birch Creek BLM take-out
211
Whistling Bird Rapid
Lambert Rocks
Bogus Creek
Owyhee R
Jordan Craters
N
0 1 2 3
MILES
Crooked Creek
Jordan Creek
95
95
Rome
Owyhee R

Because the Owyhee depends on snowmelt, the boating season is short and variable. It is usually runnable during April and May. In some years, the season may extend into early June, while in other years it may end by mid-May. The weather is also undependable, with temperatures ranging from freezing to one hundred degrees Fahrenheit and higher. Be prepared for rain or drought. The normal trip is four or five overnights. The rapids on this run are mostly class 2, making it a nice river for intermediate kayakers and rafters. However, the few class 3 and 4 rapids and the remoteness of the river demand that experienced boaters accompany less skilled boaters.

Beyond the Rome put-in, at RM 6.2 (RM is river-mile), Crooked Creek comes in on the left, marking the start of the canyon. About 6 miles below Crooked Creek is Upset Rapid, class 3, followed by Bull's Eye, class 2–3. Artillery Rapid (RM 21.1), is a straightforward class 3. After the beautiful Lambert Rocks, Bogus Creek Falls is seen on the right at RM 27.2. Another 1.5 miles farther is Dog Leg Rapid, class 3. About 1.5 miles below Dog Leg start looking for class 3+ to 4- Whistling Bird Rapid, at RM 31.

Whistling Bird is preceded by a large rock wall located 0.5 mile upstream of the rapid on the left. A dry wash on the left, a rock face and slab on the right, and the noise of the rapid mark its location. Whistling Bird Rapid should be scouted on the left by those unfamiliar with it. The current washes into a large slab that has fallen from the canyon wall, which should be avoided by aggressively moving to the left. This move becomes increasingly difficult at lower flows.

In 2.5 miles, Montgomery Rapid (RM 32.5), class 3, is located in a steep-walled canyon, after a left turn followed by a pool. It may be tricky for unsuspecting boaters at low water levels. The river drops and turns right, pushing boats toward a rock on the left. High water provides plenty of room to maneuver. About 5 miles below Montgomery Rapid is Nuisance Rapid. At low water (below 800 cfs), the right channel can require precise maneuvering. Just below Nuisance is Morcum Dam Rapid (RM 38.5). Most of the old dam has been washed away, but be careful at low water.

A campsite at Upper Greeley Bar allows access to a hot spring on the left at RM 44. At RM 48.5, pass by the Birch Creek Historic Ranch, followed shortly by a waterwheel and the Birch Creek take-out on the right at RM 49.5. For those continuing on, slack water begins around RM 54 when the reservoir is full. Owyhee Reservoir, an 8- to 12-mile flat stretch, is the toughest part of this run. Without a headwind, plan a minimum paddle time of four hours. Lazier folks (some might say smarter) may wish to arrange beforehand for a tow (see Access). Leslie Gulch comes in on the right where the lake bends left at mile 67.

Maps, access information, permit requirements, and other important information can be found online. Search for "Owyhee, Bruneau and Jarbidge Wild and Scenic Rivers Boating Guide." The guide includes the BLM's requirements for paddling the river, history, geology and useful maps. Additional information, including a waterproof river map, can be obtained from the BLM office in Vale (451-473-3144).

A camp with a magical view, lower Owyhee River (Mark Scantlebury)

Hazards

Scout Whistling Bird Rapid to avoid the large slab rock; scout Nuisance Rapid at low water. Be prepared for changeable weather as well as rattlesnakes.

Access

Shuttle service may be obtained from several local sources. Ask the BLM office in Vale for a list of recommended shuttle drivers. Some shuttle drivers can also arrange for a tow along Owyhee Reservoir to the Leslie Gulch take-out. An alternative take-out that avoids the slack water on the reservoir is the BLM boat ramp at Birch Creek.

For directions to Rome, see the run Owyhee River: Three Forks to Rome. The shuttle routes for both take-out options go through Jordan Valley. From Rome, take US 95 east 32 miles to Jordan Valley. To reach the Leslie Gulch take-out, go north from Jordan Valley on US 95 for 18 miles and then west on Succor and Leslie Gulch roads for 24 miles to the boat ramp. To reach the Birch Creek take-out, go north from Jordan Valley on US 95 for 8 miles and then west on Cow Creek and Birch Creek roads for 28 miles to the river (four-wheel drive recommended). Each access road may be impassable during wet conditions.

Gauge

Owyhee River near Rome. A flow of 1000 cfs is considered minimum, but the river has been floated as low as 400 cfs. Over 8000 cfs, big water hydraulics, large waves, and holes are found.

Dan Valens, Lance Stein, and WKCC Editors

Opposite: *Two share the wave* (Kate Howell)

Coastal Surf Kayaking

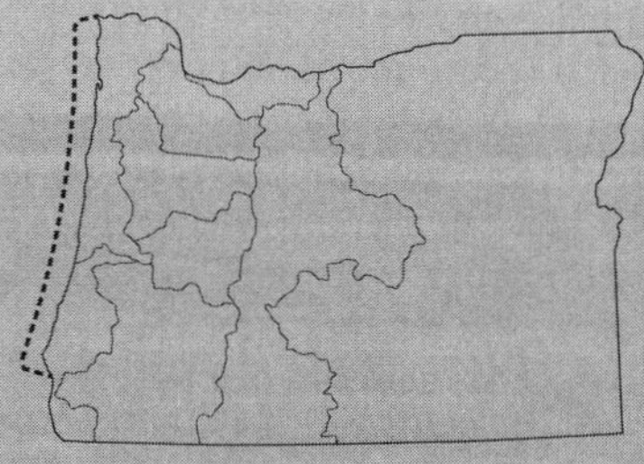

Region 10

Riding ocean waves in kayak, surf shoe, or surf ski is a thrilling form of whitewater boating that requires knowledge of ocean conditions, strong swimming skills, and suitable equipment. Rugged headlands, expansive beaches, and direct exposure to North Pacific ocean swells make the Oregon Coast one of the most spectacular surfing areas in North America. However, these same factors can produce hazardous ocean conditions that are subtle and unique to the Pacific Northwest. The following terms offer important safety tips for kayak surfing along the Oregon Coast. In addition to reading these sections, we strongly suggest that boaters unfamiliar with the ocean arrange initial trips with experienced wave riders.

Waves. Small spilling breakers in the 2- to 4-foot height range are ideal for beginning surf kayakers. Plunging breakers in the 6- to 8-foot height range can rip paddles from boaters' hands and pop spray skirts, forcing even the most skilled boater to swim for shore. Since larger waves break in deeper water, they also break farther from shore, leading surfers to greatly underestimate their size. For this reason, it is prudent to start surfing close to shore and then move out gradually to the larger surf as true wave size is confirmed. Such an approach also ensures that surfers will observe the infrequent sets of very large waves (called "cleanup sets") before committing themselves to a thorough cleaning!

Beaches, Reefs, and Points. In their search for waves, surfers usually concentrate on beaches with offshore sandbars and reefs, as well as on points such as headlands and harbor jetties. These features cause swells to refract, or bend toward shore, and produce waves that break right or left along the shore, giving long rides to surfers.

Currents. Coastal currents can be wide and with velocities of several knots, twice the speed of a swimmer. They present a great danger to boaters out of their boats. **Rip currents** are particularly dangerous because they move out to sea a distance of 0.5 mile or more.

Particularly strong rip currents occur alongside headlands and jetties. **Nearshore currents** are generated by shoaling waves that push water inshore from the breaker zone. Escaping water flows parallel to the shore in **longshore currents** and then heads back out to sea in rip currents, through gaps between offshore sandbars or reefs. Currents are intensified during conditions of large surf. The least hazardous "current" is the **undertow**, which is not really a current at all, just the backwash of a wave on a steep beach. The backwash dissipates a few yards from the beach face and is of little concern to experienced swimmers.

Rip currents heading out to sea can sometimes be identified by choppy surface water, turbid zones, or streaks of sea foam. Nearshore currents cover broad areas and can be difficult to recognize in the turbulent surf zone. Surfers and swimmers in the surf zone should keep an eye on fixed points on shore to see if they are drifting in a nearshore current. To get out of any current, swim or paddle perpendicular to the direction of current flow. In large surf, it might take 20 minutes or longer to swim out of a rip current and into shore. When an open-water rescue by other boaters is not possible, a tired or chilled swimmer should leave the boat and head for shore. Waves and wind will eventually put the boat ashore.

Equipment. Eskimos spent thousands of years developing the ultimate all-purpose sea kayak, from which modern kayaks have evolved. Flotation bags,

To the surf, mates! (Kate Howell)

support walls, and grab loops are necessary on today's boats. Boaters should use helmets and wear belted life jackets that cannot be pulled up over the shoulders by turbulent waves. Most important, a full wet suit or dry suit is essential for safe boating in cold coastal waters, where large surf can force boaters to take long swims. For winter kayak surfing, a hood and booties are worthwhile additions to the full wet suit or dry suit.

Paddling Out and Dropping In. Conflicts or collisions sometimes occur between kayak surfers and board surfers. These conflicts can be avoided if kayakers adhere to the following rules of wave etiquette.

When paddling out to the breaker zone, surfers should paddle off to the side of other surfers who are catching and riding waves. The surfer who is closest to the breaking part of the wave has the right-of-way over others riding the wave face. Other surfers trying to catch the wave should back off to avoid dropping on the surfer who is already in position. Unlike the protocol at the favorite play wave on the local river, no well-ordered lineup of boaters is waiting to catch waves out in the surf zone. Thus, all boaters must make a conscious effort to share waves and to avoid catching waves that might propel them into other surfers. In addition, most board surfers are not used to surfing with kayakers, so give them plenty of room.

Good waves, mates!

Curt Peterson, Rick Starr, and Dale Mosby

coastal access overview

	SURF AREA	COMMENTS
NORTH COAST		
212 Columbia River South Jetty	Just south of the Columbia River South Jetty	Provides some of the longest rides to be found on Oregon waves.
213 Seaside Cove	Immediately south of Seaside; north of Tillamook head	A rocky bottom and potential long swims can make Seaside Cove a poor choice for inexperienced surfers.
214 Cannon Beach and Arch Cape	Ecola State Park (Indian Beach); Cannon Beach; Arch Cape	Very popular with beginning board surfers.
215 Short Sand Beach	Oswald West State Park	Very popular area; 0.5-mile hike to beach.
216 Cape Meares	Immediately north of Cape Meares	Long way out from shore.
217 Cape Kiwanda	Just south of the tiny headland	Popular area with hang gliders and anglers.
CENTRAL COAST		
218 Gleneden Beach	Gleneden Beach County Park	Getting in and out of the surf zone can be difficult.
219 Otter Rock	South side of Otter Rock	Waves are formed over a wide range of conditions at Otter Rock, but rarely break with consistently good form.
220 Yaquina Head Cove (Agate Beach)	Just south of Yaquina Head off US 101, about 4 miles north of Newport	Some of the most consistently ridable surf on the central coast.
221 Yaquina Bay South Jetty to South Beach	1 mile south of Yaquina Bay bridge	Many surfers have frightening stories of getting caught in the South Jetty rip current during large winter surf.
222 Siuslaw River South Jetty	Just south of the Siuslaw River South Jetty	When the surf is large in the winter, ridable waves break between the jetties.
SOUTH COAST		
223 Winchester Bay South Jetty	About 5 miles south of Reedsport	Perhaps the finest jetty beach break to be found on the Oregon Coast occurs south of the Winchester Bay South Jetty.
224 Bastendorff Beach	Between the Coos Bay South Jetty and a small headland 1 mile south of the bay mouth	The beach breaks here are ridable over a wide variety of ocean swell and tide conditions, but paddling out is difficult in large winter surf when clean-up sets close-out the rip current lanes.
225 Lighthouse Beach	Beyond the Bastendorff Beach turnoff just before Sunset Beach	Probably the most popular beach in the Coos Bay area.
226 Sunset Bay	About 3 miles south of Charleston	A tiny cove that offers small waves when other breaks are closed out by large storm surf.
227 Port Orford	Between Battle Rock and Humbug Mountain, south of the tiny port of Port Orford	Some of the beach breaks form over a shallow, rocky bottom.

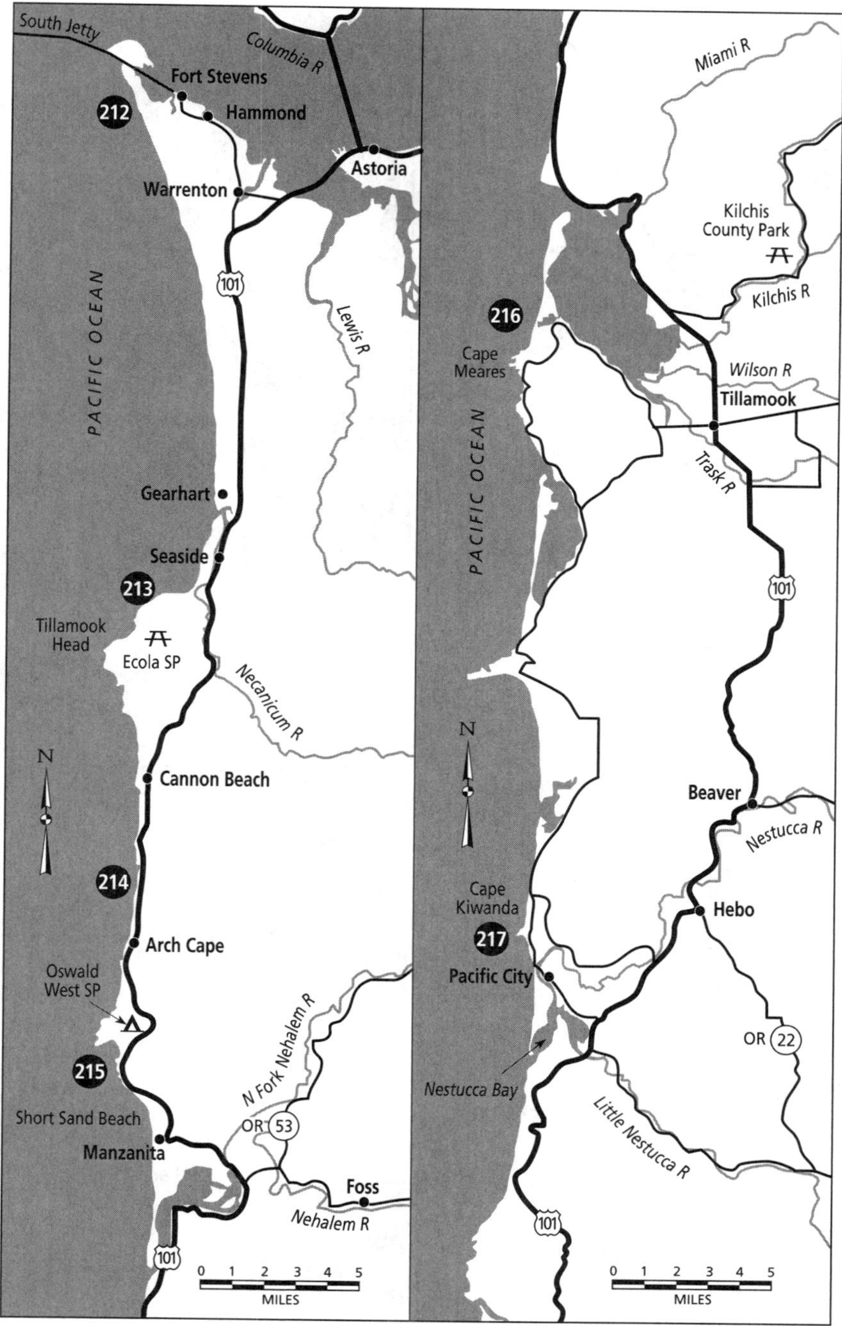
South Jetty
Columbia R
Fort Stevens
212
Hammond
Astoria
Warrenton
101
Lewis R
PACIFIC OCEAN
Gearhart
Seaside
213
Tillamook Head
Ecola SP
Necanicum R
N
Cannon Beach
214
Arch Cape
Oswald West SP
215
Short Sand Beach
N Fork Nehalem R
Manzanita
OR 53
Foss
Nehalem R
101
0 1 2 3 4 5
MILES
Miami R
Kilchis County Park
Kilchis R
216
Cape Meares
Wilson R
Tillamook
Trask R
PACIFIC OCEAN
101
N
Beaver
Nestucca R
Cape Kiwanda
Hebo
217
Pacific City
OR 22
Nestucca Bay
Little Nestucca R
101
0 1 2 3 4 5
MILES

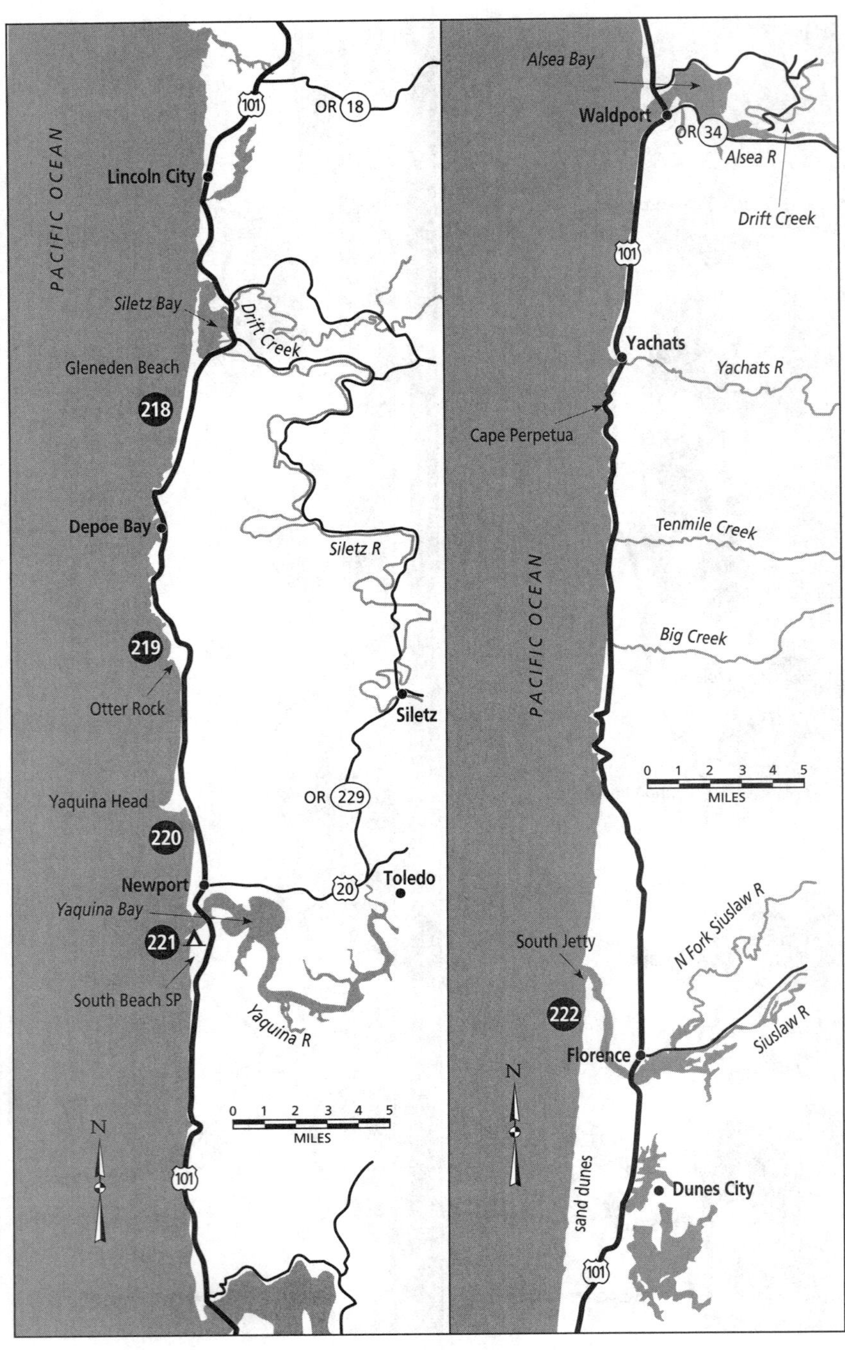

PACIFIC OCEAN
OR 18
101
Lincoln City
Siletz Bay
Drift Creek
Gleneden Beach
218
Depoe Bay
Siletz R
219
Otter Rock
Siletz
OR 229
Yaquina Head
220
Newport
OR 20
Toledo
Yaquina Bay
221
South Beach SP
Yaquina R
0 1 2 3 4 5
MILES
N
101
Alsea Bay
Waldport
OR 34
Alsea R
Drift Creek
101
Yachats
Yachats R
Cape Perpetua
Tenmile Creek
PACIFIC OCEAN
Big Creek
0 1 2 3 4 5
MILES
N Fork Siuslaw R
South Jetty
222
Siuslaw R
Florence
N
sand dunes
Dunes City
101

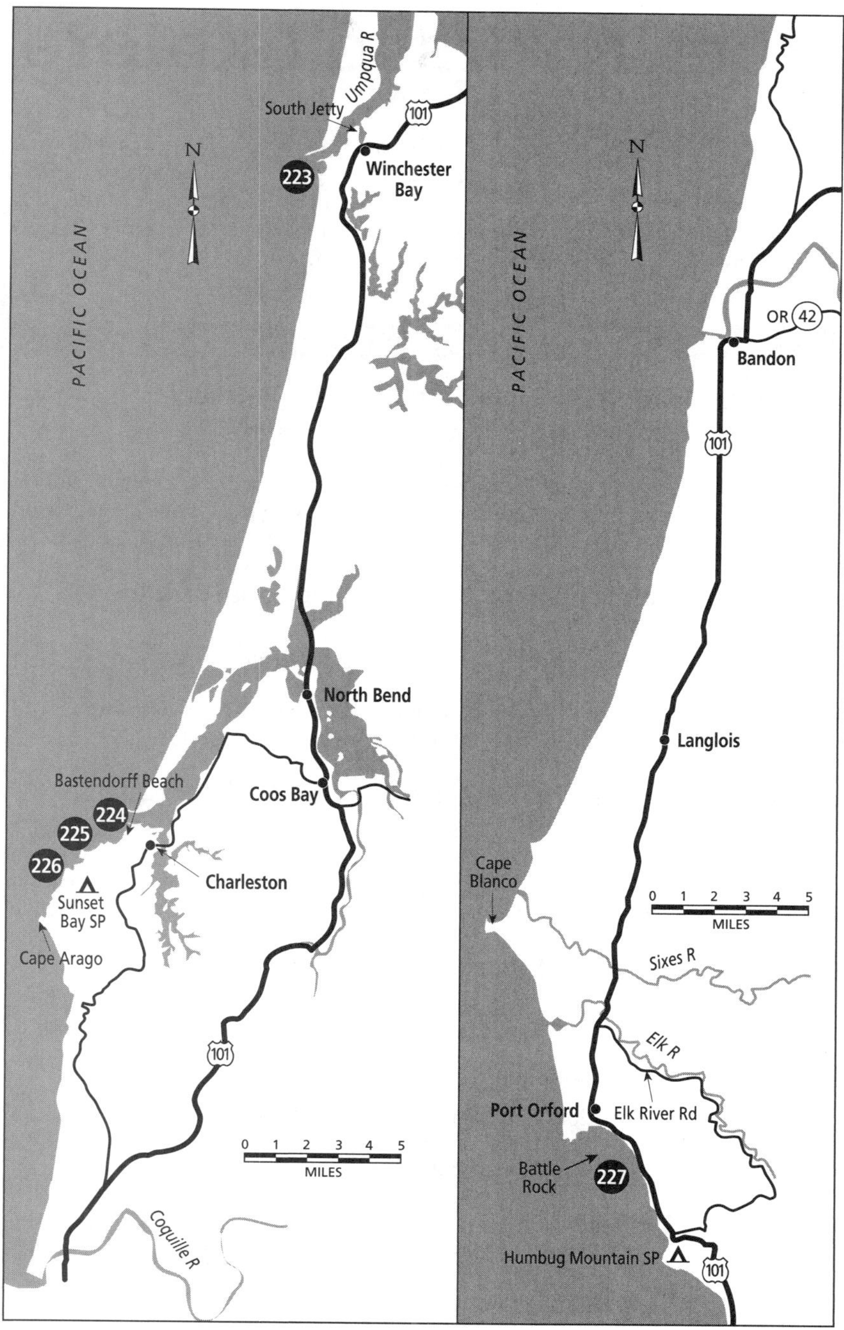
PACIFIC OCEAN
Umpqua R
South Jetty
101
223
Winchester
Bay
N
North Bend
Bastendorff Beach
Coos Bay
224
225
226
Charleston
Sunset
Bay SP
Cape Arago
101
Coquille R
MILES
0 1 2 3 4 5

PACIFIC OCEAN
N
OR 42
Bandon
101
Langlois
Cape
Blanco
0 1 2 3 4 5
MILES
Sixes R
Elk R
Port Orford
Elk River Rd
Battle
Rock
227
Humbug Mountain SP
101

other rivers to explore

The runs in this section include a few gems, many good runs, a few marginal runs and a couple of nightmares. Many of the runs have poor or limited access, numerous logs, have only recently been run or are extremely difficult. Most of the runs involved a lot of exploring by dedicated boaters looking for new challenges. There are many rivers still unexplored by boaters. Have fun, but be safe.

REGION 1: NORTH COAST RIVERS

Alsea River, North Fork: Upper Section to Fish Hatchery

| Class: 3+(4+) | Gradient: 57 fpm | Length: 7 miles |

Shuttle is confusing and long. Twenty-foot waterfall just below the put-in; run on the right. Middle section has fun class 3 rapids and one class 4–4+ ledge. Good play spots.

Alsea River, South Fork: Hubert K. McBee Memorial Park to Rock Quarry Weir

| Class: 2–3 | Gradient: 45 | Length: 6 miles |

Class 2 in first half, then class 3 below third bridge. Ends with easier water and several ledge drops. Wood-choked, numerous portages for wood.

Boulder Creek, Little: Little Boulder Creek to North Fork Siletz

| Class: 5 | Gradient: 300 fpm | Length: 3.6 miles |

This tiny tributary of Boulder Creek has several waterfalls that are difficult to scout and portage. Also prone to wood hazards. The last half is on Boulder Creek (class 3).

Clatskanie River: Upper Section to Swedetown

| Class: 2(3) | Gradient: 70 fpm | Length: 6 miles |

D River: Source to Pacific Ocean

| Class: 1 | Gradient: 50 fpm | Length: 0.5 mile |

World's second-shortest river. By Lincoln City.

Five Rivers: 10 Miles to Mouth

| Class: 1 | Gradient: 12 fpm, PD | Length: 10 miles |

Lots of wood, especially at upper part of run.

Lake Creek: Triangle Lake to Fish Creek

Class: 5   Gradient: 162 fpm   Length: 1.7 miles

Nehalem River: US 26 to Spruce Run Park

Class: 1–2   Gradient: low   Length: 5–8 miles

This run features peace and quiet, nice scenery, and easy rapids combined with good surfing that should entice both beginners and intermediates.

Nehalem River, North Fork: Fish Hatchery on Oregon 53 to Aldervale Boat Ramp

Class: 2–3   Gradient: 32 fpm   Length: 5 miles

Access is problematic due to private property.

Rock Creek: 5 Miles to Siletz River

Class: 2-   Gradient: medium-low   Length: 5 miles

Brushy, woody.

Salmonberry River, North Fork: Salmonberry Road to Salmonberry River

Class 3+(5)   Gradient: 125 fpm   Length: 3.5 miles

An alternative put-in for a run on the main Salmonberry. Boulder gardens on the first 2.5 miles, then two class 5 drops in the last mile that can be portaged on the left.

Scappoose Creek: Above Bonnie Falls to Above Scappoose

Class 3(4)   Gradient: medium   Length: 4–6 miles

Small boulder gardens and one runnable 15-foot waterfall set in a semi-urban setting.

Siletz River: Sam Creek to Old Mill Park

Class: 1   Gradient: 10 fpm, C   Length: 10 miles

Siletz River, North Fork: Valley of the Giants to Above Boulder Creek

Class: 4   Gradient 200 fpm   Length: varies based on put-in

Continuous fast water. A good level is 9 feet on the Siletz gauge.

Siletz River, South Fork: Valsetz Dam Site to North Fork Siletz

Class: 3–4 | Gradient: 86 fpm | Length: 4 miles

The hardest rapid is the rocky drop just below the lake at the put-in. Great play at high water. The minimum level is 8 feet at the Siletz gauge.

Sweet Creek: Sweet Creek Falls to Siuslaw (near Mapleton)

Class: 5 | Gradient: 500 fpm (1 mile) | Length: 2–4 miles

Slides, falls, and chutes punctuate this run. Has great access for scouting. Drive to Mapleton, take Sweet Creek Road about 12 miles to a park on the right, the take-out.

Wilson River, Upper Devils Lake Fork: Deo Creek to Oregon 6

Class: 3+ | Gradient: medium | Length: 2–3 miles

Continuous rapids through trees, with occasional logs.

REGION 2: SOUTH COAST RIVERS

Chetco River: Taggarts Bar to Tolman Ford

Class: 4 | Gradient: 46 fpm | Length: 20 miles

Ten-mile carry to the put-in, 20-mile paddle through the Kalmiopsis Wilderness.

Coos River, South Fork: Johnson Beach to Milepost 6

Class: 3 | Gradient: 23 | Length: 6.1

Weyerhaeuser land; access is now by permit only above milepost 7.

Coquille River, North Fork: Uppermost Bridge to Bridge Above Moon Creek

Class: 3 | Gradient: 40 fpm | Length: 13 miles

Coquille River, East Fork: 3 Miles East of Dora to Bridge on Gold Brick Road

Class: 3(4) | Gradient: 30 fpm | Length: 3.3 miles

Coquille River, Middle Fork: Bear Creek Campground to Bridge West of Camas Valley

Class: 3(4) | Gradient: 45 fpm | Length: 5 miles

Coquille River, South Fork: Coquille Falls to 16-Mile Bridge

Class: 5 | Gradient: 235 fpm, PD | Length: 0.8 mile

About 12 class 5 drops through huge boulder jumbles among old-growth Douglas fir and Port Orford cedar. Optimum at 1000–2000 cfs on gauge at Powers.

Goose Creek: Near Saddle Mountain Road to South Fork Smith River, California

Class: 4(5) | Gradient: 90 fpm | Length: 5.5 miles

Scenic canyon with lots of small drops and several unforgettable class 4–5 rapids. Easy scouting, pool-drop character, and crystalline water in a pristine setting.

Hurdygurdy Creek: Bear Basin Road to Big Flat Road

Class: 4–5 | Gradient: medium-high | Length: 6–7 miles

Hurdygurdy Creek is a steep, very remote tributary of South Fork Smith River, California. Once boaters enter the Devils Gap, they have no escape option but to hike downstream.

Lobster Creek: Deadline Creek to Rogue River

Class: 4 | Gradient: medium | Length: 4 miles

Millicoma River, East Fork: Bridge 19 Miles Above Allegany to Bridge at Little Creek

Class: 5 | Gradient: 150 fpm | Length: 6.3 miles

Millicoma River, West Fork: Trout Creek Road to Henrys Falls

Class: 2+ | Gradient: 53 fpm | Length: 4.5 miles

Sixes River: Bridge at Locked Gate to Sixes River Recreation Site

Class: 2(3–4) | Gradient: 37 fpm | Length: 5 miles

Smith River, South Fork: Upper Sections (California)

Class: 5 | Gradient: high | Length: 3–5 miles

REGION 3: SOUTHERN OREGON RIVERS

Big Bend Creek: 3 Miles Above Steamboat Creek to Steamboat Creek

Class: 4(5) | Gradient: unknown | Length: 3 miles

Big Butte Creek: Butte Falls Picnic Area to Crowfoot Road

| Class 3+(4) | Gradient 66 fpm | Length: 12 miles |

Fifteen-foot runnable Butte Falls at mile 1. Mostly class 3–3+ with some class 4. Expect several portages for logs and brush. Blind corners. Best at 400–900 cfs.

Boulder Creek: 3 Miles Above North Umpqua to North Umpqua

| Class: 5 | Gradient: high | Length: 3 miles |

Steep creek with many drops. Many logs in the creek.

Copeland Creek: NF 300 Bridge to North Umpqua River

| Class: 4+(5) T, P | Gradient: 125 fpm | Length: 5 miles |

Numerous ledges, boulder gardens, slides, and falls. Numerous pin spots to avoid. Much wood to be portaged and avoided.

Jackson Creek: 7 Miles Above Cover Camp to Cover Camp

| Class: 4(5) | Gradient: 120 fpm | Length: 6.5 miles |

Continuous solid class 4 with blind drops, few eddies, and pin spots galore. Most drops 3- to 5-foot range. Wood often problematic.

Little River: NF 165 to White Creek Campground

| Class: 4(5) P | Gradient: 120 fpm | Length: 7 miles |

Wood is usually in the upper part. Many fun, small ledges throughout the run, some good boulder gardens. Scenic lower half contains a fun 10-foot waterfall.

Rock Creek: Northeast Fork to North Umpqua

| Class: 3–4 P | Gradient: medium | Length: 13 miles |

Middle 6–7 miles are flat. Last mile is class 4.

Rogue River, Middle Fork: Butte Falls Road to Lost Creek Lake

| Class: 5 | Gradient: 88 fpm | Length: 6 miles |

Entire run needs scouting, class 5 gorge is 0.5 mile long with no portage option. Wood problematic. Access at take-out is no longer possible; long paddle out on the reservoir.

Rogue River, North Fork: Mill Creek Falls to Lost Creek Lake

| Class: 4+ | Gradient: 94 fpm | Length: 3 miles |

Nonstop 4+ action for the first 1.5 mile, considerable scouting/portaging needed. Logs problematic. Access at take-out is no longer possible; long paddle out on the reservoir.

Reynolds Creek: 3 Miles Above Steamboat Creek

| Class: 5(6) | Gradient: 300 fpm | Length: 3 miles |

Steamboat Creek: City Creek to Steamboat Falls

| Class: 2+(4) | Gradient: medium | Length: 10 miles |

REGION 4: UPPER WILLAMETTE AND MCKENZIE RIVERS

Big River: 7 Miles Above Coast Fork Willamette to Coast Fork Willamette River

| Class: 3 | Gradient: medium | Length: 7 miles |

Blue River: Mann Creek to Quentin Creek

| Class: 4(5) | Gradient: 240 fpm | Length: 1.5 miles |

Brice Creek: Upper NF 22 Bridge to Champion Creek

| Class: 4+(5) T, P | Gradient: 221 fpm | Length: 2.6 miles |

Upper Brice is continuous steep creeking with long boulder gardens, big holes, pin spots, falls, and ledges. Orthodontist's Nightmare is 0.6 mile above Champion Creek.

Brice Creek: Cedar Creek Campground to Layng Creek

| Class: 3 | Gradient: 75 fpm | Length: 4.5 miles |

Champion Creek: 1 Mile Up from Brice Creek Confluence

| Class: 5+, T | Gradient: 300 fpm | Length: 1 mile |

Technical boulder bashing with one runnable 20-foot waterfall and a couple of other ledges.

Christy Creek: NF 1926 Bridge to North Fork of the Middle Fork Willamette

| Class: 5–5+ T, P | Gradient: 178 fpm | Length: 6.3 miles |

Log-choked channels and boulder sieves abound. Many, many portages.

Coal Creek: 4 Miles Above Middle Fork Willamette to Middle Fork Willamette

Class: 3 — Gradient: medium — Length: 4 miles

Fall Creek: Delp Creek to Gold Creek

Class: 4 T, P — Gradient: 67 fpm — Length: 2 mile

Class 2–3 water for 0.7 mile, then an easy 11-foot falls. Just after the falls, the creek enters a mile-long tight gorge that can be best described as a logjam hell.

Fall Creek, Little: Gate on Little Fall Creek Road to Pengra Road Bridge

Class: 3 — Gradient: 25 fpm — Length: 6 miles

A small, narrow tributary of Fall Creek. Mainly class 2 with two class 3 ledges within the first 1.5 miles. Ends on Fall Creek, below the Pengra covered bridge.

Hills Creek: Upper Reaches to NF 2118 Bridge

Class: 4(5)–5 T — Gradient: 109 fpm — Length: 4 miles

Slides, falls (back-to-back 20- and 12-foot falls, choked with wood), boulder gardens, gorges, and quite a bit of wood.

Horse Creek: Trailhead Bridge to 7 Miles Above NF 2638 Bridge

Class: 3(4) T — Gradient: 114 fpm — Length: 3.5 miles

Unlike Lower Horse Creek, this section is a fairly continuous flush with few logs. Mainly class 2–3 with one class 4 at Castle Creek.

Horse Creek: 7 Miles Above NF 2638 Bridge to NF 2638 Bridge

Class: 2(3) — Gradient: 67 fpm — Length: 7 miles

Class 1–2 with one class 3. Numerous logjams, sweepers, and other dangers. (Take-out is upstream of McKenzie Bridge.)

Junetta Creek: Curran Creek to Layng Creek

Class: 5 T P — Gradient: 180 fpm — Length: 1 mile

Slow, meandering class 2 water with lots of wood for 0.7 mile, then the creek drops 160 feet for the remaining 0.3 mile. Under the main road bridge is a 12-foot falls.

Layng Creek: Junetta Creek to Layng Creek Work Center

Class: 2 — Gradient: 60 fpm — Length: 3 miles

Easy class 2–2+. Take out above the artificial 6-foot ledge. Above Junetta Creek is an unrunnable 20-plus-foot falls and class 4 boulder garden; many logjams above there.

Lookout Creek: Bridge 2.5 Miles Above Blue River Reservoir to Blue River Reservoir

Class: 3–4 | Gradient: medium | Length: 2.5 miles

McKenzie River, East Fork: 3 Miles Above Cougar Reservoir to Cougar Reservoir

Class: 4+(5) T P | Gradient: 240 fpm | Length: 3 miles

Continuous class 4 boulder gardens with one class 5 located right after a huge logjam/landslide.

McKenzie River: Clear Lake to Carmen Reservoir

Class: 5 P | Gradient: unknown | Length: 2 miles

Two huge waterfalls (50-plus feet each) that have been run but are definitely not recommended, and a 20-foot sliding falls that drops into an unrunnable logjam.

McKenzie River: Carmen Reservoir to Trail Bridge Reservoir

Class: 2–P | Gradient: medium | Length: 6 miles

After 1.2 mile, the water not diverted by Carmen Reservoir disappears into the lava; a long hike follows to the pool below the now dry Tamolitch Falls; then there are rocks and logs below.

Mohawk River: Gate on Mohawk Road to Hileman Road Bridge

Class: 2(3-) | Gradient: 39 fpm | Length: 5.8 miles

Shallow, meandering stream, mostly continuous class 2 with several ledges. A 4-foot ledge drop (class 3-) in the first mile. More than 20 portages for wood in recent runs.

Mosby Creek: Gate on Mosby Creek Road to Waldon (Row Tributary)

Class: 1+(2+) | Gradient: unknown | Length: 4.5 miles

Salt Creek: Salt Creek Falls to NF 5884 Bridge

Class: 4+(6) T P | Gradient: 193 fpm | Length: 6 miles

Class 5–6 for the first 0.33 mile. Then 80-plus-foot falls, a tough portage. Next, class 3–4. The last 0.75 mile is a nonstop class 3–4 slalom. Below: logjams galore.

Sharps Creek: Staples Creek to Row River

| Class: 2(3) | Gradient: 37 fpm | Length: 7 miles |

Staley Creek: Lower 3 Miles to the Middle Fork Willamette (above Hills Creek Reservoir)

| Class: 4(5) | Gradient: 115 fpm | Length: 3 miles |

Swift Creek: 2 Miles Above NF 21 Bridge to MF Willamette

| Class: 5 | Gradient: high | Length: 3 miles |

Logs with some rapids formed by logs.

Willamette River, North Fork of the Middle Fork: Waldo Lake to Aufderheide Drive

| Class: 5–6 P | Gradient: 270 fpm | Length: 7 miles |

Huge drops and even bigger logs and logjams. Extreme boating at its best and worst.

Willamette River, North Fork of the Middle Fork: NF 1944 Bridge to the Miracle Mile

| Class: 3 P | Gradient: 55 fpm | Length: 11 miles |

Mainly class 2 water interspersed with limbo logs, logjams, and other hazards. All but one of the class 3 rapids is created by logs/logjams.

Winberry Creek: South Fork Winberry Creek to Fall Creek Reservoir

| Class: 3+(5) T P | Gradient: 45 fpm | Length: 4.8 miles |

Logs problematic; the class 5 drop (Bridge Over Troubled Waters located 0.6 mile above take-out) has a dangerous pin spot and private property nearby, making portage difficult.

REGION 5: MID-WILLAMETTE VALLEY RIVERS

Blowout Creek: Cliff Creek to Detroit Reservoir

| Class: 4 | Gradient: 93 fpm | Length: 3.5 miles |

Calapooia River: 22 Miles Above Holley to Gate 9 Miles Above Holley

| Class: 3(4) | Gradient: 65 | Length: 13 miles |

Upper part is steep and technical, with some gorge and boulder garden rapids rating class 4. Access is now blocked by a locked gate leading to private timberland.

Calapooia River: McKercher Park to Brownsville

| Class: 1 | Gradient: 11 fpm | Length: 7 miles |

Put in below McKercher Falls for a pastoral float to Brownsville. The river below Brownsville is seldom runnable because of logjams and brush.

Canal Creek: 2.5 miles Above Quartzville Creek to Quartzville Creek

| Class: 4 | Gradient: 152 fpm | Length: 2.5 miles |

One sloping 15-foot waterfall and one class 4 boulder garden.

Canyon Creek: Elbow Creek to Owl Creek

| Class: 4(5) P | Gradient: 250 fpm | Length: 3 miles |

Very small, with wood.

Cedar Creek: Forest Road 2207 Bridge to Shady Cove Campground

| Class: 5(5+) | Gradient: 133 fpm | Length: 5 miles |

Steep, continuous boulder gardens with several demanding waterfalls. At high water, it can be extremely difficult to stop above several of the waterfalls. (Near Opal Creek.)

Crabtree Creek: North Fork Bridge to Concrete Bridge (Locked Gate)

| Class: 3–4 | Gradient: over 100 fpm | Length: 6 miles |

Technical and rocky. Wood is problematic. Access usually blocked by a locked gate leading to private timberland.

Elkhorn Creek: 3 Miles Above Little North Santiam to Little North Santiam

| Class: 5 | Gradient: high | Length: 3 miles |

Steep rapids, big boulders, and several portages set in a remote gorge. The put-in involves a 1000-foot hike down a cliff.

French Creek: 3 Miles Above Breitenbush River to Breitenbush River

| Class: 4(5) | Gradient: 200 fpm | Length: 3 miles |

Adequate flow when the Breitenbush is at 1700 cfs.

Henline Creek: Headwaters to Opal Creek Trail

Class: 5 — Gradient: high — Length: 1 mile

Many ledges and waterfalls set in a tight gorge. Some of the rapids have shallow landings and difficult entrance moves.

Indian Prairie Creek: 1 Mile Above Thomas Creek to Thomas Creek

Class: 5 — Gradient: high — Length: 1 mile

Steep rapids set in a tiny creek bed. Access usually blocked by a locked gate leading to private timberland.

Little Luckiamute River: Sams Creek to Falls City

Class: 4 — Gradient: 92 fpm — Length: 3 miles

Mostly flat with some wood hazards, with one short class 4 section in the middle.

Luckiamute River: Helmick Park to Willamette River

Class: 1 — Gradient: 1 fpm — Length: 14 miles

McDowell Creek: Majestic Falls to Logging Road

Class: 4–5 — Gradient: 225–275 fpm — Length: 2 miles

Many fun ledges and one 10-foot waterfall. The 30-foot waterfall at the put-in has been run, but it has a shallow landing. At high water, the creek becomes continuous.

Mill Creek: Cedar Creek to Mill Creek County Park

Class: 4 — Gradient: 55 fpm — Length: 8 miles

Class 3–4 rapids, a narrow gorge. Access is now blocked by a locked gate leading to private timberland. An unrunnable class 6 falls is just below the take-out park.

Moose Creek: Cub Creek to South Santiam River

Class: 3(4+) — Gradient: 105 fpm — Length: 4 miles

A tough class 4+ rapid is just upstream of the take-out bridge. Many logs to portage.

Packers Gulch: Packers Gulch Road Bridge to Quartzville Creek

Class: 4+ — Gradient: 140 fpm — Length: 1 mile

Quartzville Creek: Freezeout Creek to Gregg Creek

Class: 4+(5) — Gradient: high — Length: 3.3 miles

Santiam River, Little North:
Mill Falls (Opal Creek Wilderness) to 0.5 Mile Above Gate

Class: 5	Gradient: high	Length: 2.5 miles

Boulder gardens with rapids difficult to scout/portage; tight rapid about 0.5 mile into the run and dangerous slot a little over halfway into the run. Requires a 2.5-mile hike in through a severely burned forest.

Santiam River, Little North:
Three Pools to Salmon Falls (Opal Gorge)

Class: 5	Gradient: high	Length: 2.5 miles

Contains a vertical-walled class 5 gorge with difficult scouting.

Santiam River, Middle: Old NF 2041 Bridge to Green Peter Lake

Class: 3(4)	Gradient: 65	Length: 20 miles (6 on lake)

A pristine run through a Cascade wilderness area. A 3-mile hike in. Wood is problematic. A 5- to 6-mile flatwater paddle out on the lake.

Santiam River, South: House Rock Campground to Soda Fork

Class: 3+(5)	Gradient: 120 fpm	Length: 2 miles

Has a big, steep rapid with two waterfalls and lots of debris in the middle. Last 0.7 mile is class 2+ to 3-.

Sardine Creek:
1 Mile Above Big Cliff Reservoir to Big Cliff Reservoir

Class: 5–5+	Gradient: 320 fpm	Length: 1 mile

Big, technically demanding waterfalls; huge, mind-bendingly steep boulder gardens; severe pin potential; be sure to set safety and scout.

Soda Fork: Taylor Creek to South Santiam River

Class: 4- P	Gradient: 133 fpm	Length: 1.2 miles

Fun ledges with lots of slides.

Thomas Creek: Hall Creek to 5-Mile Bridge

Class: 3(4)	Gradient: 68 fpm	Length: 5 miles

Several ledges and a short gorge. Wood can be problematic. Access usually blocked by a locked gate leading to private timberland.

Wiley Creek: Upper Bridge to Middle Bridge

| Class 4(5-) | Gradient: 102 fpm | Length: 7 miles |

Most of the run is behind locked gates (private timberland). The 1.5 miles below the gate includes runnable Cascade Falls and some nice ledges and slides in a wonderful gorge.

Wiley Creek: Middle Bridge to South Santiam River

| Class: 2(4) | Gradient: 30 fpm | Length: 5 miles |

Toward the end of the run, there's a mandatory portage around a weir that is surrounded by private property. Wood is problematic.

Willamina Creek: Blackwell Park to Yamhill River

| Class: 1(3) | Gradient: 20 fpm | Length: 5 miles |

Yamhill River, South Fork: Sheridan to Amity-Bellevue Road

| Class: 1 | Gradient: 4 fpm, C | Length: 11 miles |

REGION 6: LOWER WILLAMETTE VALLEY AND CLACKAMAS RIVERS

Butte Creek: Butte Creek Falls to Scout Camp

| Class: 3+(5) P | Gradient: medium | Length: 8 miles |

A 25-foot runnable waterfall at the put-in, followed by 80- and 25-foot waterfalls. The next 6 miles are class 3. The last mile is difficult; a narrow class 5 rapid at take-out.

Clackamas River, North Fork: NF 4610 to 3.75 Miles Above North Fork Reservoir

| Class: 4(5) | Gradient: medium | Length: 3–3.5 miles |

Lots of wood in a tiny streambed. Includes an 18-foot waterfall followed by a 6-foot ledge and two other ledge drops.

Delph Creek: Porter Road to Eagle Creek

| Class: 3(4) | Gradient: medium | Length: 2 miles |

Elk Lake Creek: Welcome Creek to East Fork Collawash

| Class: 5 P | Gradient: medium | Length: 2 miles |

Starts mellow, followed by a sloping ledge drop, a 20-foot waterfall, and a beautiful gorge with a class 5 rapid and a difficult portage around a ledge with a logjam. Ends mellow.

Molalla River, Nasty Rock Fork: Second Bridge Above Copper Creek to Copper Creek

Class: 4(5)	Gradient: medium	Length: 2 miles

The first 1.5 miles are small with three tight rapids. The third rapid is a 25-foot waterfall that has been run. Below the bridge is one tight rapid, followed by class 3 rapids.

Molalla River, Table Rock Fork: Gorge (Gravel Pit to "Old Bridge")

Class: 5	Gradient: medium	Length: 1 mile

This short run has several fun, tight drops. Only recommended at low flows. All drops should be scouted.

Nohorn Creek: Nohorn Creek to Peg Leg Falls

Class: 3+ to 4(5)	Gradient: 140 fpm	Length: 3 miles

Small eddies above the difficult drops. Wood is problematic. Class 4 skills needed.

Pine Creek: 2 Miles Above Molalla River to Molalla River

Class: 4+	Gradient: high	Length: 2 miles

Tiny streambed (above Baby Bear) with most of the good stuff in the last 0.5 mile.

Silver Creek: Below North Falls to Lower North Falls

Class: 5	Gradient: medium	Length: 2 miles

Five runnable waterfalls are in this short section. Access is limited within Silver Falls State Park; there are strict rules prohibiting foot traffic on the banks of the creek.

REGION 7: COLUMBIA GORGE RIVERS

Eagle Creek: 6 Miles Above Historic Highway to Historic Highway

Class: 5(5+)	Gradient: high	Length: 6 miles

Big waterfalls and some other hard rapids are set in a spectacular gorge. Boaters must hike the entire distance to whatever put-in they choose.

Gordon Creek: 1 Mile Above Sandy River to Sandy River

Class: 4   Gradient: medium   Length: 1 mile

Hood River, East Fork: 10 Miles South of Mount Hood (town) to 5 Miles South of Mount Hood

Class: 4+   Gradient: unknown   Length: 5 miles

Hood River, East Fork: 6 Miles Above Parkdale to Bridge at Parkdale

Class: 4   Gradient: unknown   Length: 6 miles

Hood River, East Fork: Bridge at Parkdale to Dee

Class: 3(4) P   Gradient: 120 fpm   Length: 7–8 miles

An old dam in a steep gorge is just above the take-out in Dee; private property abuts it.

Hood River, Lake Branch Fork: Divers Creek to West Fork Hood River

Class: 4+   Gradient: 117 fpm   Length: 2.2 miles

Boulder gardens, ledges, and slots, with three major drops to be scouted from the right. The river is very narrow, so wood problems could be very dangerous.

Hood River, West Fork: NF 18 Bridge to Lake Branch Fork

Class: 3(5)   Gradient: medium   Length: 1.5 miles

Interesting gorge with many fun, small ledge drops. Fantastic scenery. Tough class 5 rapid and nasty boulder garden just above the take-out.

Panther Creek: 1 Mile Above Wind River to Wind River

Class: 4+   Gradient: high   Length: 1 mile

Steep, continuous, technical rapids. Joins the Wind River upstream of The Flume (the Wind River, Washington: High Bridge to Columbia River run).

Trout Creek: Hemlock to Wind River

Class: 4   Gradient: medium   Length: 3 miles

Washougal River, West Fork: West Fork Bridge to Washougal River

Class: 4(5)   Gradient: 100 fpm   Length: 7 miles

Teakettle Falls, a 16-foot double drop, is within the first mile. Other steep falls and rapids require portages and scrambles through thick brush. Logs can be problematic.

White Salmon River, Little: Lava Creek to Fish Hatchery

| Class: 5 | Gradient: high | Length: 2 miles |

Easier than the run downstream, this run has interesting gorge scenery. Begins with class 3 and builds to class 5 for the last part. Scout the final rapids and falls above take-out.

White Salmon River, Little: Fish Hatchery to Columbia River

| Class: 5 | Gradient: 212 fpm | Length: 4 miles |

A classic class 5 creek run. Entire run contains large drops with dangerous features, especially at high flows. Spirit Falls is a 33-foot drop; most boaters portage it.

Wind River, Upper, Upper: Above Falls Creek to Mineral Springs Road

| Class: 3–3+(4) | Gradient: 90 fpm | Length: 3.5 miles |

The fun class 3–3+ rapids are set in a tiny gorge. Toward the end is a tougher rapid. The gorge can get pretty wild with high water.

Zigzag River: Tollgate Campground to Sandy River

| Class: 3+ T | Gradient: 108 fpm, C | Length: 3.2 miles |

The first 0.5 mile is very tight. Then the run opens up for its remainder. The second half of the run is mostly class 2.

REGION 8: CENTRAL OREGON RIVERS

Crooked River, North Fork: Deep Creek Campground to Paulina Highway Bridge

| Class: 3–4 P | Gradient: 38 fpm | Length: 20 miles |

Remote wilderness canyon, two waterfalls; logjams and logs can be problematic. Extremely short season. Private land limits access near take-out.

Deschutes River: Benham Falls

| Class 5+ | Gradient: high | Length: 1 mile |

An extremely dangerous run for experts only; careful scouting mandatory.

Deschutes River: Lower Benham Falls to Slough Day Use Area

| Class: 3+ | Gradient: 60 fpm, C | Length: 1.5 miles |

Just below the falls is a short class 3+ section, then class 2, then flatwater.

Deschutes River: Slough Day Use Area to Dillon Falls

| Class: 1 | Gradient: 2 fpm | Length: 1.8 miles |

Take out before Dillon Falls (class 4+) or paddle back up to starting point.

Deschutes River, Little: Rosland Park to Harper Bridge

| Class: 1 | Gradient: low | Length: 26.2 miles |

Bridge Drive, LaPine State Recreation Area, and Montgomery Bridge are access points.

White River: Below White River Falls to Deschutes River

| Class: 3 | Gradient: medium | Length: 2 miles |

Whychus Creek: NF 1514 Bridge to Gauging Station South of Sisters

| Class: 4+ P | Gradient: high | Length: 6.5 miles |

Good-quality rapids are set in a small creek bed with a lot of logs. Severe consequences result from missing the line of many of the rapids.

REGION 9: EASTERN OREGON RIVERS

Grande Ronde River: Tony Vey Meadows to Red Bridge State Park

| Class: 3(4+) | Gradient: 54 fpm | Length: 17 miles |

Wood-choked, caused by naturally occurring logs and those placed for fish habitat. Numerous portages, especially in the steeper Stygian Steps rapid midway down the run.

Imnaha River: Indian Crossing Campground to NF 4260 Bridge near Cow Creek

| Class: 1+ to 4 | Gradient: 55 fpm | Length: 76 miles |

Mostly class 2 water, but with class 3–4 wood hazards, mostly at bridges. A fish weir (portage) several miles below Ollokot Campground; wire fencing in the river.

Imnaha River: NF 4260 (Dug Bar) Bridge near Cow Creek to Snake River Confluence

| Class: 4 | Gradient: 53 fpm | Length: 4.3 miles |

Fun, continuous class 3–4 whitewater. Requires hiking back upstream 4.3 miles through poison ivy, paddling more than 20 miles to Heller Bar on the Snake, or a long shuttle.

John Day River, North Fork: Route 52 Bridge to Dale

Class 3+(5)	Gradient: 70 fpm	Length: 41 miles

Short class 5 drop is below Granite Creek. Logjams galore, especially in the upper two-thirds of the run. Some boaters put in at Oriental Creek, 10 miles above take-out at Dale.

Joseph Creek: Headwaters to Grande Ronde River

Class: 3(4)	Gradient: 50 fpm	Length: 48

Mostly private land, including put-in areas; extremely short season; remote, isolated canyon with little to no access; tight rapids with trees and brushy banks; wood portages.

Lostine River: Williamson Campground to Picnic Area

Class: 5	Gradient: high	Length: 3.5 miles

Remote, beautiful run. Technical continuous class 3 for first half, then steeper continuous class 4+ to 5- drops and a 10-foot waterfall. Abundant wood.

Owyhee River, South Fork: YP (Petan) Ranch to East Fork Owyhee River

Class: 3	Gradient: 13 fpm	Length: 58 miles

Remote wilderness canyon, run at flows from 250 to 3000 cfs. Much class 1 water and a series of class 3s. The 45 Ranch launch site is at mile 45 of this run. Small rafts okay.

Owyhee River, West Little Fork: Anderson Crossing to Owyhee River

Class: 1(5)	Gradient: unknown	Length: about 30 miles

About 95 percent easy, 5 percent extremely difficult through narrow boulder-choked passageways, suck holes, and undercut amphitheaters. "Louse Canyon" section.

Williamson River: Klamath Marsh (Kirk Bridge) to Williamson River Campground

Class: 3(4) P	Gradient: 46 fpm	Length: 6.5 miles

Five waterfalls between 15 and 30 feet high, all but possibly one unrunnable, which makes this run an interesting combination of boating and rock climbing.

Williamson River: Collier State Park to Chiloquin County Park

Class: 1(2)	Gradient: low	Length: 6 miles

Mostly class 1 riffles; pine and aspen forest. A take-out at Chocktoot Road avoids the class 2 Chiloquin Rapid that is located just above the confluence with the Sprague.

popular and favorite runs ★

Here are some of our most popular and favorite runs. If you're visiting Oregon and only have time for a few runs, you might want to try something from this list. These are rivers that we enjoy paddling multiple times a year when they are running. The list is organized by class, and within each class, the runs are listed numerically by run number.

RUN	RIVER/CREEK	AREA	DETAILS
CLASS 1–1+			
151	Sandy River	Oxbow Park to Dabney State Recreation Area	YR
174	Deschutes River	Tenino Boat Launch to Wyeth Campground	
186	Wood River	Jackson F. Kimball State Park to Loosely Road	YR
193	John Day River	Service Creek to Clarno	O
CLASS 2–2+			
3	Kilchis River	Confluence of North Fork and South Fork to Little South Fork	
22	Lake Creek	Deadwood Creek to Tide	
63	Rogue River	Hog Creek Access to Grave Creek	YR
70	Row River	Wildwood Falls to Dorena Reservoir	
81	Middle Fork Willamette River	Hills Creek Dam to Black Canyon Campground	YR
90	McKenzie River	Paradise Campground to Bruckart Bridge	YR
92	McKenzie River	Finn Rock to Leaburg Lake	YR
97	Calapooia River	Gate 9 Miles Above Holley to McClun Wayside	
98	Calapooia River	McClun Wayside to McKercher Park	
104	Thomas Creek	5-Mile Bridge to Hannah Bridge	
116	North Santiam River	Packsaddle County Park to Mill City	YR
150	Sandy River	Dodge Park to Oxbow Park	
158	Klickitat River, Washington	Leidl Campground to Icehouse Public Access	YR
191	North Fork John Day River	Dale to Monument	O
194	John Day River	Clarno to Cottonwood Bridge	O
205	Wallowa River/Grande Ronde River	Minam to Troy	O
CLASS 3–3+			
6	Wilson River	Jones Creek Campground to Milepost 15	
7	Wilson River	Milepost 15 to Milepost 8 Boat Ramp	
9	North Fork Trask River	North Fork of North Fork Trask River to Bridge	
10	Trask River	Fish Hatchery to Cedar Creek Boat Ramp	
14	Siletz River	Buck Creek to Moonshine Park	
33	North Fork Smith River, California	Browns Flat to Gasquet	
42	South Umpqua River	Campbell Falls to Three C Rock	
49	North Umpqua River	Boulder Flat to Gravel Bin	YR
51	North Umpqua River	Bogus Creek to Susan Creek	YR
58	North Fork Rogue River	River Bridge Campground to North Fork Reservoir	YR
64	Rogue River	Grave Creek to Foster Bar	YR, O

Details: YR = usually runnable year-round   O = usually an overnight or multiday trip

RUN	RIVER/CREEK	AREA	DETAILS
77	North Fork of the Middle Fork Willamette River	Bottom of The Gorge to Westfir	
85	South Fork McKenzie River	Above French Pete Campground to Cougar Reservoir	
89	McKenzie River	Olallie Campground to Paradise Campground	YR
102	Crabtree Creek	Concrete Bridge (Locked Gate) to Larwood Covered Bridge	
105	South Santiam River	Above Soda Fork to US 20 Bridge	
113	Little North Santiam River	Elkhorn Valley Recreation Site to Mehama	
114	North Santiam River	Pamelia Creek to Blowout Road	
125	Molalla River	Table Rock Fork Confluence to Turner Bridge	
126	Molalla River	Turner Bridge to Glen Avon Bridge	
134	Eagle Creek	Fish Hatchery to Snuffin Road	
137	Clackamas River	June Creek Bridge to Collawash River	
139	Clackamas River	Three Lynx Power Station to North Fork Reservoir	YR
154	East Fork Hood River/Hood River	Dee to Tucker Bridge	
156	Klickitat River, Washington	Yakama Indian Reservation to Klickitat Salmon Hatchery	
157	Klickitat River, Washington	Klickitat Salmon Hatchery to Leidl Campground	
162	White Salmon River, Washington	BZ Corner to Husum	YR
167	Washougal River, Washington	Public Fishing Road to Milepost 3	
168	Metolius River	Source to Lake Billy Chinook	YR
173	White River	Wamic–White River Bridge to Tygh Valley	
184	Deschutes River	US 26 Bridge to Sherars Falls	YR, O
185	Deschutes River	Sherars Falls to Columbia River	YR, O
208	Snake River	Hells Canyon Dam to Heller Bar	O
211	Owyhee River	Rome to Leslie Gulch	O

CLASS 4–4+

RUN	RIVER/CREEK	AREA	DETAILS
36	Middle Fork Smith River, California	Oregon Hole Gorge	
56	North Fork Rogue River	Natural Bridge to Woodruff Bridge	YR
61	Rogue River	Fishers Ferry to Gold Hill Sports Park	YR
67	Illinois River	Miami Bar to Oak Flat	O
68	Brice Creek	Champion Creek to Cedar Creek Campground	
76	North Fork of the Middle Fork Willamette River	Miracle Mile Through The Gorge	
107	Quartzville Creek	Above Gregg Creek to Galena Creek	
108	Quartzville Creek	Galena Creek to Green Peter Reservoir	
110	Breitenbush River	Cleator Bend Campground to Detroit Reservoir	
111	Little North Santiam River	Old Mine to Three Pools (Opal Creek)	
148	Sandy River	Below Marmot Dam Site to Revenue Bridge	
152	West Fork Hood River	Lake Branch Fork to East Fork Hood River	
160	White Salmon River, Washington	Warner Road Bridge to Green Truss Bridge	
161	White Salmon River, Washington	Green Truss Bridge to BZ Corner	
165	Wind River, Washington	Stabler to High Bridge	
166	Wind River, Washington	High Bridge to Saint Martin Road	
179	Deschutes River	Meadow Camp Day Use Area to Farewell Bend Park	YR
180	Deschutes River	Sawyer Park to Tumalo State Park	
189	Klamath River	John C. Boyle Power Plant to Copco Lake	YR
199	Jarbidge River/Bruneau River	Murphy Hot Springs to 8 Miles South of Bruneau	O
210	Owyhee River	Three Forks to Rome	O

bibliography

Amaral, Grant. *Idaho The Whitewater State.* Garden Valley, Idaho: Watershed Books, 2003.

Bechdel, Les, and Slim Ray. *River Rescue: A Manual for Whitewater Safety.* 4th ed. CFS Press, 2009.

Bennett, Jeff, and Tonya Bennett. *A Guide to the Whitewater Rivers of Washington.* 2nd ed. Portland, Oregon: Swiftwater Publishing Company, 1998.

Campbell, Arthur. *John Day River: Drift and Historical Guide.* Portland, Oregon: Frank Amato Publications, Inc., 2003.

Carrey, Johnny, Cort Conley, and Ace Barton. *Snake River of Hells Canyon.* Cambridge, Idaho: Backeddy Books, 1979.

Garren, John. *Oregon River Tours.* Garren Publishing, 1991.

Jackson, Eric. *Whitewater Paddling: Strokes and Concepts. Kayaking with Eric Jackson.* Mechanicsburg, Pennsylvania: Stackpole Books, 1999.

Keller, Robb. *Paddling Oregon.* Helena, Montana: Falcon Guides, 1998.

Jones, Philip N. *Canoe and Kayak Routes of Northwest Oregon: Including Southwest Washington.* 3rd ed. Seattle: Mountaineers Books, 2007.

Moore, Greg, and Don McClaran. *Idaho Whitewater: The Complete River Guide.* McCall, Idaho: Class VI, 1989.

Nealy, William. *Kayak: The New Frontier: The Animated Manual of Intermediate and Advanced Whitewater Technique.* Birmingham, Alabama: Menasha Ridge Press, 2007.

Palmer, Tim. *Field Guide to Oregon Rivers.* Corvallis, Oregon: OSU Press, 2014.

Quinn, James M., James W. Quinn, and James G. King. *Handbook to the Deschutes River Canyon.* Medford, Oregon: Educational Adventures, Inc., 1979.

Quinn, James M., James W. Quinn, and James G. King. *Handbook to the Illinois River Canyon.* Medford, Oregon: Educational Adventures, Inc., 1979.

Quinn, James M., James W. Quinn, and James G. King. *Handbook to the Rogue River Canyon.* Medford, Oregon: Educational Adventures, Inc., 1979.

Walbridge, Charles, and Wayne A. Sundmacher. *Whitewater Rescue Manual: New Techniques for Canoeists, Kayakers, and Rafters.* Camden, Maine: International Marine/Ragged Mountain Press, 1995.

Williams, Travis. *The Willamette River Field Guide.* Portland, Oregon: Timber Press, 2009.

appendix a
river flow information

In **OREGON**, the most commonly used sources of online flow information are:
Pat Welch's My River Levels Page–current flows (and estimated flows
    for rivers without gauges)
    http://levels.wkcc.org/?P=Oregon.html
United States Geological Survey–current flows (Oregon)
    http://waterdata.usgs.gov/or/nwis/current/?type=flow
Northwest River Forecast Center–current and predicted flows for
    Oregon and Washington
    www.nwrfc.noaa.gov/rfc

NORTHERN CALIFORNIA AND WASHINGTON gauge information
    can be obtained from the following sources:
California Nevada River Forecast Center–current and predicted flows
    www.cnrfc.noaa.gov
United States Geological Survey–current flows (California)
    http://waterdata.usgs.gov/ca/nwis/current/?type=flow
United States Geological Survey–current flows (Washington)
    http://waterdata.usgs.gov/wa/nwis/current/?type=flow
Northwest River Forecast Center–current and predicted flows for Washington
    and Oregon
    www.nwrfc.noaa.gov/rfc
Dreamflows–current flows (and estimated flows for rivers without gauges) for
    numerous rivers in the Western states
    www.dreamflows.com/reports.php

MISCELLANEOUS gauges for specific rivers:
Wood River, Oregon:
Oregon Department of Water Resources
    http://apps.wrd.state.or.us/apps/sw/hydro_near_real_time
Washougal River, Washington:
    Washington State Department of Ecology
    https://fortress.wa.gov/ecy/eap/flows/station.asp?sta=28B080

appendix b
water trail paddling guides

Deschutes River

"The Deschutes River Boater's Guide" (the Lower Deschutes from
  US 26 Bridge to the Columbia River)
  by Bureau of Land Management and US Forest Service
  purchase at BLM office in Prineville (541-416-6700) or download online

"Deschutes Paddle Trail River Guide" (95 river miles from Wickiup
  Reservoir to Lower Bridge)
  by the Bend Paddle Trail Alliance
  purchase at local boating stores or download online

Grande Ronde and Wallowa Rivers

"Wallowa and Grande Ronde Rivers Boater's Guide"
  by US Bureau of Land Management and US Forest Service
  purchase at BLM office in Baker City (541-523-1256) or download online

Jarbidge and Bruneau Rivers, Idaho

"Owyhee, Bruneau, and Jarbidge Wild and Scenic Rivers Boating Guide"
  by Bureau of Land Management and US Forest Service
  purchase at BLM offices in Vale or Boise or download online

John Day River

"John Day River Recreation Guide" (Kimberly to Tumwater Falls)
  by Bureau of Land Management and others
  purchase at BLM offices in Vale (541-473-3144) or Baker City or download
  online

Nehalem River

"Tillamook County Water Trail: Nehalem River and Estuary"
  by Tillamook Estuaries Partnership
  www.tbnep.org/water_trail_guidebooks/nehalem.pdf

Nestucca River

"Tillamook County Water Trail: Nestucca and Sand Lake Watersheds"
  by Tillamook Estuaries Partnership
  www.tbnep.org/water_trail_guidebooks/nestucca-and-sandlake.pdf

North Umpqua River

"North Umpqua River Wild and Scenic Rivers Users Guide"
  by US Forest Service and Bureau of Land Management
  www.blm.gov/or/districts/roseburg/recreation/wild_and_scenic_river/

Owyhee River

"Owyhee, Bruneau, and Jarbidge Wild and Scenic Rivers Boating Guide"
  by Bureau of Land Management and US Forest Service
  purchase at BLM offices in Vale or download online

Rogue River

"Rogue River Boater's Guide" (Grants Pass to Gold Beach)
  by Bureau of Land Management and US Forest Service
  purchase at BLM offices in Medford and Grants Pass or online (as PDF)
  www.blm.gov/sites/blm.gov/files/orwa-rogue-river-boaters-guide.pdf

Sandy River

"Sandy River Water Trail Paddle Guide" by BLM and others
  www.oregonwildandscenic.com/sandy-river/Sandy_Water_Trail_2012%202.
  pdf

Snake River

"The Wild and Scenic Snake River Boater's Guide"
  by Bureau of Land Management and US Forest Service
  purchase at BLM offices in Vale and Spokane or download online

Willamette River

"Willamette River Water Trail Guide" by Willamette River Water Trail
  http://willamettewatertrail.org

appendix c
whitewater boating organizations

Lower Columbia Canoe Club
Portland, Oregon
www.l-ccc.org

Northwest Rafters Association
Roseburg, Oregon
www.nwwhitewaterrafting.org

Oregon Kayak and Canoe Club
Portland, Oregon
www.okcc.org

Oregon Ocean Paddling Society
Portland, Oregon
www.oopskayak.org

Oregon Whitewater Association
Portland, Oregon
www.oregonwhitewater.org

PDXkayaker
www.pdxkayaker.org

Southern Oregon Kayakers
www.kayak.coosweb.com

Willamette Kayak and Canoe Club, Inc.
P.O. Box 1062
Corvallis, OR 97339
www.wkcc.org

index

MOUNTAINEERS BOOKS is a leading publisher of mountaineering literature and guides—including our flagship title, *Mountaineering: The Freedom of the Hills*—as well as adventure narratives, natural history, and general outdoor recreation. Through our two imprints, Skipstone and Braided River, we also publish titles on sustainability and conservation. We are committed to supporting the environmental and educational goals of our organization by providing expert information on human-powered adventure, sustainable practices at home and on the trail, and preservation of wilderness.

The Mountaineers, founded in 1906, is a 501(c)(3) nonprofit outdoor activity and conservation organization whose mission is "to explore, study, preserve, and enjoy the natural beauty of the outdoors." One of the largest such organizations in the United States, it sponsors classes and year-round outdoor activities throughout the Pacific Northwest, including climbing, hiking, backcountry skiing, snowshoeing, bicycling, camping, paddling, and more. The Mountaineers also supports its mission through its publishing division, Mountaineers Books, and promotes environmental education and citizen engagement. For more information, visit The Mountaineers Program Center, 7700 Sand Point Way NE, Seattle, WA 98115-3996; phone 206-521-6001; www.mountaineers.org; or email info@ mountaineers.org.

Our publications are made possible through the generosity of donors and through sales of more than 600 titles on outdoor recreation, sustainable lifestyle, and conservation. To donate, purchase books, or learn more, visit us online:

MOUNTAINEERS BOOKS

1001 SW Klickitat Way, Suite 201 • Seattle, WA 98134

800-553-4453 • mbooks@mountaineersbooks.org • www.mountaineersbooks.org

Mountaineers Books is proud to be a corporate sponsor of the Leave No Trace Center for Outdoor Ethics, whose mission is to promote and inspire responsible outdoor recreation through education, research, and partnerships. • The Leave No Trace program is focused specifically on human-powered (nonmotorized) recreation. • Leave No Trace strives to educate visitors about the nature of their recreational impacts and offers techniques to prevent and minimize such impacts. • Leave No Trace is best understood as an educational and ethical program, not as a set of rules and regulations. • For more information, visit www.lnt.org or call 800-332-4100.